selected works

John Dryden
selected works

SECOND EDITION

EDITED WITH AN INTRODUCTION
AND COMMENTARIES BY WILLIAM FROST

Holt, Rinehart and Winston
New York / Chicago / San Francisco / Atlanta
Dallas / Montreal / Toronto / London / Sydney

Introduction and Commentaries copyright, © 1953, 1971 by William Frost
Printed in the United States of America
Library of Congress Catalog Card Number: 79-123477
ISBN   0-03-078795-5

012   008   9876

TO C.G.F., M.P.F.,
M.A.F., C.E.F., AND C.W.F.

Introduction

Less than eight months after the publication of Milton's *Paradise Lost* in 1667, John Dryden (then chiefly known as a playwright, though he had written a few occasional poems and some dramatic criticism) was chosen poet laureate of England. Not many years can have elapsed before a curious meeting is said to have taken place in London. According to an early biographer of Milton, the aging revolutionary received a visit from the new laureate, who wanted permission to adapt Milton's great epic for the stage. The resultant rimed opera, *The State of Innocence* (not one of Dryden's better works; it was never played), must have been completed by 1674, the year of Milton's death.

Dryden himself died a quarter of a century later, in 1700— like Milton, long out of favor with the reigning government, in comparative poverty, and bereft of his honors and emoluments. Pope, who at this time was not quite twelve years old, later claimed to have seen Dryden in London during his boyhood, a claim his modern biographer is inclined to dispute. However this may be, there exists a more significant personal connection between the last great poet of the seventeenth century and the first of the eighteenth through their mutual admiration of a dramatist whose career overlapped both epochs—William Congreve.

Six years before Dryden's death this rising young playwright had published his second comedy, *The Double Dealer*. Dryden was at this time still deriving an income from the stage, and remained, though no longer laureate, the greatest man of letters of his day.

To *The Double Dealer* he contributed a prefatory poem praising Congreve's personality—

> So much the sweetness of your manners move,
> We cannot envy you, because we love;

proclaiming him a greater dramatist than Jonson or Fletcher, the Jacobean masters; and foretelling his literary pre-eminence:

> . . . this I prophesy; thou shalt be seen
> (Though with some short parenthesis between)
> High on the throne of wit; and seated there,
> Not mine—that's little—but *thy* laurel wear.

In the concluding lines Dryden called on his presumptive successor to "be kind to my remains"; and, accordingly, in 1717, Congreve produced an edition of Dryden's dramatic works. Three years later Congreve was the recipient of an unusual honor for a mere man of letters. In those days major works of imaginative literature were ordinarily dedicated to great noblemen or statesmen who might be useful sources of financial or political aid to authors. In 1720 this custom was abruptly and notably violated by the dedication to Congreve ("one of the most valuable men, as well as finest writers, of my age and country") of the great new English *Iliad,* just completed that year, by the young admirer of Dryden, Alexander Pope.

Eighteen years after this event Pope was approaching the conclusion of his career as a poet; in May of 1738 he was bringing out, in fact, the first of the two dialogues that were to constitute his *Epilogue to the Satires.* On the same spring morning that this poem appeared, there was also published, anonymously, another verse satire stemming from the Roman classics: "London"; and as Boswell (who later wrote a life of its author) tells the story, "The first buzz of the literary circles was, 'Here is an unknown poet, greater even than Pope.'" Pope's reaction to the poem was unhesitating; having enquired who the author was and having been told "only that his name was Johnson, and that he was some obscure man," the wasp of Twickenham commented "He will soon be déterré [dug up]." The following year, having discovered on further enquiry that Johnson, who wished to be appointed to a vacant rural headmastership, was wearing himself out in hackwork for the booksellers, Pope interceded with powerful friends in the younger poet's behalf. As it turned out, his efforts were unsuccessful; Johnson—

who was in his old age to write the lives of Milton, Dryden, Congreve, and Pope—remained in London.

II

    It was fitting that he remain there, for one of the first characteristics that Milton, Dryden, Pope, and Johnson had in common was this: none of them was an exile. Far from it. Milton's career was so bound up with the course of contemporary national life that his chief biographer, Masson, devotes the first half of every chapter of his biography to an elaborate review of current events during the period covered by the chapter. Pope—though Tories called him a Whig, and Whigs a Tory—was as sensitive to the world of economic, cultural, and political affairs in the capital as a seismograph is to earthquakes. The same thing might be said of Johnson. As for Dryden, he was so much a public figure that, at the height of his literary career, the very subject of one of his major poems is believed to have been suggested to him, in private conversation, by the reigning monarch.

    Concern for national affairs, plus the fact that their opinions were often widely attended to, no doubt contributed to make all four poets accomplished arguers in verse. A recent biographer of Johnson has deprecated the poem "London" on the grounds that many of the opinions in it (it was modeled on Juvenal's second-century attack on the city of Rome) are not necessarily those of the poet—are, indeed, in some cases demonstrably opposite to Johnson's own. Johnson himself, whom Boswell represents on one occasion as briefly hesitating which side of an argument he would enter, would surely have had difficulty in understanding such an objection to his verse. Dryden, when he translated the arguments of the atheistical poet Lucretius against the immortality of the soul, undoubtedly did so (despite his own avowed religious convictions) with as much enthusiasm as Milton when he constructed the elaborate chain of reasoning by means of which Satan misleads Eve in *Paradise Lost,* or framed the great debate on classical versus Christian values which climaxes *Paradise Regained.* These poets believed, in other words, that ideas are exciting, and can be good material for poetry; and, further, that the dramatic clash of divergent ideas can fortify a poem. Even satire and philosophy, in the major works of Pope, usually assume the presence of an objecting, heckling, unconvinced interlocutor.

None of the four poets considered his private life—or the emotions, conflicts, and turmoils of his adolescence—appropriate material for much of his poetry. In a famous passage in "The Hind and the Panther" Dryden speaks briefly of his youth—

> My thoughtless youth was wing'd with vain desires,
> My manhood, long misled by wand'ring fires,
> Follow'd false lights; and when their glimpse was gone,
> My pride struck out new sparkles of her own,

and the mood of the passage can be summed up in the phrase "good-bye to all that." Although the last century and a half has set a high literary value on personal revelations of childhood and early youth—one thinks of Proust and of Wordsworth's *Prelude*—it is improbable that the thoughts and feelings of maturity should be dismissed from literature: at any rate, Boswell first encountered Johnson when Johnson was fifty-one; and his biography, though based chiefly on Johnson's life *after* that encounter, has never lacked an audience.

Any one of these four poets would have had to profess a more modest ambition than the celebrated wish of the late Irish novelist, James Joyce: Milton or Dryden was destined to forge in the smithy of his soul, not the uncreated, but the already half-created conscience of his race. In those days the creative mind of England was dominated by images of two ancient cities: Jerusalem and Rome. From Jerusalem came Bunyan's *Pilgrim's Progress* and the landings on Plymouth Rock. From Rome came Gibbon's *Decline and Fall of the Roman Empire,* as well as philosophy, rationalism, skepticism, Greek atomic science, the new thought—and, ultimately, the industrial revolution:

> Locke sank into a swoon;
> The garden died.
> God took the spinning-jenny
> Out of his side.*

In practice, no educated poet could escape the impact of *both* cities: the garden is very much alive in *Paradise Lost,* even though the texture and design of that poem emulate Homer and Virgil—

---

* From William Butler Yeats, *Collected Poems* (New York: The Macmillan Company, 1938). Reprinted with the permission of The Macmillan Company.

even though Adam discusses with the angel the latest speculations in astrophysics.

What Rome meant as a cultural symbol in areas less abstruse than astrophysics can be seen most clearly from the first volume of Gibbon's history (Gibbon was a friend of Johnson), published in that interesting year 1776. Roman civilization, for Gibbon, evidently constituted a mean between two rival cultural extremes: the decadent totalitarian monarchy of Persia in the east; and the barbarian tribal anarchy of Scotland and Germany in the west. Rome at its best, as Gibbon saw it, possessed the independent-mindedness and the vigor of the tribes, happily combined with the literacy, sophistication, and centralized government of the Persians. Here, for example, is a profile of the Emperor Carus, campaigning against a troublesomely aggressive Persian ruler:

> The successor of Artaxerxes, Varanes or Bahram, though he had subdued the Segestans, one of the most warlike nations of Upper Asia, was alarmed at the approach of the Romans, and endeavored to retard their progress by a negotiation of peace. His ambassadors entered the camp about sunset, at the time when the troops were satisfying their hunger with a frugal repast. The Persians expressed their desire of being introduced to the presence of the Roman emperor. They were at length conducted to a soldier, who was seated on the grass. A piece of stale bacon and a few hard peas composed his supper. A coarse woolen garment of purple was the only circumstance that announced his dignity. The conference was conducted with the same disregard of courtly elegance. Carus, taking off a cap which he wore to conceal his baldness, assured the ambassadors that, unless their master acknowledged the superiority of Rome, he would speedily render Persia as naked of trees as his own head was destitute of hair. Notwithstanding some traces of art and preparation, we may discover in this scene the manners of Carus, and the severe simplicity which the martial princes, who succeeded Gallienus, had already restored in the Roman camps. The ministers of the Great King trembled and retired.

Such a passage, appearing as it does in one of the best-sellers of the period, helps to explain why it was natural for Pope to take the Emperor Augustus as an ideal of which George II was evidently a blatant caricature; or why Johnson drew his melancholy parallel between Charles XII of Sweden and Alexander the Great; or why Dryden, in *All for Love,* imposed what he took to be a more classical form on material which Shakespeare had so successfully Elizabethanized in *Antony and Cleopatra.*

The cultural influences of Jerusalem and Rome, however, had to compete with certain characteristic concerns of an England—especially a London—already beginning to think of itself as "modern." In addition to the new science (Dryden was an early member of the Royal Society, created by Charles II to foster scientific thought), there was also the new wealth, rising from commerce and banking (Dryden, who had connections among the landed aristocracy, was sometimes mockingly referred to, by poets sympathetic to the new wealth, as "Squire Dryden").

Capitalism scarcely plays a major role in Gibbon's account of the palmy days of Rome. The following extract comprises one of its very few appearances on the scene:

> Another and a last labor still awaited the indefatigable Aurelian [Roman emperor 270–275 A.D.]: to suppress a dangerous though obscure rebel, who, during the revolt of Palmyra, had arisen on the banks of the Nile. Firmus, the friend and ally, as he proudly styled himself, of Odenathus and Zenobia [rulers of Palmyra], was no more than a wealthy merchant of Egypt. In the course of his trade to India, he had formed very intimate connections with the Saracens and the Blemmyes, whose situation on either coast of the Red Sea gave them an easy introduction into the upper Egypt. The Egyptians he inflamed with the hope of freedom, and, at the head of their furious multitude, broke into the city of Alexandria, where he assumed the Imperial purple, coined money, published edicts, and raised an army, which, as he vainly boasted, he was capable of maintaining from the sole profits of his paper trade. Such troops were a feeble defence against the approach of Aurelian; and it seems almost unnecessary to relate, that Firmus was routed, taken, tortured, and put to death.

Firmus's English successors were found by the English equivalents of Aurelian to be far less easy to deal with. The Roman analogy offers only a limited insight into the merchants' strength and situation; to understand them more fully it is necessary to return for a moment to Jerusalem.

In Dryden's and Pope's day the Christian tradition—the only religion of any consequence in England—had assumed in England three competing forms: the Establishment, the dissenters, and Catholicism. All three were engaged in intermittent ideological battles among themselves, as well as in continuous warfare with that philosophic skepticism which derived ultimately from ancient Greece and Rome. Roughly speaking, the Anglican Establishment, after Charles II was restored in 1660, included the aristocracy and most of the nation; dissent (that is, the various sects that had split off from the Establishment) included the commercial classes of London and a portion of the nation at large; and Roman Catholics were a tiny minority. The ideas of all three groups derived both from the Bible and the writings of a long series of Christian thinkers who had interpreted this document; but the dissenters professed to base their doctrines exclusively on the Bible itself, the Catholics exclusively on the tradition of ecclesiastical interpretation, and the Anglicans on a combination of text and tradition. Politically, the dissenters were pro-Parliament and antimonarchy; the Anglicans tended to favor a strong monarchy; and the Catholics were suspected of subversively plotting to make England a dependency of France. Milton was, of course, the greatest literary figure that dissent produced. Pope was a Catholic; Johnson an Anglican; and Dryden first (probably) a skeptic, then an Anglican, finally a Catholic.

All the elements discussed so far—Rome, Jerusalem, politics, science, philosophy—made the cultural situation complex; and each of the four poets tended to produce his best work when the symbols he created in his verse reflected a high degree of that cultural complexity. Johnson harmonized Christian and classical philosophy in his "Vanity of Human Wishes"; Pope mingled London social life and classical legend to produce "The Rape of the Lock"; and Milton paralleled the fall of Satan with the more graceful descent of the minor Roman deity Mulciber:

> from morn
> To noon he fell; from noon to dewy eve,
> A summer's day; and with the setting sun
> Dropped from the zenith like a falling star,
> On Lemnos the Aegean isle.

As for Dryden, he took advantage of two undoubted facts: first, that the dissenting merchants of London presented to the detached observer a curious spectacle of belligerent Christian piety coupled with a shrewd, hard-fisted instinct for worldly success; and, second, that he, although heir to a classical, heroic, Roman way of looking at experience, was living in a modern, urban, unheroic world.

The mixture of theology and the full cash register which permeates certain brilliant sections of "Absalom and Achitophel" embodies a criticism of western ethics by no means applicable only during Dryden's lifetime. Decades after Dryden's death Pope took up the theme in one of the most powerful of his poems, the "Epistle to Bathurst" (Moral Essay III); and in the twentieth century George Orwell reports the following anecdote of "a legendary nonconformist grocer" and his shop assistant:

"James!"
"Yessir!"
"Have you sanded the sugar?"
"Yessir!"
"Have you watered the treacle?"
"Yessir!"
"Then come up to prayers."

Though something of a scholar, translator, and admirer of old poets like Homer and Chaucer, Dryden was also an intensely interested observer of his own time and place; he loved the court, the theater, the London scene, the ferment of new ideas, and the clash of political opinions. These contrasting qualities of his personality result, in his best verse, in a kind of irony—he is involved in his own world, and at the same time is observing it from outside. He recreates the ancient Roman theme with a beautifully elevated play on the Cleopatra story, and then flanks the drama fore and aft with a slangy prologue and epilogue aimed directly at the pit and the theater critics. These—the prologue and epilogue—reveal his ambivalent feelings about the past. On the one hand, the vanished Elizabethan age was to the present day as autumn is to winter:

> And since that plenteous autumn now is past,
> Whose grapes and peaches have indulg'd your taste,
> Take in good part, from our poor poet's board,
> Such rivel'd fruits as winter can afford.

On the other hand, if any old-fashioned critics expect *him* to imitate Shakespeare, the devil take them for not understanding the problem of a poet who must face his own time!

> Yet if some antiquated lady say,
> The last age is not copied in his play;

Heav'n help the man who for that face must drudge,
Which only has the wrinkles of a judge.

The greatest literary accomplishment of classical culture, in the opinion of the educated world from Milton's time to Johnson's, was not so much tragedy as epic; and the greatest poetic visions of both Pope and Dryden came as a result of their ability to see the modern world in the distorting mirror of the epic way of life. Cowley's *Davideis,* an epic about the Old Testament ruler, was popular in England some ten years before *Paradise Lost* appeared; the first book contains a spirited description of hell (which Cowley, like Dante, puts in the center of the earth), beginning as follows:

> Beneath the silent Chambers of the Earth
> Where the sun's fruitful Beams give Metals Birth,
> Where he the Growth of Fatal Gold does see,
> Gold which above more Influence has than he,
> Beneath the Dens where unfletcht Tempests lye,
> And Infant Winds their tender Voices try,
> Beneath the mighty Ocean's wealthy Caves,
> Beneath th' eternal Fountain of all Waves,
> Where their vast Court the Mother-waters keep,
> And undisturb'd by Moons in Silence sleep,
> There is a place deep, wondrous deep below,
> Which genuine Night and Horror does o'erflow;
> No Bound controls th' unwearied Space, but Hell
> Endless as those dire Pains that in it dwell. . . .

This description struck Dryden's imagination; and he later drew on it for certain overtones in a picture of the theatrical-and-redlight district of London, a city which he evidently found had something in common with hell:

> Close to the walls which fair Augusta [London] bind,
> (The fair Augusta much to fears inclin'd,)
> An ancient fabric rais'd t' inform the sight,
> There stood of yore, and Barbican it hight:
> A watchtower once; but now, so fate ordains,
> Of all the pile an empty name remains.
> From its old ruins brothel-houses rise,
> Scenes of lewd loves, and of polluted joys,
> *Where their vast courts the mother-strumpets keep,*
> *And, undisturb'd by watch* [police], *in silence sleep.*
> Near these a Nursery erects its head,

> Where queens are form'd and future heroes bred;
> *Where unfledg'd actors learn to laugh and cry,*
> *Where infant punks their tender voices try.* . . .

III

Two hundred years after those lines were written, the ability to read such poetry seemed almost to have become a lost art among admirers of English verse. The modern world—in such an unadorned form—was not thought to be, on the whole, a very profitable theme for the Muses—or indeed, for the contemplation of an educated person. Such was the nineteenth-century point of view; and because the nineteenth-century point of view has lingered on into the twentieth century and still influences many readers' unconscious preconceptions about poetry and what poetry should contain, it is worth dramatizing the difference between the two ages by two illustrations from literature outside Dryden's own writings.

A phrase in a Sherlock Holmes story, especially significant because so casual, is as good an indication as any of the nineteenth-century outlook. Holmes is toying with the idea of retiring from crime detection and devoting himself to certain "chemical researches" which have long been his occasional hobby; he says to Watson,

"Of late I have been tempted to look into the *problems furnished by nature* rather than *those more superficial ones for which our artificial state of society is responsible.*"

The italics are mine; for a nineteenth-century reader Holmes merely echoes a point of view all but taken for granted.

A poetic example will make the contrast between the values of the two periods still clearer. Everyone, even today, knows the story of Danaë, the princess whose father, hoping to forestall the appearance of potentially dangerous grandchildren, shut her up in a tower, only to have Zeus seduce her by falling into her lap in the form of a shower of gold. This legend Tennyson incorporated briefly in his well-known lyric description of a summer evening ("Now sleeps the crimson petal, now the white"), as follows:

> Now lies the Earth all Danaë to the stars
> And all thy heart lies open unto me.

It is not so well known that Pope (to whom a famous modern student of classical myths in English poetry devotes almost no attention) also used the Danaë story, submerging it just below the surface in a description of how Satan successfully seduced a London businessman from righteousness by making him fabulously wealthy:

> The Tempter saw his time; the work he ply'd;
> Stocks and Subscriptions pour on ev'ry side,
> 'Till all the Daemon makes his full descent,
> In one abundant show'r of Cent. per Cent.,
> Sinks deep within him, and possesses whole,
> Then dubs Director, and secures his soul.

Tennyson is clearly looking into "the problems furnished by nature"—starlight and young love. Pope is evidently interested rather in "those more superficial ones for which our artificial state of society is responsible." (Today not everyone is so sure these *are* superficial, or that some sort of social context for the individual human soul is so "artificial" as the romantics once tended to assume). What is interesting about the two treatments of Danaë, from the point of view of the literary critic, is that Pope has built a piece of poetry on the myth that is at least as rich, complex, and powerful as Tennyson's—*only in a totally different manner*. The graphic, almost obscene violence of the seduction imagery; the grotesqueness of replacing charming Danaë in the role of victim by middle-aged money-grubbing Sir Balaam; the modernizing, and vitalizing, of the "golden shower" image by means of offhand technical allusions to stock-exchange operations—these things took genius; and it was the genius of a poet, not a high priest of prose and reason.

IV

Milton, Dryden, Pope, and Johnson, as poets, are probably receiving more and better critical attention today than they have received at any time these last hundred years. Milton has had the most, being the greatest of the four; and Johnson's poems the least, for he wrote the smallest quantity of verse. Dryden's distinction among the four is unquestionably his versatility: the present anthology, for example, exhibits him as satirist, dramatist, verse translator, and critic, among other literary roles. As a satirist, he produced unquestionably the greatest political poem in the language, "Absalom and Achitophel"; as a dramatist, he wrote the best verse tragedy for the stage between the era of Shakespeare and Fletcher, and the twentieth century; of his Aeneid (his most ambitious verse translation) a recent critic has written that his "merits as a translator of Virgil surpass all those of his fellow translators put together . . . whatever Modern Translation may add in detail or alternative, it has not been able to supersede, or even rival, Dryden, book for book";* and, finally, as an essayist he has been again and again proclaimed the father of English prose.

The intrinsic nature of his genius can be understood partly in the light of the sort of attacks that have been made on him; defects are often a clue to qualities. According to one influential modern critic, Dryden had "a commonplace mind"; according to another, he was, although a "great, flawed poet," "rather a boor." It has often been pointed out how essentially derivative the bulk of his work is: his best play is based on one of Shakespeare's, some of the most famous speeches of which Dryden echoes or adapts; his criticism is partly a tissue of continental ideas and attitudes; "his original poems," one of their chief editors remarks, "were all occasional productions, written not from any creative impulse, but to serve some passing purpose"; and his great translations were—after all—translations. He has even been called a journalist in verse.

All the foregoing strictures are valid clues to his peculiar greatness, as well as to the influence he has exercised over subsequent English literature even down to the present day; for what Dryden set out to be can be very simply described: a popular poet, and at the same time an excellent one. He wanted to deal with the perennial themes and interests of the great masters of world literature—Homer, Chaucer, Shakespeare—and at the same time to write verse and prose as immediately and as widely effective as the inspired vaudeville turns to which some of his racier prologues and epilogues have been aptly compared. When Dryden the satirist makes a telling point, no learned monograph on seventeenth-century controversy is required to let us know what is happening:

---

* Ernest Stuart Bates, *Modern Translation* (London: Oxford University Press, 1936), p. 29; see also Douglas Bush, *Mythology and the Romantic Tradition in English Poetry* (Cambridge, Mass.: Harvard University Press, 1937), p. 17.

> The midwife laid her hand on his thick skull,
> With this prophetic blessing: *Be thou dull;*
> Drink, swear, and roar, forbear no lewd delight
> Fit for thy bulk; do anything but write.

When Dryden the dramatist builds up to an emotional climax—the rhythms of daily speech and the rhythms of the most precise blank verse blending with each other in his dialogue—the lapse of two and one-half centuries has still not made footnotes necessary to help the modern reader over any archaisms:

> CLEOPATRA: Go; leave me, soldier
> (For you're no more a lover): leave me dying:
> Push me, all pale and panting, from your bosom,
> And, when your march begins, let one run after,
> Breathless almost for joy, and cry—she's dead.
> The soldiers shout; you then, perhaps, may sigh,
> And muster all your Roman gravity:
> Ventidius chides; and straight your brow clears up,
> As I had never been.
> ANTONY: Gods, 'tis too much; too much for man to bear.

And when Dryden the critic praises an ancient author, his readers need no initiation into a technical vocabulary or metaphysical theory to follow his argument:

> Chaucer must have been a man of a most wonderful comprehensive nature, because, as it has been truly observed of him, he has taken into the compass of his *Canterbury Tales* the various manners and humours (as we now call them) of the whole English nation, in his age. . . . We have our forefathers and great-grand-dames all before us, as they were in Chaucer's days: their general characters are still remaining in mankind, and even in England, though they are called by other names than those of Monks, and Friars, and Canons, and Lady Abbesses, and Nuns; for mankind is ever the same, and nothing lost out of Nature, though everything is altered.

Dryden certainly attained his goal of popularity; indeed, toward the end of his life, after government patronage and the theater had failed him, he became, through his achievements in verse translation, the first English author to depend for a livelihood directly on the reading public, thus foreshadowing the lifelong independence of Pope, the wide circulation of the *Spectator Papers,* and the profitable careers of the great novelists during the next two centuries.

Dryden's literary excellence, which he achieved despite some care-lessness, lies in his wit and his vigor; in the psychological penetra-tion of his satire; in the rapidity of his narrative, and the clarity of his argumentative verses; in the fluency, melody, and variety of all his poems; and in the translucent ease of his essays. His subject matter, though intimately related to his place and time, will continue to interest readers who care whether popular authors write well or ill; who enjoy a good yarn or an energetic debate about eternal verities; and who do not mind if the motives of politicians, or other mortals, are sometimes scrutinized in no very kindly light. Nor will Dryden's point of view seem out of date to those who remem-ber that, widely as his political and religious opinions differed from those of his great contemporary Milton, the two poets nevertheless saw eye to eye on one central issue, the issue discussed in *Areo-pagitica*. As Dryden puts it in "The Hind and the Panther," while arguing for the freedom of certain sects which he still feared as wolfish internal enemies of the commonweal,

> Their native walks, methinks, they might enjoy,
> Curb'd of their native malice to destroy.
> Of all the tyrannies on human kind,
> The worst is that which persecutes the mind.

NOTE ON THE 1971 EDITION

The recent attention given "The Hind and the Panther" in such works as Phillip Harth's *Contexts of Dryden's Thought* and Earl Miner's *Dryden's Poetry* suggests that it ought be included in the Rinehart Dryden complete if included at all; and the same can be said of the attention paid to "Annus Mirabilis" by Miner, by Alan Roper in *Dryden's Poetic Kingdoms,* and by others. The second edition has also given a welcome opportunity for rearranging and expanding the Bibliography.

July, 1970   W. F.

A Brief Chronology
of Dryden's Life and Works

1631   John Dryden born August 9 (old style), probably at Aldwinckle All Saints, Northamptonshire; the first of fourteen children born to Erasmus and Mary Pickering Dryden; the grandson of Sir Erasmus Driden, baronet, and the Reverend Henry Pickering, rector of Aldwinckle All Saints. Both the Dridens and the Pickerings sided with Parliament against Charles II in the Civil Wars of the 1640's, and were presumably Puritans.

ca. 1644
−1650   Dryden at Westminster School, London, under famous headmaster Dr. Busby. John Locke at Westminster during this period. Dryden publishes elegy "Upon the Death of Lord Hastings" (a school fellow), 1649.

1650
−1654   Dryden at Trinity College, Cambridge. Publishes complimentary poem to his friend John Hoddesdon, 1650; writes love letter to his eighteen-year-old cousin, Honor Dryden, ca. 1653. B.A. degree, Cambridge, January, 1654. Father dies, June, 1654, leaving Dryden a small annual income (40 pounds).

1657
−1658   Employed in London as clerk in Commonwealth (Cromwellian) government. Writes elegy, "Heroic Stanzas," on the death of Cromwell, 1658.

1660
−1662   Writes poems on the restoration of Charles II, 1660, and on his coronation; also poems addressed to Sir Robert

Howard; to the statesman Clarendon; and to the archae-
ologist Dr. Charleton. Elected to the Royal Society on
Charleton's recommendation.

1663   Dryden's first play, a prose comedy, *The Wild Gallant,* a
failure (February). Writes poem to Lady Castlemaine,
then Charles II's favorite mistress, who liked the play.
Marries, on December 1, Lady Elizabeth Howard, sister of
Sir Robert Howard and youngest daughter of the loyalist
Earl of Berkshire; a woman of some means.

1664
–1665   Produces *The Rival Ladies,* his first verse drama. Collab-
orates with Sir Robert Howard on *The Indian Queen,* a
"heroic play" in couplets. Scores success with *The Indian
Emperor* (a sequel). Plague (spring, 1665) forces Dry-
den to leave London.

1666   Eldest son, Charles, born at Charleton in Wiltshire, the
country estate of Dryden's father-in-law. Dryden publishes
"Annus Mirabilis" to commemorate the great fire which
devastated London in September, and the naval war with
Holland; and to encourage public support for the mon-
archy. Writes "An Essay of Dramatic Poesy" (published
1668). Dropped from membership in Royal Society for
nonpayment of dues.

1667   Produces a tragicomedy, *Secret Love;* a comedy adapted
from Molière, *Sir Martin Mar-All;* and, in collaboration
with the famous playwright and poet laureate Sir Wil-
liam Davenant, an adaptation of Shakespeare's *Tempest.*
Second son, John, born (1667 or 1668). Dryden so
prosperous he is able to lend Charles II 500 pounds as
an investment.

1668
–1669   Upon the death of Davenant, April, 1668, warrant issued
to create Dryden poet laureate; Dryden renews loan to
Charles II. Third son, Erasmus Henry, born (1669). Pro-
duces the comedy *An Evening's Love* (1668); and the
heroic play *Tyrannic Love* (1669), with the role of
Valeria taken by Nell Gwyn, soon to bear Charles II a son.
Dryden made an M.A. at Cambridge, 17 June 1668, "by
.the dispensation of Archbishop Sheldon in consequence
of a recommendation of King Charles II."

1670   *The Conquest of Granada,* his most famous heroic play.
Appointed historiographer royal, in addition to poet laur-
eate, with yearly pension of 200 pounds, retroactive to
1668.

1671
–1672   George Villiers, Duke of Buckingham, produces *The Re-
hearsal,* a sprightly satire of heroic plays in general; of *The
Conquest of Granada* in particular; and of Dryden, lam-
pooned as "Mr. Bayes" in allusion to his laureateship
(*bayes* = laurel wreath). Dryden's *Marriage à la Mode,*
a tragicomedy; *Amboyna,* a political (anti-Dutch) tragedy;
and *The Assignation,* a comedy. Revival of *Secret Love,*
with the actress Anne Reeves, thought by some to have
been Dryden's mistress, reading the epilogue.

1673
–1674   Prologues and Epilogues to the University of Oxford.
Pamphlet war with Elkanah Settle, a younger dramatist
much patronized by the nobility. Writes *The State of
Innocence,* an opera based on *Paradise Lost.* Dryden's loan
to Charles II repaid with interest.

1675   Dryden's *Aureng-Zebe,* a heroic play, influenced by Racine
and Shakespeare.

1676   A prologue to the University of Oxford ("He chooses
Athens in his riper age"). Mother dies (June); small in-
crease in inherited income.

1677   *All for Love.* Dryden's pension nominally increased to
300 pounds; but only half paid in fact (1677–1684).

1678   *The Kind Keeper,* a comedy; and the tragedy, *Oedipus,*
written in collaboration with Nathaniel Lee. Dryden shifts
his theatrical activities from King's Company to Duke's.
Adapts Shakespeare's *Troilus and Cressida.* Writes "Mac
Flecknoe."

1679   Essay, "The Grounds of Criticism in Tragedy." "An Essay
on Satire," by Dryden's friend, the Earl of Mulgrave, cir-
culates anonymously in manuscript; contains attacks on
the Earl of Rochester and on two of the King's mistresses.
Dryden (suspected of being the author) beaten by hired
thugs in Rose Alley, Covent Garden.

1680   *The Spanish Friar,* a tragicomedy. *Ovid's Epistles,* by a number of authors, published, with preface by Dryden; Dryden's part in the volume constitutes his first experiment in verse translation.

1681   "Absalom and Achitophel." Nine editions in two years.

1682   "The Medal." Nahum Tate's "The Second Part of Absalom and Achitophel," containing passages on Settle and Shadwell by Dryden. *The Duke of Guise,* a tragedy with elements of political satire, by Dryden and Nathaniel Lee. "Religio Laici." Unauthorized version of "Mac Flecknoe" published (the poem's first appearance in print).

1683   Writes a *Life of Plutarch,* and collaborates in translating Plutarch's *Lives.*

1684   Jacob Tonson (Dryden's publisher after he left Herringman in 1678) publishes *Miscellany Poems,* containing (with Dryden's authorization) "Mac Flecknoe," "Absalom and Achitophel," and "The Medal"; several of Dryden's prologues and epilogues; and short translations by Dryden of Theocritus, Ovid, and Virgil. Poems addressed to Roscommon (author of "An Essay on Translated Verse"), "To the Memory of Mr. Oldham." Translation of Maimbourg's *History of the League.*

1685   Death of Charles II; Dryden's elegy, "Threnodia Augustalia." Tonson publishes the anthology, *Sylvae, or the Second Part of Poetical Miscellanies,* containing a preface, and translations from Lucretius, Virgil, Theocritus, and Horace, by Dryden. "To the Memory of Anne Killigrew." *Albion and Albanius,* Dryden's first opera. A sequel, *King Arthur,* written but not acted. Dryden becomes a Catholic.

1687   "The Hind and the Panther." "A Song for St. Cecilia's Day."

1688   Translates Bouhours' *Life of St. Francis Xavier.* "Britannia Rediviva," a poem celebrating the birth of a son to James II. James II dethroned; the Protestant William III crowned. Dryden ousted as poet laureate and historiographer royal; Shadwell installed in these offices. "Epigram on Milton."

1689   For financial reasons, Dryden returns to the theater: *Don Sebastian,* a tragedy, his first independently written play in nine years.

1690   *Amphityron,* a comedy adapted from Molière.

1691   The opera *King Arthur* performed. "Eleonora," a poem in memory of the late Countess of Abingdon.

1692   *Cleomenes,* a tragedy. Dryden's *Satires of Juvenal and Persius* (prefaced by Dryden's "Discourse Concerning . . . Satire"; the Persius translated entirely by Dryden; the Juvenal by Dryden and others selected by him, including his sons Charles and John).

1693   Tonson's *Examen Poeticum: Being the Third Part of Miscellany Poems;* Dryden contributes three selections from Ovid's *Metamorphoses,* an episode from the *Iliad,* and the preface (dedication) to the volume. Translates some of Ovid's *Art of Love* (not published during his lifetime). Dryden's last play, *Love Triumphant,* a tragicomedy. Dryden begins work on his translation of Virgil.

1694   "To My Dear Friend Mr. Congreve." "To Sir Godfrey Kneller." Virgil's *Georgics III* (in Tonson's *Fourth . . . Miscellany*). His son Erasmus Henry Dryden ordained a Dominican priest in Rome, after study at Douay and Rome.

1695   "Ode on the Death of Mr. Henry Purcell." Translation of Dr. Fresnoy's *Art of Painting.* Sir Richard Blackmore attacks Dryden in the preface to his *Prince Arthur.* John Dryden, Jr.'s, comedy, *The Husband His Own Cuckold,* acted.

1697   Translation of *The Works of Virgil,* containing an essay on the *Georgics* by Addison, published. "Alexander's Feast." Dryden scotches Tonson's plan to dedicate *Works of Virgil* to William III. Dryden's profits probably about 1,200 pounds.

1698   Dryden translates Book I of Tacitus' *Annals.* Jeremy Collier's *Short View of the Immortality and Profaneness of the English Stage.* Milbourne's (hostile) *Notes on Dryden's Virgil.* Charles Dryden returns from several years in Rome at Pope's court.

1700   *Fables,* including a preface; poems to the Duchess of Ormond and to "My Honor'd Kinsman John Driden"; translations of Chaucer's *Knight's Tale, Nun's Priest's Tale, Wife of Bath's Tale,* and character of the parson from the

Prologue to *The Canterbury Tales;* translations of large parts of Ovid's *Metamorphoses;* a translation of the Middle English poem "The Flower and the Leaf"; and verse adaptations of three tales from Boccaccio's *Decameron.* Tonson pays 300 pounds for *Fables.* Prologue, Epilogue, and "Secular Masque" for Fletcher's *Pilgrim.* Death of Dryden, May 1.

A NOTE ON THE TEXT

Thanks are due to the Houghton Mifflin Company and the late Professor George R. Noyes for permission to reprint the poems included here from the text prepared by Professor Noyes for the Cambridge Edition of Dryden's *Poetical Works,* revised 1950. The text of the "Essay of Dramatic Poesy" follows Dryden's revision of 1684, rather than the first edition (1668). For reading and commenting on Introduction and Brief Chronology, respectively, I am grateful to Maynard Mack and James Osborn.

WILLIAM FROST

Santa Barbara, California
March, 1953

Selected Bibliography

BIBLIOGRAPHIES:

HUGH MACDONALD, *John Dryden: A Bibliography of Early Editions and of Drydeniana.* New York, Oxford University Press, 1939.

SAMUEL HOLT MONK, *John Dryden: A List of Critical Studies Published from 1895 to 1948.* Minneapolis, University of Minnesota Press, 1950.

O. M. BRACK, JR., C. N. FIFER, W. J. FARRELL, D. T. TORCHIANA, and C. A. ZIMANSKY, eds., *English Literature 1660–1800: A Current Bibliography,* published annually in *Philological Quarterly.*

CONCORDANCE:

GUY MONTGOMERY, *A Concordance to the Works of John Dryden.* Berkeley, University of California Press, 1957.

EDITIONS:

E. N. HOOKER, H. T. SWEDENBERG, E. MINER, *et al.,* eds., *The William Andrews Clark Edition of Dryden's Works:* Vol. I, *Poems 1649–1680* [1956]; Vol. VIII, *Wild Gallant, Rival Ladies, Indian Queen* [1962]; Vol. III, *Poems 1685–92* [1969]; Vol. X, *Tempest, Evening's Love, Tyrannic Love* [1970]; Vol. XVII, *Essay of Dramatic Poesy* [1971]; etc. Berkeley and Los Angeles, University of California Press.

SIR WALTER SCOTT and GEORGE SAINTSBURY, eds., *The Works of John Dryden*. London, William Paterson, 1882–1893.

JAMES KINSLEY, ed., *The Poems of John Dryden*. Oxford, The Clarendon Press, 1958.

———, [Selected] *Poems and Fables of John Dryden*. London and New York, Oxford University Press, 1962.

GEORGE R. NOYES, ed., *The Poetical Works of Dryden*. Cambridge, Mass., Houghton Mifflin Company, 1909; rev. ed., 1950.

W. P. KER, ed., [Selected] *Essays of John Dryden*. Oxford, The Clarendon Press, 1900.

ARTHUR C. KIRSCH, ed., *Literary Criticism of John Dryden*. Lincoln, University of Nebraska Press, 1966.

JAMES T. BOULTON, *Of Dramatick Poesy, An Essay*. London, Oxford University Press, 1964.

GEORGE WATSON, ed., *Dryden's Of Dramatic Poesy, and other Critical Essays*. London, J. M. Dent & Sons, Ltd.; New York, E. P. Dutton & Co., Inc., 1962.

JAMES KINSLEY, ed., *The Works of Virgil Translated by John Dryden*. London, Oxford University Press, 1961.

L. A. BEAURLINE and F. BOWERS, eds., *John Dryden: Four Comedies* and *John Dryden: Four Tragedies* [including *All For Love*]. Chicago and London, University of Chicago Press, 1967.

W. BRADFORD GARDNER, ed., *Dryden's Prologues and Epilogues: A Critical Edition*. New York, Columbia University Press, 1951.

CYRUS LAWRENCE DAY, ed., *The Songs of John Dryden*. Cambridge, Mass., Harvard University Press, 1932.

CHARLES E. WARD, ed., *The Letters of John Dryden, with Letters Addressed to Him*. Durham, Duke University Press, 1942.

DAVID ZESMER, ed., *Dryden: Poems, Plays and Essays*. New York, Toronto, London, Bantam Books, 1967.

LOUIS I. BREDVOLD, ed., *The Best of Dryden*. New York, The Ronald Press Company, 1933.

EARL MINER, ed., *Selected Poetry and Prose of John Dryden*, New York, Random House, 1969.

BIOGRAPHY AND HISTORICAL BACKGROUND:

JAMES M. OSBORN, *John Dryden: Some Biographical Facts and Problems*. New York, Columbia University Press, 1940; Gainesville, University of Florida Press, 1965 (rev.).

CHARLES E. WARD, *The Life of John Dryden*. Chapel Hill, University of North Carolina Press, 1961.

SIR WALTER SCOTT, "Life of Dryden," in *Works of John Dryden* (see above), Vol. I. (ed. by B. Kreissman, University of Nebraska Press, 1963).

SAMUEL JOHNSON, "Life of Dryden," in *The Lives of the Poets* (London, 1779–1781), ed. G. B. Hill. Oxford, The Clarendon Press, 1905.

GEORGE SAINTSBURY, *Dryden*. New York, Harper & Brothers, 1881.

B. N. SCHILLING, *Dryden and the Conservative Myth, A Reading of "Absalom and Achitophel."* New Haven, Yale University Press, 1961.

LOUIS I. BREDVOLD, *The Intellectual Milieu of John Dryden: Studies in Some Aspects of Seventeenth-Century Thought.* Ann Arbor, University of Michigan Press, 1934, 1956.

ALEXANDRE BELJAME, *Men of Letters and the English Public in the Eighteenth Century, 1660–1744: Dryden, Addison, Pope* (Paris, 1881), ed. Bonamy Dobree, trans. by E. O. Lorimer. London, Routledge & Kegan Paul Ltd., 1948.

GEORGE DE F. LORD and others, eds., *Poems on Affairs of State 1660–1714*, New Haven: Vol. I, 1660–1678 [1963]; Vol. II, 1678–1681 [ed. E. F. Mengel, Jr., 1965]; Vol. III, 1682–1685 [ed. H. H. Schless, 1968]; Vol. IV, 1685–1688 [ed. G. M. Crump, 1968].

CRITICISM:

PROSSER HALL FRYE, "Dryden and the Critical Canons of the Eighteenth Century." *University of Nebraska Studies*, VII (1907), 1–39.

A. W. VERRALL, *Lectures on Dryden*. Cambridge, at the University Press, 1914.

MARK VAN DOREN, *John Dryden: A Study of His Poetry*. New York, Holt, Rinehart and Winston, Inc., 1920; rev. ed., 1946.

THOMAS STEARNS ELIOT, *Homage to John Dryden: Three Essays on the Poetry of the Seventeenth Century*. London, L. and Virginia Woolf, 1924.

———, *John Dryden: The Poet, the Dramatist, the Critic*. New York: T. & Elsa Holliday, 1932.

RUTH C. WALLERSTEIN, "The Development of the Rhetoric and Metre of the Heroic Couplet, Especially in 1625–1645," *Pub. Mod. Lang. Assoc.*, L (1935), 166–209.

GEORGE WILLIAMSON, "The Rhetorical Pattern of Neoclassical Wit," *Modern Philology*, XXXIII (1935), 55–81.

MARY CLAIRE RANDOLPH, "The Structural Design of the Formal Verse Satire." *Philological Quarterly*, XXI (1942), 368–384.

F. L. HUNTLEY, *On Dryden's Essay of Dramatic Poesy*. Ann Arbor, University of Michigan, 1951, 1968.

D. W. JEFFERSON, "Aspects of Dryden's Imagery." *Essays in Criticism,* IV (1954), 20–41.

WILLIAM FROST, *Dryden and the Art of Translation.* New Haven, Yale University Press, 1955, 1969.

L. W. CAMERON, "The Cold Prose Fits of John Dryden" [on his translations of Maimbourg and Bouhours]. *Révue de Littérature Comparée,* XXX (1956), 371–379.

L. PROUDFOOT, *Dryden's Aeneid and its Seventeenth-Century Predecessors.* Manchester [England], Manchester University Press, 1960.

F. T. PRINCE, "Dryden Redivivus." *A Review of English Literature,* I (1960), 71–79.

UPALI AMARASINGHE, *Dryden and Pope in the Early Nineteenth Century; A Study of Changing Taste.* Cambridge [England], Cambridge University Press, 1962.

ARTHUR W. HOFFMAN, *John Dryden's Imagery.* Gainesville, University of Florida Press, 1962.

EUGENE R. WAITH, *The Herculean Hero in Marlowe, Shakespeare, and Dryden.* New York, Columbia University Press, 1962.

JOHN M. ADEN, *Critical Opinions of John Dryden, A Dictionary.* Nashville, Vanderbilt University Press, 1963.

A. D. HOPE, "Anne Killigrew or the Art of Modulating," *Southern Review* [University of Adelaide], No. 1 (1963), 4–14.

PETER NAZARETH, "*All for Love:* Dryden's Hybrid Play," *English Studies in Africa* VI (1963), 154–63.

BERNARD N. SCHILLING, *Dryden: A Collection of Critical Essays.* Englewood Cliffs, Prentice-Hall, 1963.

IRÈNE SIMON, "Dryden's Revision of the *Essay of Dramatic Poesy,*" *Review of English Studies* 14 (1963), 142–141.

L. P. GOGGIN, "This Bow of Ulysses" [on *All for Love*], *Duquesne Studies,* Philological Series No. 5 (1964), 49–86.

BRUCE A. ROSENBERG, "*Annus Mirabilis* Distilled," *Pub. Mod. Lang. Assoc.* 79 (1964), 254–58.

D. T. STARNES, "Imitation of Shakespeare in Dryden's *All for Love, Texas Studies in Literature and Language* 6 (1964), 39–46.

G. R. WASSERMAN, *John Dryden.* New York, Twayne, 1964.

ARTHUR C. KIRSCH, *Dryden's Heroic Drama.* Princeton University Press, 1965.

J. A. LEVINE, "Dryden's *Song for St. Cecilia's Day, 1687,*" *Philological Quarterly* 44 (1965), 38–50.

B. K. LEWALSKI, "The Scope and Function of Biblical Allusion in *Absalom and Achitophel,*" *English Language Notes* 3 (1965), 29–35.

ALAN ROPER, *Dryden's Poetic Kingdoms.* London, Routledge & Kegan Paul, 1965.

SELMA A. ZEBOUNI, *Dryden: A Study in Heroic Characterization.* Baton Rouge, Louisiana State University Press, 1965.

D. M. VIETH, "Irony in Dryden's *Ode to Anne Killigrew*," *Studies in Philology* 62 (1965), 91–100.

R. A. ANSELMENT, "Martin Marprelate: A New Source for Dryden's Fable of the Martin and the Swallows," *Review of English Studies* 17 (1966), 256–67.

BRUCE KING, *Dryden's Major Plays.* Edinburgh, Oliver and Boyd, 1966.

A. E. WALLACE MAURER, "The Design of Dryden's *The Medall*," *Papers On Language and Literature* 2 (1966), 293–304.

H. T. SWEDENBERG, JR., *Essential Articles for the Study of John Dryden.* Hamden, Conn., Archon, 1966.

J. E. WELLINGTON, "Conflicting Concepts of Man in *Absalom and Achitophel*," *Satire Newsletter* 4 (1966), 2–11.

M. W. ALSSID, "Shadwell's *Mac Flecknoe*," *Studies in English Literature,* 7 (1967), 387–402.

A. FOWLER and D. BROOKS, "The Structure of Dryden's *Song for St. Cecilia's Day, 1687*," *Essays in Criticism* 17 (1967), 434–47.

EARL MINER, *Dryden's Poetry.* Bloomington and London, Indiana University Press, 1967.

H. D. WEINBROT, "Alexas in *All for Love:* His Genealogy and Function," *Studies in Philology* 64 (1967), 629–39.

DENNIS DAVISON, *Dryden.* London, Evans Brothers, 1968.

ANNE DAVIDSON FERRY, *Milton and the Miltonic Dryden.* Cambridge, Harvard University Press, 1968.

PHILLIP HARTH, *Contexts of Dryden's Thought.* Chicago and London, University of Chicago Press, 1968. On *Religio Laici* and *The Hind and the Panther.*

BRUCE KING, *20th Century Interpretations of ALL FOR LOVE.* Englewood Cliffs, Prentice-Hall, 1968.

K. G. HAMILTON, *John Dryden and the Poetry of Statement.* East Lansing, Michigan State University Press, 1969.

JAMES H. JENSEN, *A Glossary of Dryden's Critical Terms.* Minneapolis, University of Minnesota Press, 1969.

BRUCE KING, ed., *Dryden's Mind and Art.* Edinburgh, Oliver and Boyd, 1969.

PAUL RAMSEY, *The Art of John Dryden.* Lexington, University of Kentucky Press, 1969.

MICHAEL WILDING, "Allusion and Innuendo in *Mac Flecknoe*," *Essays in Criticism* 19 (1969), 355–70.

LEON M. GUILHAMET, "Dryden's Debasement of Scripture in *Absalom and Achitophel*," *Studies in English Literature* 9 (1969): 395–413.

Contents

Satires

Commentary on the Satires

MAC FLECKNOE

Mac Flecknoe, Dryden's most exuberant and entertaining poem, appears to have been written in 1678 and circulated in manuscript among Dryden's friends. A bookseller named Green got hold of it four years later and published a somewhat inaccurate text of it, without Dryden's authority. After this, Dryden allowed it to be published—anonymously—in the publisher Tonson's anthology, *Miscellany Poems,* in 1684, but he did not publicly acknowledge his authorship of it till 1692.

As a poem, though much of the best of its humor is just as apparent to an uninstructed modern reader as it was to Dryden's contemporaries, *Mac Flecknoe* embodies in many details the special interests of the poet and his age, as described in the Introduction to this volume. Specifically, the full bite and punch of many lines will be more readily available to a modern reader specially briefed on the following topics:

1. *London Theatrical and Literary Life of the 1660's and 70's.* *T. S.* or *Sh*——, the main target of the satire, is Thomas Shadwell, a dramatist of the Restoration who felt that on him had descended the mantle of the great Elizabethan poet-playwright, Ben Jonson (d. 1637). Shadwell was the author of a number of "humor" comedies—that is, comedies featuring exaggerated personal eccentricities ("humors") in various characters, rather like certain well-known types on radio or television today. His plays, though by no means so totally devoid of merit as Dryden's satire implies, are far below Jonson's in quality (the mantle did not quite fit), and make gen-

erous use of the kind of bawdy dialogue suggested by Dryden in line 181 (where "selling bargains" means replying to an innocent question with some flippant indecency). Dryden also refers, in the blanket tossing (42) and the trap door (212), to slapstick devices Shadwell had used in two of his plays. *Mac Flecknoe* is full of allusions to the titles of these plays: *Epsom Wells, Psyche, The Miser, The Humorists, The Hypocrite,* and *The Virtuoso,* which Dryden insinuates Shadwell took five years to write (he was known to be a rather slow worker); and there are likewise allusions to various characters in them: *Sir Formal, Prince Nicander, Longvil, Raymond, Bruce.* Shadwell's works, when published, were often dedicated to the Duke of Newcastle, the location of whose country estate Dryden indicates in the phrase *northern dedications* (170).

Personally, Shadwell was a large, corpulent fellow (Dryden himself, in the words of his editor Noyes, was "a pudgy little man"), and an opium addict; in line 126 Dryden manages to imply that the soporific nature of Shadwell's writings is somehow connected with his personal use of the poppy; elsewhere (197) he remarks, *Thy tragic muse gives smiles, thy comic, sleep.* In politics —not an issue in this poem except for the fact that the publishers (probably) inserted the phrase *trueblue Protestant* into the title— Shadwell was a Whig; he was destined to become Poet Laureate after Dryden's Toryism, Catholicism, and loyalty to James II had caused his ouster from that office in 1688. Shadwell's size and sensuousness—which did *not,* however, afford him any valid *likeness* (194) to the stout Jonson—are alluded to in the *tympany* (or drum) and the *tun* and *kilderkin* (wine casks of large and small sizes) of lines 193–195.

The relations of Dryden and Shadwell appear to have been fairly cordial up to 1678, though the two men had been needling each other for some years in occasional prefaces to their published writings. In 1678, however, Shadwell made the mistake of publicly praising Buckingham's *Rehearsal,* a play that had lampooned Dryden (see Chronological Table, 1671); and *Mac Flecknoe* was, apparently, the result.

The title and central idea of the poem derive from the fact that 1678 saw the death of Richard Flecknoe, an author now totally forgotten, but known unfavorably in Dryden's day as an execrable minor poet and playwright. Dryden seized on the idea of making the dying Flecknoe bequeath to Shadwell, as his son ("Mac") and successor, the empire and laureateship of bad writing; and he made use in the poem of the facts that Flecknoe was Irish (Ireland at that time was a proverbial symbol of illiteracy and boorishness), that he was a *priest* (119), that he had once made a trip to *Portugal* (36), and that he had written a play called *Love's Kingdom* (122). As far as we know, the alleged connection between Irish Flecknoe and Shadwell existed wholly within the realm of Dryden's fertile imagination; at any rate, Shadwell's reaction to *Mac Flecknoe* (a reaction which goes far in itself to justify Dryden's allegations of obtuseness) was in part as follows: "Sure he goes a little too far in calling me the dullest, and has no more reason for that than giving me the Irish name of Mack, when he knows I never saw Ireland till I was three and twenty years old, and was there but four months"!

Since the Restoration theater was dominated by traditions deriving from the spacious days of Queen Elizabeth, Dryden associates with the Flecknoe-Shadwell succession three Elizabethan dramatists then in low repute: *Heywood, Shirley,* and *Dekker.* For contrasting symbols of literary *merit,* from which he *dis*sociates Flecknoe-Shadwell, he uses *Fletcher* and *Jonson,* as well as the Restoration poet-playwright, Sir Charles Sedley (163; Sedley figures as *Lisideius* in *An Essay of Dramatic Poesy*), and the Restoration comic dramatist "Gentle George" Etherege. According to Dryden, the follies of Etherege's characters (*Dorimant, Loveit, Cully, Cockwood, Fopling*) attest their creator's cleverness; whereas the follies of Shadwell's merely reflect their creator's folly.

Miscellaneous theatrical information incorporated in *Mac Flecknoe* includes the names of the operatic performer *Singleton,* who had appeared in the role of *Valerius* in a play by Davenant; of *Maximin,* an exaggeratedly heroic hero in an early play of Dryden's own; of *Simkin,* apparently a low-comedy part in the drama of the time; of *Panton,* a punster (*clinches,* 83, are puns); and of *St. André,* a dancing teacher. Dryden uses the traditional classical symbols for comedy and tragedy, the *sock* and *buskin,* respectively (79–80); and he derives part of his setting from the so-called *Nursery* (74), a playhouse founded in 1664 by Charles II, the theater-loving monarch, to train child actors.

To pass from the theater to the literary world generally, *Mac Flecknoe* also singles out the mediocre but much publicized hack writer *Ogleby,* who, with brilliant alliteration, is made Shadwell's uncle, just as Flecknoe is Shadwell's father (174). *Herringman,* a former publisher of both Dryden and Shadwell, also makes a brief appearance (105), in the role of a *bilked stationer,* or publisher ruined by the failure of such writers as Shadwell and Ogleby to sell. So poor have been the sales, in fact, that pages of these authors' works, Dryden asserts, are now put to humbler uses as wrapping paper in pastry shops or conveniences in privies (101). At the conclusion of the poem Dryden advises Shadwell, because he lacks talent, to eschew satire (*keen iambics*) and stick to the then equivalent of cross-word-puzzle production: anagrams, acrostics, poems printed in the shapes of objects (*wings* and *altars*), poems *set* to music as popular songs, or poems made up entirely of the letters of a single word, combined *ten thousand ways* (204–210).

2. *The London Scene Generally.* Less pleasing aspects of the London scene appear in allusions to the Thames as a sewer (50); to *Pissing Alley* (there was in fact a street of that name); to prostitution (72, 77); to the *watch* or police; and to hysterical popular suspicions about subversive "plots" (65). *Aston Hall* (48), as yet unidentified, was presumably also disreputable. To produce the general mock-heroic tone of the poem, Dryden closely combines these sordid matters with Christian and classical materials.

3. *Christian and Classical Materials.* Shadwell is compared to Jesus (the *last great prophet,* 30); Flecknoe, his predecessor, to John the Baptist (*sent before but to prepare thy way,* 32); Heywood and Shirley, "bad" poets of an earlier age, to Old Testament prefigurations (*types*) of the new revelation (29). (Like John the Baptist, Flecknoe wears simple garments: *Norwich drugget,* 33).

In another enlarging metaphor, Flecknoe is an emperor who, like Augustus, the first emperor of Rome, chooses his own successor on the basis of merit (3); moreover, he possesses the medieval scepter, ball, and sacred anointing oil as symbols of power (118–121), not to mention a *Kingdom* derived from the title of one of his plays. Shadwell himself occurs under various historical and mythological guises: as *Arion* (43), the Greek musician who charmed even the dolphins swimming about his ship (an allusion to Shadwell's high opinion of his own musical talents); as *Ascanius* (108), Flecknoe's "son"*); as *Hannibal* (112), Rome's greatest military

---

* With 173–174 compare the line Dryden later adopted from Virgil (*Aeneid* iii, 343) as a motto for a play (*The Husband His Own Cuckold*) written by his son John, Jr., and dedicated to his brother-in-law Sir Robert

the son of Rome's legendary founder Aeneas (just as Shadwell is enemy; or as *Romulus* (130), another legendary founder of the city on the Tiber. *Rome,* of course, has a double function as symbol: where Shadwell is its ruler, it stands for supreme dullness; where he appears as its *sworn foe* (113), it stands for supreme enlightenment. Epic style occurs in the appellation *Augusta* (64) for London; as well as in the archaic language of, for example, line 134 (where *honors* means hair) and 137, where Shadwell is again a *prophet,* ironically possessed or inspired, like an ancient frenzied priest, by the god of dullness.

All these various materials—myth, religion, history, greenroom gossip—Dryden unites in a subtle fabric of contrasting attitudes. Touched by the sorcery of his style, Flecknoe takes the form of an impressive monarch in the first four lines, or a romantic troubadour in the passage beginning *My warbling lute* (35). Shadwell sails down the Thames like Cleopatra, glorious on the Nile; and contemporary London derives a kind of seedy grandeur from its *old ruins* (70), *a monument of vanished minds* (82). But scarcely has grandeur or romance shown its face when it modulates into the *Nonsense, punks,* or *well-sharpened thumbs* of satire. Just as Milton in *Paradise Lost* created an unforgettable hell out of impossible combinations of attributes (like "darkness visible"), so Dryden in *Mac Flecknoe* creates a Shadwell who, though debased, is a far more impressive phenomenon in his very degradation than any actual Restoration poetaster could be or could ever have been: *And lambent dullness played about his face.* This is the apotheosis of ineptitude; this is the *genuine night* of major satire. From it Pope was to derive his *Dunciad.*

ABSALOM AND ACHITOPHEL

Dryden wrote *Absalom and Achitophel* at the age of fifty. During his lifetime England had experienced several successive forms of government: the Stuart monarchy under Charles I, beheaded in 1649; the Commonwealth or Republic (what Dryden in the poem calls a *State,* or *The Good Old Cause*), dominated by Parliament and the dissenting sects, from 1649 to 1653; the Pro-

---

Howard: *Et pater Aeneas et avunculus excitet Hector* ("Let both his father Aeneas and his uncle Hector spur him on"). Here Shadwell is again an Ascanius.

tectorate, a kind of military dictatorship under Oliver Cromwell, from 1653 to Cromwell's death in 1658 (and under his son Richard for a year afterward); and the restored Stuart monarchy under Charles II, from 1660 on. Now, in 1681, it looked as though further sudden, unconstitutional, and perhaps violent changes might be in the offing, since Charles II's legal successor, his brother James, Duke of York, was hated for his known Catholicism, because of which moves were on foot to exclude him, by act of Parliament, from the succession. A kind of anti-Catholic "witch hunt" (as we should call it now) had been in progress for three years in London. It was based on allegations of a subversive plot by a Catholic underground against Charles's life and the Protestant religion; and a party headed by the Protestant nobles Shaftesbury and Buckingham was attempting to stir up sentiment in favor of declaring the Duke of Monmouth (an illegitimate but Protestant son of Charles) the heir to the throne. Monmouth, who had won some military glory on the continent and in Scotland, had even been sent on a sort of "grass-roots" tour of the kingdom in 1680 (lines 729–744).

Not long before publication of the poem, however, public sentiment had turned in favor of Charles, who, though fond of Monmouth personally, did not want the legal succession interfered with; and Shaftesbury had been arrested on a charge of high treason. *Absalom and Achitophel,* which probably appeared shortly before Shaftesbury's trial, dramatizes and analyses the recent political imbroglios.

For the purposes of his dramatic analysis Dryden, rather like Milton in *Samson Agonistes,* had recourse to a parallel from Old Testament history—an especially appropriate kind of metaphor in an age when religion and politics were so closely intermeshed. In II Samuel 13–16, the great David, successor to the famous Saul as king of Israel, has had difficulties with a brief rebellion led by Absalom, an offspring of one of his numerous concubines. In this rebellion Absalom is counseled by a certain Achitophel, an enemy of David's government. In the Bible story the rebellion, dealt with by the astuteness of David and his advisors, fails completely. Absalom, defeated in battle, meets his death—contrary to David's express orders—at the hands of the government's victorious general. The episode concludes with David's heartbroken words: "O my son Absalom, my son, my son, Absalom! would God I had died for thee, O Absalom, my son, my son!"

Starting from a basic initial resemblance of ancient and modern situations, Dryden constructs a thoroughgoing analogy between Old Testament Israel and contemporary England. Thus, in the poem, *Israel* is England; the *Jews* (or the Israelites), the English. *Jerusalem* is London; *Hebron,* Scotland where Charles II had first been crowned); *Egypt,* France; *Gath,* Brussels (scene of Charles's exile before his restoration); the *Nile,* the Seine; *Tyrus,* Holland; and *Jordan's sand* (270) the coast at Dover where Charles landed in 1660. An *Abbethdin* is a judge; the *Sanhedrin,* the Parliament; the *Solymaean rout,* the London mob (Solyma was a name for Jerusalem); and *Pharaoh,* Louis XIV of France. The *Jebusites* are the Catholics (Jebus was an ancient name for Jerusalem); the *Jewish rabbins* (or Hebrew priests), the Church of England clergy; the *Levites,* the Presbyterians; the *ark,* the national religion; *Aaron's race,* the priesthood in general; a *rabbinical degree,* an ordination; a *Rechabite,* one who has forsworn drinking on religious grounds; and *Judge's days* (520), the Commonwealth period when the sects dominated the country. *Egyptian rites* (118) implies a comparison between the French (Catholic) doctrine of transubstantiation and the holiness of certain foods in the actual ancient Egyptian religion. *Belial* and *Beelzebub,* as in the Bible, symbolize evil. The chosen people are the English Protestants, and the heathen priesthood, the Catholic priests.

David, of course, is Charles; Dryden stresses a parallel between the two kings in their promiscuity (he gives the name of *Bathsheba,* David's most famous concubine, to the Duchess of Portsmouth, currently Charles's mistress), and also in their paternal affection, clemency, and statesmanship. *Absalom* is Monmouth (both were famous for good looks); and *Achitophel,* Shaftesbury. *Shimei,* who (in the Bible) publicly cursed David at the time of Absalom's rebellion, is Slingsby Bethel, the Whig Sheriff of London, notorious for his Puritanism, antiroyalism, and stinginess. From other Old Testament episodes Dryden took the names of the conspirator *Zimri* for Buckingham (author of *The Rehearsal:* see Chronological Table, 1671); the rebel *Corah,* for Titus Oates, instigator of action against the alleged Popish plot; and the statesman *Barzillai,* for the Duke of Ormond, friend and counselor to both Charles I and Charles II. One passage in the poem (829–861) constitutes an elegy for the death of Ormond's eldest son. These comprise the central personages of the drama.

Among the lesser figures are *Michal,* who represents Charles's queen; *Saul,* Cromwell; *Ishbosheth,* Cromwell's son Richard; and *Agag,* probably a certain Justice Scraggs, who presided at one of the trials connected with the Plot more impartially than Corah (the archwitness) liked. To various Whig nobility and gentry Dryden gives the names *Balaam, Caleb, Jonas, Issachar,* and *Nadab* (line 576 refers to the fact that Nadab was believed to have profaned the sacraments of the Church by eating the consecrated bread and wine in the form of a dish of baked apples and ale). Among the Tories are *Zadoc* (the Archbishop of Canterbury), *him of the western dome* (the Dean of Westminster), *Amiel* (a former speaker of the House of Commons), and three noblemen; *Adriel* (the poet Mulgrave), *Jotham* (a prominent Parliamentarian), and *Hushai* (First Lord of the Treasury). *Annabel* is Monmouth's wife, Anne Scott; *Amnon,* whose murder Monmouth is said to have caused, has not been certainly identified.

Such is the basic Biblical analogy; on it Dryden superimposes a second religious metaphor, mostly by implication. The structure of the poem falls into four main parts: (1) an introduction to the political situation (1–149); (2) Achitophel's temptation of Absalom (150–490); (3) a review of first Absalom's, then David's, supporters (491–932); and (4) David's assertion of his authority and power (933–1032). Of these divisions the most obviously dramatic is the second—the temptation scene. In the Christian tradition there exist, of course, two great temptation stories: the successful temptation of Adam and Eve, persuaded by the serpent to eat the apple so that they would become "as gods, knowing good and evil" (Genesis 3:5); and the unsuccessful temptation of Christ, whom Satan could not persuade to receive at his hands "all the kingdoms of the world" (Matthew 4:8). Bearing these two stories in mind, Dryden metaphorically associates David with God, Achitophel with Satan (372), the rebellious elements in the kingdom with Adam (51), and Absalom—ironically—with Christ the Messiah or Savior, the Son of God.

The association of David with God is easy and natural; for traditional political theory (both Protestant and Catholic) held that magistrates are God's representatives on earth, a belief symbolized in ritual by the anointing of a new king with holy oil. The Biblical David, moreover, had been a man "after [the Lord's] own heart" (I Samuel 13:14)—a phrase Dryden twice echoes (each time with some irony), in lines 7 and 436. The parallel is used for comic purposes—because of Charles's notorious promiscuity—at the opening of the poem, but it becomes increasingly serious as the poem progresses and David is made to share not only God's creative energy (10) but also His mercy (328), His authority (938), and His power (1006–1007, which refer to Moses' dangerous request to behold God's glory directly: "Thou canst not see my face; for there shall no man see me, and live"—Exodus 33:20).

Absalom is elaborately invited by Achitophel (230 ff.) to confuse himself with Christ: symbols used are the star of Bethlehem, Christ's predecessor Moses, the visions and predictions of the Old Testament prophets, and the epithet "Savior." In his final speech David compares Absalom to *Jacob* (982), who tricked his father Isaac into making him, instead of *Esau,* his heir (Genesis 27); and also, ironically, to *Samson* (955), whose career was traditionally interpreted as foreshadowing Christ's.

The successful temptation of Absalom, who evidently yields to the delusions suggested by Achitophel, is paralleled by the various moral and psychological aberrations of Achitophel's other followers. Some oppose David on ostensible political or economic grounds (*pretending public good, to serve their own,* 504); others for alleged religious reasons. Religion to them, however, is an anarchic affair consisting of individual *inspiration* and *enthusiasm,* as well as salvation decreed on purely arbitrary grounds (524, 530, 539); it serves as a convenient camouflage for more material aggrandizement (*spoils,* 524). Shimei, the city magistrate, though he has heaped up wealth and is, in fact, loaded with gold, frugally avoids, because of religious fastidiousness, the lavish hospitality ordinarily extended by the holder of a *shrieval* (sheriff's) office (617–625; Dryden ironically attributes the low temperature of his kitchen to a desire to avoid a second great fire of London!); but with "spiritual food" he is eminently generous (obeys a kind of golden rule, 600; gathers *two or three together,* as the Anglican prayerbook advises; and so on). Corah, the recipient of a higher education straight from the hands of the Holy Ghost (655–658), has such a rich and fertile professional *memory* for the names of supposedly subversive (pro-Catholic) ctiizens that it is exceedingly rash to doubt the truth of his testimony (665)—any doubter might suddenly find himself "remembered" as an *appendix of the plot.* Except for Zimri (a merely unstable personality), most of David's enemies combine so closely fanatic religious zeal and lust for wealth or power that it is hard to say which quality predominates in them.

Dryden's language in the poem, once the basic metaphors are grasped, is for the most part as lucid to a twentieth-century as to a seventeenth-century reader; indeed, some lines, like *peace itself is war in masquerade* (752), have an electrifying contemporaneity. The following few phrases, however, are archaic or otherwise unusual today: *proves* (44): tests; *savages* (56): wild beasts; *humor* (138): fluid; *fretted* (158): wore out; *o'erinformed* (158): filled to full; *gown* (193): (judge's) robes; *manifest of* (204): openly displaying; *metal* (310): temperament; *vare* (595): staff; *vermilion* (649): beefy complexion; *stem* (867): family; *plume* (920): pluck; *event* (1018): result. Classical allusions are few: the *Dog-star* Sirius (334) always connoted summer heat and madness; the *Hydra* (541) was a monster that grew new heads with every decapitation; *Hybla* (697) in Sicily was famous for its honey; and *th'unequal ruler of the day* (910) is Phaeton, who once unskillfully drove the sun's chariot across the heavens, with disastrous effect.

Dryden's strategy in the poem is to present each side as a mixture of strength and weakness, or morally pleasing and displeasing qualities—a method well epitomized in his notably balanced and tentative review of the political arguments (751–810)—and at the same time to develop gradually the central figure of David, who keeps reappearing at various points, from a symbol of weakness (or power dissipated by frivolity), to a symbol of stability and disinterested justice. The subtlety by which this effect is achieved has misled many commentators into suggesting that the poem "lacks unity" or that "nothing happens" in it. What happens is that our attitude toward the King, who is at first merely an *idol* (or idle) *monarch, grown in Bathsheba's embraces old,* shifts, as the whole situation is unrolled before our eyes, from almost contempt to a feeling that David is the only stable prop against sheer chaos—political, economic, and moral.

Dryden manages all this not only by the brilliance of his satiric thumbnail sketches (Zimri and the like) but also by various less obvious dramatic devices: putting the first praise of David into the mouth of his opponents (315 ff.); comparing Achitophel's judicial incorruptibility (186 ff.) with his blatant, and corrupting, flattery of Absalom; even contrasting David's sexual energy with Achitophel's bungling and futile paternity (169 ff.). Above all, Dryden presents the rebels as a loosely knit crew of variously, but always meanly, motivated destructive agencies, so that David, by the time the conclusion is reached, remains the center of public order.

That Dryden's analysis can be shown to bear a close relation to certain actual events of Charles's reign gives the poem an incidental interest as political commentary, and no doubt accounts, genetically speaking, for much of its complexity; but excessive concern for the historic Shaftesbury or Monmouth is irrelevant to a realization of the imaginative unity and variety achieved in *Absalom and Achitophel* the poem. As an analysis, and a drama, of political values it is fit to take its place in literature with such other imaginative analyses of human power as *Richard II* and *Prometheus Unbound*.

THE MEDAL

Anthony Ashley Cooper (1621–1683), first Earl of Shaftesbury, had had an active and variegated career in English politics by the time Dryden attacked him, in March, 1682, in *The Medal,* a poem which caricatures his life, person, and personality in the following detail:

He was physically small (27) and deformed (272). In his youth at the time of the Civil Wars he had fought (26) at first for Charles I, but later for the Parliamentary side (28), and had been an adviser to Cromwell (31), in whose government, however, he failed to attain great influence (46). For aiding in Charles II's restoration (51) he was rewarded (54) with a barony in 1661 and an earldom eleven years later. He was a member of the "Cabal" ministry (55) of the early 1670's, and helped dissolve England's triple alliance (65) with Holland and Sweden against France; Anglo-Dutch wars followed (68), almost as disastrous (Dryden implies), as the fall of Troy (67). Failing to strengthen the royal power when Charles refused to support some of his bolder measures, including the Declaration granting toleration to Catholics and dissenters (77–78), Shaftesbury became a leader of the opposition not only to Charles but also (according to Dryden) to the monarchy itself (80 ff.); and he associated himself with the Puritanical dissenting sects of London, with whom the dissoluteness of his personal life made him as incongruous an ally (273 ff.) as it had in Crom-

well's days (33 ff.). When witnesses in the "Popish plot" trials (see
the discussion of *Absalom and Achitophel,* above) began to for-
swear their earlier testimony and turn against those who had hired
them (151), Shaftesbury was arrested for treason, partly on the
grounds of his having planned to organize a private, extralegal
association (205) to protect Protestantism. The two sheriffs (14)
of London, however, were strong Whigs (182); and a Whig metro-
politan jury refused to indict.

To celebrate Shaftesbury's release his followers had a medal
struck, showing his title and profile on one side (10) and on the
other the London skyline, including the Tower in which he had
been imprisoned, the sun breaking through a cloud, the date
(November 24, 1681) of his acquittal, and the Latin motto
LAETAMUR: let us rejoice (12–14).* Of this scene Dryden wrote
in a prose "Epistle to the Whigs," prefixed to the poem: "Truth is,
you might have spar'd one side of your Medal: the head would be
seen to more advantage if it were placed on a spike of the Tower,
a little nearer to the sun, which would then break out to better
purpose."

In addition to Shaftesbury, Dryden also attacks the London dis-
senters (as he had in *Absalom and Achitophel*), alleging their
piousness and sharp dealing (191); the gloom of their *conventicles,*
or illegal assemblies (284), a gloom more appropriate to *Bedlam,*
the London insane asylum (285); and their doctrine of individual
interpretation of Scripture (162–166). He even implies that their
seditiousness had brought the *plague* and *fire* upon London as a
divine judgment (198); and predicts that if they succeed in their
antiroyalist designs a new series of Civil Wars will break out
(290 ff.), very likely resulting in the installation of their general
Monmouth as dictator (313), followed by his ouster for being
(after all) a son of Charles (316–317)—just as *Collatine,* the
Roman antiroyalist, had once been ousted from power.

A third subject of satire in *The Medal* is the republican doc-
trine of majority rule, bound up (as Dryden saw it) with an assump-
tion of the relativity of value: thus *Phocion* and *Socrates* (96),

---

* A standard joke about Shaftesbury's ambitious nature was that he had
once hoped to be chosen King of Poland when the throne of that elective
monarchy fell vacant some years earlier (3, 15). For a picture of the medal, see
H. H. Schless's *Poems on Affairs of State,* Vol. II, 1968, p. 39.

having been put to death in democratic Athens on charges of treason and impiety, were later honored by the Athenians.

The Medal contains a few allusions to the Bible, and one or two expressions no longer current: *Lucifer* (1): Satan; *white witches* (62); benevolent witches; *Jehu* (119): the furious driver of II Kings 9:20; *manna* (131): the vegetable food which the ungrateful Israelites complained of having to eat in the wilderness, whereupon God sent them quail, followed by a plague (Numbers 11); *Cyclops* (226): man-eating monster in the *Odyssey; Croatian* (240): ferocious; *passengers* (243): passers-by; *stum* (270): new wine used to cause a second fermentation in stale wine.

According to an eighteenth-century anecdote, the inception of *The Medal* was Charles II's remark to Dryden that "if I was a poet, and I think I am poor enough to be one, I would write a poem on such a subject in the following manner" (outlining the plan Dryden used). But Charles was not a poet, and *The Medal* is a less imaginative treatment of a theme similar to that of *Absalom and Achitophel*. Objections have been made to it as an unfair or exaggerated picture of Shaftesbury, for example. Any such objections to the temptation scene in the earlier poem would be clearly irrelevant, because this scene makes no claim to being a representation of literal fact. *The Medal* has, nevertheless, a kind of hilarious vigor; from its spirited invective Pope may have taken one or two hints for his immortal portrait of Sporus in the "Epistle to Dr. Arbuthnot."

From ABSALOM AND ACHITOPHEL, PART II

To this poem, written by Nahum Tate and published in November, 1682, Dryden contributed the lines printed in the present anthology. After dealing with Robert Ferguson (*Judas*), a dissenting preacher and antiroyalist plotter who kept a boys' school near London; with James Forbes (*Phaleg*), also a dissenting clergyman, who had been traveling tutor to the young Earl of Derby; with a certain Reverend Samuel Johnson (*Ben-Jochanan*), author of a tract on Julian the Apostate designed to show that since the early Christians had resisted the pagan Emperor Julian, modern Protestants would be equally justified in resisting a Catholic king; and with the famous preacher Gilbert Burnet (*Balak*), Dryden turns his attention from *Levi* (the priesthood), passes rapidly over two minor

writers (*Mephibosheth:* Samuel Pordage; *Uzza:* not certainly identi-
fied), and comes to two poetasters, Elkanah Settle (*Doeg*) and
Thomas Shadwell (*Og*).

Settle, a minor dramatist with whom Dryden had had a brief
pamphlet war in the 1670's, had published in April, 1682, a reply
to *Absalom and Achitophel* entitled *Absalom Senior; or, Absalom
Transposed,* in which he makes Absalom (as Dryden points out in
line 430) the Duke of York, King Charles's brother. The italicized
nonsensical phrase in line 446 is taken from the second line of
Absalom Senior. In lines 451–452 Dryden refers to Settle's Whig-
gish activity in arranging Pope burnings. In the next few lines his
picture of Settle's true vocation (that of puppet master) turned out
to be prophetic: failing as a dramatist, Settle later went into the
puppet-show business in Bartholemew Fair.

Shadwell (or *Og*) had been the protagonist of *Mac Flecknoe*
(see the comments, above, on that poem). In 1682 Dryden had
new reasons, both political and personal, for damning him to ever-
lasting fame; for he seems to have been the author of the then
recently published *Medal of John Bayes,* a long, personal, obscene,
and scurrilous attack on Dryden, written after the publication of
The Medal. In line 461 of *Absalom and Achitophel, Part II, link*
refers to the torch- (or link-) carrier who preceded a citizen about
the London streets at night; *Jew* (471) of course means Englishman;
King David (488), or the *Lord's anointed* (503), is Charles II;
and *to thee* (494) means "compared to thee." In all other respects
the attack is perfectly lucid, and among the best of its kind Dryden
ever produced.

The portraits of the several dissenting clergymen, which pre-
cede the famous Doeg-Og passage, are, though also vigorous, less
easy to explicate today. It is not known, for example, whether
Dryden had any basis for suggesting, as he does in lines 338–341
(which echo the great "dry bones" chapter [37] of Ezekiel), that
slim Phaleg had seduced the wife of some noble patron. Some de-
tails can, however, be clarified. The *drunken patriarch* (383) is
Noah, who cursed Ham's progeny under the circumstances (Genesis
9:18 ff.) Dryden refers to; Ben-Jochanan's *hot father* (392) is St.
Gregory Nazianus, an early Christian writer who had attacked the
memory of the Emperor Julian (*the Apostate*); and Samuel Pordage
(*Mephibosheth*) is called *the wizard's son* (405) because his father,
a clergyman, had been charged with having dealings with spirits.

MAC FLECKNOE
Or, A Satire Upon The True-Blue-Protestant Poet T.S.

All human things are subject to decay,
And when fate summons, monarchs must obey.
This Flecknoe found, who, like Augustus, young
Was call'd to empire, and had govern'd long;
In prose and verse, was own'd, without dispute,
Thro' all the realms of *Nonsense,* absolute.
This aged prince, now flourishing in peace,
And blest with issue of a large increase;
Worn out with business, did at length debate
To settle the succession of the State;   10
And, pond'ring which of all his sons was fit
To reign, and wage immortal war with wit,
Cried: " 'T is resolv'd; for nature pleads, that he
Should only rule, who most resembles me.
Sh—— alone my perfect image bears,
Mature in dulness from his tender years:
Sh—— alone, of all my sons, is he
Who stands confirm'd in full stupidity.
The rest to some faint meaning make pretense,
But Sh—— never deviates into sense.   20
Some beams of wit on other souls may fall,
Strike thro', and make a lucid interval;
But Sh——'s genuine night admits no ray,
His rising fogs prevail upon the day.
Besides, his goodly fabric fills the eye,
And seems design'd for thoughtless majesty;
Thoughtless as monarch oaks that shade the plain,
And, spread in solemn state, supinely reign.
Heywood and Shirley were but types of thee,
Thou last great prophet of tautology.   30
Even I, a dunce of more renown than they,
Was sent before but to prepare thy way;
And, coarsely clad in Norwich drugget, came
To teach the nations in thy greater name.

My warbling lute, the lute I whilom strung,
When to King John of Portugal I sung,
Was but the prelude to that glorious day,
When thou on silver Thames didst cut thy way,
With well-tim'd oars before the royal barge,
Swell'd with the pride of thy celestial charge;   40
And big with hymn, commander of a host,
The like was ne'er in Epsom blankets toss'd.
Methinks I see the new Arion sail,
The lute still trembling underneath thy nail.
At thy well-sharpen'd thumb from shore to shore
The treble squeaks for fear, the basses roar;
Echoes from Pissing Alley Sh—— call,
And Sh—— they resound from Aston Hall.
About thy boat the little fishes throng,
As at the morning toast that floats along.   50
Sometimes, as prince of thy harmonious band,
Thou wield'st thy papers in thy threshing hand.
St. André's feet ne'er kept more equal time,
Not ev'n the feet of thy own *Psyche's* rhyme;
Tho' they in number as in sense excel:
So just, so like tautology, they fell,
That, pale with envy, Singleton forswore
The lute and sword, which he in triumph bore,
And vow'd he ne'er would act Villerius more."
Here stopp'd the good old sire, and wept for joy   60
In silent raptures of the hopeful boy.
All arguments, but most his plays, persuade,
That for anointed dulness he was made.
   Close to the walls which fair Augusta bind,
(The fair Augusta much to fears inclin'd,)
An ancient fabric rais'd t' inform the sight,
There stood of yore, and Barbican it hight:
A watchtower once; but now, so fate ordains,
Of all the pile an empty name remains.
From its old ruins brothel-houses rise,   70
Scenes of lewd loves, and of polluted joys,
Where their vast courts the mother-strumpets keep,
And, undisturb'd by watch, in silence sleep.
Near these a Nursery erects its head,

Where queens are form'd, and future heroes bred;
Where unfledg'd actors learn to laugh and cry,
Where infant punks their tender voices try,
And little Maximins the gods defy.
Great Fletcher never treads in buskins here,
Nor greater Jonson dares in socks appear;   80
But gentle Simkin just reception finds
Amidst this monument of vanish'd minds:
Pure clinches the suburbian Muse affords,
And Panton waging harmless war with words.
Here Flecknoe, as a place to fame well known,
Ambitiously design'd his Sh——'s throne;
For ancient Dekker prophesied long since,
That in this pile should reign a mighty prince,
Born for a scourge of wit, and flail of sense;
To whom true dulness should some *Psyches* owe,   90
But worlds of *Misers* from his pen should flow;
Humorists and *Hypocrites* it should produce,
Whole Raymond families, and tribes of Bruce.
     Now Empress Fame had publish'd the renown
Of Sh——'s coronation thro' the town.
Rous'd by report of Fame, the nations meet,
From near Bunhill, and distant Watling Street.
No Persian carpets spread th' imperial way,
But scatter'd limbs of mangled poets lay;
From dusty shops neglected authors come,   100
Martyrs of pies, and relics of the bum.
Much Heywood, Shirley, Ogleby there lay,
But loads of Sh—— almost chok'd the way.
Bilk'd stationers for yeomen stood prepar'd,
And Herringman was captain of the guard.
The hoary prince in majesty appear'd,
High on a throne of his own labors rear'd.
At his right hand our young Ascanius sate,
Rome's other hope, and pillar of the State.
His brows thick fogs, instead of glories, grace,   110
And lambent dulness play'd around his face.
As Hannibal did to the altars come,
Sworn by his sire a mortal foe to Rome;
So Sh—— swore, nor should his vow be vain,

That he till death true dulness would maintain;
And, in his father's right, and realm's defense,
Ne'er to have peace with wit, nor truce with sense.
The king himself the sacred unction made,
As king by office, and as priest by trade.
In his sinister hand, instead of ball,   120
He plac'd a mighty mug of potent ale;
Love's Kingdom to his right he did convey,
At once his scepter, and his rule of sway;
Whose righteous lore the prince had practic'd young,
And from whose loins recorded *Psyche* sprung.
His temples, last, with poppies were o'erspread,
That nodding seem'd to consecrate his head.
Just at that point of time, if fame not lie,
On his left hand twelve reverend owls did fly.
So Romulus, 't is sung, by Tiber's brook,   130
Presage of sway from twice six vultures took.
Th'admiring throng loud acclamations make,
And omens of his future empire take.
The sire then shook the honors of his head,
And from his brows damps of oblivion shed
Full on the filial dulness: long he stood,
Repelling from his breast the raging god;
At length burst out in this prophetic mood:
    "Heavens bless my son, from Ireland let him reign
To far Barbadoes on the western main;   140
Of his dominion may no end be known,
And greater than his father's be his throne;
Beyond *Love's Kingdom* let him stretch his pen!"
He paus'd, and all the people cried, "Amen."
Then thus continued he: "My son, advance
Still in new impudence, new ignorance.
Success let others teach, learn thou from me
Pangs without birth, and fruitless industry.
Let *Virtuosos* in five years be writ;
Yet not one thought accuse thy toil of wit.   150
Let gentle George in triumph tread the stage,
Make Dorimant betray, and Loveit rage;
Let Cully, Cockwood, Fopling, charm the pit,
And in their folly shew the writer's wit.

Yet still thy fools shall stand in thy defense,
And justify their author's want of sense.
Let 'em be all by thy own model made
Of dulness, and desire no foreign aid;
That they to future ages may be known,
Not copies drawn, but issue of thy own.   160
Nay, let thy men of wit too be the same,
All full of thee, and differing but in name.
But let no alien S—dl—y interpose,
To lard with wit thy hungry *Epsom* prose.
And when false flowers of rhetoric thou wouldst cull,
Trust nature, do not labor to be dull;
But write thy best, and top; and, in each line,
Sir Formal's oratory will be thine:
Sir Formal, tho' unsought, attends thy quill,
And does thy northern dedications fill.   170
Nor let false friends seduce thy mind to fame,
By arrogating Jonson's hostile name.
Let father Flecknoe fire thy mind with praise,
And uncle Ogleby thy envy raise.
Thou art my blood, where Jonson has no part:
What share have we in nature, or in art?
Where did his wit on learning fix a brand,
And rail at arts he did not understand?
Where made he love in Prince Nicander's vein,
Or swept the dust in *Psyche's* humble strain?   180
Where sold he bargains, 'whip-stitch, kiss my arse,'
Promis'd a play and dwindled to a farce?
When did his Muse from Fletcher scenes purloin,
As thou whole Eth'rege dost transfuse to thine?
But so transfus'd, as oil on water's flow,
His always floats above, thine sinks below.
This is thy province, this thy wondrous way,
New humors to invent for each new play:
This is that boasted bias of thy mind,
By which one way, to dulness, 't is inclin'd;   190
Which makes thy writings lean on one side still,
And, in all changes, that way bends thy will.
Nor let thy mountain-belly make pretense
Of likeness; thine 's a tympany of sense.

A tun of man in thy large bulk is writ,
But sure thou 'rt but a kilderkin of wit.
Like mine, thy gentle numbers feebly creep;
Thy tragic Muse gives smiles, thy comic sleep.
With whate'er gall thou sett'st thyself to write,
Thy inoffensive satires never bite.   200
In thy felonious heart tho' venom lies,
It does but touch thy Irish pen, and dies.
Thy genius calls thee not to purchase fame
In keen iambics, but mild anagram.
Leave writing plays, and choose for thy command
Some peaceful province in acrostic land.
There thou may'st wings display and altars raise,
And torture one poor word ten thousand ways.
Or, if thou wouldst thy diff'rent talents suit,
Set thy own songs, and sing them to thy lute."   210
    He said: but his last words were scarcely heard;
For Bruce and Longvil had a trap prepar'd,
And down they sent the yet declaiming bard.
Sinking he left his drugget robe behind,
Borne upwards by a subterranean wind.
The mantle fell to the young prophet's part,
With double portion of his father's art.

ABSALOM AND ACHITOPHEL

In pious times, ere priestcraft did begin,
Before polygamy was made a sin;
When man on many multiplied his kind,
Ere one to one was cursedly confin'd;
When nature prompted, and no law denied
Promiscuous use of concubine and bride;
Then Israel's monarch after Heaven's own heart,
His vigorous warmth did variously impart
To wives and slaves; and, wide as his command,
Scatter'd his Maker's image thro' the land.   10
Michal, of royal blood, the crown did wear;
A soil ungrateful to the tiller's care:

Not so the rest; for several mothers bore
To godlike David several sons before.
But since like slaves his bed they did ascend,
No true succession could their seed attend.
Of all this numerous progeny was none
So beautiful, so brave, as Absalom:
Whether, inspir'd by some diviner lust,
His father got him with a greater gust;   20
Or that his conscious destiny made way,
By manly beauty, to imperial sway.
Early in foreign fields he won renown,
With kings and states allied to Israel's crown:
In peace the thoughts of war he could remove,
And seem'd as he were only born for love.
Whate'er he did, was done with so much ease,
In him alone 't was natural to please:
His motions all accompanied with grace;
And paradise was open'd in his face.   30
With secret joy indulgent David view'd
His youthful image in his son renew'd:
To all his wishes nothing he denied;
And made the charming Annabel his bride.
What faults he had, (for who from faults is free?)
His father could not, or he would not see.
Some warm excesses which the law forbore,
Were construed youth that purg'd by boiling o'er,
And Amnon's murther, by a specious name,
Was call'd a just revenge for injur'd fame.   40
Thus prais'd and lov'd the noble youth remain'd,
While David, undisturb'd, in Sion reign'd.
But life can never be sincerely blest;
Heav'n punishes the bad, and proves the best.
The Jews, a headstrong, moody, murm'ring race,
As ever tried th' extent and stretch of grace;
God's pamper'd people, whom, debauch'd with ease,
No king could govern, nor no God could please;
(Gods they had tried of every shape and size,
That god-smiths could produce, or priests devise:)   50
These Adam-wits, too fortunately free,
Began to dream they wanted liberty;

And when no rule, no precedent was found,
Of men by laws less circumscrib'd and bound;
They led their wild desires to woods and caves,
And thought that all but savages were slaves.
They who, when Saul was dead, without a blow,
Made foolish Ishbosheth the crown forego;
Who banish'd David did from Hebron bring,
And with a general shout proclaim'd him king: 60
Those very Jews, who, at their very best,
Their humor more than loyalty express'd,
Now wonder'd why so long they had obey'd
An idol monarch, which their hands had made;
Thought they might ruin him they could create,
Or melt him to that golden calf, a State.
But these were random bolts; no form'd design,
Nor interest made the factious crowd to join:
The sober part of Israel, free from stain,
Well knew the value of a peaceful reign;   70
And, looking backward with a wise affright,
Saw seams of wounds, dishonest to the sight:
In contemplation of whose ugly scars
They curs'd the memory of civil wars.
The moderate sort of men, thus qualified,
Inclin'd the balance to the better side;
And David's mildness manag'd it so well,
The bad found no occasion to rebel.
But when to sin our bias'd nature leans,
The careful Devil is still at hand with means;   80
And providently pimps for ill desires.
The Good Old Cause reviv'd, a plot requires:
Plots, true or false, are necessary things,
To raise up commonwealths, and ruin kings.
    Th' inhabitants of old Jerusalem
Were Jebusites; the town so call'd from them;
And theirs the native right——
But when the chosen people grew more strong,
The rightful cause at length became the wrong;
And every loss the men of Jebus bore,   90
They still were thought God's enemies the more.
Thus worn and weaken'd, well or ill content,

Submit they must to David's government:
Impoverish'd and depriv'd of all command,
Their taxes doubled as they lost their land;
And, what was harder yet to flesh and blood,
Their gods disgrac'd, and burnt like common wood.
This set the heathen priesthood in a flame;
For priests of all religions are the same:
Of whatsoe'er descent their godhead be,   100
Stock, stone, or other homely pedigree,
In his defense his servants are as bold,
As if he had been born of beaten gold.
The Jewish rabbins, tho' their enemies,
In this conclude them honest men and wise:
For 't was their duty, all the learned think,
T' espouse his cause, by whom they eat and drink.
From hence began that Plot, the nation's curse,
Bad in itself, but represented worse;
Rais'd in extremes, and in extremes decried;   110
With oaths affirm'd, with dying vows denied;
Not weigh'd or winnow'd by the multitude;
But swallow'd in the mass, unchew'd and crude.
Some truth there was, but dash'd and brew'd with lies,
To please the fools, and puzzle all the wise.
Succeeding times did equal folly call,
Believing nothing, or believing all.
Th' Egyptian rites the Jebusites embrac'd;
Where gods were recommended by their taste.
Such sav'ry deities must needs be good,   120
As serv'd at once for worship and for food.
By force they could not introduce these gods,
For ten to one in former days was odds;
So fraud was us'd (the sacrificer's trade):
Fools are more hard to conquer than persuade.
Their busy teachers mingled with the Jews,
And rak'd for converts even the court and stews:
Which Hebrew priests the more unkindly took,
Because the fleece accompanies the flock.
Some thought they God's anointed meant to slay   130
By guns, invented since full many a day:
Our author swears it not; but who can know

How far the Devil and Jebusites may go?
This Plot, which fail'd for want of common sense,
Had yet a deep and dangerous consequence:
For, as when raging fevers boil the blood,
The standing lake soon floats into a flood,
And ev'ry hostile humor, which before
Slept quiet in its channels, bubbles o'er;
So several factions from this first ferment   140
Work up to foam, and threat the government.
Some by their friends, more by themselves thought wise,
Oppos'd the pow'r to which they could not rise.
Some had in courts been great, and thrown from thence,
Like fiends were harden'd in impenitence.
Some, by their monarch's fatal mercy, grown
From pardon'd rebels kinsmen to the throne,
Were rais'd in pow'r and public office high;
Strong bands, if bands ungrateful men could tie.   *Earle of Shaftsbury*
    Of these the false Achitophel was first;   150
A name to all succeeding ages curst:
For close designs and crooked counsels fit;
Sagacious, bold, and turbulent of wit;
Restless, unfix'd in principles and place;
In pow'r unpleas'd, impatient of disgrace:
A fiery soul, which, working out its way,
Fretted the pigmy body to decay,
And o'er-inform'd the tenement of clay.
A daring pilot in extremity;
Pleas'd with the danger, when the waves went high,   160
He sought the storms; but, for a calm unfit,
Would steer too nigh the sands, to boast his wit.
Great wits are sure to madness near allied,
And thin partitions do their bounds divide;
Else why should he, with wealth and honor blest,
Refuse his age the needful hours of rest?
Punish a body which he could not please;
Bankrupt of life, yet prodigal of ease?
And all to leave what with his toil he won,
To that unfeather'd two-legg'd thing, a son;   170
Got, while his soul did huddled notions try;
And born a shapeless lump, like anarchy.

In friendship false, implacable in hate;
Resolv'd to ruin or to rule the State.
To compass this the triple bond he broke;
The pillars of the public safety shook;
And fitted Israel for a foreign yoke:
Then seiz'd with fear, yet still affecting fame,
Usurp'd a patriot's all-atoning name.
So easy still it proves in factious times,   *180*
With public zeal to cancel private crimes.
How safe is treason, and how sacred ill,
Where none can sin against the people's will!
Where crowds can wink, and no offense be known,
Since in another's guilt they find their own!
Yet fame deserv'd no enemy can grudge;
The statesman we abhor, but praise the judge.
In Israel's courts ne'er sat an Abbethdin
With more discerning eyes, or hands more clean;
Unbrib'd, unsought, the wretched to redress;   *190*
Swift of dispatch, and easy of access.
O, had he been content to serve the crown,
With virtues only proper to the gown;
Or had the rankness of the soil been freed
From cockle, that oppress'd the noble seed;
David for him his tuneful harp had strung,
And Heav'n had wanted one immortal song.
But wild Ambition loves to slide, not stand,
And Fortune's ice prefers to Virtue's land.
Achitophel, grown weary to possess   *200*
A lawful fame, and lazy happiness,
Disdain'd the golden fruit to gather free,
And lent the crowd his arm to shake the tree.
Now, manifest of crimes contriv'd long since,
He stood at bold defiance with his prince;
Held up the buckler of the people's cause
Against the crown, and skulk'd behind the laws.
The wish'd occasion of the Plot he takes;
Some circumstances finds, but more he makes.
By buzzing emissaries fills the ears   *210*
Of list'ning crowds with jealousies and fears
Of arbitrary counsels brought to light,

And proves the king himself a Jebusite.
Weak arguments! which yet he knew full well
Were strong with people easy to rebel.
For, govern'd by the moon, the giddy Jews
Tread the same track when she the prime renews;
And once in twenty years, their scribes record,
By natural instinct they change their lord.
Achitophel still wants a chief, and none   220
Was found so fit as warlike Absalon:
Not that he wish'd his greatness to create,
(For politicians, neither love nor hate,)
But, for he knew his title not allow'd,
Would keep him still depending on the crowd:
That kingly pow'r, thus ebbing out, might be
Drawn to the dregs of a democracy.
Him he attempts with studied arts to please,
And sheds his venom in such words as these:
    "Auspicious prince, at whose nativity   230
Some royal planet rul'd the southern sky;
Thy longing country's darling and desire;
Their cloudy pillar and their guardian fire:
Their second Moses, whose extended wand
Divides the seas, and shews the promis'd land;
Whose dawning day in every distant age
Has exercis'd the sacred prophets' rage:
The people's pray'r, the glad diviners' theme,
The young men's vision, and the old men's dream!
Thee, Savior, thee, the nation's vows confess,   240
And, never satisfied with seeing, bless:
Swift unbespoken pomps thy steps proclaim,
And stammering babes are taught to lisp thy name.
How long wilt thou the general joy detain,
Starve and defraud the people of thy reign?
Content ingloriously to pass thy days
Like one of Virtue's fools that feeds on praise;
Till thy fresh glories, which now shine so bright,
Grow stale and tarnish with our daily sight.
Believe me, royal youth, thy fruit must be   250
Or gather'd ripe, or rot upon the tree.
Heav'n has to all allotted, soon or late,

Some lucky revolution of their fate;
Whose motions if we watch and guide with skill,
(For human good depends on human will,)
Our Fortune rolls as from a smooth descent,
And from the first impression takes the bent:
But, if unseiz'd, she glides away like wind,
And leaves repenting Folly far behind.
Now, now she meets you with a glorious prize,   260
And spreads her locks before her as she flies.
Had thus old David, from whose loins you spring,
Not dar'd, when Fortune call'd him, to be king,
At Gath an exile he might still remain,
And Heaven's anointing oil had been in vain.
Let his successful youth your hopes engage;
But shun th' example of declining age:
Behold him setting in his western skies,
The shadows lengthening as the vapors rise.
He is not now, as when on Jordan's sand   270
The joyful people throng'd to see him land,
Cov'ring the beach, and black'ning all the strand;
But, like the Prince of Angels, from his height
Comes tumbling downward with diminish'd light;
Betray'd by one poor plot to public scorn,
(Our only blessing since his curst return;)
Those heaps of people which one sheaf did bind,
Blown off and scatter'd by a puff of wind.
What strength can he to your designs oppose,
Naked of friends, and round beset with foes?   280
If Pharaoh's doubtful succor he should use,
A foreign aid would more incense the Jews:
Proud Egypt would dissembled friendship bring;
Foment the war, but not support the king:
Nor would the royal party e'er unite
With Pharaoh's arms t' assist the Jebusite;
Or if they should, their interest soon would break,
And with such odious aid make David weak.
All sorts of men by my successful arts,
Abhorring kings, estrange their alter'd hearts   290
From David's rule: and 't is the general cry,
'Religion, commonwealth, and liberty.'

If you, as champion of the public good,
Add to their arms a chief of royal blood,
What may not Israel hope, and what applause
Might such a general gain by such a cause?
Not barren praise alone, that gaudy flow'r
Fair only to the sight, but solid pow'r;
And nobler is a limited command,
Giv'n by the love of all your native land,   300
Than a successive title, long and dark,
Drawn from the moldy rolls of Noah's ark."
    What cannot praise effect in mighty minds,
When flattery soothes, and when ambition blinds!
Desire of pow'r, on earth a vicious weed,
Yet, sprung from high, is of celestial seed:
In God 't is glory; and when men aspire,
'T is but a spark too much of heavenly fire.
Th' ambitious youth, too covetous of fame,
Too full of angels' metal in his frame,   310
Unwarily was led from virtue's ways,
Made drunk with honor, and debauch'd with praise.
Half loth, and half consenting to the ill,
(For loyal blood within him struggled still,)
He thus replied: "And what pretense have I
To take up arms for public liberty?
My father governs with unquestion'd right;
The faith's defender, and mankind's delight;
Good, gracious, just, observant of the laws:
And Heav'n by wonders has espous'd his cause.   320
Whom has he wrong'd in all his peaceful reign?
Who sues for justice to his throne in vain?
What millions has he pardon'd of his foes,
Whom just revenge did to his wrath expose?
Mild, easy, humble, studious of our good;
Enclin'd to mercy, and averse from blood;
If mildness ill with stubborn Israel suit,
His crime is God's beloved attribute.
What could he gain, his people to betray,
Or change his right for arbitrary sway?   330
Let haughty Pharaoh curse with such a reign
His fruitful Nile, and yoke a servile train.

If David's rule Jerusalem displease,
The Dog-star heats their brains to this disease.
Why then should I encourage the bad,
Turn rebel and run popularly mad?
Were he a tyrant, who, by lawless might
Oppress'd the Jews, and rais'd the Jebusite,
Well might I mourn; but nature's holy bands
Would curb my spirits and restrain my hands: 340
The people might assert their liberty;
But what was right in them were crime in me.
His favor leaves me nothing to require,
Prevents my wishes, and outruns desire.
What more can I expect while David lives?
All but his kingly diadem he gives:
And that"— But there he paus'd; then sighing, said—
"Is justly destin'd for a worthier head.
For when my father from his toils shall rest,
And late augment the number of the blest,   350
His lawful issue shall the throne ascend,
Or the *collat'ral* line, where that shall end.
His brother, tho' oppress'd with vulgar spite,
Yet dauntless, and secure of native right,
Of every royal virtue stands possess'd;
Still dear to all the bravest and the best.
His courage foes, his friends his truth proclaim;
His loyalty the king, the world his fame.
His mercy ev'n th' offending crowd will find;
For sure he comes of a forgiving kind.   360
Why should I then repine at Heaven's decree,
Which gives me no pretense to royalty?
Yet O that fate, propitiously inclin'd,
Had rais'd my birth, or had debas'd my mind;
To my large soul not all her treasure lent,
And then betray'd it to a mean descent!
I find, I find my mounting spirits bold,
And David's part disdains my mother's mold.
Why am I scanted by a niggard birth?
My soul disclaims the kindred of her earth;   370
And, made for empire, whispers me within,
'Desire of greatness is a godlike sin.'"

Him staggering so when hell's dire agent found,
While fainting Virtue scarce maintain'd her ground,
He pours fresh forces in, and thus replies:
  "Th' eternal God, supremely good and wise,
Imparts not these prodigious gifts in vain:
What wonders are reserv'd to bless your reign!
Against your will, your arguments have shown,
Such virtue 's only giv'n to guide a throne.   380
Not that your father's mildness I contemn;
But manly force becomes the diadem.
'Tis true he grants the people all they crave;
And more, perhaps, than subjects ought to have:
For lavish grants suppose a monarch tame,
And more his goodness than his wit proclaim.
But when should people strive their bonds to break,
If not when kings are negligent or weak?
Let him give on till he can give no more,
The thrifty Sanhedrin shall keep him poor;   390
And every shekel which he can receive,
Shall cost a limb of his prerogative.
To ply him with new plots shall be my care;
Or plunge him deep in some expensive war;
Which when his treasure can no more supply,
He must, with the remains of kingship, buy.
His faithful friends, our jealousies and fears
Call Jebusites, and Pharaoh's pensioners;
Whom when our fury from his aid has torn,
He shall be naked left to public scorn.   400
The next successor, whom I fear and hate,
My arts have made obnoxious to the State;
Turn'd all his virtues to his overthrow,
And gain'd our elders to pronounce a foe.
His right, for sums of necessary gold,
Shall first be pawn'd, and afterwards be sold;
Till time shall ever-wanting David draw,
To pass your doubtful title into law:
If not, the people have a right supreme
To make their kings; for kings are made for them.   410
All empire is no more than pow'r in trust,
Which, when resum'd, can be no longer just.

Succession, for the general good design'd,
In its own wrong a nation cannot bind;
If altering that the people can relieve,
Better one suffer than a nation grieve.
The Jews well know their pow'r: ere Saul they chose,
God was their king, and God they durst depose.
Urge now your piety, your filial name,
A father's right, and fear of future fame;   420
The public good, that universal call,
To which even Heav'n submitted, answers all.
Nor let his love enchant your generous mind;
'T is Nature's trick to propagate her kind.
Our fond begetters, who would never die,
Love but themselves in their posterity.
Or let his kindness by th' effects be tried,
Or let him lay his vain pretense aside.
God said he lov'd your father; could he bring
A better proof, than to anoint him king?   430
It surely shew'd he lov'd the shepherd well,
Who gave so fair a flock as Israel.
Would David have you thought his darling son?
What means he then, to alienate the crown?
The name of godly he may blush to bear:
'T is after God's own heart to cheat his heir.
He to his brother gives supreme command,
To you a legacy of barren land:
Perhaps th' old harp, on which he thrums his lays,
Or some dull Hebrew ballad in your praise.   440
Then the next heir, a prince severe and wise,
Already looks on you with jealous eyes;
Sees thro' the thin disguises of your arts,
And marks your progress in the people's hearts.
Tho' now his mighty soul its grief contains,
He meditates revenge who least complains;
And, like a lion, slumb'ring in the way,
Or sleep dissembling, while he waits his prey,
His fearless foes within his distance draws,
Constrains his roaring, and contracts his paws;   450
Till at the last, his time for fury found,
He shoots with sudden vengeance from the ground;

The prostrate vulgar passes o'er and spares,
But with a lordly rage his hunters tears.
Your case no tame expedients will afford:
Resolve on death, or conquest by the sword,
Which for no less a stake than life you draw;
And self-defense is nature's eldest law.
Leave the warm people no considering time;
For then rebellion may be thought a crime.   460
Prevail yourself of what occasion gives,
But try your title while your father lives;
And that your arms may have a fair pretense,
Proclaim you take them in the king's defense;
Whose sacred life each minute would expose
To plots, from seeming friends, and secret foes.
And who can sound the depth of David's soul?
Perhaps his fear his kindness may control.
He fears his brother, tho' he loves his son,
For plighted vows too late to be undone.   470
If so, by force he wishes to be gain'd;
Like women's lechery, to seem constrain'd.
Doubt not: but, when he most affects the frown,
Commit a pleasing rape upon the crown.
Secure his person to secure your cause:
They who possess the prince, possess the laws."
    He said, and this advice above the rest,
With Absalom's mild nature suited best:
Unblam'd of life, (ambition set aside,)
Not stain'd with cruelty, nor puff'd with pride;   480
How happy had he been, if destiny
Had higher plac'd his birth, or not so high!
His kingly virtues might have claim'd a throne,
And blest all other countries but his own.
But charming greatness since so few refuse,
'T is juster to lament him than accuse.
Strong were his hopes a rival to remove,
With blandishments to gain the public love;
To head the faction while their zeal was hot,
And popularly prosecute the Plot.   490
To farther this, Achitophel unites
The malcontents of all the Israelites;

Whose differing parties he could wisely join,
For several ends, to serve the same design:
The best, (and of the princes some were such,)
Who thought the pow'r of monarchy too much;
Mistaken men, and patriots in their hearts;
Not wicked, but seduc'd by impious arts.
By these the springs of property were bent,
And wound so high, they crack'd the government.   500
The next for interest sought t' embroil the State,
To sell their duty at a dearer rate;
And make their Jewish markets of the throne,
Pretending public good, to serve their own.
Others thought kings an useless heavy load,
Who cost too much, and did too little good.
These were for laying honest David by,
On principles of pure good husbandry.
With them join'd all th' haranguers of the throng,
That thought to get preferment by the tongue.   510
Who follow next, a double danger bring,
Not only hating David, but the king:
The Solymaean rout, well-vers'd of old
In godly faction, and in treason bold;
Cow'ring and quaking at a conqu'ror's sword;
But lofty to a lawful prince restor'd;
Saw with disdain an Ethnic plot begun,
And scorn'd by Jebusites to be outdone.
Hot Levites headed these; who, pull'd before
From th' ark, which in the Judges' days they bore   520
Resum'd their cant, and with a zealous cry
Pursued their old belov'd Theocracy:
Where Sanhedrin and priest enslav'd the nation,
And justified their spoils by inspiration:
For who so fit for reign as Aaron's race,
If once dominion they could found in grace.
These led the pack; tho' not of surest scent,
Yet deepest mouth'd against the government.
A numerous host of dreaming saints succeed,
Of the true old enthusiastic breed: 530
'Gainst form and order they their pow'r imploy,
Nothing to build, and all things to destroy.

But far more numerous was the herd of such,
Who think too little, and who talk too much.
These, out of mere instinct, they knew not why,
Ador'd their fathers' God and property;
And, by the same blind benefit of fate,
The Devil and the Jebusite did hate:
Born to be sav'd, even in their own despite,
Because they could not help believing right.   540
Such were the tools; but a whole Hydra more
Remains, of sprouting heads too long to score.
Some of their chiefs were princes of the land:
In the first rank of these did Zimri stand;
A man so various, that he seem'd to be
Not one, but all mankind's epitome:
Stiff in opinions, always in the wrong;
Was everything by starts, and nothing long;
But, in the course of one revolving moon,
Was chymist, fiddler, statesman, and buffoon: 550
Then all for women, painting, rhyming, drinking,
Besides ten thousand freaks that died in thinking.
Blest madman, who could every hour employ,
With something new to wish, or to enjoy!
Railing and praising were his usual themes;
And both (to shew his judgment) in extremes:
So over-violent, or over-civil,
That every man, with him, was God or Devil.
In squand'ring wealth was his peculiar art:
Nothing went unrewarded but desert.   560
Beggar'd by fools, whom still he found too late,
He had his jest, and they had his estate.
He laugh'd himself from court; then sought relief
By forming parties, but could ne'er be chief;
For, spite of him, the weight of business fell
On Absalom and wise Achitophel:
Thus, wicked but in will, of means bereft,
He left not faction, but of that was left.
    Titles and names 't were tedious to rehearse
Of lords, below the dignity of verse.   570
Wits, warriors, Commonwealth's-men, were the best;
Kind husbands, and mere nobles, all the rest.

And therefore, in the name of dulness, be
The well-hung Balaam and cold Caleb, free;
And canting Nadab let oblivion damn,
Who made new porridge for the paschal lamb.
Let friendship's holy band some names assure;
Some their own worth, and some let scorn secure.
Nor shall the rascal rabble here have place,
Whom kings no titles gave, and God no grace: 580
Not bull-fac'd Jonas, who could statutes draw
To mean rebellion, and make treason law.
But he, tho' bad, is follow'd by a worse,
The wretch who Heav'n's anointed dar'd to curse:
Shimei, whose youth did early promise bring
Of zeal to God and hatred to his king,
Did wisely from expensive sins refrain,
And never broke the Sabbath, but for gain;
Nor ever was he known an oath to vent,
Or curse, unless against the government.   590
Thus heaping wealth, by the most ready way
Among the Jews, which was to cheat and pray,
The city, to reward his pious hate
Against his master, chose him magistrate.
His hand a vare of justice did uphold;
His neck was loaded with a chain of gold.
During his office, treason was no crime;
The sons of Belial had a glorious time;
For Shimei, tho' not prodigal of pelf,
Yet lov'd his wicked neighbor as himself.   600
When two or three were gather'd to declaim
Against the monarch of Jerusalem,
Shimei was always in the midst of them;
And if they curs'd the king when he was by,
Would rather curse than break good company.
If any durst his factious friends accuse,
He pack'd a jury of dissenting Jews;
Whose fellow-feeling in the godly cause
Would free the suff'ring saint from human laws.
For laws are only made to punish those   610
Who serve the king, and to protect his foes.
If any leisure time he had from pow'r,

(Because 't is sin to misimploy an hour,)
His bus'ness was, by writing, to persuade
That kings were useless, and a clog to trade;
And, that his noble style he might refine,
No Rechabite more shunn'd the fumes of wine.
Chaste were his cellars, and his shrieval board
The grossness of a city feast abhorr'd:
His cooks, with long disuse, their trade forgot;   620
Cool was his kitchen, tho' his brains were hot.
Such frugal virtue malice may accuse,
But sure 't was necessary to the Jews;
For towns once burnt such magistrates require
As dare not tempt God's providence by fire.
With spiritual food he fed his servants well,
But free from flesh that made the Jews rebel;
And Moses' laws he held in more account,
For forty days of fasting in the mount.
      To speak the rest, who better are forgot,   630
Would tire a well-breath'd witness of the Plot.
Yet, Corah, thou shalt from oblivion pass:
Erect thyself, thou monumental brass,
High as the serpent of thy metal made,
While nations stand secure beneath thy shade.
What tho' his birth were base, yet comets rise
From earthy vapors, ere they shine in skies.
Prodigious actions may as well be done
By weaver's issue, as by prince's son.
This arch-attestor for the public good   640
By that one deed ennobles all his blood.
Who ever ask'd the witnesses' high race,
Whose oath with martyrdom did Stephen grace?
Ours was a Levite, and as times went then,
His tribe were God Almighty's gentlemen.
Sunk were his eyes, his voice was harsh and loud,
Sure signs he neither choleric was nor proud:
His long chin prov'd his wit; his saintlike grace
A church vermilion, and a Moses' face.
His memory, miraculously great,   650
Could plots, exceeding man's belief, repeat;
Which therefore cannot be accounted lies,

For human wit could never such devise.
Some future truths are mingled in his book;
But where the witness fail'd, the prophet spoke:
Some things like visionary flights appear;
The spirit caught him up, the Lord knows where;
And gave him his rabbinical degree,
Unknown to foreign university.
His judgment yet his mem'ry did excel;   660
Which piec'd his wondrous evidence so well,
And suited to the temper of the times,
Then groaning under Jebusitic crimes.
Let Israel's foes suspect his heav'nly call,
And rashly judge his writ apocryphal;
Our laws for such affronts have forfeits made:
He takes his life, who takes away his trade.
Were I myself in witness Corah's place,
The wretch who did me such a dire disgrace,
Should whet my memory, tho' once forgot,   670
To make him an appendix of my plot.
His zeal to Heav'n made him his prince despise,
And load his person with indignities;
But zeal peculiar privilege affords,
Indulging latitude to deeds and words;
And Corah might for Agag's murther call,
In terms as coarse as Samuel us'd to Saul.
What others in his evidence did join,
(The best that could be had for love or coin,)
In Corah's own predicament will fall;   680
For *witness* is a common name to all.
   Surrounded thus with friends of every sort,
Deluded Absalom forsakes the court;
Impatient of high hopes, urg'd with renown,
And fir'd with near possession of a crown.
Th' admiring crowd are dazzled with surprise,
And on his goodly person feed their eyes.
His joy conceal'd, he sets himself to show,
On each side bowing popularly low;
His looks, his gestures, and his words he frames,   690
And with familiar ease repeats their names.
Thus form'd by nature, furnish'd out with arts,

He glides unfelt into their secret hearts.
Then, with a kind compassionating look,
And sighs, bespeaking pity ere he spoke,
Few words he said; but easy those and fit,
More slow than Hybla-drops, and far more sweet.

   "I mourn, my countrymen, your lost estate;
Tho' far unable to prevent your fate:
Behold a banish'd man, for your dear cause   700
Expos'd a prey to arbitrary laws!
Yet O! that I alone could be undone,
Cut off from empire, and no more a son!
Now all your liberties a spoil are made;
Egypt and Tyrus intercept your trade,
And Jebusites your sacred rites invade.
My father, whom with reverence yet I name,
Charm'd into ease, is careless of his fame;
And, brib'd with petty sums of foreign gold,
Is grown in Bathsheba's embraces old;   710
Exalts his enemies, his friends destroys;
And all his pow'r against himself imploys.
He gives, and let him give, my right away;
But why should he his own and yours betray?
He, only he, can make the nation bleed,
And he alone from my revenge is freed.
Take then my tears, (with that he wip'd his eyes,)
'T is all the aid my present pow'r supplies:
No court-informer can these arms accuse;
These arms may sons against their fathers use: 720
And 't is my wish, the next successor's reign
May make no other Israelite complain."

   Youth, beauty, graceful action seldom fail;
But common interest always will prevail;
And pity never ceases to be shown
To him who makes the people's wrongs his own.
The crowd, that still believe their kings oppress,
With lifted hands their young Messiah bless:
Who now begins his progress to ordain
With chariots, horsemen, and a num'rous train;   730
From east to west his glories he displays,
And, like the sun, the promis'd land surveys.

Fame runs before him as the morning star,
And shouts of joy salute him from afar:
Each house receives him as a guardian god,
And consecrates the place of his abode.
But hospitable treats did most commend
Wise Issachar, his wealthy western friend.
This moving court, that caught the people's eyes,
And seem'd but pomp, did other ends disguise: 740
Achitophel had form'd it, with intent
To sound the depths, and fathom, where it went,
The people's hearts; distinguish friends from foes,
And try their strength, before they came to blows.
Yet all was color'd with a smooth pretense
Of specious love, and duty to their prince.
Religion, and redress of grievances,
Two names that always cheat and always please,
Are often urg'd; and good King David's life
Endanger'd by a brother and a wife.   750
Thus in a pageant shew a plot is made,
And peace itself is war in masquerade.
O foolish Israel! never warn'd by ill!
Still the same bait, and circumvented still!
Did ever men forsake their present ease,
In midst of health imagine a disease;
Take pains contingent mischiefs to foresee,
Make heirs for monarchs, and for God decree?
What shall we think! Can people give away,
Both for themselves and sons, their native sway?   760
Then they are left defenseless to the sword
Of each unbounded, arbitrary lord:
And laws are vain, by which we right enjoy,
If kings unquestion'd can those laws destroy.
Yet if the crowd be judge of fit and just,
And kings are only officers in trust,
Then this resuming cov'nant was declar'd
When kings were made, or is for ever barr'd.
If those who gave the scepter could not tie
By their own deed their own posterity,   770
How then could Adam bind his future race?
How could his forfeit on mankind take place?

Or how could heavenly justice damn us all,
Who ne'er consented to our father's fall?
Then kings are slaves to those whom they command,
And tenants to their people's pleasure stand.
Add, that the pow'r for property allow'd
Is mischievously seated in the crowd;
For who can be secure of private right,
If sovereign sway may be dissolv'd by might?   780
Nor is the people's judgment always true:
The most may err as grossly as the few;
And faultless kings run down, by common cry,
For vice, oppression, and for tyranny.
What standard is there in a fickle rout,
Which, flowing to the mark, runs faster out?
Nor only crowds, but Sanhedrins may be
Infected with this public lunacy,
And share the madness of rebellious times,
To murther monarchs for imagin'd crimes.   790
If they may give and take whene'er they please,
Not kings alone, (the Godhead's images,)
But government itself at length must fall
To nature's state, where all have right to all.
Yet, grant our lords the people kings can make,
What prudent men a settled throne would shake?
For whatsoe'er their sufferings were before,
That change they covet makes them suffer more.
All other errors but disturb a state,
But innovation is the blow of fate.   800
If ancient fabrics nod, and threat to fall,
To patch the flaws, and buttress up the wall,
Thus far 't is duty: but here fix the mark;
For all beyond it is to touch our ark.
To change foundations, cast the frame anew,
Is work for rebels, who base ends pursue,
At once divine and human laws control,
And mend the parts by ruin of the whole.
The tamp'ring world is subject to this curse,
To physic their disease into a worse.   810
  Now what relief can righteous David bring?
How fatal 't to be too good a king!

Friends he has few, so high the madness grows:
Who dare be such, must be the people's foes.
Yet some there were, ev'n in the worst of days;
Some let me name, and naming is to praise.
  In this short file Barzillai first appears;
Barzillai, crown'd with honor and with years.
Long since, the rising rebels he withstood
In regions waste, beyond the Jordan's flood: 820
Unfortunately brave to buoy the State;
But sinking underneath his master's fate:
In exile with his godlike prince he mourn'd;
For him he suffer'd, and with him return'd.
The court he practic'd, not the courtier's art:
Large was his wealth, but larger was his heart,
Which well the noblest objects knew to choose,
The fighting warrior, and recording Muse.
His bed could once a fruitful issue boast;
Now more than half a father's name is lost.   830
His eldest hope, with every grace adorn'd,
By me (so Heav'n will have it) always mourn'd,
And always honour'd, snatch'd in manhood's prime
B' unequal fates, and Providence's crime;
Yet not before the goal of honor won,
All parts fulfill'd of subject and of son:
Swift was the race, but short the time to run.
O narrow circle, but of pow'r divine,
Scanted in space, but perfect in thy line!
By sea, by land, thy matchless worth was known,   840
Arms thy delight, and war was all thy own:
Thy force, infus'd, the fainting Tyrians propp'd;
And haughty Pharaoh found his fortune stopp'd
O ancient honor! Our unconquer'd hand,
Whom foes unpunish'd never could withstand!
But Israel was unworthy of thy name;
Short is the date of all immoderate fame.
It looks as Heav'n our ruin had design'd,
And durst not trust thy fortune and thy mind.
Now, free from earth, thy disencumber'd soul   850
Mounts up, and leaves behind the clouds and starry pole:
From thence thy kindred legions mayst thou bring,

To aid the guardian angel of thy king.
Here stop, my Muse, here cease thy painful flight;
No pinions can pursue immortal height:
Tell good Barzillai thou canst sing no more,
And tell thy soul she should have fled before.
Or fled she with his life, and left this verse
To hang on her departed patron's hearse?
Now take thy steepy flight from heav'n, and see   860
If thou canst find on earth another *he:*
Another *he* would be too hard to find;
See then whom thou canst see not far behind.
Zadoc the priest, whom, shunning pow'r and place,
His lowly mind advanc'd to David's grace.
With him the Sagan of Jerusalem,
Of hospitable soul, and noble stem;
Him of the western dome, whose weighty sense
Flows in fit words and heavenly eloquence.
The prophets' sons, by such example led,   870
To learning and to loyalty were bred:
For colleges on bounteous kings depend,
And never rebel was to arts a friend.
To these succeed the pillars of the laws;
Who best could plead, and best can judge a cause.
Next them a train of loyal peers ascend;
Sharp-judging Adriel, the Muses' friend;
Himself a Muse—in Sanhedrin's debate
True to his prince, but not a slave of state:
Whom David's love with honors did adorn,   880
That from his disobedient son were torn.
Jotham of piercing wit, and pregnant thought;
Endued by nature, and by learning taught
To move assemblies, who but only tried
The worse a while, then chose the better side:
Nor chose alone, but turn'd the balance too;
So much the weight of one brave man can do.
Hushai, the friend of David in distress;
In public storms, of manly steadfastness:
By foreign treaties he inform'd his youth,   890
And join'd experience to his native truth.
His frugal care supplied the wanting throne;

Frugal for that, but bounteous of his own:
'T is easy conduct when exchequers flow,
But hard the task to manage well the low;
For sovereign power is too depress'd or high,
When kings are forc'd to sell, or crowds to buy.
Indulge one labor more, my weary Muse,
For Amiel: who can Amiel's praise refuse?
Of ancient race by birth, but nobler yet   900
In his own worth, and without title great:
The Sanhedrin long time as chief he rul'd,
Their reason guided, and their passion cool'd:
So dext'rous was he in the crown's defense,
So form'd to speak a loyal nation's sense,
That, as their band was Israel's tribes in small,
So fit was he to represent them all.
Now rasher charioteers the seat ascend,
Whose loose careers his steady skill commend:
They, like th' unequal ruler of the day,   910
Misguide the seasons, and mistake the way;
While he withdrawn at their mad labor smiles,
And safe enjoys the sabbath of his toils.
　These were the chief, a small but faithful band
Of worthies, in the breach who dar'd to stand,
And tempt th' united fury of the land.
With grief they view'd such powerful engines bent,
To batter down the lawful government:
A numerous faction, with pretended frights,
In Sanhedrins to plume the regal rights;   920
The true successor from the court remov'd;
The Plot, by hireling witnesses, improv'd.
These ills they saw, and, as their duty bound,
They shew'd the king the danger of the wound;
That no concessions from the throne would please,
But lenitives fomented the disease;
That Absalom, ambitious of the crown,
Was made the lure to draw the people down;
That false Achitophel's pernicious hate
Had turn'd the Plot to ruin Church and State;   930
The council violent, the rabble worse;
That Shimei taught Jerusalem to curse.

With all these loads of injuries oppress'd,
And long revolving in his careful breast
Th' event of things, at last, his patience tir'd,
Thus from his royal throne, by Heav'n inspir'd,
The godlike David spoke: with awful fear
His train their Maker in their master hear.
  "Thus long have I, by native mercy sway'd,
My wrongs dissembled, my revenge delay'd: 940
So willing to forgive th' offending age;
So much the father did the king assuage.
But now so far my clemency they slight,
Th' offenders question my forgiving right.
That one was made for many, they contend;
But 't is to rule; for that 's a monarch's end.
They call my tenderness of blood, my fear;
Tho' manly tempers can the longest bear.
Yet, since they will divert my native course,
'T is time to shew I am not good by force.   950
Those heap'd affronts that haughty subjects bring,
Are burthens for a camel, not a king.
Kings are the public pillars of the State,
Born to sustain and prop the nation's weight;
If my young Samson will pretend a call
To shake the column, let him share the fall:
But O that yet he would repent and live!
How easy 't is for parents to forgive!
With how few tears a pardon might be won
From nature, pleading for a darling son!   960
Poor pitied youth, by my paternal care
Rais'd up to all the height his frame could bear!
Had God ordain'd his fate for empire born,
He would have giv'n his soul another turn:
Gull'd with a patriot's name, whose modern sense
Is one that would by law supplant his prince;
The people's brave, the politician's tool;
Never was patriot yet, but was a fool.
Whence comes it that religion and the laws
Should more be Absalom's than David's cause?   970
His old instructor, ere he lost his place,
Was never thought indued with so much grace.

Good heav'ns, how faction can a patriot paint!
My rebel ever proves my people's saint.
Would *they* impose an heir upon the throne?
Let Sanhedrins be taught to give their own.
A king 's at least a part of government,
And mine as requisite as their consent;
Without my leave a future king to choose,
Infers a right the present to depose.   980
True, they petition me t' approve their choice;
But Esau's hands suit ill with Jacob's voice.
My pious subjects for my safety pray;
Which to secure, they take my pow'r away.
From plots and treasons Heav'n preserve my years,
But save me most from my petitioners!
Unsatiate as the barren womb or grave;
God cannot grant so much as they can crave.
What then is left, but with a jealous eye
To guard the small remains of royalty?   990
The law shall still direct my peaceful sway,
And the same law teach rebels to obey:
Votes shall no more establish'd pow'r control—
Such votes as make a part exceed the whole:
No groundless clamors shall my friends remove,
Nor crowds have pow'r to punish ere they prove;
For gods and godlike kings their care express,
Still to defend their servants in distress.
O that my pow'r to saving were confin'd!
Why am I forc'd, like Heav'n, against my mind,   1000
To make examples of another kind?
Must I at length the sword of justice draw?
O curst effects of necessary law!
How ill my fear they by my mercy scan!
Beware the fury of a patient man.
Law they require, let Law then shew her face;
They could not be content to look on Grace,
Her hinder parts, but with a daring eye
To tempt the terror of her front and die.
By their own arts, 't is righteously decreed,   1010
Those dire artificers of death shall bleed.
Against themselves their witnesses will swear,

Till viper-like their mother Plot they tear;
And suck for nutriment that bloody gore,
Which was their principle of life before.
Their Belial with their Belzebub will fight;
Thus on my foes, my foes shall do me right.
Nor doubt th' event; for factious crowds engage,
In their first onset, all their brutal rage.
Then let 'em take an unresisted course;   1020
Retire, and traverse, and delude their force;
But, when they stand all breathless, urge the fight,
And rise upon 'em with redoubled might;
For lawful pow'r is still superior found;
When long driv'n back, at length it stands the ground."

  He said. Th' Almighty, nodding, gave consent;
And peals of thunder shook the firmament.
Henceforth a series of new time began,
The mighty years in long procession ran:
Once more the godlike David was restor'd,   1030
And willing nations knew their lawful lord.

THE MEDAL

Of all our antic sights and pageantry,
Which English idiots run in crowds to see,
The Polish Medal bears the prize alone:
A monster, more the favorite of the town
Than either fairs or theaters have shown.
Never did art so well with nature strive,
Nor ever idol seem'd so much alive:
So like the man; so golden to the sight,
So base within, so counterfeit and light.
One side is fill'd with title and with face;   10
And, lest the king should want a regal place,
On the reverse, a tow'r the town surveys;
O'er which our mounting sun his beams displays.
The word, pronounc'd aloud by shrieval voice,
Laetamur, which, in Polish, is *rejoice.*
The day, month, year, to the great act are join'd;

And a new canting holiday design'd.
Five days he sate for every cast and look;
Four more than God to finish Adam took.
But who can tell what essence angels are,   20
Or how long Heav'n was making Lucifer?
O could the style that copied every grace,
And plow'd such furrows for an eunuch face,
Could it have form'd his ever-changing will,
The various piece had tir'd the graver's skill!
A martial hero first, with early care,
Blown, like a pigmy by the winds, to war.
A beardless chief, a rebel, ere a man:
(So young his hatred to his prince began.)
Next this, (how wildly will ambition steer!)   30
A vermin wriggling in th' usurper's ear.
Bart'ring his venal wit for sums of gold,
He cast himself into the saintlike mold;
Groan'd, sigh'd, and pray'd, while godliness was gain,
The loudest bagpipe of the squeaking train.
But, as 't is hard to cheat a juggler's eyes,
His open lewdness he could ne'er disguise.
There split the saint; for hypocritic zeal
Allows no sins but those it can conceal.
Whoring to scandal gives too large a scope;   40
Saints must not trade, but they may interlope.
Th' ungodly principle was all the same;
But a gross cheat betrays his partner's game.
Besides, their pace was formal, grave, and slack;
His nimble wit outran the heavy pack.
Yet still he found his fortune at a stay;
Whole droves of blockheads choking up his way:
They took, but not rewarded, his advice;
Villain and wit exact a double price.
Pow'r was his aim; but, thrown from that pretense,   50
The wretch turn'd loyal in his own defense,
And malice reconcil'd him to his prince.
Him in the anguish of his soul he serv'd,
Rewarded faster still than he deserv'd.
Behold him now exalted into trust;
His counsel 's oft convenient, seldom just.

Ev'n in the most sincere advice he gave,
He had a grudging still to be a knave.
The frauds he learnt in his fanatic years
Made him uneasy in his lawful gears: 60
At best as little honest as he could,
And, like white witches, mischievously good;
To his first bias longingly he leans,
And *rather* would be great by wicked means.
Thus, fram'd for ill, he loos'd our triple hold;
(Advice unsafe, precipitous, and bold.)
From hence those tears! that Ilium of our woe!
Who helps a pow'rful friend, forearms a foe.
What wonder if the waves prevail so far,
When he cut down the banks that made the bar?   70
Seas follow but their nature to invade,
But he by art our native strength betray'd.
So Samson to his foe his force confess'd;
And, to be shorn, lay slumb'ring on her breast.
But when this fatal counsel, found too late,
Expos'd its author to the public hate;
When his just sovereign, by no impious way,
Could be seduc'd to arbitrary sway;
Forsaken of that hope, he shifts the sail,
Drives down the current with a pop'lar gale;   80
And shews the fiend confess'd without a veil.
He preaches to the crowd that pow'r is lent,
But not convey'd to kingly government;
That claims successive bear no binding force,
That coronation oaths are things of course;
Maintains the multitude can never err,
And sets the people in the papal chair.
The reason's obvious: *int'rest never lies;*
The most have still their int'rest in their eyes;
The pow'r is always theirs, and pow'r is ever wise.   90
Almighty crowd, thou shorten'st all dispute!
Pow'r is thy essence, wit thy attribute!
Nor faith nor reason make thee at a stay,
Thou leap'st o'er all eternal truths in thy Pindaric way!
Athens no doubt did righteously decide,
When Phocion and when Socrates were tried;

As righteously they did those dooms repent;
Still they were wise, whatever way they went.
Crowds err not, tho' to both extremes they run;
To kill the father and recall the son.   100
Some think the fools were most, as times went then;
But now the world 's o'erstock'd with prudent men.
The common cry is ev'n religion's test:
The Turk's is at Constantinople best;
Idols in India; Popery at Rome;
And our own worship only true at home.
And true, but for the time; 't is hard to know
How long we please it shall continue so.
This side to-day, and that to-morrow burns;
So all are God-a'mighties in their turns.   110
A tempting doctrine, plausible and new:
What fools our fathers were, if this be true!
Who, to destroy the seeds of civil war,
Inherent right in monarchs did declare;
And, that a lawful pow'r might never cease,
Secur'd succession, to secure our peace.
Thus property and sovereign sway, at last,
In equal balances were justly cast:
But this new Jehu spurs the hot-mouth'd horse;
Instructs the beast to know his native force,   120
To take the bit between his teeth, and fly
To the next headlong steep of anarchy.
Too happy England, if our good we knew,
Would we possess the freedom we pursue!
The lavish government can give no more;
Yet we repine, and plenty makes us poor.
God tried us once: our rebel fathers fought;
He glutted 'em with all the pow'r they sought:
Till, master'd by their own usurping brave,
The freeborn subject sunk into a slave.   130
We loathe our manna, and we long for quails;
Ah, what is man, when his own wish prevails!
How rash, how swift to plunge himself in ill;
Proud of his pow'r, and boundless in his will!
That kings can do no wrong we must believe;
None can they do, and must they all receive?

Help, Heaven! or sadly we shall see an hour,
When neither wrong nor right are in their pow'r!
Already they have lost their best defense,
The benefit of laws which they dispense: 140
No justice to their righteous cause allow'd;
But baffled by an arbitrary crowd;
And medals grav'd, their conquest to record,
The stamp and coin of their adopted lord.
　　The man who laugh'd but once, to see an ass
Mumbling to make the crossgrain'd thistles pass,
Might laugh again, to see a jury chaw
The prickles of unpalatable law.
The witnesses that, leech-like, liv'd on blood,
Sucking for them were med'cinally good;   150
But when they fasten'd on *their* fester'd sore,
Then justice and religion they forswore;
Their maiden oaths debauch'd into a whore.
Thus men are rais'd by factions, and decried;
And rogue and saint distinguish'd by their side.
They rack ev'n scripture to confess their cause,
And plead a call to preach in spite of laws.
But that 's no news to the poor injur'd page:
It has been us'd as ill in every age;
And is constrain'd, with patience, all to take;   160
For what defense can Greek and Hebrew make?
Happy who can this talking trumpet seize;
They make it speak whatever sense they please!
'T was fram'd at first our oracle t' enquire;
But since our sects in prophecy grow higher,
The text inspires not them, but they the text inspire.
　　London, thou great *emporium* of our isle,
O thou too bounteous, thou too fruitful Nile!
How shall I praise or curse to thy desert;
Or separate thy sound from thy corrupted part!   170
I call'd thee Nile; the parallel will stand:
Thy tides of wealth o'erflow the fatten'd land;
Yet monsters from thy large increase we find,
Engender'd on the slime thou leav'st behind.
Sedition has not wholly seiz'd on thee,
Thy nobler parts are from infection free.

Of Israel's tribes thou hast a numerous band,
But still the Canaanite is in the land.
Thy military chiefs are brave and true,
Nor are thy disinchanted burghers few.   180
The head is loyal which thy heart commands,
But what 's a head with two such gouty hands?
The wise and wealthy love the surest way,
And are content to thrive and to obey.
But wisdom is to sloth too great a slave;
None are so busy as the fool and knave.
Those let me curse; what vengeance will they urge,
Whose ordures neither plague nor fire can purge;
Nor sharp experience can to duty bring,
Nor angry Heaven, nor a forgiving king!   190
In gospel-phrase their chapmen they betray;
Their shops are dens, the buyer is their prey.
The knack of trades is living on the spoil;
They boast, ev'n when each other they beguile.
Customs to steal is such a trivial thing,
That 't is their charter to defraud their king.
All hands unite of every jarring sect;
They cheat the country first, and then infect.
They for God's cause their monarchs dare dethrone,
And they 'll be sure to make his cause their own.   200
Whether the plotting Jesuit laid the plan
Of murth'ring kings, or the French Puritan,
Our sacrilegious sects their guides outgo,
And kings and kingly pow'r would murther too.
    What means their trait'rous combination less,
Too plain t' evade, too shameful to confess!
But treason is not own'd when 't is descried:
Successful crimes alone are justified.
The men, who no conspiracy would find,
Who doubts, but had it taken, they had join'd—   210
Join'd in a mutual cov'nant of defense,
At first without, at last against their prince?
If sovereign right by sovereign pow'r they scan,
The same bold maxim holds in God and man:
God were not safe, his thunder could they shun,
He should be forc'd to crown another son.

Thus, when the heir was from the vineyard thrown,
The rich possession was the murth'rers' own.
In vain to sophistry they have recourse:
By proving theirs no plot, they prove 't is worse;   220
Unmask'd rebellion, and audacious force;
Which tho' not actual, yet all eyes may see
'T is working in th' immediate pow'r to be;
For from pretended grievances they rise,
First to dislike, and after to despise;
Then, Cyclop-like, in human flesh to deal,
Chop up a minister at every meal;
Perhaps not wholly to melt down the king,
But clip his regal rights within the ring;
From thence t' assume the pow'r of peace and war;   230
And ease him by degrees of public care.
Yet, to consult his dignity and fame,
He should have leave to exercise the name,
And hold the cards, while commons play'd the game.
For what can pow'r give more than food and drink,
To live at ease, and not be bound to think?
These are the cooler methods of their crime,
But their hot zealots think 't is loss of time;
On utmost bounds of loyalty they stand,
And grin and whet like a Croatian band,   240
That waits impatient for the last command.
Thus outlaws open villainy maintain,
They steal not, but in squadrons scour the plain;
And, if their pow'r the passengers subdue,
The most have right, the wrong is in the few.
Such impious axioms foolishly they show,
For in some soils republics will not grow:
Our temp'rate isle will no extremes sustain
Of pop'lar sway or arbitrary reign,
But slides between them both into the best,   250
Secure in freedom, in a monarch blest;
And tho' the climate, vex'd with various winds,
Works thro' our yielding bodies on our minds,
The wholesome tempest purges what it breeds,
To recommend the calmness that succeeds.
    But thou, the pander of the people's hearts,

(O crooked soul, and serpentine in arts!)
Whose blandishments a loyal land have whor'd,
And broke the bonds she plighted to her lord;
What curses on thy blasted name will fall! 260
Which age to age their legacy shall call;
For all must curse the woes that must descend on all.
Religion thou hast none; thy *mercury*
Has pass'd thro' every sect, or theirs thro' thee.
But what thou giv'st, that venom still remains;
And the pox'd nation feels thee in their brains.
What else inspires the tongues and swells the breasts
Of all thy bellowing renegado priests,
That preach up thee for God, dispense thy laws,
And with thy stum ferment their fainting cause, 270
Fresh fumes of madness raise, and toil and sweat
To make the formidable cripple great?
Yet should thy crimes succeed, should lawless pow'r
Compass those ends thy greedy hopes devour,
Thy canting friends thy mortal foes would be,
Thy God and theirs will never long agree;
For thine (if thou hast any) must be one
That lets the world and humankind alone;
A jolly god, that passes hours too well
To promise heav'n, or threaten us with hell; 280
That unconcern'd can at rebellion sit,
And wink at crimes he did himself commit.
A tyrant theirs; the heav'n their priesthood paints
A conventicle of gloomy sullen saints;
A heav'n like Bedlam, slovenly and sad,
Foredoom'd for souls with false religion mad.
    Without a vision poets can foreshow
What all but fools by common sense may know;
If true succession from our isle should fail,
And crowds profane with impious arms prevail, 290
Not thou, nor those thy factious arts ingage,
Shall reap that harvest of rebellious rage,
With which thou flatter'st thy decrepit age.
The swelling poison of the sev'ral sects,
Which, wanting vent, the nation's health infects,
Shall burst its bag; and, fighting out their way,

The various venoms on each other prey.
The presbyter, puff'd up with spiritual pride,
Shall on the necks of the lewd nobles ride,
His brethren damn, the civil pow'r defy,   300
And parcel out republic prelacy.
But short shall be his reign: his rigid yoke
And tyrant pow'r will puny sects provoke;
And frogs and toads, and all the tadpole train,
Will croak to Heav'n for help from this devouring crane.
The cutthroat sword and clamorous gown shall jar,
In sharing their ill-gotten spoils of war;
Chiefs shall be grudg'd the part which they pretend;
Lords envy lords, and friends with every friend
About their impious merit shall contend.   310
The surly commons shall respect deny,
And justle peerage out with property.
Their gen'ral either shall his trust betray,
And force the crowd to arbitrary sway;
Or they, suspecting his ambitious aim,
In hate of kings shall cast anew the frame;
And thrust out Collatine that bore their name.
    Thus inborn broils the factions would ingage,
Or wars of exil'd heirs, or foreign rage,
Till halting vengeance overtook our age;   320
And our wild labors wearied into rest,
Reclin'd us on a rightful monarch's breast.

FROM THE SECOND PART OF

ABSALOM AND ACHITOPHEL

· · · · · ·

Next these, a troop of busy spirits press,   310
Of little fortunes, and of conscience less;
With them the tribe, whose luxury had drain'd
Their banks, in former sequestrations gain'd;
Who rich and great by past rebellions grew,
And long to fish the troubled streams anew.

Some future hopes, some present payment draws,
To sell their conscience and espouse the cause.
Such stipends those vile hirelings best befit,
Priests without grace, and poets without wit.
Shall that false Hebronite escape our curse,   320
Judas, that keeps the rebels' pension-purse;
Judas, that pays the treason-writer's fee,
Judas, that well deserves his namesake's tree;
Who at Jerusalem's own gates erects
His college for a nursery of sects;
Young prophets with an early care secures,
And with the dung of his own arts manures!
What have the men of Hebron here to do?
What part in Israel's promis'd land have you?
Here Phaleg, the lay Hebronite, is come,   330
'Cause like the rest he could not live at home;
Who from his own possessions could not drain
An omer even of Hebronitish grain,
Here struts it like a patriot, and talks high
Of injur'd subjects, alter'd property;
An emblem of that buzzing insect just,
That mounts the wheel, and thinks she raises dust.
Can dry bones live? or skeletons produce
The vital warmth of cuckoldizing juice?
Slim Phaleg could, and at the table fed,   340
Return'd the grateful product to the bed.
A waiting-man to trav'ling nobles chose,
He his own laws would saucily impose,
Till bastinado'd back again he went,
To learn those manners he to teach was sent.
Chastis'd, he ought to have retreated home,
But he reads politics to Absalom;
For never Hebronite, tho' kick'd and scorn'd,
To his own country willingly return'd.
—But leaving famish'd Phaleg to be fed,   350
And to talk treason for his daily bread,
Let Hebron, nay, let hell produce a man
So made for mischief as Ben-Jochanan.
A Jew of humble parentage was he,
By trade a Levite, tho' of low degree:

His pride no higher than the desk aspir'd,
But for the drudgery of priests was hir'd
To read and pray in linen ephod brave,
And pick up single shekels from the grave.
Married at last, and finding charge come faster,   360
He could not live by God, but chang'd his master;
Inspir'd by want, was made a factious tool,
They got a villain, and we lost a fool:
Still violent, whatever cause he took,
But most against the party he forsook;
For renegadoes, who ne'er turn by halves,
Are bound in conscience to be double knaves.
So this prose-prophet took most monstrous pains
To let his masters see he earn'd his gains.
But as the Dev'l owes all his imps a shame,   370
He chose th' Apostate for his proper theme;
With little pains he made the picture true,
And from reflection took the rogue he drew:
A wondrous work, to prove the Jewish nation
In every age a murmuring generation;
To trace 'em from their infancy of sinning,
And shew 'em factious from their first beginning;
To prove they could rebel, and rail, and mock,
Much to the credit of the chosen flock;
A strong authority, which must convince,   380
That saints own no allegiance to their prince;
As 't is a leading card to make a whore,
To prove her mother had turn'd up before.
But, tell me, did the drunken patriarch bless
The son that shew'd his father's nakedness?
Such thanks the present Church thy pen will give,
Which proves rebellion was so primitive.
Must ancient failings be examples made?
Then murtherers from Cain may learn their trade.
As thou the heathen and the saint hast drawn,   390
Methinks th' Apostate was the better man;
And thy hot father, (waiving my respect,)
Not of a mother church, but of a sect.
And such he needs must be of thy inditing;
This comes of drinking asses' milk and writing.

If Balak should be call'd to leave his place,
(As profit is the loudest call of grace,)
His temple dispossess'd of one, would be
Replenish'd with seven devils more by thee.
    Levi, thou art a load, I'll lay thee down,   400
And shew rebellion bare, without a gown;
Poor slaves in meter, dull and addle-pated,
Who rhyme below ev'n David's psalms translated;
Some in my speedy pace I must outrun,
As lame Mephibosheth the wizard's son;
To make quick way I'll leap o'er heavy blocks,
Shun rotten Uzza, as I would the pox
And hasten Og and Doeg to rehearse,
Two fools that crutch their feeble sense on verse;
Who, by my Muse, to all succeeding times   410
Shall live, in spite of their own dogg'rel rhymes.
    Doeg, tho' without knowing how or why,
Made still a blund'ring kind of melody;
Spurr'd boldly on, and dash'd thro' thick and thin,
Thro' sense and nonsense, never out nor in;
Free from all meaning, whether good or bad,
And, in one word, heroically mad:
He was too warm on picking-work to dwell,
But fagoted his notions as they fell,
And if they rhym'd and rattled, all was well.   420
Spiteful he is not, tho' he wrote a satire,
For still there goes some *thinking* to ill-nature:
He needs no more than birds and beasts to think;
All his occasions are to eat and drink.
If he call rogue and rascal from a garret,
He means you no more mischief than a parrot;
The words for friend and foe alike were made,
To fetter 'em in verse is all his trade.
For almonds he 'll cry whore to his own mother;
And call young Absalom King David's brother.   430
Let him be gallows-free by my consent,
And nothing suffer, since he nothing meant;
Hanging supposes human soul and reason,
This animal 's below committing treason.
Shall he be hang'd who never could rebel?

That 's a preferment for Achitophel.
The woman that committed buggary,
Was rightly sentenc'd by the law to die;
But 't was hard fate that to the gallows led
The dog that never heard the statute read.   *440*
Railing in other men may be a crime,
But ought to pass for mere instinct in him:
Instinct he follows, and no farther knows,
For to write verse with him is to *transpose.*
'T were pity treason at his door to lay,
Who *makes heaven's gate a lock to its own key:*
Let him rail on, let his invective Muse
Have four and twenty letters to abuse,
Which if he jumbles to one line of sense,
Indict him of a capital offense.   *450*
In fireworks give him leave to vent his spite,
Those are the only serpents he can write;
The height of his ambition is, we know,
But to be master of a puppet show:
On that one stage his works may yet appear,
And a month's harvest keeps him all the year.
   Now stop your noses, readers, all and some,
For here 's a tun of midnight work to come,
Og, from a treason-tavern rolling home.
Round as a globe, and liquor'd ev'ry chink,   *460*
Goodly and great he sails behind his link.
With all this bulk there 's nothing lost in Og,
For ev'ry inch that is not fool is rogue:
A monstrous mass of foul corrupted matter,
As all the devils had spew'd to make the batter.
When wine has given him courage to blaspheme,
He curses God, but God before curs'd him;
And if man could have reason, none has more,
That made his paunch so rich, and him so poor.
With wealth he was not trusted, for Heav'n knew   *470*
What 't was of old to pamper up a Jew;
To what would he on quail and pheasant swell,
That ev'n on tripe and carrion could rebel?
But tho' Heav'n made him poor, (with rev'rence speaking,)
He never was a poet of God's making.

The midwife laid her hand on his thick skull,
With this prophetic blessing: *Be thou dull;*
Drink, swear, and roar, forbear no lewd delight
Fit for thy bulk, do anything but write:
Thou art of lasting make, like thoughtless men,　　　　　480
A strong nativity—but for the pen;
Eat opium, mingle arsenic in thy drink,
Still thou mayst live, avoiding pen and ink.
I see, I see, 't is counsel given in vain,
For treason botch'd in rhyme will be thy bane;
Rhyme is the rock on which thou art to wreck,
'T is fatal to thy fame and to thy neck:
Why should thy meter good King David blast?
A psalm of his will surely be thy last.
Dar'st thou presume in verse to meet thy foes,　　　　　490
Thou whom the penny pamphlet foil'd in prose?
Doeg, whom God for mankind's mirth has made,
O'ertops thy talent in thy very trade;
Doeg to thee, thy paintings are so coarse,
A poet is, tho' he 's the poets' horse.
A double noose thou on thy neck dost pull,
For writing treason, and for writing dull;
To die for faction is a common evil,
But to be hang'd for nonsense is the devil.
Hadst thou the glories of thy king express'd,　　　　　500
Thy praises had been satire at the best;
But thou in clumsy verse, unlick'd, unpointed,
Hast shamefully defined the Lord's anointed:
I will not rake the dunghill of thy crimes,
For who would read thy life that reads thy rhymes?
But of King David's foes, be this the doom,
May all be like the young man Absalom;
And for my foes may this their blessing be,
To talk like Doeg, and to write like thee.

·　　·　　·　　·　　·

Odes

荘重な文体、まじめな内容
情熱的、エリスク vision り

Pindar (522? — 433 B.C.)

{
strophe　コーラスが左に動きながら歌う　　←

anti-strophe　　　　　右　　　　　　→
epode　　　静止して歌う
}

・オリンピックの勝者を誉めたたえる。

Horatian Ode
静かで、内省的。(単一のスタンザの繰り返し)

Harrisons p. 202 Pindaric ode
The Bard
·926
- 0524 - Cowley
irregular or pindaric ode

Commentary on the Odes

ANNE KILLIGREW

Dryden's ode to Mrs. (that is, Mistress) Anne Killigrew has been the subject of critical controversy. Samuel Johnson called it simply "the noblest ode that our language has ever produced." Dr. Joseph Warton, in his 1811 edition of Dryden's *Poetical Works,* objected strenuously to this judgment, and attacked the ode for bad writing, tumid expression, hyperbolical admiration, and other supposed flaws; "very inferior in all respects to the divine ode on St. Cecilia's day" was his verdict. Warton even made his note on the ode an occasion for a paragraph of personal censure of Johnson, whom he had known. Saintsbury, in his 1881 life of Dryden, defended Johnson, calling Warton's depreciation of the ode "a curious instance of the lack of catholic taste which has so often marred English criticism of poetry." In more recent times Mark Van Doren has judged most of the ode "sadly uneven" (he praises the first, fourth, and last stanzas, however); but his criticism has come under attack from E. M. W. Tillyard, who calls the ode "a masterpiece of a major poet." Tillyard's analysis, in his *Five Poems* (1948) is among the most perceptive yet written.

The chief facts about Anne Killigrew to which Dryden alludes in the ode are that she was both a poet and a painter, disciple of two of the nine Muses (88); that her father was a clergyman (79) and minor dramatist (26); that she died young, innocent, and unmarried (67; 83–87: *vestal* means virginal priestess; *Diana* is the goddess of chastity); that her brother was a naval officer (165); and that her death—like that of the poet

65

Katherine Philips, popularly known as the Matchless *Orinda*—was due to smallpox (154–164). Dryden further stresses her innocence by the assertion that even the ancient moralist Epictetus (to whom he gives a lamp like that carried by Diogenes in his quest for human integrity) would have found her unexceptionable. The *martial king* (128) is James II; his queen, Mary of Este, had been crowned in April, 1685, only two months before Anne Killigrew's death.

Though Dryden avails himself of a specific historical and biographical situation, the ode is less personal than ceremonial; Anne Killigrew is made a symbol for the high aspirations of the arts, particularly of poetry. Thus Dryden speculates as to whether she derived her talents by inheritance (*traduction, 23*) from her father, or by reincarnation of the soul of preceding great poets, from the ancient Greek poetess *Sappho* (33) to those of the present; and he implies a comparison with Plato (of whom such a legend was current) in the passage about the bees (50–51). This exaltation of the arts is one reason for the poem's large use of astronomy (the *neighboring star,* that is planet, of line 6; the star-cluster, *Pleiades,* of 175; and so on), and of astrology (the influence of unfavorable planets was neutralized at Anne Killigrew's birth by their being *in trine,* or 120 degrees apart [43]). Stanza ten of course refers to the Last Judgment ("God judges" is the etymological meaning of *Jehosaphat,* 180), when the dead (*the nations underground,* 179) will be brought to life again; this Christian conception is paralleled by the pagan idea of heroes being translated, after death, to the astronomical heavens (174–177). All these large claims for what poetry might, ideally, represent are contrasted, in stanza four, with the lubricity and folly characteristic of a great deal of Restoration literature. Thus Dryden makes the precocious and prematurely dead Mistress Killigrew seem a flash of meteoric light set against a somber background. The volume of her poems to which his ode was contributed bears the motto (compare 147): *Immodicis brevis est aetas, et rara senectus:* "For extraordinary beings life is short, and old age unusual."

THE ST. CECILIA ODES

In the 1680's and 90's a London musical society annually celebrated the feast of St. Cecilia (November 22) with a public concert. Dryden was twice engaged, in 1687 and 1697, to write odes for this event; each was set to music by one or more composers of the period (and ultimately, in the eighteenth century, by Handel). Today they are probably his most widely reprinted poems. In each he attributes to St. Cecilia, patroness of music, the invention of the organ.

The first and shorter ode, "A Song for St. Cecilia's Day," dramatizes the ancient conception of the universe as a harmony of warring elements (8) created by God out of chaos (*a heap of jarring atoms*). The translucent spheres which encased each planet, and all the fixed stars, were thought to create a divine music, inaudible to man, by their contact with one another. Thus at the conclusion of the poem the Last Trumpet, which will conclude the existence of the universe, makes a music which ends another music, that of the spheres: *Music shall untune the sky.* Dryden unites Christian and classical myths about music in his references to *Jubal* ("the father of all such as handle the harp and organ" [Genesis 4:21]) and *Orpheus,* the musician who made even animals (47) and trees *sequacious of* him—that is, his followers.

"Alexander's Feast" dramatizes the legend that Alexander, son of *Philip* of Macedon (2), conqueror of *Darius,* King of Persia (75), and lover of the courtesan *Thais* (9), was influenced by the musician *Timotheus* (20) to burn the Persian city Persepolis, in which he was feasting. Dryden—or Timotheus—attributes Alexander's true paternity to Zeus, who had seduced Alexander's mother *Olympia* (30) in the form of a dragon; this makes the divine *sov'reign of the world* father of the world's conquerer (33).

To the Pious Memory of the
Accomplish'd Young Lady

MRS. ANNE KILLIGREW

Excellent in the Two Sister-Arts
of Poesy and Painting, An Ode

I

Thou youngest virgin-daughter of the skies,
Made in the last promotion of the blest;
Whose palms, new pluck'd from paradise,

In spreading branches more sublimely rise,
Rich with immortal green above the rest:
Whether, adopted to some neighboring star,
Thou roll'st above us, in thy wand'ring race,
 Or, in procession fix'd and regular,
 Mov'd with the heavens' majestic pace;
 Or, call'd to more superior bliss,   10
Thou tread'st, with seraphims, the vast abyss:
Whatever happy region is thy place,
Cease thy celestial song a little space;
(Thou wilt have time enough for hymns divine,
 Since heav'n's eternal year is thine.)
Hear then a mortal Muse thy praise rehearse,
   In no ignoble verse;
But such as thy own voice did practice here,
When thy first fruits of poesy were giv'n,
To make thyself a welcome inmate there;   20
  While yet a young probationer,
  And candidate of heav'n.

II
 If by traduction came thy mind,
 Our wonder is the less to find
A soul so charming from a stock so good;
Thy father was transfus'd into thy blood:
So wert thou born into the tuneful strain,
(An early, rich, and inexhausted vein.)
 But if thy preëxisting soul
 Was form'd, at first, with myriads more,   30
It did thro' all the mighty poets roll,
 Who Greek or Latin laurels wore,
And was that Sappho last, which once it was before.
 If so, then cease thy flight, *O heav'n-born mind!*
 Thou hast no dross to purge from thy rich ore;
 Nor can thy soul a fairer mansion find,
 Than was the beauteous frame she left behind:
Return, to fill or mend the choir of thy celestial kind.

III
 May we presume to say, that at thy birth
New joy was sprung in heav'n, as well as here on earth?   40

For sure the milder planets did combine
On thy auspicious horoscope to shine,
And ev'n the most malicious were in trine.
Thy brother-angels at thy birth
   Strung each his lyre, and tun'd it high,
   That all the people of the sky
Might know a poetess was born on earth.
   And then, if ever, mortal ears
Had heard the music of the spheres!
And if no clust'ring swarm of bees   *50*
On thy sweet mouth distill'd their golden dew,
   'T was that such vulgar miracles
   Heav'n had no leisure to renew:
For all the blest fraternity of love
Solemniz'd there thy birth, and kept thy holiday above.

IV

   O gracious God! how far have we
Profan'd thy heav'nly gift of poesy!
Made prostitute and profligate the Muse,
Debas'd to each obscene and impious use,
Whose harmony was first ordain'd above   *60*
For tongues of angels, and for hymns of love!
O wretched we! why were we hurried down
   This lubric and adult'rate age,
   (Nay, added fat pollutions of our own,)
   T' increase the steaming ordures of the stage?
What can we say t' excuse our *second fall?*
Let this thy *vestal,* Heav'n, atone for all:
Her Arethusian stream remains unsoil'd,
Unmix'd with foreign filth, and undefil'd;
Her wit was more than man, her innocence a child!   *70*

V

   Art she had none, yet wanted none;
   For nature did that want supply:
   So rich in treasures of her own,
   She might our boasted stores defy:
Such noble vigor did her verse adorn
That it seem'd borrow'd, where 't was only born.
Her morals too were in her bosom bred,

By great examples daily fed,
What in the best of books, her father's life, she read.
And to be read herself she need not fear;   80
Each test, and ev'ry light, her Muse will bear,
Tho' Epictetus with his lamp were there.
Ev'n love (for love sometimes her Muse express'd)
Was but a *lambent flame* which play'd about her breast,
Light as the vapors of a morning dream:
So cold herself, whilst she such warmth express'd,
'T was Cupid bathing in Diana's stream.

VI
Born to the spacious empire of the Nine,
One would have thought she should have been content
To manage well that mighty government;   90
But what can young ambitious souls confine?
    To the next realm she stretch'd her sway,
    For *painture* near adjoining lay,
A plenteous province, and alluring prey.
    A chamber of dependences was fram'd,
(As conquerors will never want pretense,
    When arm'd, to justify th' offense,)
And the whole fief in right of poetry she claim'd.
The country open lay without defense;
For poets frequent inroads there had made,   100
    And perfectly could represent
    The shape, the face, with ev'ry lineament;
And all the large domains which the *Dumb Sister* sway'd,
    All bow'd beneath her government;
    Receiv'd in triumph wheresoe'er she went.
Her pencil drew whate'er her soul design'd,
And oft the happy draught surpass'd the image in her mind.
    The *sylvan* scenes of herds and flocks,
    And fruitful plains and barren rocks,
    Of shallow brooks that flow'd so clear   110
    The bottom did the top appear;
    Of deeper too and ampler floods,
    Which, as in mirrors, shew'd the woods;
    Of lofty trees, with sacred shades,
    And perspectives of pleasant glades,

Where nymphs of brightest form appear,
And shaggy satyrs standing near,
Which them at once admire and fear:
The ruins too of some majestic piece,
Boasting the pow'r of ancient Rome, or Greece,   *120*
Whose statues, friezes, columns broken lie,
And, tho' defac'd, the wonder of the eye:
What nature, art, bold fiction, e'er durst frame,
Her forming hand gave feature to the name.
So strange a concourse ne'er was seen before,
But when the peopled ark the whole creation bore.

VII

The scene then chang'd: with bold erected look
Our martial king the sight with reverence strook;
For, not content t'express his outward part,
Her hand call'd out the image of his heart: *130*
His warlike mind, his soul devoid of fear,
His high-designing thoughts were figur'd there,
As when, by magic, ghosts are made appear.
Our Phoenix queen was portray'd too so bright,
Beauty alone could beauty take so right:
Her dress, her shape, her matchless grace,
Were all observ'd, as well as heav'nly face.
With such a peerless majesty she stands,
As in that day she took the crown from sacred hands;
Before a train of heroines was seen,   *140*
In beauty foremost, as in rank the queen.
Thus nothing to her *genius* was denied,
But like a ball of fire the further thrown,
Still with a greater blaze she shone,
And her bright soul broke out on ev'ry side.
What next she had design'd, Heaven only knows;
To such immod'rate growth her conquest rose
That fate alone its progress could oppose.

VIII

Now all those charms, that blooming grace,
The well-proportion'd shape, and beauteous face,   *150*
Shall never more be seen by mortal eyes:

In earth the much-lamented virgin lies!
 Not wit, nor piety could fate prevent;
 Nor was the cruel Destiny content
 To finish all the murder at a blow,
 To sweep at once her life and beauty too;
But, like a harden'd felon, took a pride
 To work more mischievously slow,
And plunder'd first, and then destroy'd.
O double sacrilege on things divine,   *160*
To rob the relic, and deface the shrine!
  But thus Orinda died:
Heav'n, by the same disease, did both translate;
As equal were their souls, so equal was their fate.

IX

 Meantime her warlike brother on the seas
 His waving streamers to the winds displays,
And vows for his return, with vain devotion, pays.
  Ah, generous youth, that wish forbear,
  The winds too soon will waft thee here!
 Slack all thy sails, and fear to come,   *170*
Alas, thou know'st not, thou art wreck'd at home!
No more shalt thou behold thy sister's face,
Thou hast already had her last embrace.
But look aloft, and if thou kenn'st from far
Among the Pleiads a new kindled star;
If any sparkles than the rest more bright,
'T is she that shines in that propitious light.

X

 When in mid-air the golden trump shall sound,
  To raise the nations under ground;
  When in the Valley of Jehosaphat   *180*
The judging God shall close the book of fate,
  And there the last assizes keep
  For those who wake and those who sleep;
  When rattling bones together fly
  From the four corners of the sky;
When sinews o'er the skeletons are spread,
Those cloth'd with flesh, and life inspires the dead;

The sacred poets first shall hear the sound,
And foremost from the tomb shall bound,
For they are cover'd with the lightest ground;   190
And straight, with inborn vigor, on the wing,
Like mounting larks, to the new morning sing.
There thou, sweet saint, before the choir shalt go,
As harbinger of heav'n, the way to show,
The way which thou so well hast learn'd below.

A SONG FOR ST. CECILIA'S DAY, 1687

I

From harmony, from heav'nly harmony
    This universal frame began:
    When Nature underneath a heap
        Of jarring atoms lay,
    And could not heave her head,
The tuneful voice was heard from high:
        "Arise, ye more than dead."
Then cold, and hot, and moist, and dry,
In order to their stations leap,
        And Music's pow'r obey.   10
From harmony, from heav'nly harmony
    This universal frame began:
    From harmony to harmony
Thro' all the compass of the notes it ran,
The diapason closing full in Man.

II

What passion cannot Music raise and quell!
    When Jubal struck the corded shell,
    His list'ning brethren stood around,
    And, wond'ring, on their faces fell
    To worship that celestial sound.   20
Less than a god they thought there could not dwell
    Within the hollow of that shell
    That spoke so sweetly and so well.
What passion cannot Music raise and quell!

III

    The Trumpet's loud clangor
      Excites us to arms,
    With shrill notes of anger,
      And mortal alarms.
    The double double double beat
      Of the thund'ring Drum   30
Cries: "Hark! the foes come;
Charge, charge, 't is too late to retreat."

IV

    The soft complaining Flute
    In dying notes discovers
    The woes of hopeless lovers,
Whose dirge is whisper'd by the warbling Lute.

V

    Sharp Violins proclaim
Their jealous pangs, and desperation,
Fury, frantic indignation,
Depth of pains, and height of passion,   40
    For the fair, disdainful dame.

VI

    But O! what art can teach,
    What human voice can reach,
The sacred Organ's praise?
    Notes inspiring holy love,
Notes that wing their heav'nly ways
    To mend the choirs above.

VII

Orpheus could lead the savage race;
And trees unrooted left their place,
    Sequacious of the lyre;   50
But bright Cecilia rais'd the wonder high'r:
When to her Organ vocal breath was giv'n,
An angel heard, and straight appear'd,
    Mistaking earth for heav'n.

GRAND CHORUS

> *As from the pow'r of sacred lays*
> > *The spheres began to move,*
> *And sung the great Creator's praise*
> > *To all the blest above;*
> *So, when the last and dreadful hour*
> *This crumbling pageant shall devour,*   60
> *The Trumpet shall be heard on high,*
> *The dead shall live, the living die,*
> *And Music shall untune the sky.*

ALEXANDER'S FEAST

Or, The Power Of Music,

An Ode in Honor of St. Cecilia's Day

I

'T was at the royal feast, for Persia won
> By Philip's warlike son:
> > Aloft in awful state
> > The godlike hero sate
> > > On his imperial throne:
> His valiant peers were plac'd around;
Their brows with roses and with myrtles bound:
> (So should desert in arms be crown'd.)
> The lovely Thais, by his side,
> Sate like a blooming Eastern bride   10
In flow'r of youth and beauty's pride.
> > Happy, happy, happy pair!
> > None but the brave,
> > None but the brave,
> None but the brave deserves the fair.

CHORUS

> *Happy, happy, happy pair!*
> *None but the brave,*
> *None but the brave,*
> *None but the brave deserves the fair.*

II

Timotheus, plac'd on high   *20*
  Amid the tuneful choir,
  With flying fingers touch'd the lyre:
The trembling notes ascend the sky,

                                    And heav'nly joys inspire.

The song began from Jove,
Who left his blissful seats above,
(Such is the pow'r of mighty love.)
A dragon's fiery form belied the god:
Sublime on radiant spires he rode,
  When he to fair Olympia press'd;   *30*
  And while he sought her snowy breast:
Then, round her slender waist he curl'd,
And stamp'd an image of himself, a sov'reign of the world.
The list'ning crowd admire the lofty sound;
"A present deity," they shout around;
"A present deity," the vaulted roofs rebound:
  With ravish'd ears
  The monarch hears,
  Assumes the god,
  Affects to nod,   *40*
And seems to shake the spheres.

CHORUS

    With ravish'd ears
    The monarch hears,
    Assumes the god,
    Affects to nod,
  And seems to shake the spheres.

III

The praise of Bacchus then the sweet musician sung,
  Of Bacchus ever fair and ever young:
    "The jolly god in triumph comes;
    Sound the trumpets; beat the drums;   *50*
      Flush'd with a purple grace
      He shews his honest face:
Now give the hautboys breath; he comes, he comes.

    Bacchus, ever fair and young,
       Drinking joys did first ordain;
    Bacchus' blessings are a treasure,
    Drinking is the soldier's pleasure:
       Rich the treasure,
       Sweet the pleasure,
       Sweet is pleasure after pain."   60

CHORUS

    Bacchus' blessings are a treasure,
    Drinking is the soldier's pleasure:
       Rich the treasure,
       Sweet the pleasure,
    Sweet is pleasure after pain.

IV

    Sooth'd with the sound, the king grew vain;
       Fought all his battles o'er again;
And thrice he routed all his foes; and thrice he slew the slain.
The master saw the madness rise;
His glowing cheeks, his ardent eyes;   70
And, while he heav'n and earth defied,
Chang'd his hand, and check'd his pride.
    He chose a mournful Muse,
       Soft pity to infuse:
He sung Darius great and good,
       By too severe a fate,
Fallen, fallen, fallen, fallen,
       Fallen from his high estate,
       And welt'ring in his blood;
Deserted, at his utmost need,   80
By those his former bounty fed;
On the bare earth expos'd he lies,
With not a friend to close his eyes.
With downcast looks the joyless victor sate,
    Revolving in his alter'd soul
       The various turns of chance below;
    And, now and then, a sigh he stole;
       And tears began to flow.

CHORUS

> Revolving in his alter'd soul
>   The various turns of chance below;   90
> And, now and then, a sigh he stole;
>   And tears began to flow.

V

The mighty master smil'd, to see
That love was in the next degree:
'T was but a kindred sound to move,
For pity melts the mind to love.
>   Softly sweet, in Lydian measures,
>   Soon he sooth'd his soul to pleasures.
> "War," he sung, "is toil and trouble;
> Honor, but an empty bubble;   100
>   Never ending, still beginning,
> Fighting still, and still destroying:
>   If the world be worth thy winning,
> Think, O think it worth enjoying;
>   Lovely Thais sits beside thee,
>   Take the good the gods provide thee."
The many rend the skies with loud applause;
So Love was crown'd, but Music won the cause.
>   The prince, unable to conceal his pain,
>   Gaz'd on the fair   110
>   Who caus'd his care,
>   And sigh'd and look'd, sigh'd and look'd,
> Sigh'd and look'd, and sigh'd again:
At length, with love and wine at once oppress'd,
The vanquish'd victor sunk upon her breast.

CHORUS

> The prince, unable to conceal his pain,
>   Gaz'd on the fair
>   Who caus'd his care,
>   And sigh'd and look'd, sigh'd and look'd,
> Sigh'd and look'd, and sigh'd again: 120
> At length, with love and wine at once oppress'd,
> The vanquish'd victor sunk upon her breast.

VI

Now strike the golden lyre again:
A louder yet, and yet a louder strain.
Break his bands of sleep asunder,
And rouse him, like a rattling peal of thunder.

Hark, hark, the horrid sound
Has rais'd up his head:
As awak'd from the dead,
And amaz'd, he stares around.   130

"Revenge, revenge!" Timotheus cries,
"See the Furies arise!
See the snakes that they rear,
How they hiss in their hair,
And the sparkles that flash from their eyes!
Behold a ghastly band,
Each a torch in his hand!
Those are Grecian ghosts, that in battle were slain,
And unburied remain
Inglorious on the plain: 140
Give the vengeance due
To the valiant crew.
Behold how they toss their torches on high,
How they point to the Persian abodes,
And glitt'ring temples of their hostile gods!"
The princes applaud, with a furious joy;
And the king seiz'd a flambeau with zeal to destroy;
Thais led the way,
To light him to his prey,
And, like another Helen, fir'd another Troy.   150

CHORUS

And the king seiz'd a flambeau with zeal to destroy;
Thais led the way,
To light him to his prey,
And, like another Helen, fir'd another Troy.

VII

Thus, long ago,
Ere heaving bellows learn'd to blow,

While organs yet were mute;
Timotheus, to his breathing flute,
And sounding lyre,
Could swell the soul to rage, or kindle soft desire.   160
At last, divine Cecilia came,
Inventress of the vocal frame;
The sweet enthusiast, from her sacred store,
Enlarg'd the former narrow bounds,
And added length to solemn sounds,
With nature's mother wit, and arts unknown before.
Let old Timotheus yield the prize,
Or both divide the crown;
He rais'd a mortal to the skies;
She drew an angel down.   170

GRAND CHORUS

At last, divine Cecilia came,
Inventress of the vocal frame;
The sweet enthusiast, from her sacred store,
Enlarg'd the former narrow bounds,
And added length to solemn sounds,
With nature's mother wit, and arts unknown before.
Let old Timotheus yield the prize,
Or both divide the crown;
He rais'd a mortal to the skies;
She drew an angel down.   180

Songs

Commentary on the Songs

The next three divisions of this anthology—Songs; *All for Love;* Prologues and Epilogues—afford examples of Dryden's work for the stage, an important part of his career. Dates of the various plays from which the Songs are taken can be found in the Chronological Table. Though most of the songs are related in some way to their dramatic context, they are so self-sufficient that they require little commentary. It might be noted that in the seventeenth century the words *die, dying, death,* and the like could be taken to refer to the climax of physical love; once or twice, in the songs here printed, this semantic overtone is present. In "Sylvia the Fair" the term *Trimmer* (14) refers to a political party believing in compromise between Whig and Tory, at the time of the debate over exclusion of Charles II's heir (later James II) from the throne.

The "Secular Masque" from the *Pilgrim,* a play of Fletcher's revived in a benefit for Dryden during the last month of his life (according to one account, the night of his death, May 1, 1700, was the third night of its performance), sums up in epigram the poet's view of the entire century, *secular* meaning "of an age." *Momus* is the god of mockery; *Janus* of beginnings; *Diana* of hunting; *Chronos* of time; *Venus* of love; and *Mars* of war. Only the conclusion of the masque is printed here. The reference to the *chase* may be in part an allusion to the widely known love of hunting indulged by James I, who became king in 1603. The *wars* are the various civil and foreign wars of the period; the *lovers* are doubtless those of the Restoration court and stage. But the lines are general enough to be variously symbolic and need not be tied too closely to Dryden's time and country.

AN EVENING'S LOVE

I
You charm'd me not with that fair face,
  Tho' it was all divine:
To be another's is the grace
  That makes me wish you mine.

II
The gods and Fortune take their part,
  Who like young monarchs fight,
And boldly dare invade that heart
  Which is another's right.

III
First, mad with hope, we undertake
  To pull up every bar;
But, once possess'd, we faintly make
  A dull defensive war.

IV
Now, every friend is turn'd a foe,
  In hope to get our store;
And passion makes us cowards grow,
  Which made us brave before.

I
After the pangs of a desperate lover,
  When day and night I have sigh'd all in vain,
Ah what a pleasure it is to discover,
  In her eyes pity, who causes my pain.

II

When with unkindness our love at a stand is,
  And both have punish'd ourselves with the pain,
Ah what a pleasure the touch of her hand is,
  Ah what a pleasure to press it again!

III

When the denial comes fainter and fainter,
  And her eyes give what her tongue does deny,
Ah what a trembling I feel when I venture,
  Ah what a trembling does usher my joy!

IV

When, with a sigh, she accords me the blessing,
  And her eyes twinkle 'twixt pleasure and pain,
Ah what a joy 't is, beyond all expressing,
  Ah what a joy to hear: "Shall we again?"

I
DAMON.   CELIMENA, of my heart,
             None shall e'er bereave you:
           If with your good leave I may
           Quarrel with you once a day,
             I will never leave you.

II
CELIMENA. Passion's but an empty name
             Where respect is wanting:
           Damon, you mistake your aim;
           Hang your heart, and burn your flame,
             If you must be ranting.

III
DAMON.   Love as dull and muddy is
             As decaying liquor:
           Anger sets it on the lees,
           And refines it by degrees,
             Till it works it quicker.

IV

CELIMENA.   Love by quarrels to beget
    Wisely you endeavor;
   With a grave physician's wit
   Who, to cure an ague fit,
    Put me in a fever.

V

DAMON.   Anger rouses love to fight,
    And his only bait is:
   'T is the spur to dull delight,
   And is but an eager bite,
    When desire at height is.

VI

CELIMENA.   If such drops of heat can fall
    In our wooing weather;
   If such drops of heat can fall,
   We shall have the devil and all
    When we come together.

SONG FROM

TYRANNIC LOVE

I

Ah how sweet it is to love!
Ah how gay is young desire!
And what pleasing pains we prove
When we first approach love's fire!
 Pains of love be sweeter far
 Than all other pleasures are.

II

Sighs which are from lovers blown,
Do but gently heave the heart:
Ev'n the tears they shed alone,

Cure, like trickling balm, their smart.
　Lovers when they lose their breath,
　Bleed away in easy death.

III

Love and time with reverence use,
Treat 'em like a parting friend:
Nor the golden gifts refuse,
Which in youth sincere they send:
　For each year their price is more,
　And they less simple than before.

IV

Love, like spring-tides full and high,
Swells in every youthful vein;
But each tide does less supply,
Till they quite shrink in again:
　If a flow in age appear,
　'Tis but rain, and runs not clear.

SONG FROM

MARRIAGE À LA MODE

I

Why should a foolish marriage vow,
　Which long ago was made,
Oblige us to each other now,
　When passion is decay'd?
We lov'd, and we lov'd, as long as we could,
　Till our love was lov'd out in us both;
But our marriage is dead, when the pleasure is fled:
　'T was pleasure first made it an oath.

II

If I have pleasures for a friend,
　And farther love in store,
What wrong has he whose joys did end,

And who could give no more?
'T is a madness that he should be jealous of me,
  Or that I should bar him of another:
For all we can gain is to give ourselves pain,
  When neither can hinder the other.

THE SPANISH FRIAR

I
Farewell, ungrateful traitor!
  Farewell, my perjur'd swain!
Let never injur'd creature
  Believe a man again.
The pleasure of possessing
Surpasses all expressing,
But 't is too short a blessing,
  And love too long a pain.

II
'T is easy to deceive us,
  In pity of your pain;
But when we love, you leave us
  To rail at you in vain.
Before we have descried it,
There is no bliss beside it;
But she that once has tried it,
  Will never love again.

III
The passion you pretended,
  Was only to obtain;
But when the charm is ended,
  The charmer you disdain.
Your love by ours we measure,
Till we have lost our treasure;

But dying is a pleasure,
　When living is a pain.

SYLVIA THE FAIR

I

SYLVIA, the fair, in the bloom of fifteen,
Felt an innocent warmth as she lay on the green;
She had heard of a pleasure, and something she guess'd
By the towzing, and tumbling, and touching her breast.
She saw the men eager, but was at a loss,
What they meant by their sighing, and kissing so close;
　　By their praying and whining,
　　And clasping and twining,
　　And panting and wishing,
　　And sighing and kissing,
　And sighing and kissing so close.

II

"Ah!" she cried, "ah! for a languishing maid,
In a country of Christians, to die without aid!
Not a Whig, or a Tory, or Trimmer at least,
Or a Protestant parson, or Catholic priest,
To instruct a young virgin, that is at a loss,
What they meant by their sighing, and kissing so close!
　　By their praying and whining,
　　And clasping and twining,
　　And panting and wishing,
　　And sighing and kissing,
　And sighing and kissing so close."

III

Cupid, in shape of a swain, did appear,
He saw the sad wound, and in pity drew near;
Then show'd her his arrow, and bid her not fear,
For the pain was no more than a maiden may bear.
When the balm was infus'd, she was not at a loss,
What they meant by their sighing, and kissing so close;

By their praying and whining,
And clasping and twining,
And panting and wishing,
And sighing and kissing,
And sighing and kissing so close.

A Pastorial Dialogue Betwixt Thyrsis and Iris, from

AMPHITRYON

I

THYRSIS.   FAIR Iris and her swain
    Were in a shady bow'r;
Where Thyrsis long in vain
    Had sought the shepherd's hour;
At length his hand advancing upon her snowy breast,
    He said: "O kiss me longer,
    And longer yet and longer,
      If you will make me blest."

II

IRIS.   An easy yielding maid
    By trusting is undone;
Our sex is oft betray'd
    By granting love too soon.
If you desire to gain me, your suff'rings to redress,
    Prepare to love me longer,
    And longer yet, and longer,
      Before you shall possess.

III

THYRSIS.   The little care you show
    Of all my sorrows past
Makes death appear too slow
    And life too long to last.
Fair Iris, kiss me kindly, in pity of my fate;
    And kindly still, and kindly,
      Before it be too late.

IV

IRIS.   You fondly court your bliss,
        And no advances make;
    'Tis not for maids to kiss,
        But 'tis for men to take.
    So you may kiss me kindly, and I will not rebel;
        And kindly still, and kindly,
           But kiss me not and tell.

V

A RONDEAU

CHORUS. Thus at the height we love and live,
        And fear not to be poor;
    We give, and give, and give, and give,
        Till we can give no more;
    But what to-day will take away,
        To-morrow will restore.
    Thus at the heighth we love and live,
        And fear not to be poor.

SONG FROM

CLEOMENES

I

No, no, poor suff'ring heart, no change endeavor,
Choose to sustain the smart, rather than leave her;
My ravish'd eyes behold such charms about her,
I can die with her, but not live without her;
One tender sigh of hers to see me languish,
Will more than pay the price of my past anguish:
Beware, O cruel fair, how you smile on me,
'Twas a kind look of yours that has undone me.

II

Love has in store for me one happy minute,
And she will end my pain, who did begin it;
Then no day void of bliss, or pleasure, leaving,

Ages shall slide away, without perceiving:
Cupid shall guard the door, the more to please us,
And keep out Time and Death, when they would seize us;
Time and Death shall depart, and say, in flying,
Love has found out a way to live by dying.

SONG FOR A GIRL, FROM

LOVE TRIUMPHANT

I
Young I am, and yet unskill'd
How to make a lover yield;
How to keep, or how to gain,
When to love, and when to feign.

II
Take me, take me, some of you,
While I am yet young and true;
Ere I can my soul disguise,
Heave my breasts, and roll my eyes.

III
Stay not till I learn the way,
How to lie, and to betray:
He that has me first, is blest,
For I may deceive the rest.

IV
Could I find a blooming youth,
Full of love, and full of truth,
Brisk, and of a jaunty mien,
I should long to be fifteen.

FROM

THE SECULAR MASQUE

FROM

THE PILGRIM

. . . . .

MOMUS.	All, all of a piece throughout:
	Pointing to DIANA.
	Thy chase had a beast in view;
	To MARS.
	Thy wars brought nothing about;
	To VENUS.
	Thy lovers were all untrue.
JANUS.	'T is well an old age is out:
CHRONOS.	And time to begin a new.

CHORUS OF ALL.

All, all of a piece throughout:
Thy chase had a beast in view;
Thy wars brought nothing about;
Thy lovers were all untrue.
'T is well an old age is out,
And time to begin a new.

Dance of huntsmen, nymphs, warriors,
and lovers.

Drama

Commentary on
All for Love

The prologue and epilogue to *All for Love* will be found below, in the next section of the anthology. The play needs little, if any, explication; for discussions of it, see Bibliography under King (*20th-Century Interpretations*), Goggin and Ramsey. *All for Love* illustrates, at their brilliant best, both Dryden's stagecraft and his ability to create rich, musical, and highly metaphorical blank verse. Dryden's Cleopatra has something of the innocence of Shaw's, and something of the passion of Shakespeare's. His Antony, though in many respects conforming to the neoclassic pattern of a hero, is very little of a ranter. In the preface to the play Dryden wrote that he supposed the cause of the story's popularity among poets was "the excellency of the moral. For the chief persons represented were famous patterns of unlawful love; and their end accordingly was unfortunate." Yet perhaps the play's theme and tone are better represented by the fine soliloquy of Dolabella in Act IV:

> Men are but children of a larger growth;
> Our appetites as apt to change as theirs,
> And full as craving too, and full as vain;
> And yet the soul, shut up in her dark room,
> Viewing so clear abroad, at home sees nothing;
> But, like a mole in earth, busy and blind,
> Works all her folly up, and casts it outward
> To the world's open view: Thus I discovered,
> And blamed the love of ruined Antony;
> Yet wish that I were he, to be so ruined.

ALL FOR LOVE

ACT I

SCENE I.—*The Temple of Isis*

[*Enter* SERAPION, MYRIS, Priests of Isis.]

SERAPION.   Portents and prodigies have grown so frequent,
That they have lost their name. Our fruitful Nile
Flowed ere the wonted season, with a torrent
So unexpected, and so wondrous fierce,
That the wild deluge overtook the haste
Even of the hinds that watched it: Men and beasts
Were borne above the tops of trees, that grew
On the utmost margin of the water-mark.
Then, with so swift an ebb that flood drove backward,
It slipt from underneath the scaly herd: 10
Here monstrous phocae panted on the shore;
Forsaken dolphins there with their broad tails,
Lay lashing the departing waves: hard by them,
Sea horses floundering in the slimy mud,
Tossed up their heads, and dashed the ooze about them.

[*Enter* ALEXAS *behind them.*]

MYRIS.   Avert these omens, Heaven!
SERAPION.   Last night, between the hours of twelve and one,
In a lone aisle of the temple while I walked,
A whirlwind rose, that, with a violent blast,
Shook all the dome: the doors around me clapt;   20
The iron wicket, that defends the vault,
Where the long race of Ptolemies is laid,
Burst open, and disclosed the mighty dead.
From out each monument, in order placed,
An armed ghost starts up: the boy-king last
Reared his inglorious head. A peal of groans
Then followed, and a lamentable voice
Cried, Egypt is no more; My blood ran back,
My shaking knees against each other knocked;

On the cold pavement down I fell entranced,   30
And so unfinished left the horrid scene.

ALEXAS.   And dreamed you this, or did invent the story,

[*Showing himself.*]

To frighten our Egyptian boys withal,
And train them up, betimes, in fear of priesthood?

SERAPION.   My lord, I saw you not,
Nor meant my words should reach your ears; but what
I uttered was most true.

ALEXAS.   A foolish dream,
Bred from the fumes of indigested feasts,
And holy luxury.

SERAPION.   I know my duty:
This goes no further.

ALEXAS.   'Tis not fit it should;   40
Nor would the times now bear it, were it true.
All southern, from yon hills, the Roman camp
Hangs o'er us black and threatening, like a storm
Just breaking on our heads.

SERAPION.   Our faint Egyptians pray for Antony;
But in their servile hearts they own Octavius.

MYRIS.   Why then does Antony dream out his hours,
And tempts not fortune for a noble day,
Which might redeem what Actium lost?

ALEXAS.   He thinks 'tis past recovery.

SERAPION.   Yet the foe   50
Seems not to press the siege.

ALEXAS.   Oh, there's the wonder.
Maecenas and Agrippa, who can most
With Caesar, are his foes. His wife Octavia,
Driven from his house, solicits her revenge;
And Dolabella, who was once his friend,
Upon some private grudge, now seeks his ruin:
Yet still war seems on either side to sleep.

SERAPION.   'Tis strange that Antony, for some days past,
Has not beheld the face of Cleopatra;
But here, in Isis' temple, lives retired,   60
And makes his heart a prey to black despair.

ALEXAS.   'Tis true; and we much fear he hopes by absence
To cure his mind of love.

SERAPION.   If he be vanquished,
   Or make his peace, Egypt is doomed to be
   A Roman province; and our plenteous harvests
   Must then redeem the scarceness of their soil.
   While Antony stood firm, our Alexandria
   Rivalled proud Rome (dominion's other seat),
   And Fortune striding, like a vast Colossus,
   Could fix an equal foot of empire here.   70
ALEXAS.   Had I my wish, these tyrants of all nature,
   Who lord it o'er mankind, should perish,—perish,
   Each by the other's sword; but, since our will
   Is lamely followed by our power, we must
   Depend on one; with him to rise or fall.
SERAPION.   How stands the queen affected?
ALEXAS.   Oh, she dotes,
   She dotes, Serapion, on this vanquished man,
   And winds herself about his mighty ruins;
   Whom would she yet forsake, yet yield him up,
   This hunted prey, to his pursuer's hands,   80
   She might preserve us all: but 'tis in vain—
   This changes my designs, this blasts my counsels,
   And makes me use all means to keep him here,
   Whom I could wish divided from her arms,
   Far as the earth's deep centre. Well, you know
   The state of things; no more of your ill omens
   And black prognostics; labour to confirm
   The people's hearts.
[*Enter* VENTIDIUS, *talking aside with a* GENTLEMAN *of* ANTONY'S.]
SERAPION.   These Romans will o'erhear us.
   But, who's that stranger? By his warlike port,
   His fierce demeanour, and erected look,   90
   He's of no vulgar note.
ALEXAS.   Oh 'tis Ventidius,
   Our emperor's great lieutenant in the East,
   Who first showed Rome that Parthia could be conquered.
   When Antony returned from Syria last,
   He left this man to guard the Roman frontiers.
SERAPION.   You seem to know him well.
ALEXAS.   Too well. I saw him at Cilicia first,
   When Cleopatra there met Antony:

A mortal foe he was to us, and Egypt.
But,—let me witness to the worth I hate,—   100
A braver Roman never drew a sword;
Firm to his prince, but as a friend, not slave.
He ne'er was of his pleasures; but presides
O'er all his cooler hours, and morning counsels:
In short the plainness, fierceness, rugged virtue,
Of an old true-stampt Roman lives in him.
His coming bodes I know not what of ill
To our affairs. Withdraw to mark him better;
And I'll acquaint you why I sought you here,
And what's our present work.

[*They withdraw to a corner of the stage; and* VENTIDIUS, *with the
other, comes forward to the front.*]

VENTIDIUS.   Not see him, say you?   110
I say, I must, and will.

GENTLEMAN.   He has commanded,
On pain of death, none should approach his presence.

VENTIDIUS.   I bring him news will raise his drooping spirits,
Give him new life.

GENTLEMAN.   He sees not Cleopatra.

VENTIDIUS.   Would he had never seen her!

GENTLEMAN.   He eats not, drinks not, sleeps not, has no use
Of anything, but thought; or if he talks,
'Tis to himself, and then 'tis perfect raving:
Then he defies the world, and bids it pass;
Sometimes he gnaws his lip, and curses loud   120
The boy Octavius; then he draws his mouth
Into a scornful smile, and cries, "Take all,
The world's not worth my care."

VENTIDIUS.   Just, just his nature.
Virtue's his path; but sometimes 'tis too narrow
For his vast soul; and then he starts out wide,
And bounds into a vice, that bears him far
From his first course, and plunges him in ills:
But, when his danger makes him find his fault,
Quick to observe, and full of sharp remorse,
He censures eagerly his own misdeeds,   130
Judging himself with malice to himself,
And not forgiving what as man he did,

Because his other parts are more than man.—
He must not thus be lost.

                             [ALEXAS *and the* Priests *come forward.*]

ALEXAS.   You have your full instructions, now advance;
   Proclaim your orders loudly.

SERAPION.   Romans, Egyptians, hear the queen's command.
   Thus Cleopatra bids: Let labour cease;
   To pomp and triumphs give this happy day,
   That gave the world a lord: 'tis Antony's.   140
   Live, Antony; and Cleopatra live!
   Be this the general voice sent up to heaven,
   And every public place repeat this echo.

VENTIDIUS.   Fine pageantry!   [*Aside.*]

SERAPION.   Set out before your doors
   The images of all your sleeping fathers,
   With laurels crowned; with laurels wreathe your posts,
   And strew with flowers the pavement; yet the priests
   Do present sacrifice; pour out the wine,
   And call the gods to join with you in gladness.

VENTIDIUS.   Curse on the tongue that bids this general joy!
   Can they be friends of Antony, who revel   151
   When Antony's in danger? Hide, for shame,
   You Romans, your great grandsires' images,
   For fear their souls should animate their marbles,
   To blush at their degenerate progeny.

ALEXAS.   A love, which knows no bounds, to Antony;
   Would mark the day with honours, when all heaven
   Laboured for him, when each propitious star
   Stood wakeful in his orb, to watch that hour,
   And shed his better influence. Her own birthday   160
   Our queen neglected like a vulgar fate,
   That passed obscurely by.

VENTIDIUS.   Would it had slept,
   Divided far from this; till some remote
   And future age had called it out, to ruin
   Some other prince, not him!

ALEXAS.   Your emperor,
   Though grown unkind, would be more gentle, than
   To upbraid my queen for loving him too well.

VENTIDIUS.   Does the mute sacrifice upbraid the priest?

He knows him not his executioner.
Oh, she has decked his ruin with her love,   170
Led him in golden bands to gaudy slaughter,
And made perdition pleasing: She has left him
The blank of what he was.
I tell thee, eunuch, she has quite unmanned him.
Can any Roman see, and know him now,
Thus altered from the lord of half mankind,
Unbent, unsinewed, made a woman's toy,
Shrunk from the vast extent of all his honours,
And crampt within a corner of the world?
O Antony!   180
Thou bravest soldier, and thou best of friends!
Bounteous as nature; next to nature's God!
Couldst thou but make new worlds, so wouldst thou give them.
As bounty were thy being; rough in battle,
As the first Romans when they went to war;
Yet after victory more pitiful
Than all their praying virgins left at home!

ALEXAS.   Would you could add, to those more shining virtues,
His truth to her who loves him.

VENTIDIUS.   Would I could not!
But wherefore waste I precious hours with thee!   190
Thou art her darling mischief, her chief engine,
Antony's other fate. Go, tell thy queen,
Ventidius is arrived, to end her charms.
Let your Egyptian timbrels play alone,
Nor mix effeminate sounds with Roman trumpets.
You dare not fight for Antony; go pray
And keep your cowards' holiday in temples.

                                    [*Exeunt* ALEXAS, SERAPION.]
                            [*Re-enter the* GENTLEMAN *of* M. ANTONY.]

2 GENTLEMAN.   The emperor approaches, and commands,
On pain of death, that none presume to stay.

1 GENTLEMAN.   I dare not disobey him.

                                    [*Going out with the other.*]

VENTIDIUS.   Well, I dare.   200
But I'll observe him first unseen, and find
Which way his humour drives: The rest I'll venture.

                                    [*Withdraws.*]

[*Enter* ANTONY, *walking with a disturbed motion before he speaks.*]

ANTONY.   They tell me, 'tis my birthday, and I'll keep it
  With double pomp of sadness.
  'Tis what the day deserves, which gave me breath.
  Why was I raised the meteor of the world,
  Hung in the skies, and blazing as I travelled,
  Till all my fires were spent; and then cast downward,
  To be trod out by Caesar?

VENTIDIUS.   [*Aside.*] On my soul,
  'Tis mournful, wondrous mournful!

ANTONY.   Count thy gains.   210
  Now, Antony, wouldst thou be born for this?
  Glutton of fortune, thy devouring youth
  Has starved thy wanting age.

VENTIDIUS.   How sorrow shakes him!   [*Aside.*]
  So, now the tempest tears him up by the roots,
  And on the ground extends the noble ruin.

               [ANTONY *having thrown himself down.*]

  Lie there, thou shadow of an emperor;
  The place thou pressest on thy mother earth
  Is all thy empire now: now it contains thee;
  Some few days hence, and then 'twill be too large,
  When thou'rt contracted in thy narrow urn,
  Shrunk to a few cold ashes; then Octavia   220
  (For Cleopatra will not live to see it),
  Octavia then will have thee all her own,
  And bear thee in her widowed hand to Caesar;
  Caesar will weep, the crocodile will weep,
  To see his rival of the universe
  Lie still and peaceful there. I'll think no more on't.

ANTONY.   Give me some music: look that it be sad:
  I'll soothe my melancholy, till I swell,
  And burst myself with sighing.—   [*Soft music.*]
  'Tis somewhat to my humour: stay, I fancy   230
  I'm now turned wild, a commoner of nature;
  Of all forsaken, and forsaking all;
  Live in a shady forest's sylvan scene,
  Stretched at my length beneath some blasted oak,
  I lean my head upon the mossy bark,
  And look just of a piece as I grew from it;

My uncombed locks, matted like mistletoe,
Hang o'er my hoary face; a murmuring brook
Runs at my foot.
VENTIDIUS.   Methinks I fancy
Myself there too.
ANTONY.   The herd come jumping by me,   *240*
And, fearless, quench their thirst, while I look on,
And take me for their fellow-citizen.
More of this image, more; it lulls my thoughts.

[Soft music again.]

VENTIDIUS.   I must disturb him; I can hold no longer.

[Stands before him.]

ANTONY.   [*Standing up.*] Art thou Ventidius?
VENTIDIUS.   Are you Antony?
I'm liker what I was, than you to him
I left you last.
ANTONY.   I'm angry.
VENTIDIUS.   So am I.
ANTONY.   I would be private: leave me.
VENTIDIUS.   Sir, I love you,
And therefore will not leave you.
ANTONY.   Will not leave me!
Where have you learnt that answer? Who am I?   *250*
VENTIDIUS.   My emperor; the man I love next Heaven:
If I said more, I think 'twere scarce a sin:
You're all that's good, and god-like.
ANTONY.   All that's wretched.
You will not leave me then?
VENTIDIUS.   'Twas too presuming
To say I would not; but I dare not leave you:
And, 'tis unkind in you to chide me hence
So soon, when I so far have come to see you.
ANTONY.   Now thou hast seen me, are thou satisfied?
For, if a friend, thou hast beheld enough;   *260*
And, if a foe, too much.
VENTIDIUS.   Look, emperor, this is no common dew.

[Weeping.]

I have not wept this forty years; but now
My mother comes afresh into my eyes;
I cannot help her softness.

ANTONY.   By heavens, he weeps! poor good old man, he weeps!
  The big round drops course one another down
  The furrows of his cheeks.—Stop them, Ventidius,
  Or I shall blush to death: they set my shame,
  That caused them, full before me.
VENTIDIUS.   I'll do my best.   270
ANTONY.   Sure there's contagion in the tears of friends:
  See, I have caught it too. Believe me, 'tis not
  For my own griefs, but thine.—Nay, father!
VENTIDIUS.   Emperor.
ANTONY.   Emperor! Why, that's the style of victory;
  The conqu'ring soldier, red with unfelt wounds,
  Salutes his general so: but never more
  Shall that sound reach my ears.
VENTIDIUS.   I warrant you.
ANTONY.   Actium, Actium! Oh!—
VENTIDIUS.   It sits too near you.
ANTONY.   Here, here it lies, a lump of lead by day,
  And, in my short, distracted, nightly slumbers,   280
  The hag that rides my dreams.——
VENTIDIUS.   Out with it; give it vent.
ANTONY.   Urge not my shame.
  I lost a battle,——
VENTIDIUS.   So has Julius done.
ANTONY.   Thou favour'st me, and speak'st not half thou
      think'st;
  For Julius fought it out, and lost it fairly:
  But Antony——
VENTIDIUS.   Nay, stop not.
ANTONY.   Antony,—
  Well, thou wilt have it—like a coward, fled,
  Fled while his soldiers fought; fled first, Ventidius.
  Thou long'st to curse me, and I give thee leave.
  I know thou cam'st prepared to rail.
VENTIDIUS.   I did.   290
ANTONY.   I'll help thee.—I have been a man, Ventidius.
VENTIDIUS.   Yes, and a brave one; but——
ANTONY.   I know thy meaning.
  But I have lost my reason, have disgraced
  The name of soldier, with inglorious ease.

In the full vintage of my flowing honours,
Sat still, and saw it prest by other hands.
Fortune came smiling to my youth, and wooed it,
And purple greatness met my ripened years.
When first I came to empire, I was borne
On tides of people, crowding to my triumphs;   *300*
The wish of nations, and the willing world
Received me as its pledge of future peace;
I was so great, so happy, so beloved,
Fate could not ruin me; till I took pains,
And worked against my fortune, chid her from me,
And turned her loose; yet still she came again.
My careless days, and my luxurious nights,
At length have wearied her, and now she's gone,
Gone, gone, divorced for ever. Help me, soldier,
To curse this madman, this industrious fool,   *310*
Who laboured to be wretched: Pr'ythee, curse me.
VENTIDIUS.   No.
ANTONY.   Why?
VENTIDIUS.   You are too sensible already
Of what you've done, too conscious of your failings;
And, like a scorpion, whipt by others first
To fury, sting yourself in mad revenge.
I would bring balm, and pour it in your wounds,
Cure your distempered mind, and heal your fortunes.
ANTONY.   I know thou would'st.
VENTIDIUS.   I will.
ANTONY.   Ha, ha, ha, ha!
VENTIDIUS.   You laugh.
ANTONY.   I do, to see officious love
Give cordials to the dead.
VENTIDIUS.   You would be lost, then?   *320*
ANTONY.   I am.
VENTIDIUS.   I say you are not. Try your fortune.
ANTONY.   I have, to the utmost. Dost thou think me desperate,
Without just cause? No, when I found all lost
Beyond repair, I hid me from the world,
And learnt to scorn it here; which now I do
So heartily, I think it is not worth
The cost of keeping.

VENTIDIUS.   Caesar thinks not so;
  He'll thank you for the gift he could not take.
  You would be killed like Tully, would you? do,
  Hold out your throat to Caesar, and die tamely.   330
ANTONY.   No, I can kill myself! and so resolve.
VENTIDIUS.   I can die with you too, when time shall serve;
  But fortune calls upon us now to live,
  To fight, to conquer.
ANTONY.   Sure thou dream'st, Ventidius.
VENTIDIUS.   No; 'tis you dream; you sleep away your hours
  In desperate sloth, miscalled philosophy.
  Up, up, for honour's sake; twelve legions wait you,
  And long to call you chief: By painful journeys
  I led them, patient both of heat and hunger,
  Down from the Parthian marches to the Nile.   340
  'Twill do you good to see their sunburnt faces,
  Their scarred cheeks, and chopt hands: there's virtue in them.
  They'll sell those mangled limbs at dearer rates
  Than yon trim bands can buy.
ANTONY.   Where left you them?
VENTIDIUS.   I said in Lower Syria.
ANTONY.   Bring them hither;
  There may be life in these.
VENTIDIUS.   They will not come.
ANTONY.   Why didst thou mock my hopes with promised aids.
  To double my despair? They're mutinous.
VENTIDIUS.   Most firm and loyal.
ANTONY.   Yet they will not march
  To succour me. O trifler!
VENTIDIUS.   They petition.   350
  You would make haste to head them.
ANTONY.   I'm besieged.
VENTIDIUS.   There's but one way shut up: How came I hither?
ANTONY.   I will not stir.
VENTIDIUS.   They would perhaps desire
  A better reason.
ANTONY.   I have never used
  My soldiers to demand a reason of
  My actions. Why did they refuse to march?

VENTIDIUS.   They said they would not fight for Cleopatra.
ANTONY.   What was't they said?
VENTIDIUS.   They said they would not fight for Cleopatra.
Why should they fight indeed, to make her conquer,
And make you more a slave? to gain your kingdoms,
Which, for a kiss, at your next midnight feast,
You'll sell to her? Then she new-names her jewels,
And calls this diamond such or such a tax;
Each pendant in her ear shall be a province.
ANTONY.   Ventidius, I allow your tongue free licence
On all my other faults; but, on your life,
No word of Cleopatra: she deserves
More worlds than I can lose.
VENTIDIUS.   Behold, you Powers,   370
To whom you have intrusted humankind!
See Europe, Afric, Asia, put in balance,
And all weighed down by one light, worthless woman!
I think the gods are Antonies, and give,
Like prodigals, this nether world away
To none but wasteful hands.
ANTONY.   You grow presumptuous.
VENTIDIUS.   I take the privilege of plain love to speak.
ANTONY.   Plain love! plain arrogance, plain insolence!
Thy men are cowards; thou, an envious traitor;
Who, under seeming honesty, hast vented   380
The burden of thy rank, o'erflowing gall.
O that thou wert my equal; great in arms
As the first Caesar was, that I might kill thee
Without a stain to honour!
VENTIDIUS.   You may kill me;
You have done more already,—called me traitor.
ANTONY.   Art thou not one?
VENTIDIUS.   For showing you yourself,
Which none else durst have done? but had I been
That name, which I disdain to speak again,
I needed not have sought your abject fortunes,
Come to partake your fate, to die with you.   390
What hindered me to have led my conquering eagles
To fill Octavius' bands? I could have been

A traitor then, a glorious, happy traitor,
And not have been so called.

ANTONY.   Forgive me, soldier;
I've been too passionate.

VENTIDIUS.   You thought me false;
Thought my old age betrayed you: Kill me, sir,
Pray, kill me; yet you need not, your unkindness
Has left your sword no work.

ANTONY.   I did not think so;
I said it in my rage: Pr'ythee, forgive me.
Why didst thou tempt my anger, by discovery   400
Of what I would not hear?

VENTIDIUS.   No prince but you
Could merit that sincerity I used,
Nor durst another man have ventured it;
But you, ere love misled your wandering eyes,
Were sure the chief and best of human race,
Framed in the very pride and boast of nature;
So perfect, that the gods, who formed you, wondered
At their own skill, and cried—A lucky hit
Has mended our design. Their envy hindered,
Else you had been immortal, and a pattern   410
When Heaven would work for ostentation's sake
To copy out again.

ANTONY.   But Cleopatra—
Go on; for I can bear it now.

VENTIDIUS.   No more.

ANTONY.   Thou dar'st not trust my passion, but thou may'st;
Thou only lov'st, the rest have flattered me.

VENTIDIUS.   Heaven's blessing on your heart for that kind
    word!
May I believe you love me? Speak again.

ANTONY.   Indeed I do. Speak this, and this, and this.

                                        [*Hugging him.*]

Thy praises were unjust; but, I'll deserve them,
And yet mend all. Do with me what thou wilt;   420
Lead me to victory! thou know'st the way.

VENTIDIUS.   And, will you leave this——

ANTONY.   Pr'ythee, do not curse her,

And I will leave her; though, Heaven knows, I love
Beyond life, conquest, empire, all, but honour;
But I will leave her.
VENTIDIUS.   That's my royal master;
And, shall we fight?
ANTONY.   I warrant thee, old soldier.
Thou shalt behold me once again in iron;
And at the head of our old troops, that beat
The Parthians, cry aloud—Come, follow me!
VENTIDIUS.   Oh, now I hear my emperor! in that word   430
Octavius fell. Gods, let me see that day,
And, if I have ten years behind, take all:
I'll thank you for the exchange.
ANTONY.   O Cleopatra!
VENTIDIUS.   Again?
ANTONY.   I've done: In that last sigh she went.
Caesar shall know what 'tis to force a lover
From all he holds most dear.
VENTIDIUS.   Methinks, you breathe
Another soul: Your looks are more divine;
You speak a hero, and you move a god.
ANTONY.   Oh, thou hast fired me; my soul's up in arms,   440
And mans each part about me: Once again,
That noble eagerness of fight has seized me;
That eagerness with which I darted upward
To Cassius' camp: In vain the steepy hill
Opposed my way; in vain a war of spears
Sung round my head, and planted on my shield;
I won the trenches, while my foremost men
Lagged on the plain below.
VENTIDIUS.   Ye gods, ye gods,
For such another honour!
ANTONY.   Come on, my soldier!
Once more to meet our foes; that thou and I,
Like Time and Death, marching before our troops,
May taste fate to them; mow them out a passage,
And, entering where the foremost squadrons yield,
Begin the noble harvest of the field.   [*Exeunt.*]

neoclassical ○
※? Romantic ○

ACT II

SCENE I

[*Enter* CLEOPATRA, IRAS, *and* ALEXAS.]

CLEOPATRA.   What shall I do, or whither shall I turn?
  Ventidius has o'ercome, and he will go.

ALEXAS.   He goes to fight for you.

CLEOPATRA.   Then he would see me, ere he went to fight:
  Flatter me not: If once he goes, he's lost,
  And all my hopes destroyed.

ALEXAS.   Does this weak passion
  Become a mighty queen?

CLEOPATRA.   I am no queen:
  Is this to be a queen, to be besieged
  By yon insulting Roman, and to wait
  Each hour the victor's chain? These ills are small: 10
  For Antony is lost, and I can mourn
  For nothing else but him. Now come, Octavius,
  I have no more to lose! prepare thy bands;
  I'm fit to be a captive: Antony
  Has taught my mind the fortune of a slave.

IRAS.   Call reason to assist you.

CLEOPATRA.   I have none,
  And none would have: My love's a noble madness,
  Which shows the cause deserved it. Moderate sorrow
  Fits vulgar love, and for a vulgar man:
  But I have loved with such transcendent passion,   20
  I soared, at first, quite out of reason's view,
  And now am lost above it. No, I'm proud
  'Tis thus: Would Antony could see me now;
  Think you he would not sigh? though he must leave me.
  Sure he would sigh; for he is noble-natured,
  And bears a tender heart: I know him well.
  Ah, no, I know him not; I knew him once,
  But now 'tis past.

IRAS.   Let it be past with you:
  Forget him, madam.

CLEOPATRA.   Never, never, Iras.

He once was mine; and once, though now 'tis gone,   30
Leaves a faint image of possession still.

ALEXAS.   Think him inconstant, cruel, and ungrateful.

CLEOPATRA.   I cannot: If I could, those thoughts were vain.
Faithless, ungrateful, cruel, though he be,
I still must love him.

[*Enter* CHARMION.]

Now, what news, my Charmion?
Will he be kind? and will he not forsake me?
Am I to live, or die?—nay, do I live?
Or am I dead? for when he gave his answer,
Fate took the word, and then I lived or died.

CHARMION.   I found him, madam——

CLEOPATRA.   A long speech preparing?
If thou bring'st comfort, haste, and give it me,
For never was more need.

IRAS.   I know he loves you.

CLEOPATRA.   Had he been kind, her eyes had told me so,
Before her tongue could speak it: Now she studies,
To soften what he said; but give me death,
Just as he sent it, Charmion, undisguised,
And in the words he spoke.

CHARMION.   I found him, then,
Encompassed round, I think, with iron statues;
So mute, so motionless his soldiers stood,
While awfully he cast his eyes about,   50
And every leader's hopes or fears surveyed:
Methought he looked resolved, and yet not pleased.
When he beheld me struggling in the crowd,
He blushed, and bade make way.

ALEXAS.   There's comfort yet.

CHARMION.   Ventidius fixed his eyes upon my passage
Severely, as he meant to frown me back,
And sullenly gave place: I told my message,
Just as you gave it, broken and disordered;
I numbered in it all your sighs and tears,
And while I moved your pitiful request,   60
That you but only begged a last farewell,
He fetched an inward groan; and every time
I named you, sighed, as if his heart were breaking,

But, shunned my eyes, and guiltily looked down;
He seemed not now that awful Antony,
Who shook an armed assembly with his nod;
But, making show as he would rub his eyes,
Disguised and blotted out a falling tear.

CLEOPATRA.   Did he then weep? And was I worth a tear?
  If what thou hast to say be not as pleasing,   70
  Tell me no more, but let me die contented.

CHARMION.   He bid me say,—He knew himself so well,
  He could deny you nothing, if he saw you;
  And therefore——

CLEOPATRA.   Thou wouldst say, he would not see me?

CHARMION.   And therefore begged you not to use a power,
  Which he could ill resist; yet he should ever
  Respect you, as he ought.

CLEOPATRA.   Is that a word
  For Antony to use to Cleopatra?
  O that faint word, *respect!* how I disdain it!
  Disdain myself, for loving after it!   80
  He should have kept that word for cold Octavia.
  Respect is for a wife: Am I that thing,
  That dull, insipid lump, without desires,
  And without power to give them?

ALEXAS.   You misjudge;
  You see through love, and that deludes your sight;
  As, what is straight, seems crooked through the water:
  But I, who bear my reason undisturbed,
  Can see this Antony, this dreaded man,
  A fearful slave, who fain would run away,
  And shuns his master's eyes: If you pursue him,   90
  My life on't, he still drags a chain along
  That needs must clog his flight.

CLEOPATRA.   Could I believe thee!—

ALEXAS.   By every circumstance I know he loves.
  True, he's hard prest, by interest and by honour;
  Yet he but doubts, and parleys, and casts out
  Many a long look for succour.

CLEOPATRA.   He sends word,
  He fears to see my face.

ALEXAS.   And would you more?

He shows his weakness who declines the combat,
And you must urge your fortune. Could he speak
More plainly? To my ears, the message sounds—   *100*
Come to my rescue, Cleopatra, come;
Come, free me from Ventidius; from my tyrant:
See me, and give me a pretence to leave him!—
I hear his trumpets. This way he must pass.
Please you, retire a while; I'll work him first,
That he may bend more easy.

CLEOPATRA.   You shall rule me;
But all, I fear, in vain.   [*Exit with* CHARMION *and* IRAS.]

ALEXAS.   I fear so too;
Though I concealed my thoughts, to make her bold;
But 'tis our utmost means, and fate befriend it!   [*Withdraws.*
Enter LICTORS *with Fasces; one bearing the Eagle; then enter* AN-
TONY *with* VENTIDIUS, *followed by other* COMMANDERS.]

ANTONY.   Octavius is the minion of blind chance,   *110*
But holds from virtue nothing.

VENTIDIUS.   Has he courage?

ANTONY.   But just enough to season him from coward.
Oh, 'tis the coldest youth upon a charge,
The most deliberate fighter! if he ventures
(As in Illyria once, they say, he did,
To storm a town), 'tis when he cannot choose;
When all the world have fixt their eyes upon him;
And then he lives on that for seven years after;
But, at a close revenge he never fails.

VENTIDIUS.   I heard you challenged him.

ANTONY.   I did, Ventidius.   *120*
What think'st thou was his answer? 'Twas so tame!—
He said, he had more ways than one to die;
I had not.

VENTIDIUS.   Poor!

ANTONY.   He has more ways than one;
But he would choose them all before that one.

VENTIDIUS.   He first would choose an ague, or a fever.

ANTONY.   No; it must be an ague, not a fever;
He has not warmth enough to die by that.

VENTIDIUS.   Or old age and a bed.

ANTONY.   Ay, there's his choice,

He would live, like a lamp, to the last wink,
And crawl upon the utmost verge of life.   *130*
O Hercules! Why should a man like this,
Who dares not trust his fate for one great action,
Be all the care of Heaven? Why should he lord it
O'er fourscore thousand men, of whom each one
Is braver than himself?

VENTIDIUS.   You conquered for him:
Philippi knows it; there you shared with him
That empire, which your sword made all your own.

ANTONY.   Fool that I was, upon my eagle's wings
I bore this wren, till I was tired with soaring,
And now he mounts above me.   *140*
Good heavens, is this—is this the man who braves me?
Who bids my age make way? Drives me before him,
To the world's ridge, and sweeps me off like rubbish?

VENTIDIUS.   Sir, we lose time; the troops are mounted all.

ANTONY.   Then give the word to march:
I long to leave this prison of a town,
To join thy legions; and, in open field,
Once more to show my face. Lead, my deliverer.

                                        [*Enter* ALEXAS.]

ALEXAS.   Great emperor,
In mighty arms renowned above mankind,   *150*
But, in soft pity to the opprest, a god;
This message sends the mournful Cleopatra
To her departing lord.

VENTIDIUS.   Smooth sycophant!

ALEXAS.   A thousand wishes, and ten thousand prayers,
Millions of blessings wait you to the wars;
Millions of sighs and tears she sends you too,
And would have sent
As many dear embraces to your arms,
As many parting kisses to your lips;
But those, she fears, have wearied you already.   *160*

VENTIDIUS.   [*Aside.*] False crocodile!

ALEXAS.   And yet she begs not now, you would not leave her;
That were a wish too mighty for her hopes,
Too presuming
For her low fortune, and your ebbing love;

That were a wish for her more prosperous days,
    Her blooming beauty, and your growing kindness.
ANTONY.   [*Aside.*] Well, I must man it out:—What would
    the queen?
ALEXAS.   First, to these noble warriors, who attend
    Your daring courage in the chase of fame,—   170
    Too daring, and too dangerous for her quiet,—
    She humbly recommends all she holds dear,
    All her own cares and fears,—the care of you.
VENTIDIUS.   Yes, witness Actium.
ANTONY.   Let him speak, Ventidius.
ALEXAS.   You, when his matchless valour bears him forward,
    With ardour too heroic, on his foes,
    Fall down, as she would do, before his feet;
    Lie in his way, and stop the paths of death:
    Tell him, this god is not invulnerable;
    That absent Cleopatra bleeds in him;   180
    And, that you may remember her petition,
    She begs you wear these trifles, as a pawn,
    Which, at your wished return, she will redeem
                              [*Gives jewels to the* COMMANDERS.]
    With all the wealth of Egypt:
    This to the great Ventidius she presents,
    Whom she can never count her enemy,
    Because he loves her lord.
VENTIDIUS.   Tell her, I'll none on't;
    I'm not ashamed of honest poverty;
    Not all the diamonds of the east can bribe
    Ventidius from his faith. I hope to see   190
    These and the rest of all her sparkling store,
    Where they shall more deservingly be placed.
ANTONY.   And who must wear them then?
VENTIDIUS.   The wronged Octavia.
ANTONY.   You might have spared that word.
VENTIDIUS.   And he that bribe.
ANTONY.   But have I no remembrance?
ALEXAS.   Yes, a dear one;
    Your slave the queen——
ANTONY.   My mistress.
ALEXAS.   Then your mistress;

Your mistress would, she says, have sent her soul,
But that you had long since; she humbly begs
This ruby bracelet, set with bleeding hearts,
The emblems of her own, may bind your arm.   200

[*Presenting a bracelet.*]

VENTIDIUS.   Now, my best lord,—in honour's name, I ask you,
For manhood's sake, and for your own dear safety,—
Touch not these poisoned gifts,
Infected by the sender; touch them not;
Myriads of bluest plagues lie underneath them,
And more than aconite has dipt the silk.

ANTONY.   Nay, now you grow too cynical, Ventidius:
A lady's favours may be worn with honour.
What, to refuse her bracelet! On my soul,
When I lie pensive in my tent alone,   210
'Twill pass the wakeful hours of winter nights,
To tell these pretty beads upon my arm,
To count for every one a soft embrace,
A melting kiss at such and such a time:
And now and then the fury of her love,
When——And what harm's in this?

ALEXAS.   None, none, my lord,
But what's to her, that now 'tis past for ever.

ANTONY.   [*Going to tie it.*] We soldiers are so awkward—
help me tie it.

ALEXAS.   In faith, my lord, we courtiers too are awkward
In these affairs: so are all men indeed: 220
Even I, who am not one. But shall I speak?

ANTONY.   Yes, freely.

ALEXAS.   Then, my lord, fair hands alone
Are fit to tie it; she, who sent it can.

VENTIDIUS.   Hell, death! this eunuch pander ruins you.
You will not see her?

[ALEXAS *whispers an* Attendant, *who goes out.*]

ANTONY.   But to take my leave.

VENTIDIUS.   Then I have washed an Aethiop. You're undone;
Y' are in the toils; y' are taken; y' are destroyed:
Her eyes do Caesar's work.

ANTONY.   You fear too soon.
I'm constant to myself: I know my strength;
And yet she shall not think me barbarous neither, 230

Born in the depths of Afric: I am a Roman,
Bred in the rules of soft humanity.
A guest, and kindly used, should bid farewell.

VENTIDIUS.   You do not know
How weak you are to her, how much an infant:
You are not proof against a smile, or glance;
A sigh will quite disarm you.

ANTONY.   See, she comes!
Now you shall find your error.—Gods, I thank you:
I formed the danger greater than it was,
And now 'tis near, 'tis lessened.

VENTIDIUS.   Mark the end yet.   240

[*Enter* CLEOPATRA, CHARMION, *and* IRAS.]

ANTONY.   Well, madam, we are met.

CLEOPATRA.   Is this a meeting?
Then, we must part?

ANTONY.   We must.

CLEOPATRA.   Who says we must?

ANTONY.   Our own hard fates.

CLEOPATRA.   We make those fates ourselves.

ANTONY.   Yes, we have made them; we have loved each other,
Into our mutual ruin.

CLEOPATRA.   The gods have seen my joys with envious eyes;
I have no friends in heaven; and all the world,
As 'twere the business of mankind to part us,
Is armed against my love: even you yourself
Join with the rest; you, you are armed against me.   250

ANTONY.   I will be justified in all I do
To late posterity, and therefore hear me.
If I mix a lie
With any truth, reproach me freely with it;
Else, favour me with silence.

CLEOPATRA.   You command me,
And I am dumb.

VENTIDIUS.   I like this well; he shows authority.

ANTONY.   That I derive my ruin
From you alone——

CLEOPATRA.   O heavens! I ruin you!

ANTONY.   You promised me your silence, and you break it
Ere I have scarce begun.

CLEOPATRA.   Well, I obey you.   260

ANTONY.   When I beheld you first, it was in Egypt.
  Ere Caesar saw your eyes, you gave me love,
  And were too young to know it; that I settled
  Your father in his throne, was for your sake;
  I left the acknowledgment for time to ripen.
  Caesar stept in, and, with a greedy hand,
  Plucked the green fruit, ere the first blush of red,
  Yet cleaving to the bough. He was my lord,
  And was, beside, too great for me to rival;
  But, I deserved you first, though he enjoyed you.   270
  When, after, I beheld you in Cilicia,
  An enemy to Rome, I pardoned you.
CLEOPATRA.   I cleared myself——
ANTONY.   Again you break your promise.
  I loved you still, and took your weak excuses,
  Took you into my bosom, stained by Caesar,
  And not half mine: I went to Egypt with you,
  And hid me from the business of the world,
  Shut out inquiring nations from my sight,
  To give whole years to you.
VENTIDIUS.   Yes, to your shame be't spoken.   [*Aside.*]
                                                     280
ANTONY.   How I loved.
  Witness, ye days and nights, and all ye hours,
  That danced away with down upon your feet,
  As all your business were to count my passion!
  One day passed by, and nothing saw but love;
  Another came, and still 'twas only love:
  The suns were wearied out with looking on,
  And I untired with loving.
  I saw you every day, and all the day;
  And every day was still but as the first,
  So eager was I still to see you more.   290
VENTIDIUS.   'Tis all too true.
ANTONY.   Fulvia, my wife, grew jealous
  (As she indeed had reason), raised a war
  In Italy, to call me back.
VENTIDIUS.   But yet
  You went not.
ANTONY.   While within your arms I lay,
  The world fell mouldering from my hands each hour,

And left me scarce a grasp—I thank your love for't.

VENTIDIUS.   Well pushed: that last was home.

CLEOPATRA.   Yet may I speak?

ANTONY.   If I have urged a falsehood, yes; else, not.
 Your silence says, I have not. Fulvia died
 (Pardon, you gods, with my unkindness died);   *300*
 To set the world at peace, I took Octavia,
 This Caesar's sister; in her pride of youth,
 And flower of beauty, did I wed that lady,
 Whom blushing I must praise, because I left her.
 You called; my love obeyed the fatal summons:
 This raised the Roman arms; the cause was yours.
 I would have fought by land, where I was stronger;
 You hindered it: yet, when I fought at sea,
 Forsook me fighting; and (O stain to honour!
 O lasting shame!) I knew not that I fled;   *310*
 But fled to follow you.

VENTIDIUS.   What haste she made to hoist her purple sails!
 And, to appear magnificent in flight,
 Drew half our strength away.

ANTONY.   All this you caused.
 And, would you multiply more ruins on me?
 This honest man, my best, my only friend,
 Has gathered up the shipwreck of my fortunes;
 Twelve legions I have left, my last recruits.
 And you have watched the news, and bring your eyes
 To seize them too. If you have aught to answer,   *320*
 Now speak, you have free leave.

ALEXAS.   [*Aside.*] She stands confounded:
 Despair is in her eyes.

VENTIDIUS.   Now lay a sigh in the way to stop his passage:
 Prepare a tear, and bid it for his legions;
 'Tis like they shall be sold.

CLEOPATRA.   How shall I plead my cause, when you, my
  judge,
 Already have condemned me? Shall I bring
 The love you bore me for my advocate?
 That now is turned against me, that destroys me;
 For love, once past, is, at the best, forgotten;   *330*
 But oftener sours to hate: 'twill please my lord

To ruin me, and therefore I'll be guilty.
But, could I once have thought it would have pleased you,
That you would pry, with narrow searching eyes,
Into my faults, severe to my destruction,
And watching all advantages with care,
That serve to make me wretched? Speak, my lord,
For I end here. Though I deserved this usage,
Was it like you to give it?

ANTONY.   Oh, you wrong me,
   To think I sought this parting, or desired   *340*
   To accuse you more than what will clear myself,
   And justify this breach.

CLEOPATRA.   Thus low I thank you;
   And, since my innocence will not offend,
   I shall not blush to own it.

VENTIDIUS.   After this,
   I think she'll blush at nothing.

CLEOPATRA.   You seemed grieved
   (And therein you are kind), that Caesar first
   Enjoyed my love, though you deserved it better:
   I grieve for that, my lord, much more than you;
   For, had I first been yours, it would have saved
   My second choice: I never had been his,   *350*
   And ne'er had been but yours. But Caesar first,
   You say, possessed my love. Not so, my lord:
   He first possessed my person; you, my love:
   Caesar loved me; but I loved Antony.
   If I endured him after, 'twas because
   I judged it due to the first name of men;
   And, half constrained, I gave, as to a tyrant,
   What he would take by force.

VENTIDIUS.   O Syren! Syren!
   Yet grant that all the love she boasts were true,
   Has she not ruined you? I still urge that,   *360*
   The fatal consequence.

CLEOPATRA.   The consequence indeed,
   For I dare challenge him, my greatest foe,
   To say it was designed: 'tis true, I loved you,
   And kept you far from an uneasy wife,—
   Such Fulvia was.

Yes, but he'll say, you left Octavia for me;—
And, can you blame me to receive that love,
Which quitted such desert, for worthless me?
How often have I wished some other Caesar,   370
Great as the first, and as the second young,
Would court my love, to be refused for you!
VENTIDIUS.   Words, words; but Actium, sir; remember Actium.
CLEOPATRA.   Even there, I dare his malice. True, I counselled
  To fight at sea; but I betrayed you not.
  I fled, but not to the enemy. 'Twas fear;
  Would I had been a man, not to have feared!
  For none would then have envied me your friendship,
  Who envy me your love.
ANTONY.   We are both unhappy:
  If nothing else, yet our ill fortune parts us.   380
  Speak: would you have me perish by my stay?
CLEOPATRA.   If, as a friend, you ask my judgment, go;
  If, as a lover, stay. If you must perish——
  'Tis a hard word—but stay.
VENTIDIUS.   See now the effects of her so boasted love!
  She strives to drag you down to ruin with her;
  But, could she 'scape without you, oh, how soon
  Would she let go her hold, and haste to shore,
  And never look behind!
CLEOPATRA.   Then judge my love by this.
                              [*Giving* ANTONY *a writing.*]
  Could I have borne   390
  A life or death, a happiness or woe,
  From yours divided, this had given me means.
ANTONY.   By Hercules, the writing of Octavius!
  I know it well: 'tis that proscribing hand,
  Young as it was, that led the way to mine,
  And left me but the second place in murder.—
  See, see, Ventidius! here he offers Egypt,
  And joins all Syria to it, as a present;
  So, in requital, she forsake my fortunes,
  And join her arms with his.
CLEOPATRA.   And yet you leave me!   400
  You leave me, Antony; and yet I love you,
  Indeed I do: I have refused a kingdom;

That is a trifle;
For I could part with life, with anything,
But only you. Oh, let me die but with you!
Is that a hard request?

ANTONY.   Next living with you,
'Tis all that Heaven can give.

ALEXAS.   He melts; we conquer.   [*Aside.*]

CLEOPATRA.   No; you shall go: your interest calls you hence;
Yes; your dear interest pulls too strong, for these
Weak arms to hold you here.   [*Takes his hand.*]
Go; leave me, soldier   410
(For you're no more a lover) : leave me dying:
Push me, all pale and panting, from your bosom,
And, when your march begins, let one run after,
Breathless almost for joy, and cry—She's dead.
The soldiers shout; you then, perhaps, may sigh,
And muster all your Roman gravity:
Ventidius chides; and straight your brow clears up,
As I had never been.

ANTONY.   Gods, 'tis too much; too much for man to bear.

CLEOPATRA.   What is't for me then,
A weak, forsaken woman, and a lover?—   420
Here let me breathe my last: envy me not
This minute in your arms: I'll die apace,
As fast as e'er I can, and end your trouble.

ANTONY.   Die! rather let me perish; loosened nature
Leap from its hinges, sink the props of heaven,
And fall the skies, to crush the nether world!
My eyes, my soul, my all!   [*Embraces her.*]

VENTIDIUS.   And what's this toy,
In balance with your fortune, honour, fame?

ANTONY.   What is't, Ventidius?—it outweighs them all;
Why, we have more than conquered Caesar now: 430
My queen's not only innocent, but loves me.
This, this is she, who drags me down to ruin!
"But, could she 'scape without me, with what haste
Would she let slip her hold, and make to shore,
And never look behind!"
Down on thy knees, blasphemer as thou art,
And ask forgiveness of wronged innocence.

VENTIDIUS.   I'll rather die, than take it. Will you go?

ANTONY.   Go! whither? Go from all that's excellent?
  Faith, honour, virtue, all good things forbid,   440
  That I should go from her, who sets my love
  Above the price of kingdoms! Give, you gods,
  Give to your boy, your Caesar,
  This rattle of a globe to play withal,
  This gewgaw world, and put him cheaply off:
  I'll not be pleased with less than Cleopatra.
CLEOPATRA.   She's wholly yours. My heart's so full of joy.
  That I shall do some wild extravagance
  Of love, in public; and the foolish world,
  Which knows not tenderness, will think me mad.   450
VENTIDIUS.   O women! women! women! all the gods
  Have not such power of doing good to man,
  As you of doing harm.   [*Exit.*]
ANTONY.   Our men are armed:—
  Unbar the gate that looks to Caesar's camp:
  I would revenge the treachery he meant me;
  And long security makes conquest easy.
  I'm eager to return before I go;
  For, all the pleasures I have known beat thick
  On my remembrance.—How I long for night!
    That both the sweets of mutual love may try,   460
    And triumph once o'er Caesar ere we die.   [*Exeunt.*]

ACT III

SCENE I

[*At one door enter* CLEOPATRA, CHARMION, IRAS, *and*
  ALEXAS, *a Train of* Egyptians: *at the other* ANTONY
  and ROMANS. *The entrance on both sides is prepared
  by music; the trumpets first sounding on* ANTONY'S
  part: then answered by timbrels, etc., on CLEO-
  PATRA'S. CHARMION *and* IRAS *hold a laurel wreath
  betwixt them. A Dance of* Egyptians. *After the cere-
  mony,* CLEOPATRA *crowns* ANTONY.]
ANTONY.   I thought how those white arms would fold me in,

And strain me close, and melt me into love;
So pleased with that sweet image, I sprung forwards,
And added all my strength to every blow.
CLEOPATRA.   Come to me, come, my soldier, to my arms!
You've been too long away from my embraces;
But, when I have you fast, and all my own,
With broken murmurs, and with amorous sighs,
I'll say, you were unkind, and punish you,
And mark you red with many an eager kiss.   10
ANTONY.   My brighter Venus!
CLEOPATRA.   O my greater Mars!
ANTONY.   Thou join'st us well, my love!
Suppose me come from the Phlegraean plains,
Where gasping giants lay, cleft by my sword,
And mountain-tops paired off each other blow,
To bury those I slew. Receive me, goddess!
Let Caesar spread his subtle nets; like Vulcan,
In thy embraces I would be beheld
By heaven and earth at once;
And make their envy what they meant their sport.   20
Let those, who took us, blush; I would love on,
With awful state, regardless of their frowns,
As their superior gods.
There's no satiety of love in thee:
Enjoyed, thou still art new; perpetual spring
Is in thy arms; the ripened fruit but falls,
And blossoms rise to fill its empty place;
And I grow rich by giving.
                              [*Enter* VENTIDIUS, *and stands apart.*]
ALEXAS.   Oh, now the danger's past, your general comes!
He joins not in your joys, nor minds your triumphs;   30
But, with contracted brows, looks frowning on,
As envying your success.
ANTONY.   Now, on my soul, he loves me; truly loves me:
He never flattered me in any vice,
But awes me with his virtue: even this minute,
Methinks, he has a right of chiding me.
Lead to the temple: I'll avoid his presence;
It checks too strong upon me.   [*Exeunt the rest.*]
        [*As* ANTONY *is going,* VENTIDIUS *pulls him by the robe.*]

VENTIDIUS.   Emperor!

ANTONY.   'Tis the old argument; I pr'ythee, spare me.

[Looking back.]

VENTIDIUS.   But this one hearing, emperor.

ANTONY.   Let go   40
My robe; or, by my father Hercules——

VENTIDIUS.   By Hercules' father, that's yet greater,
I bring you somewhat you would wish to know.

ANTONY.   Thou see'st we are observed; attend me here,
And I'll return.   *[Exit.*

VENTIDIUS.   I am waning in his favour, yet I love him;
I love this man, who runs to meet his ruin;
And sure the gods, like me, are fond of him:
His virtues lie so mingled with his crimes,
As would confound their choice to punish one,   50
And not reward the other.

[Enter ANTONY.*]*

ANTONY.   We can conquer,
You see, without your aid.
We have dislodged their troops;
They look on us at distance, and, like curs
'Scaped from the lion's paws, they bay far off.
And lick their wounds, and faintly threaten war.
Five thousand Romans, and their faces upward,
Lie breathless on the plain.

VENTIDIUS.   'Tis well; and he,
Who lost them, could have spared ten thousand more.
Yet if, by this advantage, you could gain   60
An easier peace, while Caesar doubts the chance
Of arms——

ANTONY.   Oh, think not on't, Ventidius!
The boy pursues my ruin, he'll no peace;
His malice is considerate in advantage.
Oh, he's the coolest murderer! so staunch,
He kills, and keeps his temper.

VENTIDIUS.   Have you no friend
In all his army, who has power to move him?
Maecenas, or Agrippa, might do much.

ANTONY.   They're both too deep in Caesar's interests.
We'll work it out by dint of sword, or perish.   70

VENTIDIUS.   Fain I would find some other.

ANTONY.   Thank thy love.
  Some four or five such victories as this
  Will save thy further pains.

VENTIDIUS.   Expect no more; Caesar is on his guard:
  I know, sir, you have conquered against odds;
  But still you draw supplies from one poor town,
  And of Egyptians: he has all the world,
  And, at his beck, nations come pouring in,
  To fill the gaps you make. Pray, think again.

ANTONY.   Why dost thou drive me from myself, to search   80
  For foreign aids?—to hunt my memory,
  And range all o'er a waste and barren place,
  To find a friend? The wretched have no friends,
  Yet I had one, the bravest youth of Rome,
  Whom Caesar loves beyond the love of women:
  He could resolve his mind, as fire does wax,
  From that hard rugged image melt him down,
  And mould him in what softer form he pleased.

VENTIDIUS.   Him would I see; that man, of all the world;
  Just such a one we want.

ANTONY.   He loved me too;   90
  I was his soul; he lived not but in me:
  We were so closed within each other's breasts,
  The rivets were not found, that joined us first.
  That does not reach us yet: we were so mixt,
  As meeting streams, both to ourselves were lost;
  We were one mass; we could not give or take,
  But from the same; for he was I, I he.

VENTIDIUS.   He moves as I would wish him.   [*Aside.*]

ANTONY.   After this,
  I need not tell his name;—'twas Dolabella.

VENTIDIUS.   He's now in Caesar's camp.

ANTONY.   No matter where,   100
  Since he's no longer mine. He took unkindly,
  That I forbade him Cleopatra's sight,
  Because I feared he loved her: he confessed,
  He had a warmth, which, for my sake, he stifled;
  For 'twere impossible that two, so one,
  Should not have loved the same. When he departed,
  He took no leave; and that confirmed my thoughts.

VENTIDIUS.   It argues, that he loved you more than her,
  Else he had stayed; but he perceived you jealous,
  And would not grieve his friend: I know he loves you.   *110*
ANTONY.   I should have seen him, then, ere now.
VENTIDIUS.   Perhaps
  He has thus long been labouring for your peace.
ANTONY.   Would he were here!
VENTIDIUS.   Would you believe he loved you?
  I read your answer in your eyes, you would.
  Not to conceal it longer, he has sent
  A messenger from Caesar's camp, with letters.
ANTONY.   Let him appear.
VENTIDIUS.   I'll bring him instantly.
        [*Exit* VENTIDIUS, *and re-enters immediately with* DOLA-
                              BELLA.]
ANTONY.   'Tis he himself! himself, by holy friendship!
                        [*Runs to embrace him.*]
  Art thou returned at last, my better half?
  Come, give me all myself!
  Let me not live,   *120*
  If the young bridegroom, longing for his night,
  Was ever half so fond.
DOLABELLA.   I must be silent, for my soul is busy
  About a nobler work: she's new come home,
  Like a long-absent man, and wanders o'er
  Each room, a stranger to her own, to look
  If all be safe.
ANTONY.   Thou hast what's left of me;
  For I am now so sunk from what I was,
  Thou find'st me at my lowest water-mark.
  The rivers that ran in, and raised my fortunes,   *130*
  Are all dried up, or take another course:
  What I have left is from my native spring;
  I've still a heart that swells, in scorn of fate,
  And lifts me to my banks.
DOLABELLA.   Still you are lord of all the world to me.
ANTONY.   Why, then I yet am so; for thou art all.
  If I had any joy when thou wert absent,
  I grudged it to myself; methought I robbed
  Thee of thy part. But, O my Dolabella!
  Thou hast beheld me other than I am.   *140*

Hast thou not seen my morning chambers filled
With sceptred slaves, who waited to salute me?
With eastern monarchs, who forgot the sun,
To worship my uprising?—menial kings
Ran coursing up and down my palace-yard,
Stood silent in my presence, watched my eyes,
And, at my least command, all started out,
Like racers to the goal.

DOLABELLA.   Slaves to your fortune.

ANTONY.   Fortune is Caesar's now; and what am I?

VENTIDIUS.   What you have made yourself; I will not flatter.   *150*

ANTONY.   Is this friendly done?

DOLABELLA.   Yes; when his end is so, I must join with him;
Indeed I must, and yet you must not chide;
Why am I else your friend?

ANTONY.   Take heed, young man,
How thou upbraid'st my love: The queen has eyes,
And thou too hast a soul. Canst thou remember,
When, swelled with hatred, thou beheld'st her first,
As accessary to thy brother's death?

DOLABELLA.   Spare my remembrance; 'twas a guilty day,
And still the blush hangs here.

ANTONY.   To clear herself,   *160*
For sending him no aid, she came from Egypt.
Her galley down the silver Cydnus rowed,
The tackling silk, the streamers waved with gold;
The gentle winds were lodged in purple sails:
Her nymphs, like Nereids, round her couch were placed;
Where she, another sea-born Venus, lay.

DOLABELLA.   No more; I would not hear it.

ANTONY.   Oh, you must!
She lay, and leant her cheek upon her hand,
And cast a look so languishingly sweet,
As if, secure of all beholders' hearts,   *170*
Neglecting, she could take them: boys, like Cupids,
Stood fanning, with their painted wings, the winds,
That played about her face. But if she smiled,
A darting glory seemed to blaze abroad,
That men's desiring eyes were never wearied,
But hung upon the object: To soft flutes

The silver oars kept time; and while they played,
The hearing gave new pleasure to the sight;
And both to thought. 'Twas heaven, or somewhat more:
For she so charmed all hearts, that gazing crowds   *180*
Stood panting on the shore, and wanted breath
To give their welcome voice.
Then, Dolabella, where was then thy soul?
Was not thy fury quite disarmed with wonder?
Didst thou not shrink behind me from those eyes
And whisper in my ear—Oh, tell her not
That I accused her with my brother's death?

DOLABELLA.   And should my weakness be a plea for yours?
Mine was an age when love might be excused,
When kindly warmth, and when my springing youth   *190*
Made it a debt to nature. Yours——

VENTIDIUS.   Speak boldly.
Yours, he would say, in your declining age,
When no more heat was left but what you forced,
When all the sap was needful for the trunk,
When it went down, then you constrained the course,
And robbed from nature, to supply desire;
In you (I would not use so harsh a word)
'Tis but plain dotage.

ANTONY.   Ha!

DOLABELLA.   'Twas urged too home.—
But yet the loss was private, that I made;
'Twas but myself I lost: I lost no legions;   *200*
I had no world to lose, no people's love.

ANTONY.   This from a friend?

DOLABELLA.   Yes, Antony, a true one;
A friend so tender, that each word I speak
Stabs my own heart, before it reach your ear.
Oh, judge me not less kind, because I chide!
To Caesar I excuse you.

ANTONY.   O ye gods!
Have I then lived to be excused to Caesar?

DOLABELLA.   As to your equal.

ANTONY.   Well, he's but my equal:
While I wear this he never shall be more.

DOLABELLA.   I bring conditions from him.

ANTONY.   Are they noble?   210
  Methinks thou shouldst not bring them else; yet he
  Is full of deep dissembling; knows no honour
  Divided from his interest. Fate mistook him;
  For nature meant him for an usurer:
  He's fit indeed to buy, not conquer kingdoms.

VENTIDIUS.   Then, granting this,
  What power was theirs, who wrought so hard a temper
  To honourable terms?

ANTONY.   It was my Dolabella, or some god.

DOLABELLA.   Nor I, nor yet Maecenas, nor Agrippa:
  They were your enemies; and I, a friend,   220
  Too weak alone; yet 'twas a Roman deed.

ANTONY.   'Twas like a Roman done: show me that man,
  Who has preserved my life, my love, my honour;
  Let me but see his face.

VENTIDIUS.   That task is mine,
  And, Heaven, thou know'st how pleasing.   [*Exit* VENTIDIUS.]

DOLABELLA.   You'll remember
  To whom you stand obliged?

ANTONY.   When I forget it,
  Be thou unkind, and that's my greatest curse.
  My queen shall thank him too.

DOLABELLA.   I fear she will not.

ANTONY.   But she shall do it: The queen, my Dolabella!
  Hast thou not still some grudgings of thy fever?   230

DOLABELLA.   I would not see her lost.

ANTONY.   When I forsake her,
  Leave me my better stars! for she has truth
  Beyond her beauty. Caesar tempted her,
  At no less price than kingdoms, to betray me;
  But she resisted all: and yet thou chidest me
  For loving her too well. Could I do so?

DOLABELLA.   Yes; there's my reason.

           [*Re-enter* VENTIDIUS, *with* OCTAVIA, *leading* ANTONY's
                      two little Daughters.]

ANTONY.   Where? Octavia there!   [*Starting back.*]

VENTIDIUS.   What, is she poison to you?—a disease?
  Look on her, view her well, and those she brings:
  Are they all strangers to your eyes? has nature   240
  No secret call, no whisper they are yours?

DOLABELLA.   For shame, my lord, if not for love, receive them
　　With kinder eyes. If you confess a man,
　　Meet them, embrace them, bid them welcome to you.
　　Your arms should open, even without your knowledge,
　　To clasp them in; your feet should turn to wings,
　　To bear you to them; and your eyes dart out
　　And aim a kiss, ere you could reach the lips.

ANTONY.   I stood amazed, to think how they came hither.

VENTIDIUS.   I sent for them; I brought them in unknown   *250*
　　To Cleopatra's guards.

DOLABELLA.   Yet, are you cold?

OCTAVIA.   Thus long I have attended for my welcome;
　　Which, as a stranger, sure I might expect.
　　Who am I?

ANTONY.   Caesar's sister.

OCTAVIA.   That's unkind.
　　Had I been nothing more than Caesar's sister,
　　Know, I had still remained in Caesar's camp:
　　But your Octavia, your much injured wife,
　　Though banished from your bed, driven from your house,
　　In spite of Caesar's sister, still is yours.
　　'Tis true, I have a heart disdains your coldness,   *260*
　　And prompts me not to seek what you should offer;
　　But a wife's virtue still surmounts that pride.
　　I come to claim you as my own; to show
　　My duty first; to ask, nay beg, your kindness:
　　Your hand, my lord; 'tis mine, and I will have it.

　　　　　　　　　　　　　　　　　　[Taking his hand.]

VENTIDIUS.   Do, take it; thou deserv'st it.

DOLABELLA.   On my soul,
　　And so she does: she's neither too submissive,
　　Nor yet too haughty; but so just a mean
　　Shows, as it ought, a wife and Roman too.

ANTONY.   I fear, Octavia, you have begged my life.   *270*

OCTAVIA.   Begged it, my lord?

ANTONY.   Yes, begged it, my ambassadress!
　　Poorly and basely begged it of your brother.

OCTAVIA.   Poorly and basely I could never beg:
　　Nor could my brother grant.

ANTONY.   Shall I, who, to my kneeling slave, could say,
　　Rise up, and be a king; shall I fall down

And cry,—Forgive me, Caesar! Shall I set
A man, my equal, in the place of Jove,
As he could give me being? No; that word,
Forgive, would choke me up,   280
And die upon my tongue.

DOLABELLA.   You shall not need it.

ANTONY.   I will not need it. Come, you've all betrayed me,—
My friend too!—to receive some vile conditions.
My wife has brought me, with her prayers and tears;
And now I must become her branded slave.
In every peevish mood, she will upbraid
The life she gave: if I but look awry,
She cries—I'll tell my brother.

OCTAVIA.   My hard fortune
Subjects me still to your unkind mistakes.
But the conditions I have brought are such,   290
You need not blush to take: I love your honour,
Because 'tis mine; it never shall be said,
Octavia's husband was her brother's slave.
Sir, you are free; free, even from her you loathe,
For, though my brother bargains for your love,
Makes me the price and cement of your peace,
I have a soul like yours; I cannot take
Your love as alms, nor beg what I deserve.
I'll tell my brother we are reconciled;
He shall draw back his troops, and you shall march   300
To rule the East: I may be dropt at Athens;
No matter where. I never will complain,
But only keep the barren name of wife,
And rid you of the trouble.

VENTIDIUS.   Was ever such a strife of sullen honour!
Both scorn to be obliged.

DOLABELLA.   Oh, she has touched him in the tenderest
part;
See how he reddens with despite and shame,
To be outdone in generosity!

VENTIDIUS.   See how he winks! how he dries up a tear,   310
That fain would fall!   [*Apart.*]

ANTONY.   Octavia, I have heard you, and must praise

The greatness of your soul;
But cannot yield to what you have proposed:
For I can ne'er be conquered but by love;
And you do all for duty. You would free me,
And would be dropt at Athens; was't not so?

OCTAVIA.   It was, my lord.

ANTONY.   Then I must be obliged
To one who loves me not; who, to herself,
May call me thankless and ungrateful man:—
I'll not endure it; no.   320

VENTIDIUS.   I am glad it pinches there.   [*Aside.*]

OCTAVIA.   Would you triumph o'er poor Octavia's virtue?
That pride was all I had to bear me up;
That you might think you owed me for your life,
And owed it to my duty, not my love.
I have been injured, and my haughty soul
Could brook but ill the man who slights my bed.

ANTONY.   Therefore you love me not.

OCTAVIA.   Therefore, my lord,
I should not love you.

ANTONY.   Therefore you would leave me?

OCTAVIA.   And therefore I should leave you—if I could.   330

DOLABELLA.   Her soul's too great, after such injuries,
To say she loves; and yet she lets you see it.
Her modesty and silence plead her cause.

ANTONY.   O Dolabella, which way shall I turn?
I find a secret yielding in my soul;
But Cleopatra, who would die with me,
Must she be left? Pity pleads for Octavia;
But does it not plead more for Cleopatra?

VENTIDIUS.   Justice and pity both plead for Octavia;
For Cleopatra, neither.   340
One would be ruined with you; but she first
Had ruined you: The other, you have ruined,
And yet she would preserve you.
In everything their merits are unequal.

ANTONY.   O my distracted soul!

OCTAVIA.   Sweet Heaven compose it!—
Come, come, my lord, if I can pardon you,
Methinks you should accept it. Look on these;

Are they not yours? or stand they thus neglected,
As they are mine? Go to him, children, go;
Kneel to him, take him by the hand, speak to him;   *350*
For you may speak, and he may own you too,
Without a blush; and so he cannot all
His children: go, I say, and pull him to me,
And pull him to yourselves, from that bad woman.
You, Agrippina, hang upon his arms;
And you, Antonia, clasp about his waist:
If he will shake you off, if he will dash you
Against the pavement, you must bear it, children;
For you are mine, and I was born to suffer.

                  [Here the CHILDREN *go to him, etc.]*

VENTIDIUS.   Was ever sight so moving?—Emperor!   *360*
DOLABELLA.   Friend!
OCTAVIA.   Husband!
BOTH CHILDREN.   Father!
ANTONY.   I am vanquished: take me,
   Octavia; take me, children; share me all.   *[Embracing them.]*
   I've been a thriftless debtor to your loves,
   And run out much, in riot, from your stock;
   But all shall be amended.
OCTAVIA.   O blest hour!
DOLABELLA.   O happy change!
VENTIDIUS.   My joy stops at my tongue;
   But it has found two channels here for one,
   And bubbles out above.
ANTONY. *[to* OCTAVIA*]*.   This is thy triumph; lead me where
    thou wilt;
   Even to thy brother's camp.
OCTAVIA.   All there are yours.   *370*

                  [Enter ALEXAS *hastily.]*

ALEXAS.   The queen, my mistress, sir, and yours——
ANTONY.   'Tis past.—
   Octavia, you shall stay this night: To-morrow,
   Caesar and we are one.

        [Exit leading OCTAVIA; DOLABELLA *and the* Children *follow.]*

VENTIDIUS.   There's news for you; run, my officious eunuch,
   Be sure to be the first; haste forward:
   Haste, my dear eunuch, haste.   *[Exit.]*

ALEXAS.   This downright fighting fool, this thick-skulled hero,
    This blunt, unthinking instrument of death,
    With plain dull virtue has outgone my wit.
    Pleasure forsook my earliest infancy;   380
    The luxury of others robbed my cradle,
    And ravished thence the promise of a man.
    Cast out from nature, disinherited
    Of what her meanest children claim by kind,
    Yet greatness kept me from contempt: that's gone.
    Had Cleopatra followed my advice,
    Then he had been betrayed who now forsakes.
    She dies for love; but she has known its joys:
    Gods, is this just, that I, who know no joys,
    Must die, because she loves?
                    [*Enter* CLEOPATRA, CHARMION, IRAS, *and Train.*]
    O madam, I have seen what blasts my eyes!
    Octavia's here.
CLEOPATRA.   Peace with that raven's note.
    I know it too; and now am in
    The pangs of death.
ALEXAS.   You are no more a queen;
    Egypt is lost.
CLEOPATRA.   What tell'st thou me of Egypt?
    My life, my soul is lost! Octavia has him!—
    O fatal name to Cleopatra's love!
    My kisses, my embraces now are hers;
    While I——But thou hast seen my rival; speak,
    Does she deserve this blessing? Is she fair?   400
    Bright as a goddess? and is all perfection
    Confined to her? It is. Poor I was made
    Of that coarse matter, which, when she was finished,
    The gods threw by for rubbish.
ALEXAS.   She is indeed a very miracle.
CLEOPATRA.   Death to my hopes, a miracle!
ALEXAS.   A miracle;   [*Bowing.*]
    I mean of goodness; for in beauty, madam,
    You make all wonders cease.
CLEOPATRA.   I was too rash:
    Take this in part of recompense. But, oh!   [*Giving a ring.*]
    I fear thou flatterest me.
CHARMION.   She comes! she's here!   410

IRAS.   Fly, madam, Caesar's sister!

CLEOPATRA.   Were she the sister of the thunderer Jove,
And bore her brother's lightning in her eyes,
Thus would I face my rival.

> [*Meets* OCTAVIA *with* VENTIDIUS. OCTAVIA *bears up to
> her. Their Trains come up on either side.*]

OCTAVIA.   I need not ask if you are Cleopatra;
Your haughty carriage——

CLEOPATRA.   Shows I am a queen:
Nor need I ask you, who you are.

OCTAVIA.   A Roman:
A name, that makes and can unmake a queen.

CLEOPATRA.   Your lord, the man who serves me, is a Roman.

OCTAVIA.   He was a Roman, till he lost that name,   420
To be a slave in Egypt; but I come
To free him thence.

CLEOPATRA.   Peace, peace, my lover's Juno.
When he grew weary of that household clog,
He chose my easier bonds.

OCTAVIA.   I wonder not
Your bonds are easy: you have long been practised
In that lascivious art: He's not the first
For whom you spread your snares: Let Caesar witness.

CLEOPATRA.   I loved not Caesar; 'twas but gratitude
I paid his love: The worst your malice can,
Is but to say the greatest of mankind   430
Has been my slave. The next, but far above him
In my esteem, is he whom law calls yours,
But whom his love made mine.

OCTAVIA.   I would view nearer   [*Coming up close to her.*]
That face, which has so long usurped my right,
To find the inevitable charms, that catch
Mankind so sure, that ruined my dear lord.

CLEOPATRA.   Oh, you do well to search; for had you known
But half these charms, you had not lost his heart.

OCTAVIA.   Far be their knowledge from a Roman lady,
Far from a modest wife! Shame of our sex,   440
Dost thou not blush to own those black endearments,
That makes sin pleasing?

CLEOPATRA.   You may blush, who want them.

If bounteous nature, if indulgent Heaven
Have given me charms to please the bravest man,
Should I not thank them? Should I be ashamed,
And not be proud? I am, that he has loved me;
And, when I love not him, Heaven change this face
For one like that.

OCTAVIA.   Thou lov'st him not so well.

CLEOPATRA.   I love him better, and deserve him more.

OCTAVIA.   You do not; cannot: You have been his ruin.   450
Who made him cheap at Rome, but Cleopatra?
Who made him scorned abroad, but Cleopatra?
At Actium, who betrayed him? Cleopatra.
Who made his children orphans, and poor me
A wretched widow? only Cleopatra.

CLEOPATRA.   Yet she, who loves him best, is Cleopatra.
If you have suffered, I have suffered more.
You bear the specious title of a wife,
To gild your cause, and draw the pitying world
To favour it: the world condemns poor me.   460
For I have lost my honour, lost my fame,
And stained the glory of my royal house,
And all to bear the branded name of mistress.
There wants but life, and that too I would lose
For him I love.

OCTAVIA.   Be't so, then; take thy wish.   [*Exit with her Train.*]

CLEOPATRA.   And 'tis my wish,
Now he is lost for whom alone I lived.
My sight grows dim, and every object dances,
And swims before me, in the maze of death.
My spirits, while they were opposed, kept up;   470
They could not sink beneath a rival's scorn!
But now she's gone, they faint.

ALEXAS.   Mine have had leisure
To recollect their strength, and furnish counsel,
To ruin her, who else must ruin you.

CLEOPATRA.   Vain promiser!
Lead me, my Charmion; nay, your hand too, Iras.
My grief has weight enough to sink you both.
Conduct me to some solitary chamber,
And draw the curtains round;

Then leave me to myself, to take alone   *480*
My fill of grief:
   There I till death will his unkindness weep;
   As harmless infants moan themselves asleep.   [*Exeunt.*]

ACT IV

SCENE I

[*Enter* ANTONY *and* DOLABELLA.]

DOLABELLA.   Why would you shift it from yourself on me?
   Can you not tell her, you must part?
ANTONY.   I cannot.
   I could pull out an eye, and bid it go,
   And t'other should not weep. O Dolabella,
   How many deaths are in this word, *Depart!*
   I dare not trust my tongue to tell her so:
   One look of hers would thaw me into tears,
   And I should melt, till I were lost again.
DOLABELLA.   Then let Ventidius;
   He's rough by nature.
ANTONY.   Oh, he'll speak too harshly;   *10*
   He'll kill her with the news: Thou, only thou.
DOLABELLA.   Nature has cast me in so soft a mould,
   That but to hear a story, feigned for pleasure,
   Of some sad lover's death, moistens my eyes,
   And robs me of my manhood. I should speak
   So faintly, with such fear to grieve her heart,
   She'd not believe it earnest.
ANTONY.   Therefore,—therefore
   Thou only, thou art fit: Think thyself me;
   And when thou speak'st (but let it first be long),
   Take off the edge from every sharper sound,   *20*
   And let our parting be as gently made,
   As other loves begin: Wilt thou do this?
DOLABELLA.   What you have said so sinks into my soul,
   That, if I must speak, I shall speak just so.

ANTONY.   I leave you then to your sad task: Farewell.
  I sent her word to meet you. [*Goes to the door, and comes back.*]
  I forgot;
  Let her be told, I'll make her peace with mine:
  Her crown and dignity shall be preserved,
  If I have power with Caesar.——Oh, be sure
  To think on that.
DOLABELLA.   Fear not, I will remember.   30
              [ANTONY *goes again to the door, and comes back.*]
ANTONY.   And tell her, too, how much I was constrained;
  I did not this, but with extremest force:
  Desire her not to hate my memory,
  For I still cherish hers;——insist on that.
DOLABELLA.   Trust me, I'll not forget it.
ANTONY.   Then that's all.   [*Goes out, and returns again.*]
  Wilt thou forgive my fondness this once more?
  Tell her, though we shall never meet again,
  If I should hear she took another love,
  The news would break my heart.—Now I must go;
  For every time I have returned, I feel   40
  My soul more tender; and my next command
  Would be, to bid her stay, and ruin both.   [*Exit.*]
DOLABELLA.   Men are but children of a larger growth;
  Our appetites as apt to change as theirs,
  And full as craving too, and full as vain;
  And yet the soul, shut up in her dark room,
  Viewing so clear abroad, at home sees nothing;
  But, like a mole in earth, busy and blind,
  Works all her folly up, and casts it outward
  To the world's open view: Thus I discovered,   50
  And blamed the love of ruined Antony;
  Yet wish that I were he, to be so ruined.
                          [*Enter* VENTIDIUS *above.*]
VENTIDIUS.   Alone, and talking to himself? concerned too?
  Perhaps my guess is right; he loved her once,
  And may pursue it still.
DOLABELLA.   O friendship! friendship!
  Ill canst thou answer this; and reason, worse:
  Unfaithful in the attempt; hopeless to win;
  And if I win, undone: mere madness all.

And yet the occasion's fair. What injury
To him, to wear the robe which he throws by!   60
VENTIDIUS.   None, none at all. This happens as I wish,
To ruin her yet more with Antony.
> [*Enter* CLEOPATRA, *talking with* ALEXAS; CHARMION,
> IRAS *on the other side.*]

DOLABELLA.   She comes! What charms have sorrow on that face!
Sorrow seems pleased to dwell with so much sweetness;
Yet, now and then, a melancholy smile
Breaks loose, like lightning in a winter's night,
And shows a moment's day.
VENTIDIUS.   If she should love him too! her eunuch there?
That porc'pisce bodes ill weather. Draw, draw nearer,
Sweet devil, that I may hear.
ALEXAS.   Believe me; try   70
> [DOLABELLA *goes over to* CHARMION *and* IRAS; *seems
> to talk with them.*]

To make him jealous; jealousy is like
A polished glass held to the lips when life's in doubt;
If there be breath, 'twill catch the damp, and show it.
CLEOPATRA.   I grant you, jealousy's a proof of love,
But 'tis a weak and unavailing medicine;
It puts out the disease, and makes it show,
But has no power to cure.
ALEXAS.   'Tis your last remedy, and strongest too:
And then this Dolabella, who so fit
To practise on? He's handsome, valiant, young,   80
And looks as he were laid for nature's bait,
To catch weak women's eyes.
He stands already more than half suspected
Of loving you: the least kind word or glance
You give this youth, will kindle him with love:
Then, like a burning vessel set adrift,
You'll send him down amain before the wind.
To fire the heart of jealous Antony.
CLEOPATRA.   Can I do this? Ah, no; my love's so true,
That I can neither hide it where it is,   90
Nor show it where it is not. Nature meant me
A wife; a silly, harmless, household dove,
Fond without art, and kind without deceit;

But Fortune, that has made a mistress of me,
Has thrust me out to the wide world, unfurnished
Of falsehood to be happy.
ALEXAS.   Force yourself.
The event will be, your lover will return,
Doubly desirous to possess the good
Which once he feared to lose.
CLEOPATRA.   I must attempt it;
But oh, with what regret!   100

          [*Exit* ALEXAS. *She comes up to* DOLABELLA.]

VENTIDIUS.   So, now the scene draws near; they're in my reach.
CLEOPATRA [*to* DOLABELLA].   Discoursing with my women! might
   not I
Share in your entertainment?
CHARMION.   You have been
The subject of it, madam.
CLEOPATRA.   How! and how?
IRAS.   Such praises of your beauty!
CLEOPATRA.   Mere poetry.
Your Roman wits, your Gallus and Tibullus,
Have taught you this from Cytheris and Delia.
DOLABELLA.   Those Roman wits have never been in Egypt;
Cytheris and Delia else had been unsung:
I, who have seen——had I been born a poet,   110
Should choose a nobler name.
CLEOPATRA.   You flatter me.
But, 'tis your nation's vice: All of your country
Are flatterers, and all false. Your friend's like you.
I'm sure, he sent you not to speak these words.
DOLABELLA.   No, madam; yet he sent me——
CLEOPATRA.   Well, he sent you——
DOLABELLA.   Of a less pleasing errand.
CLEOPATRA.   How less pleasing?
Less to yourself, or me?
DOLABELLA.   Madam, to both;
For you must mourn, and I must grieve to cause it.
CLEOPATRA.   You, Charmion, and your fellow, stand at distance.—
Hold up, my spirits. [*Aside*]——Well, now your mournful
   matter!   120
For I'm prepared, perhaps can guess it too.

DOLABELLA.   I wish you would; for 'tis a thankless office,
　　To tell ill news: And I, of all your sex,
　　Most fear displeasing you.
CLEOPATRA.   Of all your sex,
　　I soonest could forgive you, if you should.
VENTIDIUS.   Most delicate advances! Women! women!
　　Dear, damned, inconstant sex!
CLEOPATRA.   In the first place,
　　I am to be forsaken; is't not so?
DOLABELLA.   I wish I could not answer to that question.
CLEOPATRA.   Then pass it o'er, because it troubles you:　　130
　　I should have been more grieved another time.
　　Next, I'm to lose my kingdom——Farewell, Egypt
　　Yet, is there any more?
DOLABELLA.   Madam, I fear
　　Your too deep sense of grief has turned your reason.
CLEOPATRA.   No, no, I'm not run mad; I can bear fortune:
　　And love may be expelled by other love,
　　As poisons are by poisons.
DOLABELLA.   You o'erjoy me, madam,
　　To find your griefs so moderately borne.
　　You've heard the worst; all are not false like him.
CLEOPATRA.   No; Heaven forbid they should.
DOLABELLA.   Some men are constant.　　140
CLEOPATRA.   And constancy deserves reward, that's certain.
DOLABELLA.   Deserves it not; but give it leave to hope.
VENTIDIUS.   I'll swear, thou hast my leave. I have enough:
　　But how to manage this! Well, I'll consider.　　[*Exit.*]
DOLABELLA.   I came prepared
　　To tell you heavy news; news, which I thought
　　Would fright the blood from your pale cheeks to hear:
　　But you have met it with a cheerfulness,
　　That makes my task more easy; and my tongue,
　　Which, on another's message was employed,　　150
　　Would gladly speak its own.
CLEOPATRA.   Hold, Dolabella.
　　First tell me, were you chosen by my lord?
　　Or sought you this employment?
DOLABELLA.   He picked me out; and, as his bosom friend,
　　He charged me with his words.

CLEOPATRA.   The message then
  I know was tender, and each accent smooth,
  To mollify that rugged word, *Depart.*
DOLABELLA.   Oh, you mistake: He chose the harshest words;
  With fiery eyes, and with contracted brows,
  He coined his face in the severest stamp;   160
  And fury shook his fabric, like an earthquake;
  He heaved for vent, and burst like bellowing Aetna,
  In sounds scarce human—"Hence away for ever,
  Let her begone, the blot of my renown,
  And bane of all my hopes!"
      [*All the time of this speech,* CLEOPATRA *seems more and*
              more concerned, till she sinks quite down.]
  "Let her be driven, as far as men can think,
  From man's commerce! she'll poison to the centre."
CLEOPATRA.   Oh, I can bear no more!
DOLABELLA.   Help, help!—O wretch! O cursed, cursed wretch!
  What have I done!
CHARMION.   Help, chafe her temples, Iras.   170
IRAS.   Bend, bend her forward quickly.
CHARMION.   Heaven be praised,
  She comes again.
CLEOPATRA.   Oh, let him not approach me.
  Why have you brought me back to this loathed being,
  The abode of falsehood, violated vows,
  And injured love? For pity, let me go;
  For, if there be a place of long repose,
  I'm sure I want it. My disdainful lord
  Can never break that quiet; nor awake
  The sleeping soul, with hollowing in my tomb
  Such words as fright her hence.—Unkind, unkind!   180
DOLABELLA.   Believe me, 'tis against myself I speak; [*Kneeling.*
  That sure desires belief; I injured him:
  My friend ne'er spoke those words. Oh, had you seen
  How often he came back, and every time
  With something more obliging and more kind,
  To add to what he said; what dear farewells;
  How almost vanquished by his love he parted,
  And leaned to what unwillingly he left!
  I, traitor as I was, for love of you

(But what can you not do, who made me false?)   190
I forged that lie; for whose forgiveness kneels
This self-accused, self-punished criminal.

CLEOPATRA. With how much ease believe we what we wish!
Rise, Dolabella; if you have been guilty,
I have contributed, and too much love
Has made me guilty too.
The advance of kindness, which I made, was feigned,
To call back fleeting love by jealousy;
But 'twould not last. Oh, rather let me lose,
Than so ignobly trifle with his heart.   200

DOLABELLA. I find your breast fenced round from human reach,
Transparent as a rock of solid crystal;
Seen through, but never pierced. My friend, my friend,
What endless treasure hast thou thrown away;
And scattered, like an infant, in the ocean,
Vain sums of wealth, which none can gather thence!

CLEOPATRA. Could you not beg
An hour's admittance to his private ear?
Like one, who wanders through long barren wilds
And yet foreknows no hospitable inn   210
Is near to succour hunger, eats his fill,
Before his painful march;
So would I feed a while my famished eyes
Before we part; for I have far to go,
If death be far, and never must return.

                    [VENTIDIUS *with* OCTAVIA, *behind.*]

VENTIDIUS. From hence you may discover—oh, sweet, sweet!
Would you indeed? The pretty hand in earnest?

DOLABELLA. I will, for this reward.   [*Takes her hand.*]
Draw it not back.
'Tis all I e'er will beg.

VENTIDIUS. They turn upon us.

OCTAVIA. What quick eyes has guilt!   220

VENTIDIUS. Seem not to have observed them, and go on.

                                              [*They enter.*]

DOLABELLA. Saw you the emperor, Ventidius?

VENTIDIUS. No.
I sought him; but I heard that he was private,
None with him but Hipparchus, his freedman.

DOLABELLA.   Know you his business?

VENTIDIUS.   Giving him instructions,
  And letters to his brother Caesar.

DOLABELLA.   Well,
  He must be found.   [*Exeunt* DOLABELLA *and* CLEOPATRA.]

OCTAVIA.   Most glorious impudence!

VENTIDIUS.   She looked, methought,
  As she would say—Take your old man, Octavia;
  Thank you, I'm better here.—
  Well, but what use   230
  Make we of this discovery?

OCTAVIA.   Let it die.

VENTIDIUS.   I pity Dolabella; but she's dangerous;
  Her eyes have power beyond Thessalian charms,
  To draw the moon from heaven; for eloquence,
  The sea-green Syrens taught her voice their flattery;
  And, while she speaks, night steals upon the day,
  Unmarked of those that hear: Then she's so charming,
  Age buds at sight of her, and swells to youth:
  The holy priests gaze on her when she smiles;
  And with heaved hands, forgetting gravity,   240
  They bless her wanton eyes: Even I, who hate her,
  With a malignant joy behold such beauty;
  And, while I curse, desire it. Antony
  Must needs have some remains of passion still,
  Which may ferment into a worse relapse,
  If now not fully cured. I know, this minute,
  With Caesar he's endeavouring her peace.

OCTAVIA.   You have prevailed:———But for a further purpose
                                                         [*Walks off.*]
  I'll prove how he will relish this discovery.
  What, make a strumpet's peace! it swells my heart: 250
  It must not, shall not be.

VENTIDIUS.   His guards appear.
  Let me begin, and you shall second me.

                                                        [*Enter* ANTONY.]

ANTONY.   Octavia, I was looking you, my love:
  What, are your letters ready? I have given
  My last instructions.

OCTAVIA.   Mine, my lord, are written.

ANTONY.   Ventidius.   [*Drawing him aside.*]

VENTIDIUS.   My lord?

ANTONY.   A word in private.—
When saw you Dolabella?

VENTIDIUS.   Now, my lord,
He parted hence; and Cleopatra with him.

ANTONY.   Speak softly.—'Twas by my command he went,
To bear my last farewell.

VENTIDIUS.   It looked indeed   [*Aloud.*]
Like your farewell.

ANTONY.   More softly.—My farewell?   261
What secret meaning have you in those words
Of—My farewell? He did it by my order.

VENTIDIUS.   Then he obeyed your order. I suppose   [*Aloud.*]
You bid him do it with all gentleness,
All kindness, and all—love.

ANTONY.   How she mourned,
The poor forsaken creature!

VENTIDIUS.   She took it as she ought; she bore your parting
As she did Caesar's, as she would another's,
Were a new love to come.

ANTONY.   Thou dost belie her;   [*Aloud.*]
Most basely, and maliciously belie her.   271

VENTIDIUS.   I thought not to displease you; I have done.

OCTAVIA.   You seemed disturbed, my lord.   [*Coming up.*]

ANTONY.   A very trifle.
Retire, my love.

VENTIDIUS.   It was indeed a trifle.
He sent——

ANTONY.   No more. Look how thou disobey'st me;   [*Angrily.*]
Thy life shall answer it.

OCTAVIA.   Then 'tis no trifle.

VENTIDIUS.   [*to* OCTAVIA]. 'Tis less; a very nothing: You too
saw it,
As well as I, and therefore 'tis no secret.

ANTONY.   She saw it!

VENTIDIUS.   Yes: She saw young Dolabella——

ANTONY.   Young Dolabella!

VENTIDIUS.   Young, I think him young,   280
And handsome too; and so do others think him.

But what of that? He went by your command,
Indeed 'tis probable, with some kind message;
For she received it graciously; she smiled;
And then he grew familiar with her hand,
Squeezed it, and worried it with ravenous kisses;
She blushed, and sighed, and smiled, and blushed again;
At last she took occasion to talk softly,
And brought her cheek up close, and leaned on his;
At which, he whispered kisses back on hers;   *290*
And then she cried aloud—That constancy
Should be rewarded.

OCTAVIA.   This I saw and heard.

ANTONY.   What woman was it, whom you heard and saw
So playful with my friend?
Not Cleopatra?

VENTIDIUS.   Even she, my lord.

ANTONY.   My Cleopatra?

VENTIDIUS.   Your Cleopatra;
Dolabella's Cleopatra; every man's Cleopatra.

ANTONY.   Thou liest.

VENTIDIUS.   I do not lie, my lord.
Is this so strange? Should mistresses be left,
And not provide against a time of change?   *300*
You know she's not much used to lonely nights.

ANTONY.   I'll think no more on't.
I know 'tis false, and see the plot betwixt you.—
You needed not have gone this way, Octavia.
What harms it you that Cleopatra's just?
She's mine no more. I see, and I forgive:
Urge it no further, love.

OCTAVIA.   Are you concerned,
That she's found false?

ANTONY.   I should be, were it so;
For, though 'tis past, I would not that the world
Should tax my former choice, that I loved one   *310*
Of so light note; but I forgive you both.

VENTIDIUS.   What has my age deserved, that you should think
I would abuse your ears with perjury?
If Heaven be true, she's false.

ANTONY.   Though heaven and earth

Should witness it, I'll not believe her tainted.

VENTIDIUS.   I'll bring you, then, a witness

From hell, to prove her so.—Nay, go not back;

> [*Seeing* ALEXAS *just entering, and starting back.*]

For stay you must and shall.

ALEXAS.   What means my lord?

VENTIDIUS.   To make you do what most you hate,—speak truth.

You are of Cleopatra's private counsel,   320

Of her bed-counsel, her lascivious hours;

Are conscious of each nightly change she makes,

And watch her, as Chaldeans do the moon,

Can tell what signs she passes through, what day.

ALEXAS.   My noble lord!

VENTIDIUS.   My most illustrious pander,

No fine set speech, no cadence, no turned periods,

But a plain homespun truth, is what I ask:

I did, myself, o'erhear your queen make love

To Dolabella. Speak; for I will know,

By your confession, what more passed betwixt them;   330

How near the business draws to your employment;

And when the happy hour.

ANTONY.   Speak truth, Alexas; whether it offend

Or please Ventidius, care not: Justify

Thy injured queen from malice: Dare his worst.

OCTAVIA.   [*Aside.*] See how he gives him courage! how he fears

To find her false! and shuts his eyes to truth,

Willing to be misled!

ALEXAS.   As far as love may plead for woman's frailty,

Urged by desert and greatness of the lover,   340

So far, divine Octavia, may my queen

Stand even excused to you for loving him

Who is your lord: so far, from brave Ventidius,

May her past actions hope a fair report.

ANTONY.   'Tis well, and truly spoken: mark, Ventidius.

ALEXAS.   To you, most noble emperor, her strong passion

Stands not excused, but wholly justified.

Her beauty's charms alone, without her crown,

From Ind and Meroe drew the distant vows

Of sighing kings; and at her feet were laid   350

The sceptres of the earth, exposed on heaps,

To choose where she would reign:
She thought a Roman only could deserve her,
And, of all Romans, only Antony;
And, to be less than wife to you, disdained
Their lawful passion.
ANTONY. 'Tis but truth.
ALEXAS. And yet, though love, and your unmatched desert,
Have drawn her from the due regard of honour,
At last Heaven opened her unwilling eyes
To see the wrongs she offered fair Octavia,   360
Whose holy bed she lawlessly usurped.
The sad effects of this improsperous war
Confirmed those pious thoughts.
VENTIDIUS. [*Aside.*] Oh, wheel you there?
Observe him now; the man begins to mend,
And talk substantial reason.—Fear not, eunuch;
The emperor has given thee leave to speak.
ALEXAS. Else had I never dared to offend his ears
With what the last necessity has urged
On my forsaken mistress; yet I must not
Presume to say, her heart is wholly altered.   370
ANTONY. No, dare not for thy life, I charge thee dare not
Pronounce that fatal word!
OCTAVIA. Must I bear this? Good Heaven, afford me patience.
     [*Aside.*]

VENTIDIUS. On, sweet eunuch; my dear half-man, proceed.
ALEXAS. Yet Dolabella
Has loved her long; he, next my god-like lord,
Deserves her best; and should she meet his passion,
Rejected, as she is, by him she loved——
ANTONY. Hence from my sight! for I can bear no more:
Let furies drag thee quick to hell; let all   380
The longer damned have rest; each torturing hand
Do thou employ, till Cleopatra comes;
Then join thou too, and help to torture her!
     [*Exit* ALEXAS, *thrust out by* ANTONY.]
OCTAVIA. 'Tis not well,
Indeed, my lord, 'tis much unkind to me,
To show this passion, this extreme concernment,
For an abandoned, faithless prostitute.

ANTONY.   Octavia, leave me; I am much disordered:
Leave me, I say.

OCTAVIA.   My lord!

ANTONY.   I bid you leave me.

VENTIDIUS.   Obey him, madam: best withdraw a while,   *390*
And see how this will work.

OCTAVIA.   Wherein have I offended you, my lord,
That I am bid to leave you? Am I false,
Or infamous? Am I a Cleopatra?
Were I she,
Base as she is, you would not bid me leave you;
But hang upon my neck, take slight excuses,
And fawn upon my falsehood.

ANTONY.   'Tis too much.
Too much, Octavia; I am pressed with sorrows
Too heavy to be borne; and you add more: *400*
I would retire, and recollect what's left
Of man within, to aid me.

OCTAVIA.   You would mourn,
In private, for your love, who has betrayed you.
You did but half return to me: your kindness
Lingered behind with her. I hear, my lord,
You make conditions for her,
And would include her treaty. Wondrous proofs
Of love to me!

ANTONY.   Are you my friend, Ventidius?
Or are you turned a Dolabella too,
And let this fury loose?

VENTIDIUS.   Oh, be advised,   *410*
Sweet madam, and retire.

OCTAVIA.   Yes, I will go; but never to return.
You shall no more be haunted with this Fury.
My lord, my lord, love will not always last,
When urged with long unkindness and disdain:
Take her again, whom you prefer to me;
She stays but to be called. Poor cozened man!
Let a feigned parting give her back your heart,
Which a feigned love first got; for injured me,
Though my just sense of wrongs forbid my stay,   *420*
My duty shall be yours.

To the dear pledges of our former love
My tenderness and care shall be transferred,
And they shall cheer, by turns, my widowed nights:
So, take my last farewell; for I despair
To have you whole, and scorn to take you half.   [*Exit.*]
VENTIDIUS. I combat Heaven, which blasts my best designs:
My last attempt must be to win her back;
But oh! I fear in vain.   [*Exit.*]
ANTONY. Why was I framed with this plain, honest
heart,   430
Which knows not to disguise its griefs and weakness,
But bears its workings outward to the world?
I should have kept the mighty anguish in,
And forced a smile at Cleopatra's falsehood:
Octavia had believed it, and had stayed.
But I am made a shallow-forded stream,
Seen to the bottom: all my clearness scorned,
And all my faults exposed.—See where he comes,

[*Enter* DOLABELLA.]

Who has profaned the sacred name of friend,
And worn it into vileness!   440
With how secure a brow, and specious form
He gilds the secret villain! Sure that face
Was meant for honesty; but Heaven mismatched it,
And furnished treason out with nature's pomp,
To make its work more easy.
DOLABELLA.   O my friend!
ANTONY. Well, Dolabella, you performed my message?
DOLABELLA.   I did, unwillingly.
ANTONY. Unwillingly?
Was it so hard for you to bear our parting?
You should have wished it.
DOLABELLA.   Why?
ANTONY. Because you love me.
And she received my message with as true,   450
With as unfeigned a sorrow as you brought it?
DOLABELLA.   She loves you, even to madness.
ANTONY. Oh, I know it.
You, Dolabella, do not better know
How much she loves me. And should I

Forsake this beauty? This all-perfect creature?

DOLABELLA.   I could not, were she mine.

ANTONY.   And yet you first
Persuaded me: How come you altered since?

DOLABELLA.   I said at first I was not fit to go:
I could not hear her sighs, and see her tears,
But pity must prevail: And so, perhaps,   460
It may again with you; for I have promised,
That she should take her last farewell: And, see,
She comes to claim my word.

> [*Enter* CLEOPATRA.]

ANTONY.   False Dolabella!

DOLABELLA.   What's false, my lord?

ANTONY.   Why, Dolabella's false,
And Cleopatra's false; both false and faithless.
Draw near, you well-joined wickedness, you serpents,
Whom I have in my kindly bosom warmed,
Till I am stung to death.

DOLABELLA.   My lord, have I
Deserved to be thus used?

CLEOPATRA.   Can Heaven prepare
A newer torment? Can it find a curse   470
Beyond our separation?

ANTONY.   Yes, if fate
Be just, much greater: Heaven should be ingenious
In punishing such crimes. The rolling stone,
And gnawing vulture, were slight pains, invented
When Jove was young, and no examples known
Of mighty ills; but you have ripened sin,
To such a monstrous growth, 'twill pose the gods
To find an equal torture. Two, two such!—
Oh, there's no further name,—two such! to me,
To me, who locked my soul within your breasts,   480
Had no desires, no joys, no life, but you;
When half the globe was mine, I gave it you
In dowry with my heart; I had no use,
No fruit of all, but you: A friend and mistress
Was what the world could give. O Cleopatra!
O Dolabella! how could you betray
This tender heart, which with an infant fondness

    Lay lulled betwixt your bosoms, and there slept,
    Secure of injured faith?

DOLABELLA.   If she has wronged you,
    Heaven, hell, and you revenge it.

ANTONY.   If she has wronged me!   490
    Thou wouldst evade thy part of guilt; but swear
    Thou lov'st not her.

DOLABELLA.   Not so as I love you.

ANTONY.   Not so? Swear, swear, I say, thou dost not love her.

DOLABELLA.   No more than friendship will allow.

ANTONY.   No more?
    Friendship allows thee nothing: Thou are perjured—
    And yet thou didst not swear thou lov'st her not;
    But not so much, no more. O trifling hypocrite,
    Who dar'st not own to her, thou dost not love,
    Nor own to me, thou dost! Ventidius heard it;
    Octavia saw it.

CLEOPATRA.   They are enemies.   500

ANTONY.   Alexas is not so: He, he confessed it;
    He, who, next hell, best knew it, he avowed it.
    Why do I seek a proof beyond yourself?   [*To* DOLABELLA.]
    You, whom I sent to bear my last farewell,
    Returned, to plead her stay.

DOLABELLA.   What shall I answer?
    If to have loved be guilt, then I have sinned;
    But if to have repented of that love
    Can wash away my crime, I have repented.
    Yet, if I have offended past forgiveness,
    Let not her suffer: She is innocent.   510

CLEOPATRA.   Ah, what will not a woman do, who loves?
    What means will she refuse, to keep that heart,
    Where all her joys are placed? 'Twas I encouraged,
    'Twas I blew up the fire that scorched his soul,
    To make you jealous, and by that regain you.
    But all in vain; I could not counterfeit:
    In spite of all the dams my love broke o'er,
    And drowned my heart again: fate took the occasion;
    And thus one minute's feigning has destroyed
    My whole life's truth.

ANTONY.   Thin cobweb arts of falsehood;   520

Seen, and broke through at first.

DOLABELLA.   Forgive your mistress.

CLEOPATRA.   Forgive your friend.

ANTONY.   You have convinced yourselves,
  You plead each other's cause: What witness have you,
  That you but meant to raise my jealousy?

CLEOPATRA.   Ourselves, and Heaven.

ANTONY.   Guilt witnesses for guilt. Hence, love and friendship!
  You have no longer place in human breasts,
  These two have driven you out: Avoid my sight!
  I would not kill the man whom I have loved,
  And cannot hurt the woman; but avoid me: 530
  I do not know how long I can be tame;
  For, if I stay one minute more, to think
  How I am wronged, my justice and revenge
  Will cry so loud within me, that my pity
  Will not be heard for either.

DOLABELLA.   Heaven has but
  Our sorrow for our sins; and then delights
  To pardon erring man: Sweet mercy seems
  Its darling attribute, which limits justice;
  As if there were degrees in infinite,
  And infinite would rather want perfection   540
  Than punish to extent.

ANTONY.   I can forgive
  A foe; but not a mistress and a friend.
  Treason is there in its most horrid shape,
  Where trust is greatest; and the soul resigned,
  Is stabbed by its own guards: I'll hear no more;
  Hence from my sight for ever!

CLEOPATRA.   How? for ever!
  I cannot go one moment from your sight,
  And must I go for ever?
  My joys, my only joys, are centred here:
  What place have I to go to? My own kingdom?   550
  That I have lost for you: Or to the Romans?
  They hate me for your sake: Or must I wander
  The wide world o'er, a helpless, banished woman,
  Banished for love of you; banished from you?
  Ay, there's the banishment! Oh, hear me; hear me,

With strictest justice: For I beg no favour;
And if I have offended you, then kill me,
But do not banish me.
ANTONY.   I must not hear you.
I have a fool within me takes your part;
But honour stops my ears.
CLEOPATRA.   For pity hear me!   560
Would you cast off a slave who followed you?
Who crouched beneath your spurn?—He has no pity!
See, if he gives one tear to my departure;
One look, one kind farewell: O iron heart!
Let all the gods look down, and judge betwixt us,
If he did ever love!
ANTONY.   No more: Alexas!
DOLABELLA.   A perjured villain!
ANTONY.   [*To* CLEOPATRA.] Your Alexas; yours.
CLEOPATRA.   Oh, 'twas his plot; his ruinous design,
To engage you in my love by jealousy.
Hear him; confront him with me; let him speak.   570
ANTONY.   I have; I have.
CLEOPATRA.   And if he clear me not——
ANTONY.   Your creature! one, who hangs upon your smiles!
Watches your eye, to say or to unsay,
Whate'er you please! I am not to be moved.
CLEOPATRA.   Then must we part? Farewell, my cruel lord!
The appearance is against me; and I go,
Unjustified, for ever from your sight.
How I have loved, you know; how yet I love,
My only comfort is, I know myself:
I love you more, even now you are unkind,   580
Than when you loved me most; so well, so truly
I'll never strive against it; but die pleased,
To think you once were mine.
ANTONY.   Good heaven, they weep at parting!
Must I weep too? that calls them innocent.
I must not weep; and yet I must, to think
That I must not forgive.——
Live, but live wretched; 'tis but just you should,
Who made me so: Live from each other's sight:
Let me not hear you meet. Set all the earth,   590

And all the seas, betwixt your sundered loves:
View nothing common but the sun and skies.
Now, all take several ways;
    And each your own sad fate, with mine, deplore;
    That you were false, and I could trust no more.

                                   [Exeunt severally.]

ACT V

SCENE I

             [Enter CLEOPATRA, CHARMION, *and* IRAS.]

CHARMION. Be juster, Heaven; such virtue punished thus,
    Will make us think that chance rules all above,
    And shuffles, with a random hand, the lots,
    Which man is forced to draw.

CLEOPATRA. I could tear out these eyes, that gained his heart,
    And had not power to keep it. O the curse
    Of doting on, even when I find it dotage!
    Bear witness, gods, you heard him bid me go;
    You, whom he mocked with imprecating vows
    Of promised faith!——I'll die; I will not bear it.   10
    You may hold me——

               [She pulls out her dagger, and they hold her.]
    But I can keep my breath; I can die inward,
    And choke this love.

                        [Enter ALEXAS.]

IRAS. Help, O Alexas, help!
    The queen grows desperate; her soul struggles in her
    With all the agonies of love and rage,
    And strives to force its passage.

CLEOPATRA. Let me go.
    Art thou there, traitor!—O,
    O for a little breath, to vent my rage,
    Give, give me way, and let me loose upon him.

ALEXAS. Yes, I deserve it, for my ill-timed truth.   20
    Was it for me to prop

  The ruins of a falling majesty?
  To place myself beneath the mighty flaw,
  Thus to be crushed, and pounded into atoms,
  By its o'erwhelming weight? 'Tis too presuming
  For subjects to preserve that wilful power,
  Which courts its own destruction.
CLEOPATRA. I would reason
  More calmly with you. Did not you o'errule,
  And force my plain, direct, and open love,
  Into these crooked paths of jealousy?   *30*
  Now, what's the event? Octavia is removed;
  But Cleopatra's banished. Thou, thou villain,
  Hast pushed my boat to open sea: to prove,
  At my sad cost, if thou canst steer it back.
  It cannot be; I'm lost too far; I'm ruined:
  Hence, thou impostor, traitor, monster, devil!—
  I can no more: Thou, and my griefs, have sunk
  Me down so low, that I want voice to curse thee.
ALEXAS. Suppose some shipwrecked seaman near the shore,
  Dropping and faint with climbing up the cliff, *40*
  If, from above, some charitable hand
  Pull him to safety, hazarding himself,
  To draw the other's weight; would he look back,
  And curse him for his pains? The case is yours;
  But one step more, and you have gained the height.
CLEOPATRA. Sunk, never more to rise.
ALEXAS. Octavia's gone, and Dolabella banished.
  Believe me, madam, Antony is yours.
  His heart was never lost, but started off
  To jealousy, love's last retreat and covert;
  Where it lies hid in shades, watchful in silence,
  And listening for the sound that calls it back.
  Some other, any man ('tis so advanced),
  May perfect this unfinished work, which I
  (Unhappy only to myself) have left
  So easy to his hand.
CLEOPATRA. Look well thou do't; else——
ALEXAS. Else, what your silence threatens.—Antony
  Is mounted up the Pharos; from whose turret,
  He stands surveying our Egyptian galleys,

Engaged with Caesar's fleet. Now death or conquest!   60
If the first happen, fate acquits my promise;
If we o'ercome, the conqueror is yours.

[*A distant shout within.*]

CHARMION.   Have comfort, madam: Did you mark that shout?

[*Second shout nearer.*]

IRAS.   Hark! they redouble it.

ALEXAS.   'Tis from the port.
The loudness shows it near: Good news, kind heavens!

CLEOPATRA.   Osiris make it so!

[*Enter* SERAPION.]

SERAPION.   Where, where's the queen?

ALEXAS.   How frightfully the holy coward stares
As if not yet recovered of the assault,
When all his gods, and, what's more dear to him,
His offerings, were at stake.

SERAPION.   O horror, horror!
Egypt has been; our latest hour has come:
The queen of nations, from her ancient seat,
Is sunk for ever in the dark abyss:
Time has unrolled her glories to the last,
And now closed up the volume.

CLEOPATRA.   Be more plain:
Say, whence thou comest; though fate is in thy face,
Which from thy haggard eyes looks wildly out,
And threatens ere thou speakest.

SERAPION.   I came from Pharos;
From viewing (spare me, and imagine it)
Our land's last hope, your navy——

CLEOPATRA.   Vanquished?

SERAPION.   No: 80
They fought not.

CLEOPATRA.   Then they fled.

SERAPION.   Nor that. I saw,
With Antony, your well-appointed fleet
Row out; and thrice he waved his hand on high,
And thrice with cheerful cries they shouted back:
'Twas then false Fortune, like a fawning strumpet,
About to leave the bankrupt prodigal,
With a dissembled smile would kiss at parting,

And flatter to the last; the well-timed oars,
Now dipt from every bank, now smoothly run
To meet the foe; and soon indeed they met,   *90*
But not as foes. In few, we saw their caps
On either side thrown up; the Egyptian galleys,
Received like friends, passed through, and fell behind
The Roman rear: And now, they all come forward,
And ride within the port.

CLEOPATRA.   Enough, Serapion:
I've heard my doom.—This needed not, you gods:
When I lost Antony, your work was done;
'Tis but superfluous malice.—Where's my lord?
How bears he this last blow?

SERAPION.   His fury cannot be expressed by words: *100*
Thrice he attempted headlong to have fallen
Full on his foes, and aimed at Caesar's galley:
Withheld, he raves on you; cries,—He's betrayed.
Should he now find you——

ALEXAS.   Shun him; seek your safety,
Till you can clear your innocence.

CLEOPATRA.   I'll stay.

ALEXAS.   You must not; haste you to your monument,
While I make speed to Caesar.

CLEOPATRA.   Caesar! No,
I have no business with him.

ALEXAS.   I can work him
To spare your life, and let this madman perish.

CLEOPATRA.   Base fawning wretch! wouldst thou betray him
    too?   *110*
Hence from my sight! I will not hear a traitor;
'Twas thy design brought all this ruin on us.—
Serapion, thou are honest; counsel me:
But haste, each moment's precious.

SERAPION.   Retire; you must not yet see Antony.
He who began this mischief,
'Tis just he tempt the danger; let him clear you:
And, since he offered you his servile tongue,
To gain a poor precarious life from Caesar,
Let him expose that fawning eloquence,   *120*
And speak to Antony.

ALEXAS.   O heavens! I dare not;
  I meet my certain death.

CLEOPATRA.   Slave, thou deservest it.—
  Not that I fear my lord, will I avoid him;
  I know him noble: when he banished me,
  And thought me false, he scorned to take my life;
  But I'll be justified, and then die with him.

ALEXAS.   O pity me, and let me follow you.

CLEOPATRA.   To death, if thou stir hence. Speak, if thou canst,
  Now for thy life, which basely thou wouldst save;
  While mine I prize at—this! Come, good Serapion.   *130*
      [*Exeunt* CLEOPATRA, SERAPION, CHARMION, *and* IRAS.]

ALEXAS.   O that I less could fear to lose this being,
  Which, like a snowball in my coward hand,
  The more 'tis grasped, the faster melts away.
  Poor reason! what a wretched aid art thou!
  For still, in spite of thee,
  These two long lovers, soul and body, dread
  Their final separation. Let me think:
  What can I say, to save myself from death?
  No matter what becomes of Cleopatra.

ANTONY.   Which way? where?   [*Within.*]

VENTIDIUS.   This leads to the monument.   [*Within.*]

ALEXAS.   Ah me! I hear him; yet I'm unprepared: *141*
  My gift of lying's gone;
  And this court-devil, which I so oft have raised,
  Forsakes me at my need. I dare not stay;
  Yet cannot far go hence.   [*Exit.*]
      [*Enter* ANTONY *and* VENTIDIUS.]

ANTONY.   O happy Caesar! thou hast men to lead:
  Think not 'tis thou hast conquered Antony;
  But Rome has conquered Egypt. I'm betrayed.

VENTIDIUS.   Curse on this treacherous train!
  Their soil and heaven infect them all with baseness: *150*
  And their young souls come tainted to the world
  With the first breath they draw.

ANTONY.   The original villain sure no god created;
  He was a bastard of the sun, by Nile,
  Aped into man; with all his mother's mud
  Crusted about his soul.

VENTIDIUS.   The nation is
    One universal traitor; and their queen
    The very spirit and extract of them all.
ANTONY.   Is there yet left
    A possibility of aid from valour?   *160*
    Is there one god unsworn to my destruction?
    The least unmortgaged hope? for, if there be,
    Methinks I cannot fall beneath the fate
    Of such a boy as Caesar.
    The world's one half is yet in Antony;
    And from each limb of it, that's hewed away,
    The soul comes back to me.
VENTIDIUS.   There yet remain
    Three legions in the town. The last assault
    Lopt off the rest; if death be your design,—
    As I must wish it now,—these are sufficient   *170*
    To make a heap about us of dead foes,
    An honest pile for burial.
ANTONY.   They are enough.
    We'll not divide our stars; but, side by side,
    Fight emulous, and with malicious eyes
    Survey each other's acts: So every death
    Thou giv'st, I'll take on me, as a just debt,
    And pay thee back a soul.
VENTIDIUS.   Now you shall see I love you. Not a word
    Of chiding more. By my few hours of life,
    I am so pleased with this brave Roman fate,   *180*
    That I would not be Caesar, to outlive you.
    When we put off this flesh, and mount together,
    I shall be shown to all the ethereal crowd,—
    Lo, this is he who died with Antony!
ANTONY.   Who knows, but we may pierce through all their
      troops,
    And reach my veterans yet? 'tis worth the 'tempting,
    To o'erleap this gulf of fate,
    And leave our wandering destinies behind.
                          [*Enter* ALEXAS, *trembling.*]
VENTIDIUS.   See, see, that villain!
    See Cleopatra stamped upon that face,
    With all her cunning, all her arts of falsehood!   *190*

How she looks out through those dissembling eyes!
How he sets his countenance for deceit,
And promises a lie, before he speaks!
Let me despatch him first.   [*Drawing.*]

ALEXAS.   O spare me, spare me!

ANTONY.   Hold; he's not worth your killing.—On thy life,
Which thou may'st keep, because I scorn to take it,
No syllable to justify thy queen;
Save thy base tongue its office.

ALEXAS.   Sir, she is gone,
Where she shall never be molested more
By love, or you.

ANTONY.   Fled to her Dolabella!   200
Die, traitor! I revoke my promise! die!   [*Going to kill him.*]

ALEXAS.   O hold! She is not fled.

ANTONY.   She is: my eyes
Are open to her falsehood; my whole life
Has been a golden dream of love and friendship;
But, now I wake, I'm like a merchant, roused
From soft repose, to see his vessel sinking,
And all his wealth cast over. Ungrateful woman!
Who followed me, but as the swallow summer,
Hatching her young ones in my kindly beams,
Singing her flatteries to my morning wake: 210
But, now my winter comes, she spreads her wings,
And seeks the spring of Caesar.

ALEXAS.   Think not so:
Her fortunes have, in all things, mixed with yours.
Had she betrayed her naval force to Rome,
How easily might she have gone to Caesar,
Secure by such a bribe!

VENTIDIUS.   She sent it first,
To be more welcome after.

ANTONY.   'Tis too plain;
Else would she have appeared, to clear herself.

ALEXAS.   Too fatally she has: she could not bear
To be accused by you; but shut herself   220
Within her monument; looked down and sighed;
While, from her unchanged face, the silent tears
Dropt, as they had not leave, but stole their parting.

Some indistinguished words she inly murmured;
At last, she raised her eyes; and, with such looks
As dying Lucrece cast——

ANTONY.   My heart forebodes——

VENTIDIUS.   All for the best:—Go on.

ALEXAS.   She snatched her poniard,
And, ere we could prevent the fatal blow,
Plunged it within her breast; then turned to me:
Go, bear my lord, said she, my last farewell;   230
And ask him, if he yet suspect my faith.
More she was saying, but death rushed betwixt.
She half pronounced your name with her last breath,
And buried half within her.

VENTIDIUS.   Heaven be praised!

ANTONY.   Then art thou innocent, my poor dear love,
And art thou dead?
O those two words! their sound should be divided:
Hadst thou been false, and died; or hadst thou lived,
And hadst been true—But innocence and death!
This shows not well above. Then what am I,   240
The murderer of this truth, this innocence!
Thoughts cannot form themselves in words so horrid
As can express my guilt!

VENTIDIUS.   Is't come to this? The gods have been too gracious;
And thus you thank them for it!

ANTONY.   [*To* ALEXAS.] Why stayest thou here?
Is it for thee to spy upon my soul,
And see its inward mourning? Get thee hence;
Thou art not worthy to behold, what now
Becomes a Roman emperor to perform.

ALEXAS.   He loves her still: 250
His grief betrays it. Good! the joy to find
She's yet alive, completes the reconcilement.
I've saved myself, and her. But, oh! the Romans!
Fate comes too fast upon my wit,
Hunts me too hard, and meets me at each double.
                                            [*Aside. Exit.*]

VENTIDIUS.   Would she had died a little sooner, though!
Before Octavia went, you might have treated:
Now 'twill look tame, and would not be received.

Come, rouse yourself, and let's die warm together.
ANTONY.   I will not fight: there's no more work for war.   *260*
The business of my angry hours is done.
VENTIDIUS.   Caesar is at your gates.
ANTONY.   Why, let him enter;
He's welcome now.
VENTIDIUS.   What lethargy has crept into your soul?
ANTONY.   'Tis but a scorn of life, and just desire
To free myself from bondage.
VENTIDIUS.   Do it bravely.
ANTONY.   I will; but not by fighting. O Ventidius!
What should I fight for now?—my queen is dead.
I was but great for her; my power, my empire,
Were but my merchandise to buy her love;   *270*
And conquered kings, my factors. Now she's dead,
Let Caesar take the world,—
An empty circle, since the jewel's gone
Which made it worth my strife: my being's nauseous;
For all the bribes of life are gone away.
VENTIDIUS.   Would you be taken?
ANTONY.   Yes, I would be taken;
But, as a Roman ought,—dead, my Ventidius:
For I'll convey my soul from Caesar's reach,
And lay down life myself. 'Tis time the world
Should have a lord, and know whom to obey.   *280*
We two have kept its homage in suspense,
And bent the globe, on whose each side we trod,
Till it was dented inwards. Let him walk
Alone upon't: I'm weary of my part.
My torch is out; and the world stands before me,
Like a black desert at the approach of night:
I'll lay me down, and stray no farther on.
VENTIDIUS.   I could be grieved,
But that I'll not outlive you: choose your death;
For, I have seen him in such various shapes,   *290*
I care not which I take: I'm only troubled,
The life I bear is worn to such a rag,
'Tis scarce worth giving. I could wish, indeed,
We threw it from us with a better grace;

That, like two lions taken in the toils,
We might at last thrust out our paws, and wound
The hunters that inclose us.
ANTONY.   I have thought on it.
Ventidius, you must live.
VENTIDIUS.   I must not, sir.
ANTONY.   Wilt thou not live, to speak some good of me?
To stand by my fair fame, and guard the approaches
From the ill tongues of men?
VENTIDIUS.   Who shall guard mine,
For living after you?
ANTONY.   Say, I command it.
VENTIDIUS.   If we die well, our deaths will speak themselves
And need no living witness.
ANTONY.   Thou has loved me,
And fain I would reward thee. I must die;
Kill me, and take the merit of my death,
To make thee friends with Caesar.
VENTIDIUS.   Thank your kindness.
You said I loved you; and in recompense,
You bid me turn a traitor: Did I think
You would have used me thus?—that I should die   *310*
With a hard thought of you?
ANTONY.   Forgive me, Roman.
Since I have heard of Cleopatra's death,
My reason bears no rule upon my tongue,
But lets my thoughts break all at random out.
I've thought better; do not deny me twice.
VENTIDIUS.   By Heaven I will not.
Let it not be to outlive you.
ANTONY.   Kill me first,
And then die thou; for 'tis but just thou serve
Thy friend before myself.
VENTIDIUS.   Give me your hand.
We soon shall meet again. Now, farewell, emperor!—

                                                                    [*Embrace.*]

Methinks that word's too cold to be my last: *320*
Since death sweeps all distinctions, farewell, friend!
That's all——

I will not make a business of a trifle;
And yet I cannot look on you, and kill you;
Pray turn your face.

ANTONY.   I do: strike home, be sure.

VENTIDIUS.   Home as my sword will reach.   [*Kills himself.*]

ANTONY.   Oh, thou mistak'st;
That wound was not of thine; give it me back;
Thou robb'st me of my death.

VENTIDIUS.   I do indeed;
But think 'tis the first time I e'er deceived you,   330
If that may plead my pardon.—And you, gods,
Forgive me, if you will; for I die perjured,
Rather than kill my friend.   [*Dies.*]

ANTONY.   Farewell! Ever my leader, even in death!
My queen and thou have got the start of me,
And I'm the lag of honour.—Gone so soon?
Is Death no more? he used him carelessly,
With a familiar kindness: ere he knocked,
Ran to the door, and took him in his arms,
As who should say—You're welcome at all hours,   340
A friend need give no warning. Books had spoiled him;
For all the learned are cowards by profession.
'Tis not worth
My further thought; for death, for aught I know,
Is but to think no more. Here's to be satisfied.
                              [*Falls on his sword.*]

I've missed my heart. O unperforming hand!
Thou never couldst have erred in a worse time.
My fortune jades me to the last; and death,
Like a great man, takes state, and makes me wait
For my admittance.——   [*Trampling within.*]
Some, perhaps, from Caesar:
If he should find me living, and suspect
That I played booty with my life! I'll mend
My work, ere they can reach me.   [*Rises upon his knees.*]
                    [*Enter* CLEOPATRA, CHARMION, *and* IRAS.]

CLEOPATRA.   Where is my lord? where is he?

CHARMION.   There he lies,
And dead Ventidius by him.

CLEOPATRA. My fears were prophets; I am come too late.
O that accursed Alexas!   [*Runs to him.*]
ANTONY. Art thou living?
Or am I dead before I knew, and thou
The first kind ghost that meets me?
CLEOPATRA. Help me seat him.
Send quickly, send for help!   [*They place him in a chair.*]
ANTONY. I am answered.   360
We live both. Sit thee down, my Cleopatra:
I'll make the most I can of life, to stay
A moment more with thee.
CLEOPATRA. How is it with you?
ANTONY. 'Tis as with a man
Removing in a hurry; all packed up,
But one dear jewel that his haste forgot;
And he, for that, returns upon the spur:
So I come back for thee.
CLEOPATRA. Too long, ye heavens, you have been cruel to me:
Now show your mended faith, and give me back
His fleeting life!
ANTONY. It will not be, my love;   370
I keep my soul by force.
Say but, thou art not false.
CLEOPATRA. 'Tis now too late
To say I'm true: I'll prove it, and die with you.
Unknown to me, Alexas feigned my death:
Which, when I knew, I hasted to prevent
This fatal consequence. My fleet betrayed
Both you and me.
ANTONY. And Dolabella——
CLEOPATRA. Scarce
Esteemed before he loved; but hated now.
ANTONY. Enough: my life's not long enough for more.
Thou say'st, thou wilt come after: I believe thee;   380
For I can now believe whate'er thou sayest,
That we may part more kindly.
CLEOPATRA. I will come:
Doubt not, my life, I'll come, and quickly too:
Caesar shall triumph o'er no part of thee.

ANTONY.   But grieve not, while thou stayest,
  My last disastrous times:
  Think we have had a clear and glorious day
  And Heaven did kindly to delay the storm,
  Just till our close of evening. Ten years' love,
  And not a moment lost, but all improved   390
  To the utmost joys,—what ages have we lived?
  And now to die each other's; and, so dying,
  While hand in hand we walk in groves below,
  Whole troops of lovers' ghosts shall flock about us,
  And all the train be ours.
CLEOPATRA.   Your words are like the notes of dying swans,
  Too sweet to last. Were there so many hours
  For your unkindness, and not one for love?
ANTONY.   No, not a minute.—This one kiss—more worth
  Than all I leave to Caesar.   [*Dies.*]
CLEOPATRA.   O tell me so again,   401
  And take ten thousand kisses for that word.
  My lord, my lord! speak, if you yet have being;
  Sign to me, if you cannot speak; or cast
  One look! Do anything that shows you live.
IRAS.   He's gone too far to hear you;
  And this you see, a lump of senseless clay,
  The leavings of a soul.
CHARMION.   Remember, madam,
  He charged you not to grieve.
CLEOPATRA.   And I'll obey him.
  I have not loved a Roman, not to know   410
  What should become his wife; his wife, my Charmion!
  For 'tis to that high title I aspire;
  And now I'll not die less. Let dull Octavia
  Survive, to mourn him dead: My nobler fate
  Shall knit our spousals with a tie, too strong
  For Roman laws to break.
IRAS.   Will you then die?
CLEOPATRA.   Why should'st thou make that question?
IRAS.   Caesar is merciful.
CLEOPATRA.   Let him be so
  To those that want his mercy: My poor lord
  Made no such covenant with him, to spare me   420

When he was dead. Yield me to Caesar's pride?
What! to be led in triumph through the streets,
A spectacle to base plebeian eyes;
While some dejected friend of Antony's,
Close in a corner, shakes his head, and mutters
A secret curse on her who ruined him!
I'll none of that.

CHARMION.   Whatever you resolve,
I'll follow, even to death.

IRAS.   I only feared
For you; but more should fear to live without you.

CLEOPATRA.   Why, now, 'tis as it should be. Quick, my friends,
Despatch: ere this, the town's in Caesar's hands: 431
My lord looks down concerned, and fears my stay,
Lest I should be surprised;
Keep him not waiting for his love too long.
You, Charmion, bring my crown and richest jewels;
With them, the wreath of victory I made
(Vain augury!) for him, who now lies dead:
You, Iras, bring the cure of all our ills.

IRAS.   The aspics, madam?

CLEOPATRA.   Must I bid you twice?

[Exit CHARMION *and* IRAS.]

'Tis sweet to die, when they would force life on me,   440
To rush into the dark abode of death,
And seize him first; if he be like my love,
He is not frightful, sure.
We're now alone, in secrecy and silence;
And is not this like lovers? I may kiss
These pale, cold lips; Octavia does not see me:
And, oh! 'tis better far to have him thus,
Than see him in her arms.—Oh, welcome, welcome!

[Enter CHARMION *and* IRAS.]

CHARMION.   What must be done?

CLEOPATRA.   Short ceremony, friends;
But yet it must be decent. First, this laurel   450
Shall crown my hero's head: he fell not basely,
Nor left his shield behind him.—Only thou
Couldst triumph o'er thyself; and thou alone
Wert worthy so to triumph.

CHARMION.   To what end
  These ensigns of your pomp and royalty?
CLEOPATRA.   Dull, that thou art! why 'tis to meet my love;
  As when I saw him first, on Cydnus' bank,
  All sparkling, like a goddess: so adorned,
  I'll find him once again; my second spousals
  Shall match my first in glory. Haste, haste, both,   460
  And dress the bride of Antony.
CHARMION.   'Tis done.
CLEOPATRA.   Now seat me by my lord. I claim this place;
  For I must conquer Caesar too, like him,
  And win my share of the world.—Hail, you dear relics
  Of my immortal love!
  O let no impious hand remove you hence:
  But rest for ever here! Let Egypt give
  His death that peace, which it denied his life.—
  Reach me the casket.
IRAS.   Underneath the fruit
  The aspic lies.
CLEOPATRA.   Welcome, thou kind deceiver!
                              [*Putting aside the leaves.*]
  Thou best of thieves; who, with an easy key,   471
  Dost open life, and, unperceived by us,
  Even steal us from ourselves; discharging so
  Death's dreadful office, better than himself;
  Touching our limbs so gently into slumber,
  That Death stands by, deceived by his own image,
  And thinks himself but sleep.
SERAPION.   The queen, where is she?   [*Within.*]
  The town is yielded, Caesar's at the gates.
CLEOPATRA.   He comes too late to invade the rights of death.
  Haste, bare my arm, and rouse the serpent's fury.   480
                      [*Holds out her arm, and draws it back.*]
  Coward flesh,
  Wouldst thou conspire with Caesar to betray me,
  As thou wert none of mine? I'll force thee to it,
  And not be sent by him,
  But bring, myself, my soul to Antony.
                      [*Turns aside, and then shows her arm bloody.*]
  Take hence; the work is done.

SERAPION.   Break ope the door,   [*Within.*]
 And guard the traitor well.
CHARMION.   The next is ours.
IRAS.   Now, Charmion, to be worthy
 Of our great queen and mistress.   [*They apply the aspics.*]
CLEOPATRA.   Already, death, I feel thee in my veins: 490
 I go with such a will to find my lord,
 That we shall quickly meet.
 A heavy numbness creeps through every limb,
 And now 'tis at my head: My eyelids fall
 And my dear love is vanquished in a mist.
 Where shall I find him, where? O turn me to him,
 And lay me on his breast!—Caesar, thy worst;
 Now part us, if thou canst.   [*Dies.*]
        [IRAS *sinks down at her feet, and dies;* CHARMION
                stands behind her chair, as dressing her head.]
        [*Enter* SERAPION, *two* Priests, ALEXAS *bound,* EGYP-
                                                         TIANS.]

PRIEST.   Behold, Serapion,
 What havoc death has made!
SERAPION.   'Twas what I feared.—
 Charmion, is this well done?   500
CHARMION.   Yes, 'tis well done, and like a queen, the last
 Of her great race: I follow her.   [*Sinks down: dies.*]
ALEXAS.   'Tis true,
 She has done well: Much better thus to die,
 Than live to make a holiday in Rome.
SERAPION.   See how the lovers sit in state together,
 As they were giving laws to half mankind!
 The impression of a smile, left in her face,
 Shows she died pleased with him for whom she lived,
 And went to charm him in another world.
 Caesar's just entering: grief has now no leisure.   510
 Secure that villain, as our pledge of safety,
 To grace the imperial triumph.—Sleep, blest pair,
 Secure from human chance, long ages out,
 While all the storms of fate fly o'er your tomb;
  And fame to late posterity shall tell,
  No lovers lived so great, or died so well.   [*Exeunt.*]

Prologues
and
Epilogues

Commentary on the Prologues and Epilogues

Prologues and epilogues in verse were used on the English stage at least as early as Shakespeare's day—see, for example, the famous prologue to *Romeo and Juliet* (*ca.* 1590)—and lasted at least till the time of Samuel Johnson, whose prologue spoken at the opening of the Drury Lane Theatre, 1747, is one of his best short poems. They were not necessarily written by the author of the play they were attached to; Pope, for example, wrote the prologue to Addison's *Cato,* 1713. Nor were they necessarily related, in content, to the plot of the play; they became, in fact, an independent form of spoken poetry, existing in their own right.

Dryden was by far the most successful prologue-and-epilogue writer of his or any other period. The story goes that when in 1682 the young dramatist, Thomas Southerne, came to him to secure a prologue for his first play, *The Loyal Brother,* Dryden raised his usual price of four guineas to six, "which [said he], young man, not out of disrespect to you; but the players [actors] have had my goods too cheap." Six guineas (about $31.50) was no mean fee in a day when a playwright's total profits from the play itself might easily go as low as twenty pounds ($100), and were considered excellent if they ran as high as fifty pounds.

But good prologues and epilogues were good investments; if well written, they served to catch the attention and ensure the good will of the small, restive, homogeneous, witty, self-absorbed, and highly sophisticated London audience. If this audience could be argued, jollied, laughed, cajoled, or surprised into interest and attention, the play's success might be partly assured.

The result of such a situation was that a Restoration prologue or epilogue could easily—in fact, often did—turn out to be a more finished work of art than the play itself. It had to be composed in easy colloquial language, yet in flawless verse; to have an air of complete casualness, but an arresting content; to be perfectly clear on a first hearing, but never flat. Since many of Dryden's prologues and epilogues, about a third of which are included in this anthology, of course allude to very specific contemporary situations, a brief running commentary is supplied below.

P: Rival Ladies. Dryden contemns the contemporary rage for scenic or other incidental effects—elaborate costumes (*habits,* 11), tricks with lighting (14), witty prologues (!), and so forth—and the neglect of good writing in the play itself.

P: Secret Love. Corneille's (6): probably pronounced with three syllables (rimes with "jellies"). For a discussion of the doctrine of the unities, see the *Essay of Dramatic Poesy* below. *Salvage* (47): savage. *Throw, set, lay* (54–55): metaphors from gambling. *on tick* (58): on credit.

P: Wild Gallant Reviv'd. This, Dryden's first play, was, despite its initial failure, apparently revived in 1667. *Whetstone's Park* (8): street of brothels.

P: Sir Martin Mar-All. It is easy for the town to make a fop, for a single anecdote about a man will give him the reputation of being an ass: a poet [playwright], however, needs a dozen such anecdotes to create a single foppish character. The poet's method is to observe, in private life, the absurdities of those who now constitute his audience. *Regalios* (2): delightful pieces of cookery, only served on special occasions.

E: Sir Martin Mar-All. Lilly (13): a contemporary astrologer and almanac maker.

P: The Tempest. Next to Shakespeare himself, *Fletcher* and *Jonson* (6) were the two Elizabethan writers most admired, in Dryden's age, for tragedy and comedy, respectively. The prologue well indicates the shift in attitude toward the supernatural that had been taking place between the time James I wrote a treatise on witchcraft, and the time Charles II founded the Royal Society to promote scientific investigation: Dryden feels called on to apologize to his audience for *Shakespeare's magic* (19, 25–26). By his metaphor of the traditional enchanted ring, or *circle* (20), however, he pays a compliment to his predecessor's overwhelming genius; and concludes with a joke at the expense of the cast. Dryden's versatile manipulation of a single image is nowhere better displayed than in this poem.

E: *The Tempest.* Dryden suggests (5) the sources, in Spain and France, of the use of rime and elaborate melodramatic plots in many Restoration tragedies. *King Richard's vision* (9) occurs in the fifth act of Shakespeare's *Richard III.*

P: *Albumazar.* Dryden supposed, from internal resemblances, that this play of Thomas Tomkis's had influenced Jonson's *Alchemist;* but the dates (*Alchemist* 1610, *Albumazar* 1615) show that any influence must have been the other way around. The prologue goes on to castigate a kind of unwarranted influence, or "borrowing," attributed by Dryden to contemporary playwrights, who, like footpads (*padders,* 19), not only steal lines and phrases from living authors (24), but even have the temerity to defile dead ones (*mummies of the Muses,* 29), as Egyptian undertakers were said (by Herodotus) to rape corpses. *Subtle* (7): leading character in Jonson's *Alchemist. Stand . . . deliver* (22): "Stick 'em up!" *of the hand* (36): that is, pickpockets. *wink* (44): keep one's eyes shut.

E: *Tyrannic Love.* Mrs. (that is, Mistress) Ellen was Nell Gwyn, who at about this time became Charles II's mistress. The *bearers* are the stagehands. *Sprites* (7, 11) are spirits or ghosts; *taking* (13) means putting under a spell or an enchantment; and restless ghosts were traditionally supposed to *walk* (15), just as Nelly is now walking, having refused to be carried off on a stretcher. The *poet* (17), that is, playwright, is Dryden himself. Note that lines 25–26 (*make haste to me*) refer back to the location (*hell*), specified in line 10. *St. Catherine* (pronounced in colloquial speech to rime with *slattern*) was another name for the play itself (*Tyrannic Love*).

This epilogue, one of the poet's most piquant, is a variation on a theme of Sir Toby Belch's: "Dost thou think, that because thou art virtuous, there shall be no more cakes and ale?"

P: *Conquest of Granada, I.* The prologue is a satire on Shadwell and other playwrights who, according to Dryden, rely more heavily on costumes and properties for comic effects than on witty dialogue. Shadwell had recently written a comedy in which *Nokes* (7) and Angel—the *best comedians* of line (19)—appeared wearing waist-belts and other finery designed to poke fun at French styles; this play was put on by the rival theatrical company (*t' other house,* 1), the Duke's (Dryden's was the King's). *blocks* (20): probably "dummies on which to display hats," with a pun on the meaning "blockhead."

E: Conquest of Granada, II. Dryden accuses Jonson and his contemporaries of confusing low horseplay (*mechanic humor,* 3) with wit. Cobb, in one of Jonson's comedies, carried a tankard about on the stage; and Otter, in another, habitually referred to his pot of ale as his horse, or bull, or bear. Today, when critics *weigh* (13) the language of a comedy word by word, none of their plays could *pass* (16) present standards without at least some small concessions (*grains for weight,* 16).

P: The Assignation. As the prologue would indicate, *fop, coxcomb,* and *fool* meant about the same thing. *Mamamouchi* (30) was the title of a contemporary comedy by Ravenscroft, who introduced as Turkish the gibberish quoted by Dryden in lines 35–36; *marabarah salem* was supposed to mean, "ah, how much in love am I." *Mamamouchi,* though condemned by the critics, as Dryden indicates (39), was a success; *The Assignation* failed. Dryden's strictures on the taste of the typical audience seem to have been well based.

P: to Oxford at the Acting of The Silent Woman. Pallas (3): goddess of Athens and of wisdom, to whom the olive tree (5) was sacred. *Lycaeum* (14): Aristotle's school of philosophy at Athens. *empiric* (22): a rule-of-thumb practitioner. *science* (27): knowledge. *Lucretian* (32): Lucretius thought nature was created by the chance collisions of various atoms. *cits* (37): citizens (of London). *plaudit* (39): applause. *Praetorian bands* (40): soldiers who elected Roman emperors when the true power should have been exercised by the Senate (41). *wreath* (43): Dryden's own laureateship, granted by Charles II (45).

P: to Oxford, 1674. In the second couplet *following nature* means studying reality, as a scientist or philosopher might; and *wit,* besides its usual meaning, connotes also "works of the imagination" (such as plays). Thus the theater sets before scholars an image of *man, the little world* (or microcosm) just as, in Spenser's *Faerie*

Queene (iii·2·21) Merlin's *sphere of crystal* (a kind of miniature planetarium) had displayed *the great* world, the universe or macrocosm (13–14). The prologue, and the epilogue which follows it, are probably two of the most eloquent tributes to academic life on record.

E: to Oxford, 1674. The *I* of line 3 is Mrs. Marshall, the actress who spoke the prologue (compare *our sex*, 26). Ralph *Bathurst* (17), a distinguished president of Trinity College, Oxford, and a writer of Latin verse, was at this time Vice Chancellor of the University.

P: Aureng-Zebe. What Dryden means by calling *Aureng-Zebe* his most *correct* play (12) is indicated by the first ten lines of the epilogue, which follows the prologue in this anthology. Here, in the prologue, he gives his estimate of his own achievement in drama so far: he is the best playwright of his own age, but *hindmost of the last* (22)—that is, inferior to the great dramatists of Shakespeare's time. Writing has not supported him, for poetry (*wit*) can only flourish in England (*northern climates*) if it is partly financed by patronage (*housed from snow*); audiences alone will not support it (32–34). The two London theatrical companies (*We and our neighbors,* 37) are ruined by competition with each other; while the play-going public, as neutral as the *wise English* (39) were at the moment in respect to certain continental wars, watches unmoved the downfall of the theater (*the tragedy of wit,* 40).

Aureng-Zebe was Dryden's last heroic play; his next production (see lines 8–15) was *All for Love,* a version in blank verse of the story treated in Shakespeare's *Antony and Cleopatra.*

E: Aureng-Zebe. target (18): shield—the reference is to battles on the stage. *silk-weavers* (21): English silks were at this time in unsuccessful competition with French. *gens barbare* (25): barbarous race. The attitude to the French in this prologue is ambivalent: on the one hand, the *filthy* foreigners are supercilious fops, inferior in virility to the English; on the other hand, their standards of criticism with respect to public entertainment are so superior that they make the English seem uncivilized—or a mere nation of shopkeepers—by comparison.

P: to Oxford [1676?] The alternative *fop gallants* or *city folly* (11) compares the poor taste of the aristocratic with the poor taste of the commercial middle class elements in the London audience; Oxford provides a *nicer pit*—more discriminating theater-goers. The Thebes-Athens (that is, Cambridge-Oxford) contrast in the final couplet depends on the facts (*a*) that Athenians traditionally regarded Thebans as stupid; and (*b*) that Dryden was a Cambridge graduate. *made free of* (30): became full citizens of. *want* (2): lack.

P: *All for Love.* The story *as sad as Dido's* (9; Dido died for unrequited love of Aeneas) is of course that of Antony and Cleopatra, subject of one of Shakespeare's greatest tragedies. Dryden was well aware of the older poet's supremacy, to which he seems to refer in the *plenteous autumn* of line 37 (though some critics take this merely as an allusion to the season of the year when *All for Love* was produced). *keeping* (15): keeping mistresses. *Tonies:* short for *Antonies,* stupid fellows. *Hector* (22): braggart.

E: *All for love.* Mr. *Bayes* (17): a name under which Dryden had been satirized (see Chronological Table, 1671). *writ of ease:* (19): certificate of discharge from employment. *The last age* (24): the period of Shakespeare (d. 1616), with whose *Antony and Cleopatra* this play was certain to be compared.

E: *Mithridates. faithful lovers die* (1): Lee's *Mithridates,* published 1678, was a tragedy. *punk* (13): whore. *cullies* (20): "suckers." *sophisticated* (21): adulterated. *half-crown* (24): "a common harlot's price" (P: *The Mistakes,* 22).

P: *Oedipus.* This prologue combines vigorous classicism with offhand allusion to current events: both the battle of *Mons* (25), in which British troops took part against French, and the passage of the Woolen Act, requiring (to encourage the English wool trade) the use of wool in shrouds (36), occurred in the summer of 1678. On the other hand, *the first four councils* (28) of the early Christian church, which among Anglicans had equal authority with Scripture, took place in the third and fourth centuries. The metaphor of *private spirit* (30) and *fanatics* (31) alludes to the dissenting sects.

E: *to the King at Oxford, 1681.* This epilogue, which followed a performance of Charles Saunders' *Tamerlane the Great,* was presented under unusual circumstances. In the midst of the political furor over the question of excluding the Duke of York (later James II) from the throne (see above, introduction to *Absalom and Achitophel*), Charles II summoned Parliament to meet at Oxford so that he would be away from the excited London populace. *Tamer-*

lane was played before an audience which included the Parliament, the King, and two of the King's mistresses (Nell Gwyn and the Duchess of Portsmouth); and at a time when, it was widely feared, civil war would break out. Thus Dryden refers to the *civil rage* (19) of thirty years earlier. An *optic glass* (1) is a lens used to throw an inverted image of distant, external objects on a paper screen in a dark room.

P: *Don Sebastian.* The tragedy *Don Sebastian* (1689) was Dryden's first play after the Revolution of 1688 lost him his laureateship and pension (4) and subjected him to various anti-Catholic statutes, including one forbidding the ownership of a *horse,* or horses, assessed at five pounds or more (41, 44). *my lord* (1): title given judges in England (judgeship symbolizes laureateship). *cast* (3): loser in a lawsuit. *alike* (15): impartial (toward the warring Italians and Trojans during Aeneas' conquest of Italy). *mighty monarch* (22): Louis XIV, unpopular in England for his Catholicism, his support of the Stuarts, and his power; Dryden implies that French *wines* are popular, however. *poet* (24): playwright (Dryden). *this noddle* (25): that is, the actress speaking the prologue.

P: *The Prophetess.* This prologue was suppressed after its first performance, and printed copies of it so effectively confiscated that only two of the first edition are known to exist. The reason seems to have been that national events taken seriously by the government are here treated with facetious wit, and that the prologue contains phrases that could be taken as subversive of William III's recently established monarchy.

In the spring of 1690, when Fletcher's *Prophetess,* with additions to the text by Betterton and music by Purcell, was revived as an opera in London, William was about to embark on a summer campaign in Ireland (*Bogland,* 31—*Teague,* 27, was a slang term for Irishman), and was to leave Queen Mary in charge of the kingdom as Regent (compare 51). Under these circumstances it seems clear that the prologue's first twelve lines, ostensibly a commentary on the heavy expense and uncertain profit of producing an opera, could also be taken as covert criticism of the expense to the nation of the approaching military expedition—especially since the *hopes of better days* (8) looks like a clear dig at William III's newly established monarchy, and since the next few lines (13–20) apparently allude in metaphor to the many changes in the English government, kingship, and constitution during this period, including James II's ouster two years earlier.

The campaign itself is described as an undignified expedition against an unworthy enemy, and likely to result only in the *rich spoils* of butter, whiskey (*usquebaugh,* 28), and perhaps a few Irish slaves with copper collars to replace the silver-collared Negro slaves then in vogue in London. Such dubious *honor* (21) is to be achieved by *doughty knights* (40) whose normal occupations are ogling, chatting, obscene repartee (*selling bargains,* 46), and *dumfounding* (57), which meant tapping someone heavily on the shoulder in such a way as to make him uncertain who did it.

Such a national event will be worthily celebrated in poetry by *pious Muses* (35); no doubt the line *We want not poets fit to sing your fights* (38), taken in connection with the mention of laurel two lines earlier, is an ironic reference to the modest literary talents of Shadwell (see *Mac Flecknoe,* above), now poet laureate of England. Indeed, according to one (poorly authenticated) tradition, it was Shadwell who drew the attention of the authorities to this excellent prologue, and caused its further performance to be prevented.

The following explanations may be helpful.

Nostradame (1): French sixteenth-century astrologer. *prospective set right* (3): telescope used correctly, so as to magnify distant objects—when the *tube* is *turned* (5) it diminishes them. *Bilbo* (22): sword noted for temper and elasticity. *proper* (32): handsome.

P: Amphitryon. Julian (17): notorious libeler of the period. *second jig* (20): apparently a small top fitted inside a larger one, so that when the larger was spun, the smaller would pop out and spin. *after yours* (32): God made Adam first, then Eve. *Hence, ye profane* (37): the words of the underworld goddess Hecate when she appears to Aeneas in the sacred grove (*Aeneid* vi, 258).

E: Amphitryon. The legend of Amphitryon, which concerns one of Jove's numerous adulteries, remains today a popular plot for plays. This epilogue undoubtedly has political overtones; Dryden's attitude toward Restoration court morals (Charles II, with his several mistresses and illegitimate children, is an obvious parallel to Jove) was ambivalent: compare, for example, the opening lines of *Absalom and Achitophel* to the fourth stanza of "Anne Killigrew." This epilogue, written in 1690, five years after Charles's death and two after the accession of the Protestant William III, regrets the passing of the Merry Monarch who treated his mistresses generously despite the limitations of his exchequer (9–10), and who loaded his illegitimate sons (for example, Monmouth) with many honors. Despite the fact that he was an idolator (3), and was worshiped falsely (25), the epilogue looks forward to a future Merry Monarchy (29–32)—possibly to a Jacobite restoration. *Severity of life* (26): Puritanism; the dissenting sects all supported William. *cuckolds* (17): husbands of unfaithful wives. *star* (20): emblem of a court honor.

Phaedra, the character who delivers the Epilogue, is a witty and mercenary maid-servant wooed by Mercury, god of thieves, while her mistress, Alcmena, is seduced by Jupiter in Amphitryon's form and conceives Hercules.

P: The Mistakes. Mr. Williams, the speaker of the prologue, was in real life something of a toper. *Cork* (10): besieged by Marlborough in 1690. *squibs* (16): firecrackers. *pelf* (17): cash. *Peace and the butt* (35): phrase Dryden and Davenant's *Tempest* had made proverbial (*butt:* wine cask).

E: King Arthur. The *cits* (2) are the London commercial citizens, whose proverbial stinginess (19, 33, 35), dislike of the aristocracy (*beaux,* 34), and propensity to be easily deceived husbands (29) are alluded to. *Bow Street* (2): fashionable residential street. *Whitehall* (3): palace of King; government center. *Temple* (3): district known for lawyers and law students. *Bridges Street* (17): in commercial district (?). *my sign* (31): her face would be painted on the sign outside his shop. Mrs. (that is, Mistress) Bracegirdle was perhaps the most famous, and most attractive, actress of the period.

E: Cleomenes. *die* (4,6): See Commentary on the Songs, pg. 83. *misses* (18): mistresses. *Fuller* (22): he claimed to have knowledge of a subversive Jacobite plot, but was unable to produce evidence; was proclaimed impostor, cheat, and false accuser by The House of Commons early in 1692, the year *Cleomenes* was acted. *person* (27): body. *half a crown* (36): price of admission to pit.

E: Henry II. The famous actress, Mrs. Bracegirdle, who spoke this prologue, had acted *Rosamond* (5), who dies after being given poison (34) by *Queen Eleanor* (3). *Haynes* (20) became a Catholic during the reign of the Catholic James II, but a Protestant again after the accession of the Protestant William II; *Mother Church* evidently means the Church of England. *Chapels of ease* (22) were placed in outlying districts for the convenience of parishioners who could not get to a church. *chaffer* (24): bargain.

    E: The Husband His Own Cuckold. Dryden's son John, Jr., author of this play, had probably been living in Italy for four years (see the concluding couplet) when it was published in 1696. *third day* (13): on this day any profits went to the author. *induction* (13): formal possession of a church. *clipp'd money* (32): coins were sometimes illegally clipped around the edge for the silver. *immortal species never dies* (36): a Virgilian phrase (*Georgics* iv, 208).

PROLOGUE

THE RIVAL LADIES

'T is much desir'd, you judges of the town
Would pass a vote to put all prologues down:
For who can show me, since they first were writ,
They e'er converted one hard-hearted wit?
Yet the world 's mended well: in former days
Good prologues were as scarce as now good plays.
For the reforming poets of our age,
In this first charge, spend their poetic rage:
Expect no more when once the prologue's done;
The wit is ended ere the play 's begun.   10
You now have habits, dances, scenes, and rhymes;
High language often; aye, and sense, sometimes.
As for a clear contrivance, doubt it not;
They blow out candles to give light to th' plot.
And for surprise, two bloody-minded men
Fight till they die, then rise and dance again.
Such deep intrigues you 're welcome to this day:
But blame yourselves, not him who writ the play;
Tho' his plot 's dull, as can be well desir'd,
Wit stiff as any you have e'er admir'd: 20
He 's bound to please, not to write well; and knows

There is a mode in plays as well as clothes;
Therefore, kind judges—

[A second PROLOGUE enters.]

   2.   Hold; would you admit
For judges all you see within the pit?
   1. Whom would he then except, or on what score?
   2. All who (like him) have writ ill plays before;
For they, like thieves condemn'd, are hangmen made,
To execute the members of their trade.
All that are writing now he would disown,   30
But then he must except—ev'n all the town;
All chol'ric, losing gamesters, who, in spite,
Will damn to-day, because they lost last night;
All servants, whom their mistress' scorn upbraids;
All maudlin lovers, and all slighted maids;
All who are out of humor, or severe;
All that want wit, or hope to find it here.

PROLOGUE TO

SECRET LOVE
Or, the Maiden Queen

I
He who writ this, not without pains and thought
From French and English theaters has brought
Th' exactest rules by which a play is wrought:

II
The unities of action, place, and time;
The scenes unbroken; and a mingled chime
Of Jonson's humor with Corneille's rhyme.

III
But while dead colors he with care did lay,
He fears his wit or plot he did not weigh,
Which are the living beauties of a play.

IV

Plays are like towns, which, howe'er fortified   10
By engineers, have still some weaker side
By the o'er-seen defendant unespied.

V

And with that art you make approaches now;
Such skilful fury in assaults you show,
That every poet without shame may bow.

VI

Ours therefore humbly would attend your doom,
If, soldier-like, he may have terms to come
With flying colors and with beat of drum.

> [*The* PROLOGUE *goes out, and stays while a tune is play'd,*
> *after which he returns again.*

SECOND PROLOGUE

I had forgot one half, I do protest,
And now am sent again to speak the rest.   20
He bows to every great and noble wit;
But to the little Hectors of the pit
Our poet's sturdy, and will not submit.
He 'll be beforehand with 'em, and not stay
To see each peevish critic stab his play:
Each puny censor, who, his skill to boast,
Is cheaply witty on the poet's cost.
No critic's verdict should of right stand good;
They are excepted all, as men of blood;
And the same law should shield him from their fury   30
Which has excluded butchers from a jury.
You 'd all be wits—
But writing 's tedious, and that way may fail;
The most compendious method is to rail;
Which you so like, you think yourselves ill us'd
When in smart prologues you are not abus'd.
A civil prologue is approv'd by no man;
You hate it as you do a civil woman:

Your fancy 's pall'd, and liberally you pay
To have it quicken'd, ere you see a play;   40
Just as old sinners, worn from their delight,
Give money to be whipp'd to appetite.
But what a pox keep I so much ado
To save our poet? He is one of you;
A brother judgment, and, as I hear say,
A cursed critic as e'er damn'd a play.
Good salvage gentlemen, your own kind spare;
He is, like you, a very wolf or bear.
Yet think not he 'll your ancient rights invade,
Or stop the course of your free damning trade;   50
For he, he vows, at no friend's play can sit,
But he must needs find fault to shew his wit.
Then, for his sake, ne'er stint your own delight;
Throw boldly, for he sets to all that write:
With such he ventures on an even lay,
For they bring ready money into play.
Those who write not, and yet all writers nick,
Are bankrupt gamesters, for they damn on tick.

PROLOGUE TO

THE WILD GALLANT,
Reviv'd

As some raw squire, by tender mother bred,
Till one and twenty keeps his maidenhead,
(Pleas'd with some sport, which he alone does find,
And thinks a secret to all humankind,)
Till mightily in love, yet half afraid,
He first attempts the gentle dairymaid.
Succeeding there, and led by the renown
Of Whetstone's Park, he comes at length to town,
Where enter'd, by some school-fellow or friend,
He grows to break glass windows in the end: 10

His valor too, which with the watch began,
Proceeds to duel, and he kills his man.
By such degrees, while knowledge he did want,
Our unfletch'd author writ a *Wild Gallant*.
He thought him monstrous lewd (I'll lay my life)
Because suspected with his landlord's wife;
But, since his knowledge of the town began,
He thinks him now a very civil man;
And, much asham'd of what he was before,
Has fairly play'd him at three wenches more.   20
'T is some amends his frailties to confess:
Pray pardon him his want of wickedness.
He 's towardly, and will come on apace;
His frank confession shows he has some grace.
You balk'd him when he was a young beginner,
And almost spoil'd a very hopeful sinner;
But, if once more you slight his weak indeavor,
For aught I know, he may turn tail for ever.

PROLOGUE AND EPILOGUE TO

SIR MARTIN MAR-ALL
Or, the Feign'd Innocence

PROLOGUE

Fools, which each man meets in his dish each day,
Are yet the great regalios of a play;
In which to poets you but just appear,
To prize that highest which cost them so dear.
Fops in the town more easily will pass;
One story makes a statutable ass:
But such in plays must be much thicker sown,
Like yolks of eggs, a dozen beat to one.
Observing poets all their walks invade,
As men watch woodcocks gliding thro' a glade;   10
And when they have enough for comedy,

They stow their several bodies in a pie:
The poet's but the cook to fashion it,
For, gallants, you yourselves have found the wit.
To bid you welcome would your bounty wrong;
None welcome those who bring their cheer along.

EPILOGUE

As country vicars, when the sermon 's done,
Run huddling to the benediction;
Well knowing, tho' the better sort may stay,
The vulgar rout will run unblest away:
So we, when once our play is done, make haste
With a short epilogue to close your taste.
In thus withdrawing we seem mannerly,
But when the curtain 's down we peep and see
A jury of the wits who still stay late,
And in their club decree the poor play's fate: 10
Their verdict back is to the boxes brought;
Thence all the town pronounces it their thought.
Thus, gallants, we like Lilly can foresee;
But if you ask us what our doom will be,
We by to-morrow will our fortune cast,
As he tells all things when the year is past.

PROLOGUE AND EPILOGUE TO

THE TEMPEST
Or, the Enchanted Island

PROLOGUE

As, when a tree's cut down, the secret root
Lives under ground, and thence new branches shoot;
So from old Shakespeare's honor'd dust, this day
Springs up and buds a new reviving play:

Shakespeare, who (taught by none) did first impart
To Fletcher wit, to laboring Jonson art.
He, monarch-like, gave those, his subjects, law;
And is that nature which they paint and draw.
Fletcher reach'd that which on his heights did grow,
Whilst Jonson crept, and gather'd all below.   10
This did his love, and this his mirth digest:
One imitates him most, the other best.
If they have since outwrit all other men,
'T is with the drops which fell from Shakespeare's pen.
The storm which vanish'd on the neighb'ring shore,
Was taught by Shakespeare's *Tempest* first to roar.
That innocence and beauty which did smile
In Fletcher, grew on this *Enchanted Isle.*
But Shakespeare's magic could not copied be;
Within that circle none durst walk but he.   20
I must confess 't was bold, nor would you now
That liberty to vulgar wits allow,
Which works by magic supernatural things;
But Shakespeare's pow'r is sacred as a king's.
Those legends from old priesthood were receiv'd,
And he then writ, as people then believ'd.
But if for Shakespeare we your grace implore,
We for our theater shall want it more:
Who by our dearth of youths are forc'd t' employ
One of our women to present a boy;   30
And that 's a transformation, you will say,
Exceeding all the magic in the play.
Let none expect in the last act to find
Her sex transform'd from man to womankind.
Whate'er she was before the play began,
All you shall see of her is perfect man.
Or if your fancy will be farther led
To find her woman, it must be abed.

EPILOGUE

Gallants, by all good signs it does appear
That sixty-seven 's a very damning year,
For knaves abroad, and for ill poets here.

Among the Muses there 's a gen'ral rot:
The rhyming Mounsieur and the Spanish plot,
Defy or court, all 's one, they go to pot.

The ghosts of poets walk within this place,
And haunt us actors wheresoe'er we pass,
In visions bloodier than King Richard's was.

For this poor wretch he has not much to say,   10
But quietly brings in his part o' th' play,
And begs the favor to be damn'd to-day.

He sends me only like a sh'riff's man here,
To let you know the malefactor 's near,
And that he means to die *en cavalier*.

For if you should be gracious to his pen,
Th' example will prove ill to other men,
And you 'll be troubled with 'em all again.

PROLOGUE TO

ALBUMAZAR
Reviv'd

To say, this comedy pleas'd long ago,
Is not enough to make it pass you now.
Yet, gentlemen, your ancestors had wit;
When few men censur'd, and when fewer writ.
And Jonson, of those few the best, chose this,
As the best model of his masterpiece.
Subtle was got by our Albumazar,
That Alchymist by his Astrologer;
Here he was fashion'd, and we may suppose
He lik'd the fashion well, who wore the clothes.   10
But Ben made nobly his what he did mold;
What was another's lead becomes his gold:
Like an unrighteous conqueror he reigns,

Yet rules that well, which he unjustly gains.
But this our age such authors does afford,
As make whole plays, and yet scarce write one word;
Who, in this anarchy of wit, rob all,
And what 's their plunder, their possession call;
Who, like bold padders, scorn by night to prey,
But rob by sunshine, in the face of day: 20
Nay, scarce the common ceremony use
Of: "Stand, sir, and deliver up your Muse;"
But knock the poet down, and, with a grace,
Mount Pegasus before the owner's face.
Faith, if you have such country Toms abroad,
'T is time for all true men to leave that road.
Yet it were modest, could it but be said,
They strip the living, but these rob the dead;
Dare with the mummies of the Muses play,
And make love to them the Egyptian way;   30
Or, as a rhyming author would have said,
Join the dead living to the living dead.
Such men in poetry may claim some part:
They have the license, tho' they want the art;
And might, where theft was prais'd, for Laureats stand,
Poets, not of the head, but of the hand.
They make the benefits of others' studying,
Much like the meals of politic Jack-Pudding,
Whose dish to challenge no man has the courage;
'T is all his own, when once h' has spit i' th' porridge.   40
But, gentlemen, you 're all concern'd in this;
You are in fault for what they do amiss:
For they their thefts still undiscover'd think,
And durst not steal, unless you please to wink.
Perhaps, you may award by your decree,
They should refund; but that can never be.
For should you letters of reprisal seal,
These men write that which no man else would steal.

EPILOGUE TO

TYRANNIC LOVE

Spoken by MRS. ELLEN, when she was to be carried off by the bearers

[*To the Bearer.*]

Hold, are you mad? you damn'd confounded dog,
I am to rise, and speak the epilogue.

[*To the Audience.*]

I come, kind gentlemen, strange news to tell ye,
I am the ghost of poor departed Nelly.
Sweet ladies, be not frighted, I 'll be civil;
I'm what I was, a little harmless devil:
For after death, we sprites have just such natures
We had for all the world, when human creatures;
And therefore, I that was an actress here,
Play all my tricks in hell, a goblin there.   10
Gallants, look to 't, you say there are no sprites;
But I'll come dance about your beds at nights.
And faith you 'll be in a sweet kind of taking,
When I surprise you between sleep and waking.
To tell you true, I walk because I die
Out of my calling in a tragedy.
O poet, damn'd dull poet, who could prove
So senseless! to make Nelly die for love!
Nay, what 's yet worse, to kill me in the prime
Of Easter term, in tart and cheese-cake time!   20
I 'll fit the fop, for I 'll not one word say
T' excuse his godly out-of-fashion play:
A play, which if you dare but twice sit out,
You 'll all be slander'd, and be thought devout.
But farewell, gentlemen, make haste to me;
I 'm sure ere long to have your company.
As for my epitaph, when I am gone,
I 'll trust no poet, but will write my own:

Here Nelly lies, who, tho' she liv'd a slattern,
Yet died a princess, acting in St. Cathar'n.
Yet died a princess, acting in St. Cathar'n.   30

PROLOGUE TO

THE CONQUEST OF GRANADA
BY THE SPANIARDS, I

PROLOGUE TO THE FIRST PART,

Spoken by MRS. ELLEN GWYN *in a*
broad-brimm'd hat, and waist-belt

This jest was first of t'other house's making,
And, five times tried, has never fail'd of taking;
For 't were a shame a poet should be kill'd
Under the shelter of so broad a shield.
This is that hat, whose very sight did win ye
To laugh and clap as tho' the devil were in ye.
As then, for Nokes, so now I hope you 'll be
So dull, to laugh, once more, for love of me.
"I 'll write a play," says one, "for I have got
A broad-brimm'd hat, and waist-belt, tow'rds a plot."   10
Says t'other: "I have one more large than that."
Thus they out-write each other with a hat!
The brims still grew with every play they writ;
And grew so large, they cover'd all the wit.
Hat was the play; 't was language, wit, and tale:
Like them that find meat, drink, and cloth in ale.
What dulness do these mungril wits confess,
When all their hope is acting of a dress!
Thus, two the best comedians of the age
Must be worn out, with being blocks o' th' stage;
Like a young girl who better things has known,
Beneath their poet's impotence they groan.

See now what charity it was to save!
They thought you lik'd, what only you forgave;
And brought you more dull sense, dull sense much worse
Than brisk gay nonsense, and the heavier curse.
They bring old ir'n and glass upon the stage,
To barter with the Indians of our age.
Still they write on, and like great authors show;
But 't is as rollers in wet garden grow   30
Heavy with dirt, and gath'ring as they go.
May none, who have so little understood,
To like such trash, presume to praise what 's good!
And may those drudges of the stage, whose fate
Is damn'd dull farce more dully to translate,
Fall under that excise the State thinks fit
To set on all French wares, whose worst is wit.
French farce, worn out at home, is sent abroad;
And, patch'd up here, is made our English mode.
Henceforth, let poets, ere allow'd to write,   40
Be search'd, like duelists, before they fight,
For wheel-broad hats, dull humor, all that chaff
Which makes you mourn, and makes the vulgar laugh:
For these, in plays, are as unlawful arms,
As, in a combat, coats of mail and charms.

EPILOGUE TO

THE CONQUEST OF GRANADA, II

They who have best succeeded on the stage
Have still conform'd their genius to their age.
Thus Jonson did mechanic humor show,
When men were dull, and conversation low.
Then comedy was faultless, but 't was coarse:
Cob's tankard was a jest, and Otter's horse.
And, as their comedy, their love was mean;
Except, by chance, in some one labor'd scene

Which must atone for an ill-written play.
They rose, but at their height could seldom stay.   *10*
Fame then was cheap, and the first comer sped;
And they have kept it since, by being dead.
But, were they now to write, when critics weigh
Each line, and ev'ry word, throughout a play,
None of 'em, no, not Jonson in his height,
Could pass, without allowing grains for weight.
Think it not envy, that these truth are told;
Our poet 's not malicious, tho' he 's bold.
'T is not to brand 'em, that their faults are shown,
But, by their errors, to excuse his own.   *20*
If love and honor now are higher rais'd,
'T is not the poet, but the age is prais'd.
Wit 's now arriv'd to a more high degree;
Our native language more refin'd and free.
Our ladies and our men now speak more wit
In conversation, than those poets writ.
Then, one of these is, consequently, true;
That what this poet writes come short of you,
And imitates you ill, (which most he fears,)
Or else his writing is not worse than theirs.   *· 30*
Yet, tho' you judge (as sure the critics will)
That some before him writ with greater skill,
In this one praise he has their fame surpass'd,
To please an age more gallant than the last.

PROLOGUE TO

THE ASSIGNATION
Or, Love in a Nunnery

Prologues, like bells to churches, toll you in
With chiming verse, till the dull plays begin:
With this sad difference, tho', of pit and pew,
You damn the poet, but the priest damns you.
But priests can treat you at your own expense,

And gravely call you fools, without offense.
Poets, poor devils, have ne'er your folly shown,
But, to their cost, you prov'd it was their own;
For, when a fop 's presented on the stage,
Straight all the coxcombs in the town ingage: 10
For his deliverance and revenge they join,
And grunt, like hogs, about their captive swine.
Your poets daily split upon this shelf:
You must have fools, yet none will have himself;
Or, if in kindness you that leave would give,
No man could write you at that rate you live;
For some of you grow fops with so much haste,
Riot in nonsense, and commit such waste,
'T would ruin poets should they spend so fast.
He who made this, observ'd what farces hit,   20
And durst not disoblige you now with wit.
But, gentlemen, you overdo the mode;
You must have fools out of the common road.
Th' unnatural strain'd buffoon is only taking;
No fop can please you now of God's own making.
Pardon our poet, if he speaks his mind;
You come to plays with your own follies lin'd:
Small fools fall on you, like small showers, in vain;
Your own oil'd coats keep out all common rain.
You must have Mamamouchi, such a fop   30
As would appear a monster in a shop:
He 'll fill your pit and boxes to the brim,
Where, ramm'd in crowds, you see yourselves in him.
Sure there 's some spell our poet never knew,
In *hullababilah da,* and *chu, chu, chu.*
But *marabarah sahem* most did touch you;
That is: "O how we love the Mamamouchi!"
Grimace and habit sent you pleas'd away:
You damn'd the poet, and cried up the play.
     This thought had made our author more uneasy,   40
But that he hopes I 'm fool enough to please ye.
But here 's my grief: tho' nature, join'd with art,
Have cut me out to act a fooling part,
Yet, to your praise, the few wits here will say,
'T was imitating you taught Haynes to play.

PROLOGUE TO

THE UNIVERSITY OF OXFORD
Spoken by MR. HART, *at the acting*
of the silent woman

What Greece, when learning flourish'd, only knew,
Athenian judges, you this day renew.
Here too are annual rites to Pallas done,
And here poetic prizes lost or won.
Methinks I see you, crown'd with olives, sit,
And strike a sacred horror from the pit.
A day of doom is this of your decree,
Where even the best are but by mercy free:
A day, which none but Jonson durst have wish'd to see.
Here they, who long have known the useful stage,   10
Come to be taught themselves to teach the age.
As your commissioners our poets go,
To cultivate the virtue which you sow;
In your Lycaeum first themselves refin'd,
And delegated thence to humankind.
But as embassadors, when long from home,
For new instructions to their princes come;
So poets, who your precepts have forgot,
Return, and beg they may be better taught:
Follies and faults elsewhere by them are shown,   20
But by your manners they correct their own.
Th' illiterate writer, empiric-like, applies
To minds diseas'd, unsafe, chance remedies:
The learn'd in schools, where knowledge first began,
Studies with care th' anatomy of man;
Sees virtue, vice, and passions in their cause,
And fame from science, not from fortune, draws.
So poetry, which is in Oxford made
An art, in London only is a trade.
There haughty dunces, whose unlearned pen   30
Could ne'er spell grammar, would be reading men.
Such build their poems the Lucretian way;

So many huddled atoms make a play;
And if they hit in order by some chance,
They call that nature, which is ignorance.
To such a fame let mere town-wits aspire,
And their gay nonsense their own cits admire.
Our poet, could he find forgiveness here,
Would wish it rather than a *plaudit* there.
He owns no crown from those Praetorian bands,   40
But knows *that* right is in this senate's hands.
Not impudent enough to hope your praise,
Low at the Muses' feet his wreath he lays,
And, where he took it up, resigns his bays.
Kings make their poets whom themselves think fit,
But 't is your suffrage makes authentic wit.

PROLOGUE AND EPILOGUE TO

THE UNIVERSITY OF OXFORD, 1674

PROLOGUE

Spoken by MR. HART

Poets, your subjects, have their parts assign'd
T' unbend, and to divert their sovereign's mind:
When tir'd with following nature, you think fit
To seek repose in the cool shades of wit,
And, from the sweet retreat, with joy survey
What rests, and what is conquer'd, of the way.
Here, free yourselves from envy, care, and strife,
You view the various turns of human life:
Safe in our scene, thro' dangerous courts you go,
And, undebauch'd, the vice of cities know.   10
Your theories are here to practice brought,
As in mechanic operations wrought;
And man, the little world, before you set,

As once the sphere of crystal shew'd the great.
Blest sure are you above all mortal kind,
If to your fortunes you can suit your mind:
Content to see, and shun, those ills we show,
And crimes on theaters alone to know,
With joy we bring what our dead authors writ,
And beg from you the value of their wit: 20
That Shakespeare's, Fletcher's, and great Jonson's claim
May be renew'd from those who gave them fame.
None of our living poets dare appear;
For Muses so severe are worshipp'd here,
That, conscious of their faults, they shun the eye,
And, as profane, from sacred places fly,
Rather than see th' offended God, and die.
We bring no imperfections but our own;
Such faults as made are by the makers shown:
And you have been so kind, that we may boast,
The greatest judges still can pardon most.
Poets must stoop, when they would please our pit,
Debas'd even to the level of their wit;
Disdaining that which yet they know will take,
Hating themselves what their applause must make.
But when to praise from you they would aspire,
Tho' they like eagles mount, your Jove is higher.
So far your knowledge all their pow'r transcends
As what *should* be, beyond what *is,* extends.

EPILOGUE

Spoken by MRS. MARSHALL

Oft has our poet wish'd, this happy seat
Might prove his fading Muse's last retreat:
I wonder'd at his wish, but now I find
He here sought quiet, and content of mind;
Which noiseful towns and courts can never know,
And only in the shades like laurels grow.
Youth, ere it sees the world, here studies rest,
And age returning thence concludes it best.

What wonder if we court that happiness
Yearly to share, which hourly you possess,   10
Teaching ev'n you, while the vex'd world we show,
Your peace to value more, and better know?
'T is all we can return for favors past,
Whose holy memory shall ever last,
For patronage from him whose care presides
O'er every noble art, and every science guides:
Bathurst, a name the learn'd with rev'rence know,
And scarcely more to his own Virgil owe;
Whose age enjoys but what his youth deserv'd,
To rule those Muses whom before he serv'd.   20
His learning, and untainted manners too,
We find, Athenians, are deriv'd to you:
Such ancient hospitality there rests
In yours, as dwelt in the first Grecian breasts,
Where kindness was religion to their guests.
Such modesty did to our sex appear,
As, had there been no laws, we need not fear,
Since each of you was our protector here.
Converse so chaste, and so strict virtue shown,
As might Apollo with the Muses own.   30
Till our return, we must despair to find
Judges so just, so knowing, and so kind.

PROLOGUE AND EPILOGUE TO

AURENG-ZEBE

PROLOGUE

Our author, by experience, finds it true,
'T is much more hard to please himself than you;
And out of no feign'd modesty, this day
Damns his laborious trifle of a play:
Not that it 's worse than what before he writ,
But he has now another taste of wit;

And, to confess a truth, (tho' out of time,)
Grows weary of his long-lov'd mistress, Rhyme.
Passion 's too fierce to be in fetters bound,
And nature flies him like enchanted ground.   10
What verse can do, he has perform'd in this,
Which he presumes the most correct of his;
But spite of all his pride, a secret shame
Invades his breast at Shakespeare's sacred name:
Aw'd when he hears his godlike Romans rage,
He, in a just despair, would quit the stage;
And to an age less polish'd, more unskill'd,
Does, with disdain, the foremost honors yield.
As with the greater dead he dares not strive,
He would not match his verse with those who live: 20
Let him retire, betwixt two ages cast,
The first of this, and hindmost of the last.
A losing gamester, let him sneak away;
He bears no ready money from the play.
The fate which governs poets thought it fit
He should not raise his fortunes by his wit.
The clergy thrive, and the litigious bar;
Dull heroes fatten with the spoils of war:
All southern vices, Heav'n be prais'd, are here;
But wit 's a luxury you think too dear.   30
When you to cultivate the plant are loth,
'T is a shrewd sign 't was never of your growth;
And wit in northern climates will not blow,
Except, like orange trees, 't is hous'd from snow.
There needs no care to put a playhouse down,
'T is the most desart place of all the town:
We and our neighbors, to speak proudly, are,
Like monarchs, ruin'd with expensive war;
While, like wise English, unconcern'd you sit,
And see us play the tragedy of wit.   40

EPILOGUE

A pretty task! and so I told the fool,
Who needs would undertake to please by rule:
He thought that, if his characters were good,

The scenes entire, and freed from noise and blood,
The action great, yet circumscrib'd by time,
The words not forc'd, but sliding into rhyme,
The passions rais'd and calm'd by just degrees,
As tides are swell'd, and then retire to seas;
He thought, in hitting these, his bus'ness done,
Tho' he, perhaps, has fail'd in ev'ry one;   10
But, after all, a poet must confess,
His art's like physic, but a happy guess.
Your pleasure on your fancy must depend:
The lady 's pleas'd, just as she likes her friend.
No song! no dance! no show! he fears you 'll say
You love all naked beauties but a play.
He much mistakes your methods to delight,
And, like the French, abhors our target fight,
But those damn'd dogs can never be i' th' right.
True English hate your Monsieurs' paltry arts,   20
For you are all silk-weavers in your hearts.
Bold Britons, at a brave Bear Garden fray,
Are rous'd; and, clatt'ring sticks, cry: "Play, play, play!"
Meantime, your filthy foreigner will stare
And mutter to himself: "*Ha, gens barbare!*"
And, gad, 't is well he mutters; well for him;
Our butchers else would tear him limb from limb.
'T is true, the time may come, your sons may be
Infected with this French civility;
But this in after-ages will be done: 30
Our poet writes a hundred years too soon.
This age comes on too slow, or he too fast;
And early springs are subject to a blast!
Who would excel, when few can make a test
Betwixt indiff'rent writing and the best?
For favors cheap and common who would strive,
Which, like abandon'd prostitutes, you give?
Yet scatter'd here and there I some behold
Who can discern the tinsel from the gold:
To these he writes; and, if by them allow'd,   40
'T is their prerogative to rule the crowd.
For he more fears, like a presuming man,
Their votes who cannot judge, than theirs who can.

PROLOGUE TO

THE UNIVERSITY OF OXFORD [1676?]

Tho' actors cannot much of learning boast,
Of all who want it, we admire it most:
We love the praises of a learned pit,
As we remotely are allied to wit.
We speak our poet's wit, and trade in ore,
Like those who touch upon the golden shore:
Betwixt our judges can distinction make,
Discern how much, and why, our poems take:
Mark if the fools, or men of sense, rejoice;
Whether th' applause be only sound or voice.   10
When our fop gallants, or our city folly
Clap over-loud, it makes us melancholy;
We doubt that scene which does their wonder raise,
And, for their ignorance, contemn their praise.
Judge then, if we who act, and they who write,
Should not be proud of giving you delight.
London likes grossly; but this nicer pit
Examines, fathoms all the depths of wit;
The ready finger lays on every blot;
Knows what should justly please, and what should not.   20
Nature herself lies open to your view;
You judge by her, what draught of her is true,
Where outlines false, and colors seem too faint,
Where bunglers daub, and where true poets paint.
But, by the sacred genius of this place,
By every Muse, by each domestic grace,
Be kind to wit, which but endeavors well,
And, where you judge, presumes not to excel.
Our poets hither for adoption come,
As nations sued to be made free of Rome: 30
Not in the suffragating tribes to stand,
But in your utmost, last, provincial band.
If his ambition may those hopes pursue,
Who with religion loves your arts and you,

Oxford to him a dearer name shall be,
Than his own mother-university.
Thebes did his green, unknowing youth ingage;
He chooses Athens in his riper age.

PROLOGUE AND EPILOGUE TO

ALL FOR LOVE
Or, the World Well Lost

PROLOGUE

What flocks of critics hover here to-day,
As vultures wait on armies for their prey,
All gaping for the carcass of a play!
With croaking notes they bode some dire event,
And follow dying poets by the scent.
Ours gives himself for gone; y' have watch'd your time!
He fights this day unarm'd,—without his rhyme;—
And brings a tale which often has been told;
As sad as Dido's; and almost as old.
His hero, whom you wits his bully call,   10
Bates of his mettle, and scarce rants at all:
He 's somewhat lewd, but a well-meaning mind;
Weeps much, fights little, but is wondrous kind.
In short, a pattern, and companion fit,
For all the keeping Tonies of the pit.
I could name more: a wife, and mistress too;
Both (to be plain) too good for most of you:
The wife well-natur'd, and the mistress true.
  Now, poets, if your fame has been his care,
Allow him all the candor you can spare.   20
A brave man scorns to quarrel once a day;
Like Hectors, in at every petty fray.
Let those find fault whose wit 's so very small,
They 've need to show that they can think at all;
Errors, like straws, upon the surface flow;

He who would search for pearls must dive below.
Fops may have leave to level all they can,
As pigmies would be glad to lop a man.
Half-wits are fleas; so little and so light.
We scarce could know they live, but that they bite.
But, as the rich, when tir'd with daily feasts,
For change, become their next poor tenant's guests,
Drink hearty draughts of ale from plain brown bowls,
And snatch the homely rasher from the coals;
So you, retiring from much better cheer,
For once, may venture to do penance here.
And since that plenteous autumn now is past,
Whose grapes and peaches have indulg'd your taste,
Take in good part, from our poor poet's board,
Such rivel'd fruits as winter can afford.   40

EPILOGUE

Poets, like disputants, when reasons fail,
Have one sure refuge left—and that's to rail.
Fop, coxcomb, fool, are thunder'd thro' the pit,
And this is all their equipage of wit.
We wonder how the devil this diff'rence grows,
Betwixt our fools in verse, and yours in prose:
For, 'faith, the quarrel rightly understood,
'T is civil war with their own flesh and blood.
The threadbare author hates the gaudy coat,
And swears at the gilt coach, but swears afoot: 10
For 't is observ'd of every scribbling man,
He grows a fop as fast as e'er he can;
Prunes up, and asks his oracle, the glass,
If pink or purple best become his face.
For our poor wretch, he neither rails nor prays;
Nor likes your wit just as you like his plays;
He has not yet so much of Mr. Bayes.
He does his best; and if he cannot please,
Would quietly sue out his *writ of ease*.
Yet, if he might his own grand jury call,   20
By the fair sex he begs to stand or fall.

Let Caesar's power the men's ambition move,
But grace you him who lost the world for love!
Yet if some antiquated lady say,
The last age is not copied in his play;
Heav'n help the man who for that face must drudge,
Which only has the wrinkles of a judge.
Let not the young and beauteous join with those;
For, should you raise such numerous hosts of foes,
Young wits and sparks he to his aid must call;   30
'T is more than one man's work to please you all.

EPILOGUE TO

MITHRIDATES, KING OF PONTUS

You've seen a pair of faithful lovers die:
And much you care, for most of you will cry,
'T was a just judgment on their constancy.
For, Heav'n be thank'd, we live in such an age,
When no man dies for love, but on the stage:
And ev'n those martyrs are but rare in plays;
A cursed sign how much true faith decays.
Love is no more a violent desire;
'T is a mere metaphor, a painted fire.
In all our sex, the name, examin'd well,   10
Is pride to gain, and vanity to tell.
In woman, 't is of subtile int'rest made:
Curse on the punk that made it first a trade!
She first did wit's prerogative remove,
And made a fool presume to prate of love.
Let honor and preferment go for gold,
But glorious beauty is not to be sold:
Or, if it be, 't is at a rate so high,
That nothing but adoring it should buy.
Yet the rich cullies may their boasting spare;   20
They purchase but sophisticated ware.

'T is prodigality that buys deceit,
Where both the giver and the taker cheat.
Men but refine on the old half-crown way;
And women fight, like Swizzers, for their pay.

PROLOGUE TO

OEDIPUS

When Athens all the Grecian state did guide,
And Greece gave laws to all the world beside;
Then Sophocles with Socrates did sit,
Supreme in wisdom one, and one in wit:
And wit from wisdom differ'd not in those,
But as 't was sung in verse, or said in prose.
Then, Oedipus, on crowded theaters,
Drew all admiring eyes and list'ning ears:
The pleas'd spectator shouted every line,
The noblest, manliest, and the best design!   10
And every critic of each learned age,
By this just model has reform'd the stage.
Now, should it fail, (as Heav'n avert our fear!)
Damn it in silence, lest the world should hear.
For were it known this poem did not please,
You might set up for perfect salvages:
Your neighbors would not look on you as men,
But think the nation all turn'd Picts again.
Faith, as you manage matters, 't is not fit
You should suspect yourselves of too much wit: 20
Drive not the jest too far, but spare this piece;
And, for this once, be not more wise than Greece.
See twice! do not pellmell to damning fall,
Like true-born Britons, who ne'er think at all:
Pray be advis'd; and tho' at Mons you won,
On pointed cannon do not always run.
With some respect to ancient wit proceed;

You take the four first councils for your creed.
But, when you lay tradition wholly by,
And on the private spirit alone rely,
You turn fanatics in your poetry.
If, notwithstanding all that we can say,
You needs will have your pen'worths of the play,
And come resolv'd to damn, because you pay,
Record it, in memorial of the fact,
The first play buried since the Woolen Act.

THE EPILOGUE SPOKEN TO

THE KING AT THE OPENING OF THE PLAYHOUSE AT OXFORD
On Saturday Last, Being March the Nineteenth, 1681

As from a darken'd room some optic glass
Transmits the distant species as they pass
(The world's large landscape is from far descried
And men contracted on the paper glide),
Thus crowded Oxford represents mankind
And in these walls Great Britain seems confin'd.
Oxford is now the public theater,
And you both audience are and actors here.
The gazing world on the new scene attend,
Admire the turns, and wish a prosp'rous end.   10
This place, the seat of peace, the quiet cell
Where arts remov'd from noisy business dwell,
Should calm your wills, unite the jarring parts,
And with a kind contagion seize your hearts:
O may its genius like soft music move
And tune you all to concord and to love!
Our ark that has in tempests long been toss'd
Could never land on so secure a coast.
From hence you may look back on civil rage
And view the ruins of the former age.   20

Here a new world its glories may unfold
And here be sav'd the remnants of the old.
  But while your days on public thoughts are bent,
Past ills to heal and future to prevent,
Some vacant hours allow to your delight:
Mirth is the pleasing business of the night,
The king's prerogative, the people's right.
Were all your hours to sullen cares confin'd,
The body would be jaded by the mind.
'T is wisdom's part betwixt extremes to steer: 30
Be gods in senates, but be mortals here.

PROLOGUE TO

DON *SEBASTIAN*
Spoken by a woman

The judge remov'd, tho' he 's no more my lord,
May plead at bar, or at the council board:
So may cast poets write; there 's no pretension
To argue loss of wit, from loss of pension.
Your looks are cheerful; and in all this place
I see not one that wears a damning face.
The British nation is too brave, to show
Ignoble vengeance on a vanquish'd foe.
At least be civil to the wretch imploring,
And lay your paws upon him without roaring.   10
Suppose our poet was your foe before,
Yet now, the bus'ness of the field is o'er;
'T is time to let your civil wars alone,
When troops are into winter quarters gone.
Jove was alike to Latian and to Phrygian;
And you well know, a play 's of no religion.
Take good advice, and please yourselves this day
No matter from what hands you have the play.
Among good fellows ev'ry health will pass,

That serves to carry round another glass: 20
When with full bowls of Burgundy you dine,
Tho' at the mighty monarch you repine;
You grant him still Most Christian in his wine.
    Thus far the poet; but his brains grow addle,
And all the rest is purely from this noddle.
You 've seen young ladies at the senate door
Prefer petitions, and your grace implore:
However grave the legislators were,
Their cause went ne'er the worse for being fair.
Reasons as weak as theirs, perhaps, I bring;   30
But I could bribe you with as good a thing.
I heard him make advances of good nature;
That he, for once, would sheathe his cutting satire.
Sign but his peace, he vows he 'll ne'er again
The sacred names of fops and beaus profane.
Strike up the bargain quickly; for I swear,
As times go now, he offers very fair.
Be not too hard on him with statutes neither;
Be kind; and do not set your teeth together,
To stretch the laws, as cobblers do their leather.   40
Horses by Papists are not to be ridden,
But sure the Muses' horse was ne'er forbidden;
For in no rate-book it was ever found
That Pegasus was valued at five pound;
Fine him to daily drudging and inditing,
And let him pay his taxes out in writing.

PROLOGUE TO

THE PROPHETESS

Spoken by MR. BETTERTON

What *Nostradame,* with all his art, can guess
The fate of our approaching *Prophetess?*
A play, which, like a prospective set right,

Presents our vast expenses close to sight;
But turn the tube, and there we sadly view
Our distant gains; and those uncertain too:
A sweeping tax, which on ourselves we raise,
And all, like you, in hopes of better days.
When will our losses warn us to be wise!
Our wealth decreases, and our charges rise.   10
Money, the sweet allurer of our hopes,
Ebbs out in oceans and comes in by drops.
We raise new objects to provoke delight,
But you grow sated ere the second sight.
False men, even so you serve your mistresses:
They rise three stories in their tow'ring dress;
And, after all, you love not long enough
To pay the rigging, ere you leave 'em off:
Never content with what you had before,
But true to change, and Englishmen all o'er.   20
New honor calls you hence, and all your care
Is to provide the horrid pomp of war.
In plume and scarf, jack boots, and Bilbo blade,
Your silver goes, that should support our trade.
Go, unkind heroes, leave our stage to mourn,
Till rich from vanquish'd rebels you return;
And the fat spoils of Teague in triumph draw,
His firkin butter, and his usquebaugh.
Go, conquerors of your male and female foes;
Men without hearts, and women without hose.   30
Each bring his love a Bogland captive home;
Such proper pages will long trains become;
With copper collars, and with brawny backs,
Quite to put down the fashion of our blacks.
Then shall the pious Muses pay their vows,
And furnish all their laurels for your brows;
Their tuneful voice shall rise for your delights;
We want not poets fit to sing your fights.
But you, bright beauties, for whose only sake
These doughty knights such dangers undertake,   40
When they with happy gales are gone away,
With your propitious presence grace our play,
And with a sigh their empty seats survey:

Then think: "On that bare bench my servant sate;
I see him ogle still, and hear him chat,
Selling facetious bargains, and propounding
That witty recreation, call'd dumfounding."
Their loss with patience we will try to bear;
And would do more, to see you often here!
That our dead stage, reviv'd by your fair eyes,   *50*
Under a female regency may rise.

PROLOGUE AND EPILOGUE TO

AMPHITRYON
Or, the Two Sosias

PROLOGUE
Spoken by MRS. BRACEGIRDLE

The lab'ring bee, when his sharp sting is gone,
Forgets his golden work, and turns a drone:
Such is a satire, when you take away
That rage in which his noble vigor lay.
What gain you by not suffering him to tease ye?
He neither can offend you, now, nor please ye.
The honey-bag and venom lay so near,
That both together you resolv'd to tear;
And lost your pleasure, to secure your fear.
How can he show his manhood, if you bind him   *10*
To box, like boys, with one hand tied behind him?
This is plain leveling of wit, in which
The poor has all th' advantage, not the rich.
The blockhead stands excus'd for wanting sense,
And wits turn blockheads in their own defense.
Yet, tho' the stage's traffic is undone,
Still Julian's interloping trade goes on:
Tho' satire on the theater you smother,
Yet, in lampoons, you libel one another.
The first produces still a second jig;   *20*

You whip 'em out, like schoolboys, till they gig,
And with the same success, we readers guess.
For ev'ry one still dwindles to a less;
And much good malice is so meanly dress'd,
That we would laugh, but cannot find the jest.
If no advice your rhyming rage can stay,
Let not the ladies suffer in the fray:
Their tender sex is privileg'd from war;
'T is not like knights, to draw upon the fair.
What fame expect you from so mean a prize?   30
We wear no murd'ring weapons but our eyes.
Our sex, you know, was after yours design'd;
The last perfection of the Maker's mind:
Heav'n drew out all the gold for us, and left your dross behind.
Beauty for valor's best reward he chose;
Peace, after war; and after toil, repose.
Hence, ye profane, excluded from our sights;
And, charm'd by day with honor's vain delights,
Go, make your best of solitary nights.
Recant betimes, 't is prudence to submit;   40
Our sex is still your overmatch in wit:
We never fail with new, successful arts,
To make fine fools of you, and all your parts.

EPILOGUE

Spoken by PHAEDRA, MRS. MOUNTFORT

I 'm thinking (and it almost makes me mad)
How sweet a time those heathen ladies had.
Idolatry was ev'n their gods' own trade;
They worship'd the fine creatures they had made.
Cupid was chief of all the deities,
And love was all the fashion in the skies.
When the sweet nymph held up the lily hand,
Jove was her humble servant at command.
The treasury of heav'n was ne'er so bare,

But still there was a pension for the fair.   10
In all his reign adult'ry was no sin,
For Jove the good example did begin.
Mark, too, when he usurp'd the husband's name,
How civilly he sav'd the lady's fame.
The secret joys of love he wisely hid;
But you, sirs, boast of more than e'er you did.
You tease your cuckolds; to their face torment 'em:
But Jove gave his new honors to content 'em;
And, in the kind remembrance of the fair,
On each exalted son bestow'd a star.   20
For those good deeds, as by the date appears,
His godship flourish'd full two thousand years.
At last, when he and all his priests grew old,
The ladies grew in their devotion cold,
And that false worship would no longer hold.
   Severity of life did next begin,
(And always does, when we no more can sin.)
That doctrine, too, so hard in practice lies,
That the next age may see another rise.
Then pagan gods may once again succeed,   30
And Jove or Mars be ready, at our need,
To get young godlings, and so mend our breed.

PROLOGUE TO

THE MISTAKES
Or, the False Report

[*Enter* MR. BRIGHT]

   Gentlemen, we must beg your pardon; here 's no prologue to
be had to-day; our new play is like to come on without a frontis-
piece, as bald as one of you young beaux without your periwig. I
left our young poet sniveling and sobbing behind the scenes, and
cursing somebody that has deceiv'd him.

[*Enter* MR. BOWEN]

Hold your prating to the audience: here's honest Mr. Williams, just come in, half mellow, from the Rose Tavern. He swears he is inspir'd with claret, and will come on, and that *extempore* too, either with a prologue of his own or something like one. O here he comes to his trial, at all adventures; for my part I wish him a good deliverance.

[*Exeunt* MR. BRIGHT *and* MR. BOWEN]

[*Enter* MR. WILLIAMS]

Save ye, sirs, save ye! I am in a hopeful way,
I should speak something, in rhyme, now, for the play:
But the deuce take me, if I know what to say.
I 'll stick to my friend the author, that I can tell ye,
To the last drop of claret in my belly.
So far I 'm sure 't is rhyme—that needs no granting:
And, if my verses' feet stumble—you see my own are wanting.
Our young poet has brought a piece of work,
In which, tho' much of art there does not lurk,
It may hold out three days—and that 's as long as Cork.   10
But, for this play—(which till I have done, we show not)
What may be its fortune—by the Lord—I know not.
This I dare swear, no malice here is writ:
'T is innocent of all things; ev'n of wit.
He 's no high-flyer; he makes no sky-rockets,
His squibs are only level'd at your pockets.
And if his crackers light among your pelf,
You are blown up; if not, then he 's blown up himself.
By this time, I'm something recover'd of my fluster'd madness:
And now a word or two in sober sadness.   20
Ours is a common play; and you pay down
A common harlot's price—just half a crown.
You 'll say, I play the pimp on my friend's score;
But since 't is for a friend, your gibes give o'er:
For many a mother has done that before.
How 's this, you cry? an actor write?—we know it;
But Shakespeare was an actor and a poet.
Has not great Jonson's learning often fail'd?
But Shakespeare's greater genius still prevail'd.
Have not some writing actors, in this age,
Deserv'd and found success upon the stage?
To tell the truth, when our old wits are tir'd,
Not one of us but means to be inspir'd.

Let your kind presence grace our homely cheer;
'Peace and the butt' is all our bus'ness here:
So much for that—and the Devil take small beer.

EPILOGUE TO

KING ARTHUR
Spoken by MRS. BRACEGIRDLE

I 've had to-day a dozen *billets-doux*
From fops, and wits, and cits, and Bow Street *beaux;*
Some from Whitehall, but from the Temple more:
A Covent Garden porter brought me four.
I have not yet read all; but, without feigning,
We maids can make shrewd guesses at your meaning.
What if, to shew your styles, I read 'em here?
Methinks I hear one cry: "O Lord, forbear!
No, madam, no; by Heav'n, that 's too severe."
Well then, be safe—   10
But swear henceforwards to renounce all writing,
And take this solemn oath of my inditing,
As you love ease, and hate campaigns and fighting.
Yet, faith, 't is just to make same few examples:
What if I shew'd you one or two for samples?
(*Pulls one out.*) Here 's one desires my ladyship to meet
At the kind couch above in Bridges Street.
O sharping knave! that would have you know what,
For a poor sneaking treat of chocolate.
(*Pulls out another.*) Now, in the name of luck, I 'll break this
     open,   20
Because I dreamt last night I had a token:
The superscription is exceeding pretty:
To the desire of all the town and city.
Now, gallants, you must know, this precious fop
Is foreman of a haberdasher's shop:
One who devoutly cheats, demure in carriage,
And courts me to the holy bands of marriage;

But with a civil innuendo too,
My overplus of love shall be for you.
(*Reads.*) "Madam, I swear your looks are so divine,   30
When I set up, your face shall be my sign:
Tho' times are hard, to shew how I adore you,
Here 's my whole heart, and half a guinea for you.
But have a care of *beaux;* they 're false, my honey;
And, which is worse, have not one rag of money."
    See how maliciously the rogue would wrong ye!
But I know better things of some among ye.
My wisest way will be to keep the stage,
And trust to the good nature of the age;
And he that likes the music and the play   40
Shall be my favorite gallant to-day.

EPILOGUE TO

CLEOMENES

Spoken by MRS. BRACEGIRDLE

This day the poet, bloodily inclin'd,
Has made me die, full sore against my mind!
Some of you naughty men, I fear, will cry:
"Poor rogue! would I might teach thee how to die!"
Thanks for your love; but I sincerely say,
I never mean to die, your wicked way.
Well, since it is decreed all flesh must go,
(And I am flesh—at least for aught you know)
I first declare, I die with pious mind,
In perfect charity with all mankind.   10
Next for my will: I have in my dispose,
Some certain movables would please you beaux;
As, first, my youth; for, as I have been told,
Some of you modish sparks are dev'lish old.
My chastity I need not leave among ye;
For, to suspect old fops, were much to wrong ye.
You swear y' are sinners; but, for all your haste,

Your misses shake their heads, and find you chaste.
I give my courage to those bold commanders
That stay with us, and dare not go to Flanders.   20
I leave my truth (to make his plot more clear)
To Mr. Fuller, when he next shall swear.
I give my judgment, craving all your mercies,
To those that leave good plays for damn'd dull farces.
My small devotion let the gallants share,
That come to ogle us at evening pray'r.
I give my person—let me well consider—
Faith, e'en to him that is the fairest bidder;
To some rich hunks, if any be so bold
To say those dreadful words, *To have and hold*.   30
But stay—to give, and be bequeathing still,
When I'm so poor, is just like Wickham's will:
Like that notorious cheat, vast sums I give,
Only that you may keep me while I live.
Buy a good bargain, gallants, while you may;
I'll cost you but your half a crown a day.

EPILOGUE TO

HENRY THE SECOND, KING OF ENGLAND

WITH THE DEATH OF ROSAMOND

Spoken by MRS. BRACEGIRDLE

Thus you the sad catastrophe have seen,
Occasion'd by a mistress and a queen.
Queen Eleanor the proud was French, they say;
But English manufacture got the day.
Jane Clifford was her name, as books aver;
Fair Rosamond was but her *nom de guerre*.
Now tell me, gallants, would you lead your life
With such a mistress, or with such a wife?

If one must be your choice, which d' ye approve,
The curtain lecture, or the curtain love?   10
Would ye be godly with perpetual strife,
Still drudging on with homely Joan your wife,
Or take your pleasure in a wicked way,
Like honest whoring Harry in the play?
I guess your minds: the mistress would be taking,
And nauseous matrimony sent a packing.
The devil 's in ye all; mankind 's a rogue;
You love the bride, but you detest the clog.
After a year, poor spouse is left i' th' lurch,
And you, like Haynes, return to Mother Church.   20
Or, if the name of Church comes cross your mind,
Chapels of ease behind our scenes you find.
The playhouse is a kind of market place;
One chaffers for a voice, another for a face:
Nay, some of you, I dare not say how many,
Would buy of me a pen'worth for your penny.
Ev'n this poor face, which with my fan I hide,
Would make a shift my portion to provide,
With some small perquisites I have beside.
Tho' for your love, perhaps, I should not care,   30
I could not hate a man that bids me fair.
What might ensue, 't is hard for me to tell;
But I was drench'd to-day for loving well,
And fear the poison that would make me swell.

EPILOGUE TO

THE HUSBAND
HIS OWN CUCKOLD
Spoken by MRS. BRACEGIRDLE

Like some raw sophister that mounts the pulpit,
So trembles a young poet at a full pit.
Unus'd to crowds, the parson quakes for fear,

And wonders how the devil he durst come there;
Wanting three talents needful for the place,
Some beard, some learning, and some little grace;
Nor is the puny poet void of care;
For authors, such as our new authors are,
Have not much learning, nor much wit to spare;
And as for grace, to tell the truth, there 's scarce one   10
But has as little as the very parson.
Both say, they preach and write for your instruction;
But 't is for a third day, and for induction.
The difference is, that tho' you like the play,
The poet's gain is ne'er beyond his day;
But with the parson 't is another case;
He, without holiness, may rise to grace.
The poet has one disadvantage more,
That if his play be dull, he 's damn'd all o'er,
Not only a damn'd blockhead, but damn'd poor.   20
But dulness well becomes the sable garment;
I warrant that ne'er spoil'd a priest's preferment:
Wit 's not his business, and, as wit now goes,
Sirs, 't is not so much yours as you suppose,
For you like nothing now but nauseous beaux.
You laugh not, gallants, as by proof appears,
At what his beauship says, but what he wears;
So 't is your eyes are tickled, not your ears:
The tailor and the furrier find the stuff,
The wit lies in the dress, and monstrous muff.   30
The truth on 't is, the payment of the pit
Is like for like, clipp'd money for clipp'd wit.
You cannot from our absent author hope,
He should equip the stage with such a fop:
Fools change in England, and new fools arise;
For tho' th' immortal species never dies,
Yet ev'ry year new maggots make new flies.
But where he lives abroad, he scarce can find
One fool, for million that he left behind.

Verse
Essays

Commentary on the Verse Essays

RELIGIO LAICI

When the great controversy between science and religion broke out in England in the last half of the nineteenth century, after the researches of Darwin and the geologists had cast doubt on the Old Testament stories of creation, certain peculiarities of the Bible as a document—either in the original or in the most widely read translations—had already been known to scholarship, and to intelligent laymen familiar with the best scholarship, for at least two centuries. A landmark in the history of Biblical criticism, for example, had appeared in 1678, when Father Simon's *Critical History of the Old Testament* was printed in Paris. The French authorities immediately suppressed it, but a few copies survived, and an English translation by a young friend of Dryden's, Henry Dickinson, was the occasion, in 1682, for Dryden's poem *Religio Laici* (*A Layman's Statement of Faith*).

Father Simon's idea had been to defend Roman Catholicism by proving that the Old Testament, in the state in which we now possess it, was an untrustworthy document: that the authorship of various books was uncertain, the manuscript imperfect, the best readings of the text doubtful, the work in part a compilation of lost older works, and so forth. To prove the Bible untrustworthy may seem a strange way to defend Catholicism; but Catholicism claimed to derive its authenticity from an unbroken tradition of Biblical interpretation, a tradition itself divinely inspired; whereas

church | the Bible

Church of England

Protestantism, especially in some of its forms, laid great stress on
a return to the actual Biblical text. Thus if the actual Biblical text
was undermined (or so Father Simon reasoned), a religiously in-
clined person could have no recourse but to cleave to the institution
which embodied the purest, most authentic Christian tradition—
in other words, the Roman Catholic Church. The question was,
should one rely on an inspired Church or on an inspired Book?
Protestant emphasis tended to be on the Book, Catholic emphasis
on the Church; hence an attack on the authenticity of the Book pur-
ported to be a defense of authenticity of the Church. That the
French authorities did not think it a good defense is shown by
their suppression of the original edition of Father Simon's work;
and that Dryden supposed Father Simon to conceal a "secret [irre-
ligious] meaning" beneath an ostensible Catholicism is shown by
his calling him "not too much a priest" (252–253). Dryden felt
that Simon's demonstration of the fallibility of the Hebrew tradi-
tions which had produced the Bible logically implied an equal
skepticism toward the Roman Catholic traditions the Bible had
produced. If the first tradition could be shown to be corrupt, why
not the second?

Where, then, was certainty in religion to be found? Dryden's
answer is that, although many details of both text and tradition may
be debatable—although "infallibility" has often "fail'd"—neverthe-
less the central doctrines of Christianity are clearly enough estab-
lished, both by the Bible and by the interpretations given it in the
early Church, to command assent. Catholics and the dissenting
Puritan sects (Dryden thought) err alike by insisting on too much
belief in respect to irrelevant details: the Catholics, by arrogating
to a specially trained priesthood sole right of Biblical interpreta-
tion, had created during the Middle Ages a self-seeking obscurantist
monopoly in religion which ultimately led to the Reformation
(370–397); more recently, the dissenting sects, by turning over
the immensely complex text of Scripture to every half-educated
layman who might suppose himself divinely inspired to interpret
its obscurest passages, had produced nothing but pointless bicker-
ing about nonessential fine points of theology (398–424). There
remained Dryden's own faith, that of the Church of England, which
accepted, in general, the central doctrines of the Bible and the
written traditions of the early, premedieval Catholic church. If our
"private Reason" should detect discrepancies in the bases of this

religion, it is the part of wisdom to submit to general opinion and established authority—for certainly reason is a faculty quite as fallible as any text, tradition, or institution; indeed, probably more so. The attitude taken in the conclusion of the poem is quite comparable to that taken toward the established monarchy in *Absalom and Achitophel,* 753–810.

In addition to the Catholics and the dissenting Puritan sects Dryden deals with one other group who differ from him in belief: the Deists. Their position was that no single religion of any sort could claim divine inspiration and authenticity; but that mankind, simply by nature, everywhere tended to believe in a God, an afterlife, and an ethical code. Dryden devotes roughly the first half of the poem (1–223) to defending Christianity against the basic objections of deism; and he concedes a point to his opponents in granting that, contrary to the professed beliefs of his own church, heathens ignorant of Scripture can attain salvation by the light of their own conscience and reason.

The poem is, as Dryden intended, both clearly and cogently written; one scarcely has the feeling that the arguments could have been better stated in prose; or that, conversely, a more metaphorical, image-ridden sort of poetry would have done better justice to the central themes and ideas. *Religio Laici* is an outstandingly successful instance of the sort of ideological poetry represented also, for example, by Pope's *Essay on Man,* Lucretius' *De Rerum Natura,* various parts of Wordsworth's *Prelude,* and various parts of Eliot's *Four Quartets.* The versification is musical, terse, and close to the language spoken by ordinary men; the opinions are mature and of continuing interest, although their immediate occasion has passed into history. A few notes on particular phrases follow.

Stagirite (20): Aristotle. Εὔρεκα (43): "I have found it." *apostle* (199): St. Paul. *bishop* (213): Athanasius (the Athanasian creed restricted salvation to believers). *Arius* (220): fourth-century heretic, disbeliever in Trinity, opponent of Athanasius. *Junius, Tremellius* (241): sixteenth-century commentators on the Bible. *Esdras* (291): "I shall write all that has been done in the world since the beginning . . ." (II Esdras 14:22). *Socinian* (312): holdier of the doctrine described in the next line; Socinus was a sixteenth-century Italian theologian. *next* (339): nearest. *Pelagius* (346): fifth-century heretic who denied original sin. *provoke* (346): appeal. *the Fathers* (440): theologians of the early Catholic church. *Sternhold* (456): mediocre versifier of the Psalms; for *Shadwell,* see *Mac Flecknoe,* above.

THE HIND AND THE PANTHER

The basic arguments in *Religio Laici* are in favor of tradition and authority in religion; at the time he wrote it (1682), Dryden was unable to accept the Roman Church as the embodiment of such authority, but lines 282–283:—

> Such an omniscient Church we wish indeed;
> 'T were worth both Testaments; and cast in the
>   Creed—

show a predisposition of temperament, at least, in its favor.

In the spring of 1685 the Catholic James II became king; and sometime during the same year, Dryden converted to the Catholic faith, in which he remained throughout the rest of his life. Skeptical and rationalistic by nature, thoroughly conversant with the arguments for and against the various forms of Christianity of his day, suspicious throughout his life of all priesthoods as venal and self-seeking, Dryden could yet write to a relative in 1699, when it might have been to his advantage to change his religion:

> . . . I can neither take the Oaths [supporting William III's government], nor forsake my Religion, because I know not what Church to go to, if I leave the Catholique: they are all so divided amongst themselves in matters of faith, necessary to salvation: & yet all assuming the name of Protestants. . . . Truth is but one. . . .

The Hind and the Panther, written in 1687, is an allegorical dramatization of the religio-political situation in England during James II's brief reign. Not all the details of the allegory have been fully and certainly interpreted, but the main outlines are clear: the *Hind* is Roman Catholicism; the *Panther,* the Church of England; the *Bear,* the Independents (now Congregationalists); the *Hare,* the Quakers (who would not take oaths); the *Ape,* the atheists, or freethinkers (who included some courtiers); the *Boar,* the Baptists (a sect which had earlier been involved in certain revolutions in Germany); *Reynard the Fox,* the Unitarians (who believed Christ to have been human, not divine; Dryden traces their origins to the ancient opponents of the theologian Athanasius, and to the sixteenth-century theologian Socinus); the *Wolves,* the Presbyterians (whose clergy wore skullcaps over their short hair, and believed in Predestination); the *Lion,* King James II (who had recently issued a declaration of religious tolerance in England); *Caledonia,* England; and *Pan* (1282), Christ. In the fable of the *Swallows* (Part III), the *Swallows* are the English Catholics; the *Martins,* a priest or party of priests who were in favor of strong pro-Catholic measures on the part of James II; the unnaturally clement winter is James's reign; and the disasters at the close of the story, Dryden's prediction of the plight of the Catholics after James (a middle-aged man at the time he became king) no longer rules, and a Protestant heir is on the throne. Dryden defends his use of allegory for subject matter of this kind by an allusion to Aesop (1300) and to Spenser's *Mother Hubbard's Tale* (1302), a political allegory of Queen Elizabeth's reign.

Though the poem is less unified than *Religio Laici,* it is more ambitious, both in imaginative brilliance and dialectic vigor. Some explication of particular passages are given below. The fullest explanation of the poem's details yet written is given in Volume III of the California Dryden (ed. Earl Miner, 1969). For easy consultation of this authority, separate line numbers have been supplied, in brackets, for Parts II and III.

THE FIRST PART

Scythian (6): in other words, poisoned. *her young* (9): the Catholics in England who had been subject to persecutions during Dryden's lifetime for alleged "Plots" against the state. *Captive Israel* (19): in Egypt (see Exodus 1). *corps* (23): corpses. *common hunt* (27): other animals (that is, religions). *sovereign power* (28): that of James II. *Unlick'd to form* (36): bearcubs were supposed to be *licked* into shape after birth; the Independent church abolished many ceremonies. *grace* (47): divine favor. *borrow'd name* (50): Dryden implies that many sects had Baptist political principles, without calling themselves Baptists. *Revers'd* (58): the metaphor is of a telescope (*optics*) when the user looks through the wrong end. *her* (70): the Catholic Church. *three in one* (79): the doctrine of the Trinity, which entails the divinity of Christ.

sight . . . touch . . . taste (86): Dryden here approaches one of the chief points dividing the Anglican and Roman Catholic churches. Catholics believed that the bread and wine used in the Mass *became* the body and blood of Christ, and that they only appeared to remain bread and wine; Anglicans believed that this was contrary to the evidence of our senses. Dryden argues that, just as we must follow faith, not reason, in accepting the Trinity, so we must trust *revelation,* not our *imperfect sense,* in accepting transubstantiation. He also argues that if Christ's body (in one of the miracles after the resurrection: see John 20), although it was itself *impassible,* nevertheless passed through closed doors (*bolts and bars*) to appear to the disciples, then who are we to demand that it should be seen (*descried*) when it appears in the bread and wine (*host*)? (See *Absalom and Achitophel* 118–121 for Dryden's attitude toward transubstantiation before his conversion.)

bilanders (128): coastwise vessels. *try* (141): test. *apostate* (151): (the Socinians). *Polonian* (152): Polish.

salvage (156): savage. *rul'd a while* (168): the Presbyterians were temporarily in power during the Civil War period. *Cambria* (171): Wales, where wolves were supposed to have been extirpated in the early Middle Ages. Dryden implies that medieval church reformers (*Wycliffe's brood*) were the ancestors of the later Calvinists in *Geneva* and *France. Zuinglius* (180): Swiss (*Helvetian*) reformer of Calvin's period; *Lake Leman* (179) is in Switzerland. *Sanhedrim* (183): Old Testament assembly of elders; the Presbyterian church was governed by such an assembly, called a *class* (189). Dryden ironically traces their origin, however, to Corah's rebellion against Moses and Aaron, who wore the priestly *ephod,* or robe symbolizing authority. Corah and his followers were swallowed up in an earthquake (Numbers 16). *Dog* (193): Dryden implies that Presbyterianism and Unitarianism amount to about the same thing; that is, that Presbyterians disbelieved in the Trinity.

Your fangs . . . . your town (202–3): Geneva, home of Calvin, formerly ruled by a bishop, became a republic after 1535. *puddle* (205): Lake Geneva. *wall:* the city wall or the Alps (?) *Tweed* (209): = Scotland. *for physic* (222): to induce vomiting. *Colchis* (232): home of the sorceress Medea. *Celtic* (235): (probably) British. *informing* (251): vitalizing. *Confessing still* (270): always bearing witness to. *coronation day* (271): (often signalized by general pardons or amnesties). *milk* (274): (of human kindness).

Pan (284): = Christ. *British Lion* (289): James II. *awfully* (304): awesomely. *conventicles* (313): religious gatherings of dissenters. *cannot bend her* (336): James II (*her injur'd Lion*) had been unable to win Church of England support for his toleration of Catholics. Dryden (correctly) implies that the Anglicans are beginning to contemplate his deposition. *A Lion* (351): Henry VIII. *compress'd* (352): mated with. *left-hand* (353): = bigamous (Henry's marriage to Ann Boleyn took place secretly, three months before his formal divorce from Catherine of Aragon; difficulties over this led to the break with Rome and the English Reformation). *luxury* (362): lust. *Confessions . . . set aside* (364): (the monasteries were dissolved and many Catholic observances abolished). *supply* (367): take the place of (a married clergy replaced a celibate one). *hatter'd out* (371): worn out, exhausted. *Mussulman* (377): Mohammedan. *Alcoran* (381): Koran. *presum'd of* (388): counted on. *ethereal pastures* (389): the church. *flock:* (of clergymen). *Burnish'd* (390): fat. *batt'ning:* fattening. *careful* (391): full of care, hardworking. *these* (392): (Lutherans). *head:* allegiance (to the Pope). *crosier* (395): bishop's staff. *miter:* bishop's hat. *affectation* (397): outward liking for. *phylacteries* (399): boxes containing texts of scripture, worn by Jews at prayer. *Nice* (408): fastidious. *one . . . . contends* (411): Roman Catholicism said that the bread and wine of the communion service *became* Christ's body and blood; Calvinism said they merely *signified* it. The English Church formulated a compromise position which Dryden (429) attacks as incomprehensible. *practice* (433): (alluding to church opposition to James II). *Indian wife* (442): (alluding to sacrifice of Indian wives on husbands' funeral pyres: suttee). *bear the sun* (447): (in the fable, the wind couldn't get the traveller's coat off, but the sun could). *Isgrim* (449): wolf's name in medieval Reynard-the-Fox beast epic. *by text* (460): by reference to the text of Scripture. *during* (496): only so long as (the State pleases). *the whole* (500): the whole (Roman Catholic) church. *salvage* (507): savage. *vanish'd train* (514): Dryden implies that the dissenting sects are the followers of the Church of England, but that they have deserted her morning and evening receptions (*levées and couchées*). *flood* (523): water hole. *monster* (537): phenomenon in Revelations 17 applied by Protestants to Roman Catholicism. *seen him first* (552): if a wolf saw a man first, it made the man speechless; the hind has reverse power over Dryden's wolf.

wait (557): accompany. *Plot* (563): see the Commentary for "Absalom and Achitophel", above.

THE SECOND PART

Philistines (574): (extreme anti-Catholic and anti-Anglican dissenters). *toils* (575): nets, snares. *sagacious* (577): keen-scented. *younger Lion* (579): James II, then Duke of York, popularly suspected of involvement in the supposed plot. *priestly calves* (580): Jesuits and other Catholic priests (some were executed). *Test* (602): Test Act of 1678 requiring Church of England members to renounce Transubstantiation, the doctrine that the bread and and wine of the mass became Christ's body and blood. *salvo* (606): saving answer. *cannon* (635): with pun on "canon" (=rule, law). *subterranean Rome* (639): the catacombs. *emission or reception* (647): a sending-out or a receiving process (something ancient physicists [*philosophers*] hadn't decided about). *Jehu* (692): furious driver (2 Kings 9: 20). *Mahomet* (702): The idea is that Mahomet treated all his followers alike, whereas *Christ and Moses* distinguished sheep from goats among theirs. *Word* (716): the Bible. *piles* (733): javelins. *Councils* (741): officially recognized in 1559 as authoritative for the English church. *traditive* (768): traditional. *depend* (774): remain undetermined. *rounds* (792): rungs. *omen* (799): = the gallows. *fam'd for sweet* (800): a traditional belief about Panthers, here used to suggest deceptive affability. *Blatant Beast* (802): symbol of slander in *Faerie Queene*, Books V and VI; here, = wolf. *elder* (809): a still older one (dispossesses it). *excepts* (815): makes objections. *thins:* makes smaller. *Fathers* (820): (of the early church). *blind* (824): place of concealment. *shelf* (829): reef. *cozenage* (830): deception. purging *fires* (858): purgatory (believed in by Catholics, but not by Anglicans). *episcopacy* (859): use of bishops (practiced by both Catholics and Anglicans).

Thus she (869): The Hind has been speaking. *Saint* (916): Peter (see II Peter 3: 16). *primitive* (928): age of the early church. *Hungary* (954): territory fought over by Austrians and Turks in the seventeenth century. *his words* (970): of Jesus to Pilate's officers (see John 18). *Polish diet* (979): Poland had an elective monarchy, and office called *crown-general* (982), and *liberty* of *rebellion* (987). *Curtana* (991): ancient sword, lacking a *point,* carried at British coronations, symbolizing mercy. *hit the blots* (995): detect the mistakes. *hardhead* (1015): head-butting. *consubstantiating Church* (1026): Lutherans. *you restrain* (1028): Hugenot immigrants weren't made English clergy. *royalties* (1062): sovereign rights. *As when of old* . . . (1071 ff.): (as dramatized in *Paradise Lost,* Book III). *Egyptian sorcerers* (1110): (See Exodus 7–9). *Magi* (1117): (the sorcerers). *dishonest* (1119): dishonorable. *Our sailing ships,* etc. (1130): (undesirables were subject to transportation to overseas colonies). *common shores* (1130): public sewage-deposit sites. *stews* (1132): brothels. *disembogue* (1134): pour forth. *palliards* (1135): sex-criminals. *some* (1140): the Dutch, alleged to have bought the right to trade in Japan by renouncing Christianity. *needle* (1143): compass needle. *chart:* mariner's chart. *Japonian* (1144): Japanese. *Old heresies* (1157): Wyclif's doctrines. *plantations* (1174): plantings. *standard* (1175): (perhaps) trees left standing when timber is cut (for growth purposes). *digits* (1181): units measuring size of an eclipse. *sev'n* . . . *ages* (1202): perhaps referring to the 800 years from England's conversion to Wyclif's era (about 600 to 1400 A.D.). *prevent* (1213): anticipate (= welcome). *Joseph* (1214): (see Genesis 43: 29, 30). *refuse your gold* (1219): the English Benedictine monks had given up their claim to their confiscated possessions. *obscene* (1224): of ill omen. *triumphs of the sky* (1226): possibly aurora borealis on the night of the battle of Sedgemoor (6 July 1685), when James crushed Monmouth's rebellion. *three* (1233): England, Scotland, and Wales (?). *nuntius* (1234): messenger. *grace cup* (1252): cup of thanksgiving. *wilder'd* (1254): led astray. *victorious of the Stygian race* (1281): victorious over the underworld deities, that is, Satan and the rebel angels. *Pan* (1283): Christ. *cates* (1293): food.

THE THIRD PART

Caledon (1297): Scotland (here, Great Britain generally). *Phrygia* (1301): ancient nation of Asia Minor. *Mother Hubbard* (1302): poem of Spenser's in which the royal powers of the lion (Queen Elizabeth) are usurped by the ape and the fox. *The wanted* . . . *supply* (1307): supply something now wanted to perform the function formerly served by their words. *endite* (1310): indict. *round* (1313): perfect (because circles symbolize perfection).

Lion's (1315): James II's. *salvage* (1316): savage (= wild beast). *furry sons in frequent senate* (1319): fur-hooded clergy in crowded Church convocation. *commons* (1322): food. *want* (1323): lack.

exil'd heir (1336): (James II had been sent abroad at the time of the plot.) *offices* (1352): obligations. *fell* (1364): cruel. *rest* (1379): remnant. *spooms* (1390): scuds ahead. *labor'd* (1394): well-tilled. *German quarrel* (1415): French phrase for quarrel without sufficient cause (the next line suggests that the French are now powerful enough to engage in such quarrels often). *winch* (1427): wince. *renounces* (1437): is repugnant. *revenues* (1442): accented "reVENues." *grandame* (1443): = inherited. *crazy* (1445): rickety. *temper:* constitution. *declin'd:* deteriorated. *sons of latitude* (1454): those who want to extend and modify the English church to accommodate the Presbyterians. *Scorpio* (1462): (to which the genitals were assigned in astrology). *French proselytes* (1467): Huguenots. *cures* (1479): clergyman's jobs; paying parishes. *chamber practice* (1480): being personal chaplain to a nobleman or his household. *silent:* (because it doesn't advance one's reputation). *Delphic* (1485): ambiguous (like many prophecies of the Delphic oracle). *argent* (1488): silver (suggests ostensible purity against a dark—*sable*—background). *grim logician* (1495): term recently applied to each other by Dryden and Stillingfleet, an Anglican controversialist whose arguments about Henry VIII's motives Dryden parodies in the next few lines. *dame* (1499): Anne Boleyn. *ghostly* (1505): spiritual. *Treatise of Humility* (1508): Dryden had alleged that Protestants seldom wrote about, or with, humility; Stillingfleet had cited a Protestant treatise, and argued that the Bible was actually the best treatment of the subject. *The Lion buys no converts* (1519): There's no practical advantage in converting to James II's religion. *stay the market of another reign* (1522): wait for the approaching reign of William and Mary (James's heirs), firm Protestants. *broad-way sons* (1523): followers of the *broad way* to hell rather than the strait and narrow path in the other direction. *nice:* choosy. *close with* (1524): made a deal with. *rais'd three steeples high'r* (1525): given enough promotion or other ecclesiastical advantage. *cassock* (1526): Anglican clergyman's garment. *canting-coat:* garment in which dissenting Puritan preachers whined hypocritically (*canted*). *How they should speed, their fortune is untried* (1535): Their fortune has not tried out any way by means of which they might succeed (they don't seek favors). *pass* (1540): pass by. *your:* (emphatic). *Hudibras* (1541): Samuel "Hudibras" Butler, anti-Puritan satirist who died (1680) unprosperous though much quoted. *Imprimatur* (1550): = "let it be printed": official licence needed for theological treatise. *virtue* (1557): strength. *pursued* (1592): went on. *your child* (1600): Dryden's opponent Stillingfleet, here accused of having *reviled* Charles II and James's first wife (*a king and princess dead*) in his attack on papers purportedly written by them defending Catholicism. *Shimei* (1602): See "Absalom and Achitophel," 585 ff. *he* (1605): Bishop Gilbert Burnet. *tend* (1606): extend. *tire* (1611): tier or row of cannon. *Henry* (1614): Henry VIII. *springs* (1618): (unworthy) motives. *paean* (1622): song of rejoicing. *is found* (1623): Stillingfleet said one had been recently published; Dryden retorted that it was an unacknowledged translation from a Spanish work. (They may not have meant the same book.) *my . . . son* (1627): = a Catholic. *make himself a saver* (1638): collect for damages. *Algerine* (1642): N. African pirate. *greater* (1646): greater (Christian) law. *characters* (1649): satiric portraits worthwhile for some one *to write. son of mine* (1660): apparently unidentified. *nod* (1665): waver. *neighborhood:* nearness. *laws* (1675): anti-Catholic laws not always strictly enforced. *protracted* (1677): deferred. *Admire* (1682): Be surprised. *int'rest* (1688): self-interest.

travail (1705): labor; travel. *prole* (1707): prowl. *chancel* (1725): space around altar. *mack'rel gale* (1750): strong breeze. *Sibyl* (1783): ancient Roman prophetess in a grotto at Cumae. *Chelidonian* (1788): that is, of swallows. *stager* (1791): person of experience. *Scales* (1799): Libra, a sign of the Zodiac associated with September. *grosser atoms* (1809): a reference to the Lucretian theory of matter. *Nostradamus* (1814): sixteenth-century astrologer. *priest, prince* (1822): perhaps an allusion to influences exerted over James II by the Jesuit Father Peter, who advised stronger pro-Catholic measures than many English Catholics thought wise. *Ram* (1830): Aries, sign of the Zodiac associated with March. *prime:* young. *Ahaz' dial* (1832): sundial on which Isaiah caused the shadow to go backward ten degrees (II Kings 20). *Joshua's day:* when the sun and moon stood still (Joshua 10:12–14). *Chapel . . . of ease* (1834): chapel built for the convenience of parishioners living far from a church (here, the royal chapel, in which Catholic services could be held in London). *Swifts* (1841): possibly, the hopeful Irish Catholics. *Gibeonites* (1843): doomed to be "hewers of wood and drawers of water" (Joshua 9:23). *Cuckow* (1853): Dryden himself (according to Walter Scott). *St. Martin's day* (1859): November 11. *Lucinda* (1878): Roman goddess of child-birth. *Capricorn* (1892): zodiacal sign of December. *Virgin Balance* (1894): August–September. *dorp* (1905): village. *Boreas* (1914): the north wind. *poll'd* (1925): clip or strip (trees). *laws* (1927): Catholic priests were not allowed in England. *prophetic bill* (1932): a dead swallow, suspended in air, was supposed to predict changes of wind in this way. *Fanatic author* (1949): John White, Puritan author of a tract (*The First Century of Scandalous Malignant Priests*) attacking the Anglican clergy. *it would soon be night* (1954): in other words, James II would die, and under a Protestant sovereign the English Catholics would suffer as the fable describes.

   trims (1960): vacillates. *Pardelis* (1961): "pantheress." *that prince* (1974): Louis XIV. *of:* for. *mandate* (1975): in 1685 Louis repealed the Edict of Nantes (1598), granting the protestant Huguenots (*Gallic friends*) toleration. *scorpion* (1984): Reho-boam (I Kings 12) threatened greater tyranny than his father Solomon's: "My little finger shall be thicker than my father's loins. . . . My father hast chastised you with whips, but I will chastise you with scorpions." *Test* (1992): See line 602, and commentary. *disseiz'd* (2005): wrongfully dispossessed. *to* (2007): by. *heir* (2008): inherit. *Oates . . . Plot* (2013): see "Absalom and Achitophel." *uncas'd* (2021): stripped (compare the stripping of Duessa in *Faerie Queene,* Book I, Canto viii). *miter'd seats* (2027): seats of the Anglican bishops in the House of Lords. *David's* = the monarch's (there were no Catholic places on Parliaments benches, though the monarch was Catholic). *atheists* (2033): (who would not object to renouncing Transubstantiation). *places* (2036): government positions. *writ of ease* (2039): certificate of discharge from employment. *pretense* (2040): claim. *sterve* (2043): starve. *censing* (2047): incense-burning. *fume:* fumigate. *Toby's rival* (2048): devil driven away by smell from burning fish liver (Tobit 6–8). *'butt and peace'* (2053): in Dryden's *Tempest* Trinculo includes a butt of wine in the peace terms. *in forma pauperis* (2055):

as a pauper. *Aeneas* (2061): the newcomer in Italy, suitor for King Latinus' daughter. *poppits* (2074): dolls, idols. *Lion* (2084): James II. *own* (2107): acknowledge (guilt by association with the dissenters). *Proteus* (2112): shape-shifting sea-god in the Odyssey. *tripod* (2113): where the priestess of Phoebus Apollo sat at Delphi. *Gordian* (2116): = undissolvable. *Int'rest* (2118): self-interest. *authentic* (2132): of genuine value. *planet* (2150): the Protestant William of Orange, James's successor. *neighbor nation* (2159): Holland (the *low* countries or Netherlands). *friends oppress'd* (2170): Huguenot refugees. *plain good man* (2200): = James II. *rack'd* (2211): tortured. *overlook'd* (2213): supervised. *as* (2228): as if. *Gave* (2233): gave to. *fabric* (2235): Catholic chapel built by James at royal palace of Whitehall in London. *Doves* (2240): Anglican clergy. *gall* (2241): an organ doves were proverbially not supposed to have. *salt* (2245): "salt-money" was a term for church endowments; salt was associated with lust; and Protestant clergy were non-celibate. *crops* (2253): gullets. *corny:* full of grain. *Harpies* (2254): winged scavenging monsters in the Aeneid. *Dan . . . Beersheba* (2259): from Dan to Beersheba = the entire country. *Levi's kind* (2261): the priesthood. *lay-preferment* (2262): secular advantage. *breeding melancholy blood* (2271): it was thought pigeon-meat did this. *bran* (2279): skin or husk. *faces* (2282): presence. *commons* (2286): food. *salt manure:* pigeon dung was thought to be uncommonly salty. *poor domestic poultry* (2289): Catholic clergy. *cruse* (2294): small container. *bird that warn'd* (2300): cock. *uncivil hours* (2304): cock-crow is proverbially early; the Anglicans had given up many Catholic nocturnal rites. *Chanticleers in cloister'd walls* (2316): monks. *sister Partlet* (2318): nuns. *restiff* (2320): restive, intractable. *good works* (2327): Protestant emphasis was on faith; Catholic on good works. *frontless* (2234): unblushing, shameless. *hideous figure* (2236): grotesque caricature. *Ptolemy* (2341): the Egyptian astronomer. *emblem* (2350): allegorical drawing. *birds of Venus* (2358): doves (pigeons), as symbols of lust. *law* (2361): law expelling priests from England under death penalty. *henbane juice* (2375): = hemlock. *emissary Pigeons* (2391): Medieval legend alleged that Mohammed trained a pigeon to peck grain in his ear to make his followers think the bird was bringing him divine messages. *suffer'd* (2397): permitted. *protractive:* delaying. *reduce*

(2398): persuade. *clos'd* (2400): made a deal. *haggard* (2410): wild. *eyry:* nest. *pounc'd* (2411): equipped with talons. *wreak* (2412): avenge. *Musket* (2413): sparrow-hawk. *Coystrel:* kestrel (small hawk). *Buzzard* (2415): Bishop Gilbert Burnet, who in youth had attacked the Scottish bishops. *Cramm'd* (2423): stuffed. *son of Anak* (2436): giant (Numbers 13: 33). *genial bent* (2441): inborn inclination. *Int'rest* (2433): self-interest. *fled* (2446): Out of favor with Charles and James, he was self-exiled in Holland. *shakes the dust against* (2455): agitates against. *race:* the English. *ordures* (2456): manure. *The hero and the tyrant change their style* (2459): he calls ("styles") a king one or the other according to how generous the king is to him. *nice* (2466): delicate. *A Greek, and bountiful . . .* (2468): "I fear the Greeks, even bearing gifts"—Aeneid, Book II. *th' accusing Sathan* (2475): the word "Satan" means adversary. Burnet had testified against the Duke of Lauderdale, a former friend of his. *Moloch* (2476): battle-god worshipped with human sacrifice. *runs an Indian muck* (2482): runs amuck [attacking people] like an Indian. *report* (2483): fame; explosive noise. *Captain* (2486): champion (of the Test Act). *But made* (2494): only made. *into question call* (2497): raise a question about (James's alleged promise to maintain the established English church). *press* (2504): crowd. *stews* (2507): brothels. *suff'ring* (2524): permitting. *doom* (2527): judgement —the Declaration of Indulgence (4 April 1627) suspending the Test Act and giving both Catholics and dissenters freedom of worship. *but* (2530): except for. *tried* (2533): experienced. *their* (2534): the pigeons'. *fowl of nature* (2537): wild fowl (the dissenters). *republic* (2545): favoring a republic rather than a monarchy. *Rubicon* (2449): crucial boundary. *Shiloh* (2552): lawgiver who gathers the people to him (Genesis 49: 10). *Dionysius* (2554): tyrant of Syracuse, later schoolmaster at Corinth. *smiths* (2562): forgers. *Nimrods* (2568): hunters. *Two Czars* (2572): Peter the Great and his brother Ivan were jointly crowned in 1682. *benting* (2577): lean (when pigeons have to feed on *bents,* a coarse grass, and their feather *molt*). *tumultuous college* (2580): Bees fight in Virgil's fourth Georgic. *Tyrant . . . below* (2582): possibly Satan. *(And . . . be)* (2383): italicized because quoted from Orrery. *require* (2586): seek.

RELIGIO LAICI

Or, A Layman's Faith

Dim as the borrow'd beams of moon and stars
To lonely, weary, wand'ring travelers,
Is Reason to the soul; and, as on high
Those rolling fires discover but the sky,
Not light us here, so Reason's glimmering ray
Was lent, not to assure our doubtful way,
But guide us upward to a better day.
And as those nightly tapers disappear,
When day's bright lord ascends our hemisphere;
So pale grows Reason at Religion's sight;   10
So dies, and so dissolves in supernatural light.
Some few, whose lamp shone brighter, have been led
From cause to cause, to nature's secret head;
And found that one first principle must be:
But what, or who, that UNIVERSAL HE;
Whether some soul incompassing this ball,
Unmade, unmov'd; yet making, moving all;
Or various atoms' interfering dance
Leapt into form, (the noble work of chance;)
Or this great all was from eternity;   20
Not ev'n the Stagirite himself could see,
And Epicurus guess'd as well as he:
As blindly grop'd they for a future state;
As rashly judg'd of providence and fate:
But least of all could their endeavors find
What most concern'd the good of humankind;
For happiness was never to be found,
But vanish'd from 'em like enchanted ground.
One thought content the good to be enjoy'd;
This every little accident destroy'd: 30
The wiser madmen did for virtue toil,
A thorny, or at best a barren soil;
In pleasure some their glutton souls would steep,
But found their line too short, the well too deep,

And leaky vessels which no bliss could keep.
Thus anxious thoughts in endless circles roll,
Without a center where to fix the soul;
In this wild maze their vain endeavors end:
How can the less the greater comprehend?
Or finite reason reach Infinity?   40
For what could fathom Good were more than He.
The Deist thinks he stands on firmer ground;
Cries: "Εὔρεκα, the mighty secret's found!
God is that spring of good; supreme and best;
We, made to serve, and in that service blest."
If so, some rules of worship must be given,
Distributed alike to all by Heaven:
Else God were partial, and to some denied
The means his justice should for all provide.
This general worship is to PRAISE and PRAY,   50
One part to borrow blessings, one to pay;
And when frail nature slides into offense,
The sacrifice for crimes is penitence.
Yet, since th' effects of providence, we find,
Are variously dispens'd to humankind;
That vice triumphs, and virtue suffers here,
(A brand that sovereign justice cannot bear;)
Our reason prompts us to a future state,
The last appeal from fortune and from fate:
Where God's all-righteous ways will be declar'd,   60
The bad meet punishment, the good reward.
    Thus man by his own strength to heaven would soar,
And would not be oblig'd to God for more.
Vain, wretched creature, how art thou misled
To think thy wit these godlike notions bred!
These truths are not the product of thy mind,
But dropp'd from heaven, and of a nobler kind.
Reveal'd Religion first inform'd thy sight,
And Reason saw not, till Faith sprung the light.
Hence all thy natural worship takes the source: 70
'T is revelation what thou think'st discourse.
Else, how com'st thou to see these truths so clear,
Which so obscure to heathens did appear?
Not Plato these, nor Aristotle found;

Nor he whose wisdom oracles renown'd.
Hast thou a wit so deep, or so sublime,
Or canst thou lower dive, or higher climb?
Canst thou, by Reason, more of Godhead know
Than Plutarch, Seneca, or Cicero?
Those giant wits, in happier ages born,   80
(When arms and arts did Greece and Rome adorn,)
Knew no such system; no such piles could raise
Of natural worship, built on pray'r and praise,
To One Sole GOD:
Nor did remorse to expiate sin prescribe,
But slew their fellow creatures for a bribe:
The guiltless victim groan'd for their offense,
And cruelty and blood was penitence.
If sheep and oxen could atone for men,
Ah! at how cheap a rate the rich might sin!   90
And great oppressors might Heaven's wrath beguile,
By offering his own creatures for a spoil!
     Dar'st thou, poor worm, offend Infinity?
And must the terms of peace be given by thee?
Then thou art Justice in the last appeal:
Thy easy God instructs thee to rebel;
And, like a king remote, and weak, must take
What satisfaction thou art pleas'd to make.
     But if there be a pow'r too just and strong
To wink at crimes, and bear unpunish'd wrong;   100
Look humbly upward, see his will disclose
The forfeit first, and then the fine impose:
A mulct thy poverty could never pay,
Had not eternal wisdom found the way,
And with celestial wealth supplied thy store:
His justice makes the fine, his mercy quits the score.
See God descending in thy human frame;
Th' offended suff'ring in th' offender's name;
All thy misdeeds to him imputed see,
And all his righteousness devolv'd on thee.   110
     For granting we have sinn'd, and that th' offense
Of man is made against Omnipotence,
Some price that bears proportion must be paid,
And infinite with infinite be weigh'd.

See then the Deist lost: remorse for vice,
Not paid; or paid, inadequate in price:
What farther means can Reason now direct,
Or what relief from human wit expect?
That shews us sick; and sadly are we sure
Still to be sick, till Heav'n reveal the cure: 120
If then Heav'n's will must needs be understood,
(Which must, if we want cure, and Heaven be good,)
Let all records of will reveal'd be shown;
With Scripture all in equal balance thrown,
And our one sacred book will be that one.
     Proof needs not here, for whether we compare
That impious, idle, superstitious ware
Of rites, lustrations, offerings, (which before,
In various ages, various countries bore,)
With Christian faith and virtues, we shall find   130
None answ'ring the great ends of humankind,
But this one rule of life, that shews us best
How God may be appeas'd, and mortals blest.
Whether from length of time its worth we draw,
The world is scarce more ancient than the law:
Heav'n's early care prescrib'd for every age;
First, in the soul, and after, in the page.
Or, whether more abstractedly we look,
Or on the writers, or the written book,
Whence, but from heav'n, could men unskill'd in arts,   140
In several ages born, in several parts,
Weave such agreeing truths, or how, or why,
Should all conspire to cheat us with a lie?
Unask'd their pains, ungrateful their advice,
Starving their gain, and martyrdom their price.
     If on the book itself we cast our view,
Concurrent heathens prove the story true;
The doctrine, miracles; which must convince,
For Heav'n in them appeals to human sense:
And tho' they prove not, they confirm the cause,   150
When what is taught agrees with nature's laws.
Then for the style; majestic and divine,
It speaks no less than God in every line:
Commanding words; whose force is still the same

As the first fiat that produc'd our frame.
All faiths beside or did by arms ascend,
Or sense indulg'd has made mankind their friend:
This only doctrine does our lusts oppose,
Unfed by nature's soil, in which it grows;
Cross to our interests, curbing sense and sin;   160
Oppress'd without, and undermin'd within,
It thrives thro' pain; its own tormentors tires;
And with a stubborn patience still aspires.
To what can Reason such effects assign,
(Transcending nature,) but to laws divine?
Which in that sacred volume are contain'd;
Sufficient, clear, and for that use ordain'd.

   But stay: the Deist here will urge anew,
No supernatural worship can be true;
Because a general law is that alone   170
Which must to all, and everywhere, be known:
A style so large as not this book can claim,
Nor aught that bears reveal'd Religion's name.
'T is said the sound of a Messiah's birth
Is gone thro' all the habitable earth;
But still that text must be confin'd alone
To what was then inhabited, and known:
And what provision could from thence accrue
To Indian souls, and worlds discover'd new?
In other parts it helps, that, ages past,   180
The Scriptures there were known, and were imbrac'd,
Till Sin spread once again the shades of night:
What 's that to these who never saw the light?

   Of all objections this indeed is chief
To startle Reason, stagger frail Belief:
We grant, 't is true, that Heav'n from human sense
Has hid the secret paths of Providence;
But boundless wisdom, boundless mercy, may
Find ev'n for those bewilder'd souls a way:
If from his nature foes may pity claim,   190
Much more may strangers who ne'er heard his name.
And tho' no name be for salvation known,
But that of his eternal Son's alone;
Who knows how far transcending goodness can

Extend the merits of that Son to man?
Who knows what reasons may his mercy lead,
Or ignorance invincible may plead?
Not only charity bids hope the best,
But more the great apostle has express'd:
That if the Gentiles (whom no law inspir'd)   200
By nature did what was by law requir'd;
They, who the written rule had never known,
Were to themselves both rule and law alone:
To nature's plain indictment they shall plead,
And by their conscience be condemn'd or freed.
Most righteous doom! because a rule reveal'd
Is none to those from whom it was conceal'd.
Then those who follow'd Reason's dictates right,
Liv'd up, and lifted high their natural light;
With Socrates may see their Maker's face,   210
While thousand rubric-martyrs want a place.
    Nor does it balk my charity, to find
Th' Egyptian bishop of another mind:
For tho' his creed eternal truth contains,
'T is hard for man to doom to endless pains
All who believ'd not all his zeal requir'd,
Unless he first could prove he was inspir'd.
Then let us either think he meant to say
This faith, where publish'd, was the only way;
Or else conclude that, Arius to confute,   220
The good old man, too eager in dispute,
Flew high; and, as his Christian fury rose,
Damn'd all for heretics who durst oppose.
    Thus far my charity this path has tried;
(A much unskilful, but well-meaning guide:)
Yet what they are, ev'n these crude thoughts were bred
By reading that which better thou hast read:
Thy matchless author's work; which thou, my friend,
By well translating better dost commend:
Those youthful hours which of thy equals most   230
In toys have squander'd, or in vice have lost,
Those hours hast thou to nobler use employ'd;
And the severe delights of truth enjoy'd.
Witness this weighty book, in which appears

The crabbed toil of many thoughtful years,
Spent by thy author in the sifting care
Of Rabbins' old sophisticated ware
From gold divine; which he who well can sort
May afterwards make algebra a sport:
A treasure, which if country curates buy,   240
They Junius and Tremellius may defy;
Save pains in various readings and translations,
And without Hebrew make most learn'd quotations:
A work so full with various learning fraught,
So nicely ponder'd, yet so strongly wrought,
As nature's height and art's last hand requir'd;
As much as man could compass, uninspir'd.
Where we may see what errors have been made
Both in the copier's and translator's trade;
How Jewish, Popish interests have prevail'd,   250
And where infallibility has fail'd.
    For some, who have his secret meaning guess'd,
Have found our author not too much a priest:
For fashion sake he seems to have recourse
To Pope, and councils, and tradition's force;
But he that old traditions could subdue,
Could not but find the weakness of the new:
If Scripture, tho' deriv'd from heav'nly birth,
Has been but carelessly preserv'd on earth;
If God's own people, who of God before   260
Knew what we know, and had been promis'd more,
In fuller terms, of Heaven's assisting care,
And who did neither time nor study spare
To keep this book untainted, unperplex'd,
Let in gross errors to corrupt the text,
Omitted paragraphs, embroil'd the sense,
With vain traditions stopp'd the gaping fence,
Which every common hand pull'd up with ease;
What safety from such brushwood-helps as these?
If written words from time are not secur'd,   270
How can we think have oral sounds endur'd?
Which thus transmitted, if one mouth has fail'd,
Immortal lies on ages are intail'd;
And that some such have been, is prov'd too plain;

If we consider interest, Church, and gain,
    "O, but," says one, "tradition set aside,
Where can we hope for an unerring guide?
For since th' original Scripture has been lost,
All copies disagreeing, maim'd the most,
Or Christian faith can have no certain ground,   280
Or truth in Church tradition must be found."
    Such an omniscient Church we wish indeed;
'T were worth both Testaments; and cast in the Creed:
But if this mother be a guide so sure,
As can all doubts resolve, all truth secure,
Then her infallibility as well
Where copies are corrupt or lame can tell;
Restore lost canon with as little pains,
As truly explicate what still remains;
Which yet no council dare pretend to do,   290
Unless like Esdras they could write it new:
Strange confidence, still to interpret true,
Yet not be sure that all they have explain'd,
Is in the blest original contain'd.
More safe, and much more modest 't is, to say
God would not leave mankind without a way;
And that the Scriptures, tho' not everywhere
Free from corruption, or intire, or clear,
Are uncorrupt, sufficient, clear, intire,
In all things which our needful faith require.   300
If others in the same glass better see,
'T is for themselves they look, but not for me:
For MY salvation must its doom receive,
Not from what OTHERS but what *I* believe.
    Must all tradition then be set aside?
This to affirm were ignorance or pride.
Are there not many points, some needful sure
To saving faith, that Scripture leaves obscure?
Which every sect will wrest a several way
(For what one sect interprets, all sects may):   310
We hold, and say we prove from Scripture plain,
That Christ is GOD; the bold Socinian
From the same Scripture urges he 's but MAN.
Now what appeal can end th' important suit;

Both parts talk loudly, but the rule is mute?
    Shall I speak plain, and in a nation free
Assume an honest layman's liberty?
I think (according to my little skill,
To my own Mother Church submitting still)
That many have been sav'd, and many may, 320
Who never heard this question brought in play.
Th' unletter'd Christian, who believes in gross,
Plods on to heaven, and ne'er is at a loss;
For the strait gate would be made straiter yet,
Were none admitted there but men of wit.
The few by nature form'd, with learning fraught,
Born to instruct, as others to be taught,
Must study well the sacred page, and see
Which doctrine, this, or that, does best agree
With the whole tenor of the work divine, 330
And plainliest points to Heaven's reveal'd design;
Which exposition flows from genuine sense,
And which is forc'd by wit and eloquence.
Not that tradition's parts are useless here,
When general, old, disinteress'd and clear:
[That ancient Fathers thus expound the page]
Gives truth the reverend majesty of age;
Confirms its force, by biding every test;
For best authority's next rules are best.
And still the nearer to the spring we go, 340
More limpid, more unsoil'd the waters flow.
Thus, first traditions were a proof alone,
Could we be certain such they were, so known;
But since some flaws in long descent may be,
They make not truth, but probability.
Even Arius and Pelagius durst provoke
To what the centuries preceding spoke.
Such difference is there in an oft-told tale;
But truth by its own sinews will prevail.
Tradition written therefore more commends 350
Authority, than what from voice descends;
And this, as perfect as its kind can be,
Rolls down to us the sacred history,
Which, from the Universal Church receiv'd,

Is tried, and after for itself believ'd.
　The partial Papists would infer from hence
Their Church, in last resort, should judge the sense;
But first they would assume, with wondrous art,
Themselves to be the whole, who are but part
Of that vast frame, the Church; yet grant they were   360
The handers down, can they from thence infer
A right t' interpret? or would they alone
Who brought the present, claim it for their own?
The book 's a common largess to mankind,
Not more for them than every man design'd;
The welcome news is in the letter found;
The carrier 's not commission'd to expound.
It speaks itself, and what it does contain,
In all things needful to be known, is plain.
　(In times o'ergrown with rust and ignorance,)   370
A gainful trade their clergy did advance;
When want of learning kept the laymen low,
And none but priests were authoriz'd to know;
When what small knowledge was, in them did dwell,
And he a god who could not read or spell;
Then Mother Church did mightily prevail;
She parcell'd out the Bible by retail;
But still expounded what she sold or gave,
To keep it in her power to damn and save:
Scripture was scarce, and, as the market went,   380
Poor laymen took salvation on content;
As needy men take money, good or bad:
God's word they had not, but the priest's they had.
Yet, whate'er false conveyances they made,
The lawyer still was certain to be paid.
　In those dark times they learn'd their knack so well,
That by long use they grew infallible:
At last, a knowing age began t' enquire
If they the book, or that did them inspire;
And, making narrower search, they found, tho' late,   390
That what they thought the priest's was their estate,
Taught by the will produc'd, (the written word,)
How long they had been cheated on record.
Then every man who saw the title fair
Claim'd a child's part, and put in for a share;

Consulted soberly his private good,
And sav'd himself as cheap as e'er he could.
    'T is true, my friend, (and far be flattery hence,)
This good had full as bad a consequence:
The book thus put in every vulgar hand,   400
Which each presum'd he best could understand,
The common rule was made the common prey,
And at the mercy of the rabble lay.
The tender page with horny fists was gall'd,
And he was gifted most that loudest bawl'd:
The spirit gave the doctoral degree;
And every member of a company
Was of his trade and of the Bible free.
Plain truths enough for needful use they found,
But men would still be itching to expound: 410
Each was ambitious of th' obscurest place,
No measure ta'en from knowledge, all from GRACE.
Study and pains were now no more their care;
Texts were explain'd by fasting and by prayer:
This was the fruit the private spirit brought,
Occasion'd by great zeal and little thought.
While crowds unlearn'd, with rude devotion warm,
About the sacred viands buzz and swarm,
The fly-blown text creates a crawling brood,
And turns to maggots what was meant for food.   420
A thousand daily sects rise up and die;
A thousand more the perish'd race supply:
So all we make of Heaven's discover'd will
Is, not to have it, or to use it ill.
The danger 's much the same; on several shelves
If others wreck us, or we wreck ourselves.
    What then remains, but, waving each extreme,
The tides of ignorance and pride to stem?
Neither so rich a treasure to forego;
Nor proudly seek beyond our pow'r to know: 430
Faith is not built on disquisitions vain;
The things we must believe are few and plain:
But since men will believe more than they need,
And every man will make himself a creed,
In doubtful questions 't is the safest way
To learn what unsuspected ancients say;

For 't is not likely we should higher soar
In search of heav'n, than all the Church before;
Nor can we be deceiv'd, unless we see
The Scripture and the Fathers disagree.   440
If, after all, they stand suspected still,
(For no man's faith depends upon his will;)
'T is some relief that points not clearly known
(Without much hazard) may be let alone:
And after hearing what our Church can say,
If still our Reason runs another way,
That private Reason 't is more just to curb,
Than by disputes the public peace disturb.
For points obscure are of small use to learn;
But common quiet is mankind's concern.   450

   Thus have I made my own opinions clear;
Yet neither praise expect, nor censure fear:
And this unpolish'd, rugged verse, I chose,
As fittest for discourse, and nearest prose;
For while from sacred truth I do not swerve,
Tom Sternhold's, or Tom Sha—ll's rhymes will serve.

THE HIND AND THE PANTHER
A Poem in Three Parts

—Antiquam exquirite matrem.
Et vera, incessu, patuit dea.—VIRGIL

THE FIRST PART

A MILK-WHITE Hind, immortal and unchang'd,
Fed on the lawns, and in the forest rang'd;
Without unspotted, innocent within,
She fear'd no danger, for she knew no sin.
Yet had she oft been chas'd with horns and hounds
And Scythian shafts; and many winged wounds
Aim'd at her heart; was often forc'd to fly,

Antiquam . . . dea: Seek out your ancient mother. Her way of walking
has shown her true divinity.—*Aeneid* III, 96; I, 405.

And doom'd to death, tho' fated not to die.
   Not so her young; for their unequal line
Was hero's make, half human, half divine.   10
Their earthly mold obnoxious was to fate,
Th' immortal part assum'd immortal state.
Of these a slaughter'd army lay in blood,
Extended o'er the Caledonian wood,
Their native walk; whose vocal blood arose,
And cried for pardon on their perjur'd foes.
Their fate was fruitful, and the sanguine seed,
Endued with souls, encreas'd the sacred breed.
So captive Israel multiplied in chains,
A numerous exile, and enjoy'd her pains.   20
With grief and gladness mix'd, their mother view'd
Her martyr'd offspring, and their race renew'd;
Their corps to perish, but their kind to last,
So much the deathless plant the dying fruit surpass'd.
   Panting and pensive now she rang'd alone,
And wander'd in the kingdoms, once her own.
The common hunt, tho' from their rage restrain'd
By sov'reign pow'r, her company disdain'd;
Grinn'd as they pass'd, and with a glaring eye
Gave gloomy signs of secret enmity.   30
'T is true, she bounded by, and tripp'd so light,
They had not time to take a steady sight;
For Truth has such a face and such a mien,
As to be lov'd needs only to be seen.
   The bloody Bear, an *Independent* beast,
Unlick'd to form, in groans her hate express'd.
Among the timorous kind the *Quaking* Hare
Profess'd neutrality, but would not swear.
Next her the *buffoon* Ape, as atheists use,
Mimick'd all sects, and had his own to choose: 40
Still when the Lion look'd, his knees he bent,
And paid at church a courtier's compliment.
   The bristled *Baptist* Boar, impure as he,
(But whiten'd with the foam of sanctity,)
With fat pollutions fill'd the sacred place,
And mountains level'd in his furious race:
So first rebellion founded was in grace.
But since the mighty ravage which he made

In German forests had his guilt betray'd,
With broken tusks, and with a borrow'd name,
He shunn'd the vengeance, and conceal'd the shame;
So lurk'd in sects unseen. With greater guile
False Reynard fed on consecrated spoil:
The graceless beast by Athanasius first
Was chas'd from Nice; then, by Socinus nurs'd,
His impious race their blasphemy renew'd,
And nature's King thro' nature's optics view'd.
Revers'd, they view'd him lessen'd to their eye,
Nor in an infant could a God descry:
New swarming sects to this obliquely tend,
Hence they began, and here they all will end.   61

    What weight of ancient witness can prevail,
If private reason hold the public scale?
But, gracious God, how well dost thou provide
For erring judgments an unerring guide!
Thy throne is darkness in th' abyss of light,
A blaze of glory that forbids the sight.
O teach me to believe thee thus conceal'd,
And search no farther than thyself reveal'd;
But her alone for my director take,   70
Whom thou hast promis'd never to forsake!
My thoughtless youth was wing'd with vain desires,
My manhood, long misled by wand'ring fires,
Follow'd false lights; and, when their glimpse was gone,
My pride struck out new sparkles of her own.
Such was I, such by nature still I am;
Be thine the glory, and be mine the shame.
Good life be now my task: my doubts are done:
(What more could fright my faith, than three in one?)
Can I believe eternal God could lie   80
Disguis'd in mortal mold and infancy?
That the great Maker of the world could die?
And after that trust my imperfect sense,
Which calls in question his omnipotence?
Can I my reason to my faith compel,
And shall my sight, and touch, and taste rebel?
Superior faculties are set aside;
Shall their subservient organs be my guide?
Then let the moon usurp the rule of day,

And winking tapers shew the sun his way;   90
For what my senses can themselves perceive,
I need no revelation to believe.
Can they who say the host should be descried
By sense, define a body glorified?
Impassible, and penetrating parts?
Let them declare by what mysterious arts
He shot that body thro' th' opposing might
Of bolts and bars impervious to the light,
And stood before his train confess'd in open sight.
    For since thus wondrously he pass'd, 't is plain,   100
One single place two bodies did contain.
And sure the same Omnipotence as well
Can make one body in more places dwell.
Let Reason then at her own quarry fly,
But how can finite grasp infinity?
    'T is urg'd again that faith did first commence
By miracles, which are appeals to sense,
And thence concluded, that our sense must be
The motive still of credibility.
For latter ages must on former wait,   110
And what began belief, must propagate.
    But winnow well this thought, and you shall find
'T is light as chaff that flies before the wind.
Were all those wonders wrought by pow'r divine,
As means or ends of some more deep design?
Most sure as means, whose end was this alone,
To prove the Godhead of th' eternal Son.
God thus asserted: man is to believe
Beyond what sense and reason can conceive,
And for mysterious things of faith rely   120
On the proponent, Heav'n's authority.
If then our faith we for our guide admit,
Vain is the farther search of human wit;
As, when the building gains a surer stay,
We take th' unuseful scaffolding away.
Reason by sense no more can understand;
The game is play'd into another hand.
Why choose we then like *bilanders* to creep
Along the coast, and land in view to keep,
When safely we may launch into the deep?   130

In the same vessel which our Savior bore,
Himself the pilot, let us leave the shore,
And with a better guide a better world explore.
Could he his Godhead veil with flesh and blood,
And not veil these again to be our food?
His grace in both is equal in extent,
The first affords us life, the second nourishment.
And if he can, why all this frantic pain
To construe what his clearest words contain,
And make a riddle what he made so plain?   *140*
To take up half on trust, and half to try,
Name it not faith, but bungling bigotry.
Both knave and fool the merchant we may call,
To pay great sums, and to compound the small:
For who would break with Heav'n, and would not break for all?
Rest then, my soul, from endless anguish freed:
Nor sciences thy guide, nor sense thy creed.
Faith is the best ensurer of thy bliss;
The bank above must fail before the venture miss.
But heav'n and heav'n-born faith are far from thee,   *150*
Thou first apostate to divinity.
Unkennel'd range in thy Polonian plains;
A fiercer foe th' insatiate Wolf remains.
    Too boastful Britain, please thyself no more,
That beasts of prey are banish'd from thy shore:
The Bear, the Boar, and every salvage name,
Wild in effect, tho' in appearance tame,
Lay waste thy woods, destroy thy blissful bow'r,
And, muzzled tho' they seem, the mutes devour.
More haughty than the rest, the *wolfish* race   *160*
Appear with belly gaunt, and famish'd face:
Never was so deform'd a beast of grace.
His ragged tail betwixt his legs he wears,
Close clapp'd for shame; but his rough crest he rears,
And pricks up his predestinating ears.
His wild disorder'd walk, his haggard eyes,
Did all the bestial citizens surprise.
Tho' fear'd and hated, yet he rul'd a while,
As captain or companion of the spoil.
Full many a year his hateful head had been   *170*

For tribute paid, nor since in Cambria seen:
The last of all the litter scap'd by chance,
And from Geneva first infested France.
Some authors thus his pedigree will trace,
But others write him of an upstart race;
Because of Wycliffe's brood no mark he brings,
But his innate antipathy to kings.
These last deduce him from th' Helvetian kind,
Who near the Leman lake his consort lin'd:
That fi'ry Zuinglius first th' affection bred,
And meager Calvin bless'd the nuptial bed.
In Israel 'some believe him whelp'd long since,   182
When the proud Sanhedrim oppress'd the prince,
Or, since he will be Jew, derive him high'r,
When Corah with his brethren did conspire
From Moses' hand the sov'reign sway to wrest,
And Aaron of his ephod to devest:
Till opening earth made way for all to pass,
And could not bear the burden of a *class.*
The Fox and he came shuffled in the dark,   190
If ever they were stow'd in Noah's ark:
Perhaps not made; for all their barking train
The Dog (a common species) will contain.
And some wild curs, who from their masters ran,
Abhorring the supremacy of man,
In woods and caves the rebel-race began.
   Oh happy pair, how well have you encreas'd!
What ills in Church and State have you redress'd!
With teeth untried, and rudiments of claws,
Your first essay was on your native laws: 200
Those having torn with ease, and trampled down,
Your fangs you fasten'd on the miter'd crown,
And freed from God and monarchy your town.
What tho' your native kennel still be small,
Bounded betwixt a puddle and a wall;
Yet your victorious colonies are sent
Where the north ocean girds the continent.
Quicken'd with fire below, your monsters breed

Line 182: *Vid.* pref. to Heyl. *Hist. of Presb.*

In fenny Holland, and in fruitful Tweed:
And, like the first, the last effects to be   210
Drawn to the dregs of a democracy.
As, where in fields the fairy rounds are seen,
A rank sour herbage rises on the green;
So, springing where these midnight elves advance,
Rebellion prints the footsteps of the dance.
Such are their doctrines, such contempt they show
To Heav'n above, and to their prince below,
As none but traitors and blasphemers know.
God, like the tyrant of the skies, is plac'd,
And kings, like slaves, beneath the crowd debas'd.   220
So fulsome is their food that flocks refuse
To bite, and only dogs for physic use.
As, where the lightning runs along the ground,
No husbandry can heal the blasting wound;
Nor bladed grass, nor bearded corn succeeds,
But scales of scurf and putrefaction breeds:
Such wars, such waste, such fiery tracks of dearth
Their zeal has left, and such a teemless earth.
But, as the poisons of the deadliest kind
Are to their own unhappy coasts confin'd;   230
As only Indian shades of sight deprive,
And magic plants will but in Colchos thrive;
So Presbyt'ry and pestilential zeal
Can only flourish in a commonweal.
    From Celtic woods is chas'd the *wolfish* crew;
But ah! some pity e'en to brutes is due:
Their native walks, methinks, they might enjoy,
Curb'd of their native malice to destroy.
Of all the tyrannies on humankind,
The worst is that which persecutes the mind.   240
Let us but weigh at what offense we strike;
'T is but because we cannot think alike.
In punishing of this, we overthrow
The laws of nations and of nature too.
Beasts are the subjects of tyrannic sway,
Where still the stronger on the weaker prey;
Man only of a softer mold is made,

Not for his fellows' ruin, but their aid:
Created kind, beneficent, and free,
The noble image of the Deity.   250
    One portion of informing fire was giv'n
To brutes, th' inferior family of heav'n:
The smith divine, as with a careless beat,
Struck out the mute creation at a heat;
But, when arriv'd at last to human race,
The Godhead took a deep consid'ring space;
And, to distinguish man from all the rest,
Unlock'd the sacred treasures of his breast;
And mercy mix'd with reason did impart,
One to his head, the other to his heart: 260
Reason to rule, but mercy to forgive;
The first is law, the last prerogative.
And like his mind his outward form appear'd,
When, issuing naked to the wond'ring herd,
He charm'd their eyes; and, for they lov'd, they fear'd:
Not arm'd with horns of arbitrary might,
Or claws to seize their furry spoils in fight,
Or with increase of feet t' o'ertake 'em in their flight;
Of easy shape, and pliant ev'ry way;
Confessing still the softness of his clay,   270
And kind as kings upon their coronation day;
With open hands, and with extended space
Of arms, to satisfy a large embrace.
Thus kneaded up with milk, the new-made man
His kingdom o'er his kindred world began;
Till knowledge misapplied, misunderstood,
And pride of empire sour'd his balmy blood.
Then, first rebelling, his own stamp he coins;
The murth'rer Cain was latent in his loins:
And blood began its first and loudest cry   280
For diff'ring worship of the Deity.
Thus persecution rose, and farther space
Produc'd the mighty hunter of his race.
Not so the blessed Pan his flock encreas'd,
Content to fold 'em from the famish'd beast:
Mild were his laws; the Sheep and harmless Hind

Were never of the persecuting kind.
Such pity now the pious Pastor shows,
Such mercy from the British Lion flows,
That both provide protection for their foes.   290
   O happy regions, Italy and Spain,
Which never did those monsters entertain!
The Wolf, the Bear, the Boar, can there advance
No native claim of just inheritance.
And self-preserving laws, severe in show,
May guard their fences from th' invading foe.
Where birth has plac'd 'em, let 'em safely share
The common benefit of vital air.
Themselves unharmful, let them live unharm'd;
Their jaws disabled, and their claws disarm'd: 300
Here, only in nocturnal howlings bold,
They dare not seize the Hind, nor leap the fold.
More pow'rful, and as vigilant as they,
The Lion awfully forbids the prey.
Their rage repress'd, tho' pinch'd with famine sore,
They stand aloof, and tremble at his roar:
Much is their hunger, but their fear is more.
   These are the chief; to number o'er the rest,
And stand, like Adam, naming ev'ry beast,
Were weary work: nor will the Muse describe   310
A slimy-born and sun-begotten tribe;
Who, far from steeples and their sacred sound,
In fields their sullen conventicles found.
These gross, half-animated lumps I leave;
Nor can I think what thoughts they can conceive.
But if they think at all, 't is sure no high'r
Than matter, put in motion, may aspire:
Souls that can scarce ferment their mass of clay:
So drossy, so divisible are they,
As would but serve pure bodies for allay: 320
Such souls as *shards* produce, such beetle things
As only buzz to heav'n with ev'ning wings;
Strike in the dark, offending but by chance,
Such are the blindfold blows of ignorance.
They know not beings, and but hate a name;
To them the Hind and Panther are the same.

    The Panther, sure the noblest, next the Hind,
And fairest creature of the spotted kind;
O, could her inborn stains be wash'd away,
She were too good to be a beast of prey!
How can I praise, or blame, and not offend,   *331*
Or how divide the frailty from the friend!
Her faults and virtues lie so mix'd that she
Nor wholly stands condemn'd, nor wholly free.
Then, like her injur'd Lion, let me speak;
He cannot bend her, and he would not break.
Unkind already, and estrang'd in part,
The Wolf begins to share her wand'ring heart.
Tho, unpolluted yet with actual ill,
She half commits, who sins but in her will.
If, as our dreaming Platonists report,   *341*
There could be spirits of a middle sort,
Too black for heav'n, and yet too white for hell,
Who just dropp'd halfway down, nor lower fell;
So pois'd, so gently she descends from high,
It seems a soft dismission from the sky.
Her house not ancient, whatsoe'er pretense
Her clergy heralds make in her defense;
A second century not halfway run,
Since the new honors of her blood begun.
A Lion, old, obscene, and furious made   *351*
By lust, compress'd her mother in a shade;
Then, by a left-hand marriage, weds the dame,
Cov'ring adult'ry with a specious name:
So Schism begot; and Sacrilege and she,
A well-match'd pair, got graceless Heresy.
God's and kings' rebels have the same good cause,
To trample down divine and human laws;
Both would be call'd reformers, and their hate
Alike destructive both to Church and State: *360*
The fruit proclaims the plant; a lawless prince
By luxury reform'd incontinence;
O, with what ease we follow such a guide,
By ruins, charity; by riots, abstinence.
Confessions, fasts, and penance set aside;
Where souls are starv'd, and senses gratified;

Where marriage pleasures midnight pray'r supply,
And matin bells (a melancholy cry)
Are tun'd to merrier notes, *encrease* and *multiply!*
Religion shows a rosy-color'd face;   370
Not hatter'd out with drudging works of grace:
A downhill reformation rolls apace.
What flesh and blood would crowd the narrow gate,
Or, till they waste their pamper'd paunches, wait?
All would be happy at the cheapest rate.

    Tho' our lean faith these rigid laws has giv'n,
The full-fed Mussulman goes fat to heav'n;
For his Arabian prophet with delights
Of sense allur'd his Eastern proselytes.
The jolly Luther, reading him, began   380
T' interpret Scriptures by his Alcoran;
To grub the thorns beneath our tender feet,
And make the paths of paradise more sweet:
Bethought him of a wife ere halfway gone,
(For 't was uneasy travailing alone;)
And, in this masquerade of mirth and love,
Mistook the bliss of heav'n for Bacchanals above.
Sure he presum'd of praise, who came to stock
Th' ethereal pastures with so fair a flock,
Burnish'd, and batt'ning on their food, to show   390
The diligence of careful herds below.

    Our Panther, tho' like these she chang'd her head,
Yet, as the mistress of a monarch's bed,
Her front erect with majesty she bore,
The crosier wielded, and the miter wore.
Her upper part of decent discipline
Shew'd affectation of an ancient line;
And Fathers, councils, Church and Church's head,
Were on her reverend phylacteries read.
But what disgrac'd and disavow'd the rest,   400
Was Calvin's brand, that stigmatiz'd the beast.
Thus, like a creature of a double kind,
In her own labyrinth she lives confin'd;
To foreign lands no sound of her is come,
Humbly content to be despis'd at home.

Such is her faith; where good cannot be had,
At least she leaves the refuse of the bad:
Nice in her choice of ill, tho' not of best,
And least deform'd, because reform'd the least.
In doubtful points betwixt her diff'ring friends,   410
Where one for substance, one for sign contends,
Their contradicting terms she strives to join;
Sign shall be substance, substance shall be sign.
A real presence all her sons allow,
And yet 't is flat idolatry to bow,
Because the Godhead's there they know not how.
Her novices are taught that bread and wine
Are but the visible and outward sign,
Receiv'd by those who in communion join;
But th' inward grace, or the thing signified,   420
His blood and body, who to save us died:
The faithful this thing signified receive.
What is 't those faithful then partake or leave?
For what is signified and understood,
Is, by her own confession, flesh and blood.
Then, by the same acknowledgment, we know
They take the sign, and take the substance too.
The lit'ral sense is hard to flesh and blood,
But nonsense never can be understood.

   Her wild belief on ev'ry wave is toss'd;   430
But sure no Church can better morals boast;
True to her king her principles are found;
O that her practice were but half so sound!
Steadfast in various turns of state she stood,
And scal'd her vow'd affection with her blood:
Nor will I meanly tax her constancy,
That int'rest or obligement made the tie
(Bound to the fate of murder'd monarchy.)
Before the sounding ax so falls the vine,
Whose tender branches round the poplar twine.   440
She chose her ruin, and resign'd her life,
In death undaunted as an Indian wife:
A rare example! but some souls we see
Grow hard, and stiffen with adversity:

Yet these by fortune's favors are undone;
Resolv'd, into a baser form they run,
And bore the wind, but cannot bear the sun.
Let this be Nature's frailty, or her fate,
Or *Isgrim's counsel, her new-chosen mate;
Still she's the fairest of the fallen crew,   450
No mother more indulgent, but the true.
   Fierce to her foes, yet fears her force to try,
Because she wants innate auctority;
For how can she constrain them to obey,
Who has herself cast off the lawful sway?
Rebellion equals all, and those who toil
In common theft will share the common spoil.
Let her produce the title and the right
Against her old superiors first to fight;
If she reform by text, ev'n that's as plain   460
For her own rebels to reform again.
As long as words a diff'rent sense will bear,
And each may be his own interpreter,
Our airy faith will no foundation find;
The word 's a weathercock for ev'ry wind:
The Bear, the Fox, the Wolf, by turns prevail;
The most in pow'r supplies the present gale.
The wretched Panther cries aloud for aid
To Church and councils, whom she first betray'd;
No help from Fathers or tradition's train: 470
Those ancient guides she taught us to disdain,
And by that Scripture which she once abus'd
To reformation stands herself accus'd.
What bills for breach of laws can she prefer,
Expounding which she owns herself may err?
And, after all her winding ways are tried,
If doubts arise, she slips herself aside,
And leaves the private conscience for the guide.
If then that conscience set th' offender free,
It bars her claim to Church auctority.   480
How can she censure, or what crime pretend,

---

* The Wolf.

But Scripture may be construed to defend?
Ev'n those whom for rebellion she transmits
To civil pow'r, her doctrine first acquits;
Because no disobedience can ensue,
Where no submission to a judge is due;
Each judging for himself, by her consent,
Whom thus absolv'd she sends to punishment.
Suppose the magistrate revenge her cause,
'T is only for transgressing human laws.   490
How answ'ring to its end a Church is made,
Whose pow'r is but to counsel and persuade?
O solid rock, on which secure she stands!
Eternal house, not built with mortal hands!
O sure defense against th' infernal gate,
A patent during pleasure of the State!
    Thus is the Panther neither lov'd nor fear'd,
A mere mock queen of a divided herd,
Whom soon by lawful pow'r she might control,
Herself a part submitted to the whole.   500
Then, as the moon who first receives the light
By which she makes our nether regions bright,
So might she shine, reflecting from afar
The rays she borrow'd from a better star;
Big with the beams which from her mother flow,
And reigning o'er the rising tides below:
Now, mixing with a salvage crowd, she goes,
And meanly flatters her invet'rate foes;
Rul'd while she rules, and losing ev'ry hour
Her wretched remnants or precarious pow'r.   510
    One evening, while the cooler shade she sought,
Revolving many a melancholy thought,
Alone she walk'd, and look'd around in vain,
With rueful visage, for her vanish'd train:
None of her sylvan subjects made their court;
Levées and couchées pass'd without resort.
So hardly can usurpers manage well
Those whom they first instructed to rebel:
More liberty begets desire of more;
The hunger still encreases with the store.   520

Without respect they brush'd along the wood,
Each in his clan, and, fill'd with loathsome food,
Ask'd no permission to the neighb'ring flood.
The Panther, full of inward discontent,
Since they would go, before 'em wisely went;
Supplying want of pow'r by drinking first,
As if she gave 'em leave to quench their thirst.
Among the rest, the Hind, with fearful face,
Beheld from far the common wat'ring place,
Nor durst approach; till with an awful roar   530
The sovereign Lion bade her fear no more.
Encourag'd thus she brought her younglings nigh,
Watching the motions of her patron's eye,
And drank a sober draught; the rest amaz'd
Stood mutely still, and on the stranger gaz'd;
Survey'd her part by part, and sought to find
The ten-horn'd monster in the harmless Hind,
Such as the Wolf and Panther had design'd.
They thought at first they dream'd; for 't was offense
With them to question certitude of sense,   540
Their guide in faith; but nearer when they drew,
And had the faultless object full in view,
Lord, how they all admir'd her heav'nly hue!
Some, who before her fellowship disdain'd,
Scarce, and but scarce, from inborn rage restrain'd,
Now frisk'd about her, and old kindred feign'd.
Whether for love or int'rest, ev'ry sect
Of all the salvage nation shew'd respect:
The viceroy Panther could not awe the herd;
The more the company, the less they fear'd.   550
The surly Wolf with secret envy burst,
Yet could not howl; the Hind had seen him first:
But what he durst not speak, the Panther durst.
    For when the herd, suffis'd, did late repair
To ferny heaths, and to their forest lair,
She made a mannerly excuse to stay,
Proff'ring the Hind to wait her half the way;
That, since the sky was clear, an hour of talk
Might help her to beguile the tedious walk.
With much good will the motion was embrac'd,   560

To chat a while on their adventures pass'd;
Nor had the grateful Hind so soon forgot
Her friend and fellow-suff'rer in the Plot.
Yet wond'ring how of late she grew estrang'd,
Her forehead cloudy, and her count'nance chang'd,
She thought this hour th' occasion would present
To learn her secret cause of discontent,
Which well she hop'd might be with ease redress'd,
Consid'ring her a well-bred civil beast,
And more a gentlewoman than the rest.   570
After some common talk what rumors ran,
The lady of the spotted muff began.

THE SECOND PART

"Dame," said the Panther, "times are mended well,
Since late among the Philistines you fell.
The toils were pitch'd, a spacious tract of ground
With expert huntsmen was encompass'd round;
Th' enclosure narrow'd; the sagacious pow'r
Of hounds and death drew nearer ev'ry hour.
'T is true, the younger Lion scap'd the snare,
But all your priestly calves lay struggling there,   580
As sacrifices on their altars laid;
While you, their careful mother, wisely fled,   [10]
Not trusting destiny to save your head.
For, whate'er promises you have applied
To your unfailing Church, the surer side
Is four fair legs in danger to provide.
And whate'er tales of Peter's chair you tell,
Yet, saving reverence of the miracle,
The better luck was yours to scape so well."
    "As I remember," said the sober Hind,   590
"Those toils were for your own dear self design'd,
As well as me; and with the selfsame throw,   [20]
To catch the quarry and the vermin too:
(Forgive the sland'rous tongues that call'd you so.)
Howe'er you take it now, the common cry

Then ran you down for your rank loyalty.
Besides, in Popery they thought you nurs'd,
(As evil tongues will ever speak the worst,)
Because some forms, and ceremonies some
You kept, and stood in the main question dumb.   600
Dumb you were born indeed; but, thinking long,
The Test it seems at last has loos'd your tongue.   [30]
And, to explain what your forefathers meant,
By real presence in the sacrament,
(After long fencing, push'd against a wall,)
Your *salvo* comes, that he's not there at all:
There chang'd your faith, and what may change may fall.
Who can believe what varies every day,
Nor ever was, nor will be at a stay?"
   "Tortures may force the tongue untruths to tell,   610
And I ne'er own'd myself infallible,"
Replied the Panther: "grant such presence were,   [40]
Yet in your sense I never own'd it there.
A real *virtue* we by faith receive,
And that we in the sacrament believe."
   "Then," said the Hind, "as you the matter state,
Not only Jesuits can equivocate;
For *real* as you now the word expound,
From solid substance dwindles to a sound.
Methinks an Æsop's fable you repeat;   620
You know who took the shadow for the meat:
Your Church's substance thus you change at will,   [50]
And yet retain your former figure still.
I freely grant you spoke to save your life,
For then you lay beneath the butcher's knife.
Long time you fought, redoubled batt'ry bore,
But, after all, against yourself you swore:
Your former self; for ev'ry hour your form
Is chopp'd and chang'd, like winds before a storm.
Thus fear and int'rest will prevail with some;   630
For all have not the gift of martyrdom."
   The Panther grinn'd at this, and thus replied: [60]
"That men may err was never yet denied.
But, if that common principle be true,
The cannon, dame, is level'd full at you.

But, shunning long disputes, I fain would see
That wondrous wight Infallibility.
Is he from heav'n, this mighty champion, come,
Or lodg'd below in subterranean Rome?
First, seat him somewhere, and derive his race,   640
Or else conclude that nothing has no place."
    "Suppose, (tho' I disown it,)" said the Hind,   [70]
"The certain mansion were not yet assign'd;
The doubtful residence no proof can bring
Against the plain existence of the thing.
Because philosophers may disagree,
If sight b' emission or reception be,
Shall it be thence inferr'd, I do not see?
But you require an answer positive,
Which yet, when I demand, you dare not give;   650
For fallacies in universals live.
I then affirm that this unfailing guide   [80]
In Pope and gen'ral councils must reside;
Both lawful, both combin'd: what one decrees
By numerous votes, the other ratifies:
On this undoubted sense the Church relies.
'T is true, some doctors in a scantier space,
I mean, in each apart, contract the place.
Some, who to greater length extend the line,
The Church's after-acceptation join.   660
This last circumference appears too wide;
The Church diffus'd is by the council tied;   [90]
As members by their representatives
Oblig'd to laws which prince and senate gives.
Thus some contract, and some enlarge the space;
In Pope and council who denies the place,
Assisted from above with God's unfailing grace?
Those canons all the needful points contain;
Their sense so obvious, and their words so plain,
That no disputes about the doubtful text   670
Have, hitherto, the lab'ring world perplex'd.
If any should in aftertimes appear,   [100]
New councils must be call'd, to make the meaning clear;
Because in them the pow'r supreme resides,
And all the promises are to the guides.

This may be taught with sound and safe defense;
But mark how sandy is your own pretense,
Who, setting councils, Pope, and Church aside,
Are ev'ry man his own presuming guide.
The sacred books, you say, are full and plain,   680
And ev'ry needful point of truth contain:
All, who can read, interpreters may be.   [*110*]
Thus, tho' your sev'ral Churches disagree,
Yet ev'ry saint has to himself alone
The secret of this philosophic stone.
These principles your jarring sects unite,
When diff'ring doctors and disciples fight.
Tho' Luther, Zuinglius, Calvin, holy chiefs,
Have made a battle-royal of beliefs;
Or, like wild horses, sev'ral ways have whirl'd   690
The tortur'd text about the Christian world;
Each Jehu lashing on with furious force,   [*120*]
That Turk or Jew could not have us'd it worse;
No matter what dissension leaders make,
Where ev'ry private man may save a stake:
Rul'd by the Scripture and his own advice,
Each has a blind by-path to Paradise;
Where, driving in a circle, slow or fast,
Opposing sects are sure to meet at last.
A wondrous charity you have in store   700
For all reform'd to pass the narrow door
So much, that Mahomet had scarcely more: [*130*]
For he, kind prophet, was for damning none;
But Christ and Moses were to save their own:
Himself was to secure his chosen race,
Tho' reason good for Turks to take the place,
And he allow'd to be the better man,
In virtue of his holier Alcoran."
    "True," said the Panther, "I shall ne'er deny
My brethren may be sav'd as well as I: 710
Tho' Huguenots contemn our ordination,
Succession, ministerial vocation;   [*140*]
And Luther, more mistaking what he read,
Misjoins the sacred body with the bread:
Yet, *lady,* still remember I maintain,
The word in needful points is only plain."

"Needless, or needful, I not now contend,
For still you have a loophole for a friend;"
Rejoin'd the matron: "but the rule you lay
Has led whole flocks, and leads them still astray   720
In weighty points, and full damnation's way.
For did not Arius first, Socinus now,   [*150*]
The Son's eternal Godhead disavow?
And did not these by gospel texts alone
Condemn our doctrine, and maintain their own?
Have not all heretics the same pretense
To plead the Scriptures in their own defense?
How did the Nicene Council then decide
That strong debate? was it by Scripture tried?
No, sure to those the rebel would not yield;   730
Squadrons of texts he marshal'd in the field;
That was but civil war, an equal set,   [*160*]
Where piles with piles, and eagles eagles met.
With texts point-blank and plain he fac'd the foe:
And did not Sathan tempt our Savior so?
The good old bishops took a simpler way;
Each ask'd but what he heard his father say,
Or how he was instructed in his youth,
And by tradition's force upheld the truth."
    The Panther smil'd at this: "And when," said she,   740
"Were those first councils disallow'd by me?
Or where did I at sure tradition strike,   [*170*]
Provided still it were apostolic?"
    "Friend," said the Hind, "you quit your former ground,
Where all your faith you did on Scripture found:
Now 't is tradition join'd with Holy Writ;
But thus your memory betrays your wit."
    "No," said the Panther, "for in that I view
When your tradition's forg'd, and when 't is true.
I set 'em by the rule, and, as they square,   750
Or deviate from undoubted doctrine there,
This oral fiction, that old faith declare."   [*180*]
    (*Hind.*) "The Council steer'd, it seems, a diff'rent course:
They tried the Scripture by tradition's force:
But you tradition by the Scripture try;
Pursued by sects, from this to that you fly,
Nor dare on one foundation to rely.

The word is then depos'd, and in this view
You rule the Scripture, not the Scripture you."
Thus said the *dame,* and, smiling, thus pursued: 760
"I see, tradition then is disallow'd,
When not evinc'd by Scripture to be true,   [*190*]
And Scripture, as interpreted by you.
But here you tread upon unfaithful ground;
Unless you could infallibly expound:
Which you reject as odious Popery,
And throw that doctrine back with scorn on me.
Suppose we on things traditive divide,
And both appeal to Scripture to decide;
By various texts we both uphold our claim,   770
Nay, often ground our titles on the same:
After long labor lost, and time's expense,   [*200*]
Both grant the words, and quarrel for the sense.
Thus all disputes for ever must depend,
For no dumb rule can controversies end.
Thus, when you said tradition must be tried
By Sacred Writ, whose sense yourselves decide,
You said no more, but that yourselves must be
The judges of the Scripture sense, not we.
Against our Church-tradition you declare,   780
And yet your clerks would sit in Moses' chair:
At least 't is prov'd against your argument,   [*210*]
The rule is far from plain, where all dissent."
    "If not by Scriptures, how can we be sure,"
Replied the Panther, "what tradition's pure?
For you may palm upon us new for old:
All, as they say, that glitters is not gold."
    "How but by following her," replied the dame,
"To whom deriv'd from sire to son they came;
Where ev'ry age does on another move,   790
And trusts no farther than the next above;
Where all the rounds like Jacob's ladder rise,   [*220*]
The lowest hid in earth, the topmost in the skies."
    Sternly the salvage did her answer mark,
Her glowing eyeballs glitt'ring in the dark,
And said but this: "Since lucre was your trade,
Succeeding times such dreadful gaps have made,

'T is dangerous climbing: to your sons and you
I leave the ladder, and its omen too."
   (*Hind.*) "The Panther's breath was ever fam'd for sweet;   800
But from the Wolf such wishes oft I meet:
You learn'd this language from the Blatant Beast,   [230]
Or rather did not speak, but were possess'd.
As for your answer, 't is but barely urg'd:
You must evince tradition to be forg'd;
Produce plain proofs; unblemish'd authors use,.
As ancient as those ages they accuse;
Till when, 't is not sufficient to defame:
An old possession stands, till elder quits the claim.
Then for our int'rest, which is nam'd alone   810
To load with envy, we retort your own.
For when traditions in your faces fly,   [240]
Resolving not to yield, you must decry.
As, when the cause goes hard, the guilty man
Excepts, and thins his jury all he can;
So, when you stand of other aid bereft,
You to the twelve apostles would be left.
Your friend the Wolf did with more craft provide
To set those toys, traditions, quite aside;
And Fathers too, unless when, reason spent,   820
He cites 'em but sometimes for ornament.
But, madam Panther, you, tho' more sincere,   [250]
Are not so wise as your adulterer:
The private spirit is a better blind
Than all the dodging tricks your authors find.
For they, who left the Scripture to the crowd,
Each for his own peculiar judge allow'd;
The way to please 'em was to make 'em proud.
Thus, with full sails, they ran upon the shelf:
Who could suspect a cozenage from himself?   830
On his own reason safer 't is to stand,
Than be deceiv'd and damn'd at second hand.   [260]
But you, who Fathers and traditions take,
And garble some, and some you quite forsake,
Pretending Church auctority to fix,
And yet some grains of private spirit mix,
Are like a mule made up of diff'ring seed,

And that's the reason why you never breed;
At least not propagate your kind abroad,
For home dissenters are by statutes aw'd.
And yet they grow upon you ev'ry day,
While you (to speak the best) are at a stay,   [270]   842
For sects that are extremes abhor a middle way.
Like tricks of state, to stop a raging flood,
Or mollify a mad-brain'd senate's mood,
Of all expedients never one was good.
Well may they argue, (nor can you deny,)
If we must fix on Church auctority,
Best on the best, the fountain, not the flood;
That must be better still, if this be good.
Shall she command, who has herself rebell'd?   851
Is Antichrist by Antichrist expell'd?   [280]
Did we a lawful tyranny displace,
To set aloft a bastard of the race?
Why all these wars to win the Book, if we
Must not interpret for ourselves, but she?
Either be wholly slaves, or wholly free.
For *purging* fires traditions must not fight,
But they must prove episcopacy's right.
Thus those led horses are from service freed;   860
You never mount 'em but in time of need.
Like mercenaries, hir'd for home defense,   [290]
They will not serve against their native prince.
Against domestic foes of *hierarchy*
These are drawn forth, to make Fanatics fly;
But, when they see their countrymen at hand,
Marching against 'em under Church command,
Straight they forsake their colors, and disband."
     Thus she, nor could the Panther well enlarge
With weak defense against so strong a charge;   870
But said: "For what did Christ his word provide,
If still his Church must want a living guide?   [300]
And if all saving doctrines are not there,
Or sacred penmen could not make 'em clear,
From after ages we should hope in vain
For truths which men inspir'd could not explain."
     "Before the word was written," said the Hind,

"Our Savior preach'd his faith to humankind:
From his apostles the first age receiv'd
Eternal truth, and what they taught believ'd.   880
Thus by tradition faith was planted first;
Succeeding flocks succeeding pastors nurs'd.   [310]
This was the way our wise Redeemer chose,
(Who sure could all things for the best dispose,)
To fence his fold from their encroaching foes.
He could have writ himself, but well foresaw
Th' event would be like that of Moses' law;
Some difference would arise, some doubts remain,
Like those which yet the jarring Jews maintain.
No written laws can be so plain, so pure,
But wit may gloss, and malice may obscure;   891
Not those indited by his first command—   [320]
A prophet grav'd the text, an angel held his hand.
Thus faith was ere the written word appear'd,
And men believ'd, not what they read, but heard.
But since th' apostles could not be confin'd
To these, or those, but severally design'd
Their large commission round the world to blow,
To spread their faith, they spread their labors too.
Yet still their absent flock their pains did share;   900
They harken'd still, for love produces care.
And, as mistakes arose, or discords fell,   [330]
Or bold seducers taught 'em to rebel;
As charity grew cold, or faction hot,
Or long neglect their lessons had forgot;
For all their wants they wisely did provide,
And preaching by epistles was supplied:
So great physicians cannot all attend,
But some they visit, and to some they send.
Yet all those letters were not writ to all;
Nor first intended, but occasional,   911
Their absent sermons; nor if they contain   [340]
All needful doctrines, are those doctrines plain.
Clearness by frequent preaching must be wrought,
They writ but seldom, but they daily taught.
And what one saint has said of holy Paul,
He darkly writ, is true applied to all.

For this obscurity could Heav'n provide
More prudently than by a living guide,
As doubts arose, the difference to decide?
A guide was therefore needful, therefore made;   *921*
And, if appointed, sure to be obey'd.   *[350]*
Thus, with due rev'rence to th' apostles' writ,
By which my sons are taught, to which submit;
I think, those truths their sacred works contain,
The Church alone can certainly explain;
That following ages, leaning on the past,
May rest upon the primitive at last.
Nor would I thence the word no rule infer,
But none without the Church interpreter;
Because, as I have urg'd before, 't is mute,
And is itself the subject of dispute.   *[360]* *932*
But what th' apostles their successors taught,
They to the next, from them to us is brought,
Th' undoubted sense which is in Scripture sought.
From hence the Church is arm'd, when errors rise,
To stop their entrance, and prevent surprise;
And, safe entrench'd within, her foes without defies.
By these all fest'ring sores her counsels heal,
Which time or has disclos'd, or shall reveal;   *940*
For discord cannot end without a last appeal.
Nor can a council national decide,   *[370]*
But with subordination to her guide:
(I wish the cause were on that issue tried.)
Much less the Scripture; for suppose debate
Betwixt pretenders to a fair estate,
Bequeath'd by some legator's last intent;
(Such is our dying Savior's testament:)
The will is prov'd, is open'd, and is read;
The doubtful heirs their diff'ring titles plead: *950*
All vouch the words their int'rest to maintain,
And each pretends by those his cause is plain.   *[380]*
Shall then the testament award the right?
No, that's the Hungary for which they fight;
The field of battle, subject of debate;
The thing contended for, the fair estate.
The sense is intricate, 't is only clear

What vowels and what consonants are there.
Therefore 't is plain, its meaning must be tried
Before some judge appointed to decide."   960
    "Suppose," the fair apostate said, "I grant
The faithful flock some living guide should want,   [390]
Your arguments an endless chase pursue:
Produce this vaunted leader to our view,
This mighty Moses of the chosen crew."
    The dame, who saw her fainting foe retir'd,
With force renew'd, to victory aspir'd;
And, looking upward to her kindred sky,
As once our Savior own'd his deity,
Pronounc'd his words—*She whom ye seek am I.*   970
Nor less amaz'd this voice the Panther heard,
Than were those Jews to hear a god declar'd.   [400]
Then thus the matron modestly renew'd:
"Let all your prophets and their sects be view'd,
And see to which of 'em yourselves think fit
The conduct of your conscience to submit:
Each proselyte would vote his doctor best,
With absolute exclusion to the rest;
Thus would your Polish diet disagree,
And end, as it began, in anarchy.   980
Yourself the fairest for election stand,
Because you seem crown-gen'ral of the land;   [410]
But soon against your superstitious lawn
Some Presbyterian saber would be drawn:
In your establish'd laws of sov'reignty
The rest some fundamental flaw would see,
And call rebellion gospel-liberty.
To Church decrees your articles require
Submission modified, if not entire;
Homage denied, to censures you proceed: 990
But when *Curtana* will not do the deed,
You lay that pointless clergy-weapon by,   [420]
And to the laws, your sword of justice, fly.
Now this your sects the more unkindly take,
(Those prying varlets hit the blots you make,)
Because some ancient friends of yours declare,
Your only rule of faith the Scriptures are,

Interpreted by men of judgment sound,
Which ev'ry sect will for themselves expound;
Nor think less rev'rence to their doctors due   *1000*
For sound interpretation, than to you.
If then by able heads are understood   [430]
Your brother prophets, who reform'd abroad,
Those able heads expound a wiser way,
That their own sheep their shepherd should obey.
But if you mean yourselves are only sound,
That doctrine turns the Reformation round,
And all the rest are false reformers found;
Because in sundry points you stand alone,
Not in communion join'd with any one;   *1010*
And therefore must be all the Church, or none.
Then, till you have agreed whose judge is best,   [440]
Against this forc'd submission they protest:
While *sound* and *sound* a diff'rent sense explains,
Both play at hardhead till they break their brains;
And from their chairs each other's force defy,
While unregarded thunders vainly fly.
I pass the rest, because your Church alone
Of all usurpers best could fill the throne.
But neither you, nor any sect beside,   *1020*
For this high office can be qualified
With necessary gifts requir'd in such a guide.   [450]
For that which must direct the whole must be
Bound in one bond of faith and unity,
But all your sev'ral Churches disagree.
The *consubstantiating* Church and priest
Refuse communion to the Calvinist:
The French reform'd from preaching you restrain,
Because you judge their ordination vain;
And so they judge of yours, but donors must ordain.   *1030*
In short, in doctrine, or in discipline,
Not one reform'd can with another join: [460]
But all from each as from damnation fly;
No union they pretend, but in *non-Popery*.
Nor, should their members in a synod meet,
Could any Church presume to mount the seat
Above the rest, their discords to decide;

None would obey, but each would be the guide;
And face to face dissensions would encrease,
For only distance now preserves the peace.
All in their turns accusers, and accus'd,   1041
Babel was never half so much confus'd.   [470]
What one can plead, the rest can plead as well;
For amongst equals lies no last appeal,
And all confess themselves are fallible.
Now since you grant some necessary guide,
All who can err are justly laid aside:
Because a trust so sacred to confer
Shows want of such a sure interpreter;
And how can he be needful who can err?   1050
Then, granting that unerring guide we want,
That such there is you stand oblig'd to grant: [480]
Our Savior else were wanting to supply
Our needs, and obviate that necessity.
It then remains, that Church can only be
The guide, which owns unfailing certainty;
Or else you slip your hold, and change your side,
Relapsing from a necessary guide.
But this annex'd condition of the crown,
Immunity from errors, you disown;   1060
Here then you shrink, and lay your weak pretensions down.
For petty royalties you raise debate,   [490]
But this unfailing universal State
You shun, nor dare succed to such a glorious weight;
And for that cause those promises detest,
With which our Savior did his Church invest;
But strive t' evade, and fear to find 'em true,
As conscious they were never meant to you:
All which the Mother Church asserts her own,
And with unrival'd claim ascends the throne.   1070
So when of old th' Almighty Father sate
In council, to redeem our ruin'd state,   [500]
Millions of millions, at a distance round,
Silent the sacred consistory crown'd,
To hear what mercy mix'd with justice could propound;
All prompt, with eager pity, to fulfil
The full extent of their Creator's will:

But when the stern conditions were declar'd,
A mournful whisper thro' the host was heard,
And the whole hierarchy, with heads hung down,   1080
Submissively declin'd the pond'rous proffer'd crown.
Then, not till then, th' eternal Son from high   [510]
Rose in the strength of all the Deity;
Stood forth t' accept the terms, and underwent
A weight which all the frame of heav'n had bent,
Nor he himself could bear, but as omnipotent.
Now, to remove the least remaining doubt,
That ev'n the blear-ey'd sects may find her out,
Behold what heav'nly rays adorn her brows,
What from his wardrobe her belov'd allows   1090
To deck the wedding day of his unspotted spouse.
Behold what marks of majesty she brings;   [520]
Richer than ancient heirs of Eastern kings:
Her right hand holds the scepter and the keys,
To shew whom she commands, and who obeys;
With these to bind, or set the sinner free,
With that t' assert spiritual royalty.
    "One in herself, not rent by schism, but sound,
Entire, one solid shining diamond;
Not sparkles shatter'd into sects like you: 1100
One is the Church, and must be to be true;
One central principle of unity.   [530]
    "As undivided, so from errors free,
As one in faith, so one in sanctity.
Thus she, and none but she, th' insulting rage
Of heretics oppos'd from age to age:
Still when the giant-brood invades her throne,
She stoops from heav'n, and meets 'em halfway down,
And with paternal thunder vindicates her crown.   1109
But like Egyptian sorcerers you stand,
And vainly lift aloft your magic wand,
To sweep away the swarms of vermin from the land: [540]
You could, like them, with like infernal force,
Produce the plague, but not arrest the course.
But when the boils and botches, with disgrace
And public scandal, sat upon the face,

Line 1100: Marks of the Catholic Church from the Nicene Creed.

Themselves attack'd, the *Magi* strove no more,
They saw God's finger, and their fate deplore;
Themselves they could not cure of the dishonest sore.

   "Thus one, thus pure, behold her largely spread,   *1120*
Like the fair ocean from her mother-bed;
From east to west triumphantly she rides,   *[550]*
All shores are water'd by her wealthy tides:
The gospel-sound diffus'd from pole to pole,
Where winds can carry, and where waves can roll;
The selfsame doctrine of the sacred page
Convey'd to ev'ry clime, in ev'ry age.

   "Here let my sorrow give my satire place,
To raise new blushes on my British race;
Our sailing ships like common shores we use,   *1130*
And thro' our distant colonies diffuse
The draughts of dungeons, and the stench of stews;   *[560]*
Whom, when their home-bred honesty is lost,
We disembogue on some far Indian coast;
Thieves, panders, palliards, sins of ev'ry sort;
Those are the manufacturers we export;
And these the *missioners* our zeal has made:
For, with my country's pardon be it said,
Religion is the least of all our trade.

   "Yet some improve their traffic more than we;   *1140*
For they on gain, their only god, rely;
And set a public price on piety.   *[570]*
Industrious of the needle and the chart,
They run full sail to their Japonian mart;
Prevention fear, and, prodigal of fame,
Sell all of Christian to the very name;
Nor leave enough of that to hide their naked shame.

   "Thus, of three marks, which in the Creed we view,
Not one of all can be applied to you:
Much less the fourth; in vain, alas, you seek   *1150*
Th' ambitious title of apostolic:
Godlike descent! 't is well your blood can be   *[580]*
Prov'd noble in the third or fourth degree:
For all of ancient that you had before
(I mean what is not borrow'd from our store)
Was error fulminated o'er and o'er;
Old heresies condemn'd in ages past,

By care and time recover'd from the blast.
" 'T is said with ease, but never can be prov'd,
The Church her old foundations has remov'd,   *1160*
And built new doctrines on unstable sands:
Judge that, ye winds and rains; you prov'd her, yet she stands.
Those ancient doctrines, charg'd on her for new,   [*591*]
Shew when, and how, and from what hands they grew.
We claim no pow'r, when heresies grow bold,
To coin new faith, but still declare the old.
How else could that obscene disease be purg'd,
When controverted texts are vainly urg'd?
To prove tradition new, there's somewhat more
Requir'd, than saying: ' 'T was not us'd before.'   *1170*
Those monumental arms are never stirr'd,
Till schism or heresy call down Goliah's sword.   [*600*]
    "Thus, what you call corruptions are, in truth,
The first plantations of the gospel's youth;
Old standard faith; but cast your eyes again,
And view those errors which new sects maintain,
Or which of old disturb'd the Church's peaceful reign;
And we can point each period of the time,
When they began, and who begot the crime;   *1179*
Can calculate how long th' eclipse endur'd,
Who interpos'd, what digits were obscur'd:
Of all which are already pass'd away,   [*610*]
We know the rise, the progress, and decay.
    "Despair at our foundations then to strike,
Till you can prove your faith apostolic;
A limpid stream drawn from the native source;
Succession lawful in a lineal course.
Prove any Church, oppos'd to this our head,
So one, so pure, so unconfin'dly spread,
Under one chief of the spiritual State,   *1190*
The members all combin'd, and all subordinate.
Shew such a seamless coat, from schism so free,   [*620*]
In no communion join'd with heresy.
If such a one you find, let truth prevail;
Till when, your weights will in the balance fail:
A Church unprincipled kicks up the scale.
    "But if you cannot think (nor sure you can

Suppose in God what were unjust in man)
That he, the fountain of eternal grace,
Should suffer Falsehood, for so long a space,   1200
To banish Truth, and to usurp her place;
That sev'n successive ages should be lost,   [630]
And preach damnation at their proper cost;
That all your erring ancestors should die,
Drown'd in th' abyss of deep idolatry;
If piety forbid such thoughts to rise,
Awake, and open your unwilling eyes:
God has left nothing for each age undone,
From this to that wherein he sent his Son:
Then think but well of him, and half your work is done.   1210
    "See how his Church, adorn'd with ev'ry grace,
With open arms, a kind forgiving face,   [640]
Stands ready to prevent her long-lost son's embrace.
Not more did Joseph o'er his brethren weep,
Nor less himself could from discovery keep,
When in the crowd of suppliants they were seen,
And in their crew his best-beloved Benjamin.
That pious Joseph in the Church behold,
To feed your famine, and refuse your gold;
The Joseph you exil'd, the Joseph whom you sold."   1220
    Thus, while with heav'nly charity she spoke,
A streaming blaze the silent shadows broke;   [650]
Shot from the skies a cheerful azure light;
The birds obscene to forests wing'd their flight,
And gaping graves receiv'd the wand'ring guilty sprite.
    Such were the pleasing triumphs of the sky
For James his late nocturnal victory;
The pledge of his Almighty Patron's love,
The fireworks which his angel made above.
I saw myself the lambent easy light   1230
Gild the brown horror, and dispel the night.
The messenger with speed the tidings bore;   [660]
News which three lab'ring nations did restore;
But heav'n's own *nuntius* was arriv'd before.

Lines 1218–1220: The renunciation of the Benedictines to the Abbey Lands.

Line 1230: *Poeta loquitur:* the poet (himself) speaks.

By this, the Hind had reach'd her lonely cell,
And vapors rose, and dews unwholesome fell.
When she, by frequent observation wise,
As one who long on heav'n had fix'd her eyes,
Discern'd a change of weather in the skies.
The western borders were with crimson spread,   1240
The moon descending look'd all flaming red;
She thought good manners bound her to invite   [670]
The stranger dame to be her guest that night.
'T is true, coarse diet, and a short repast,
(She said,) were weak inducements to the taste
Of one so nicely bred, and so unus'd to fast;
But what plain fare her cottage could afford,
A hearty welcome at a homely board,
Was freely hers; and, to supply the rest,
An honest meaning, and an open breast:
Last, with content of mind, the poor man's wealth,   1251
A grace cup to their common patron's health.   [680]
This she desir'd her to accept, and stay,
For fear she might be wilder'd in her way,
Because she wanted an unerring guide;
And then the dewdrops on her silken hide
Her tender constitution did declare,
Too lady-like a long fatigue to bear,
And rough inclemencies of raw nocturnal air.
But most she fear'd that, traveling so late,   1260
Some evil-minded beasts might lie in wait,
And without witness wreak their hidden hate.   [690]
    The Panther, tho' she lent a list'ning ear,
Had more of Lion in her than to fear:
Yet wisely weighing, since she had to deal
With many foes, their numbers might prevail,
Return'd her all the thanks she could afford,
And took her friendly hostess at her word;
Who, ent'ring first her lowly roof, (a shed
With hoary moss and winding ivy spread,   1270
Honest enough to hide an humble hermit's head,)
Thus graciously bespoke her welcome guest: [700]
"So might these walls, with your fair presence blest,
Become your dwelling place of everlasting rest,

Not for a night, or quick revolving year;
Welcome an owner, not a sojourner.
This peaceful seat my poverty secures;
War seldom enters but where wealth allures:
Nor yet despise it; for this poor abode
Has oft receiv'd, and yet receives a god;
A god victorious of the Stygian race   1281
Here laid his sacred limbs, and sanctified the place.   [710]
This mean retreat did mighty Pan contain:
Be emulous of him, and pomp disdain,
And dare not to debase your soul to gain."
   The silent stranger stood amaz'd to see
Contempt of wealth, and wilful poverty;
And, tho' ill habits are not soon controll'd,
Awhile suspended her desire of gold;
But civilly drew in her sharpen'd paws,
Not violating hospitable laws,   1291
And pacified her tail, and lick'd her frothy jaws.   [720]
   The Hind did first her country cates provide;
Then couch'd herself securely by her side.

THE THIRD PART

Much malice mingled with a little wit,
Perhaps, may censure this mysterious writ;
Because the Muse has peopled Caledon
With Panthers, Bears, and Wolves, and beasts unknown,
As if we were not stock'd with monsters of our own.
Let Æsop answer, who has set to view   1300
Such kinds as Greece and Phrygia never knew;
And Mother Hubbard, in her homely dress,
Has sharply blam'd a British Lioness,
That queen, whose feast the factious rabble keep,   [10]
Expos'd obscenely naked and asleep.
Led by those great examples, may not I
The wanted organs of their words supply?
If men transact like brutes, 't is equal then
For brutes to claim the privilege of men.

Others our Hind of folly will endite,   *1310*
To entertain a dang'rous guest by night.
Let those remember that she cannot die
Till rolling time is lost in round eternity;
Nor need she fear the Panther, tho' untam'd,   [20]
Because the Lion's peace was now proclaim'd:
The wary salvage would not give offense,
To forfeit the protection of her prince;
But watch'd the time her vengeance to complete,
When all her furry sons in frequent senate met;
Meanwhile she quench'd her fury at the flood,   *1320*
And with a lenten salad cool'd her blood.
Their commons, tho' but coarse, were nothing scant,
Nor did their minds an equal banquet want.

   For now the Hind, whose noble nature strove   [30]
T' express her plain simplicity of love,
Did all the honors of her house so well,
No sharp debates disturb'd the friendly meal.
She turn'd the talk, avoiding that extreme,
To common dangers past, a sadly pleasing theme;
Rememb'ring ev'ry storm which toss'd the State,   *1330*
When both were objects of the public hate,
And dropp'd a tear betwixt for her own children's fate.
   Nor fail'd she then a full review to make
Of what the Panther suffer'd for her sake: [40]
Her lost esteem, her truth, her loyal care,
Her faith unshaken to an exil'd heir,
Her strength t' endure, her courage to defy;
Her choice of honorable infamy.
On these, prolixly thankful, she enlarg'd;
Then with acknowledgments herself she charg'd;   *1340*
For friendship, of itself an holy tie,
Is made more sacred by adversity.
Now should they part, malicious tongues would say,
They met like chance companions on the way,   [50]
Whom mutual fear of robbers had possess'd:
While danger lasted, kindness was profess'd;
But that once o'er, the short-liv'd union ends;
The road divides, and there divide the friends.
   The Panther nodded when her speech was done,

And thank'd her coldly in a hollow tone,   1350
But said her gratitude had gone too far
For common offices of Christian care:
If to the lawful heir she had been true,
She paid but Caesar what was Caesar's due.   [60]
"I might," she added, "with like praise describe
Your suff'ring sons, and so return your bribe;
But incense from my hands is poorly priz'd,
For gifts are scorn'd where givers are despis'd.
I serv'd a turn, and then was cast away;
You, like the gaudy fly, your wings display,   1360
And sip the sweets, and bask in your great *patron's* day."
     This heard, the matron was not slow to find
What sort of malady had seiz'd her mind:
Disdain, with gnawing envy, fell despite,   [70]
And canker'd malice stood in open sight;
Ambition, int'rest, pride without control,
And jealousy, the jaundice of the soul;
Revenge, the bloody minister of ill,
With all the lean tormentors of the will.
'T was easy now to guess from whence arose   1370
Her new-made union with her ancient foes,
Her forc'd civilities, her faint embrace,
Affected kindness with an alter'd face:
Yet durst she not too deeply probe the wound,   [80]
As hoping still the nobler parts were sound;
But strove with anodynes t' assuage the smart,
And mildly thus her med'cine did impart.
     "Complaints of lovers help to ease their pain;
It shows a rest of kindness to complain,
A friendship loth to quit its former hold,
And conscious merit may be justly bold.
But much more just your jealousy would show,   1382
If others' good were injury to you:
Witness, ye heav'ns, how I rejoice to see   [90]
Rewarded worth and rising loyalty.
Your warrior offspring that upheld the crown,
The scarlet honors of your peaceful gown,
Are the most pleasing objects I can find,
Charms to my sight, and cordials to my mind:

When virtue spooms before a prosp'rous gale,   1390
My heaving wishes help to fill the sail;
And if my pray'rs for all the brave were heard,
Caesar should still have such, and such should still reward.
    "The labor'd earth your pains have sow'd and till'd;   [100]
'T is just you reap the product of the field:
Yours be the harvest; 't is the beggar's gain
To glean the fallings of the loaded wain.
Such scatter'd ears as are not worth your care
Your charity for alms may safely spare,
And alms are but the vehicles of pray'r.
My daily bread is lit'rally implor'd;   1401
I have no barns nor granaries to hoard;
If Caesar to his own his hand extends,
Say which of yours his charity offends: [110]
You know he largely gives to more than are his friends.
Are you defrauded when he feeds the poor?
Our mite decreases nothing of your store.
I am but few, and by your fare you see
My crying sins are not of luxury.
Some juster motive sure your mind withdraws,   1410
And makes you break our friendship's holy laws;
For barefac'd envy is too base a cause.
    "Show more occasion for your discontent;
Your love, the Wolf, would help you to invent: [120]
Some German quarrel, or, as times go now,
Some French, where force is uppermost, will do.
When at the fountain's head, as merit ought
To claim the place, you take a swilling draught,
How easy 't is an envious eye to throw,
And tax the sheep for troubling streams below;   1420
Or call her (when no farther cause you find)
An enemy profess'd of all your kind.
But then, perhaps, the wicked world would think
The Wolf design'd to eat as well as drink."   [130]
    This last allusion gall'd the Panther more,
Because indeed it rubb'd upon the sore.
Yet seem'd she not to winch, tho' shrewdly pain'd,
But thus her passive character maintain'd.
    "I never grudg'd, whate'er my foes report,
Your flaunting fortune in the Lion's court.   1430

You have your day, or you are much belied,
But I am always on the suff'ring side:
You know my doctrine, and I need not say
I will not, but I cannot disobey.   [140]
On this firm principle I ever stood;
He of my sons who fails to make it good,
By one rebellious act renounces to my blood."
    "Ah," said the Hind, "how many sons have you
Who call you mother, whom you never knew!
But most of them who that relation plead,
Are such ungracious youths as wish you dead.   1441
They gape at rich revenues which you hold,
And fain would nibble at your grandame gold;
Enquire into your years, and laugh to find   [150]
Your crazy temper shews you much declin'd.
Were you not dim, and doted, you might see
A pack of cheats that claim a pedigree,
No more of kin to you, than you to me.
Do you not know, that for a little coin
Heralds can foist a name into the line;   1450
They ask you blessing but for what you have,
But once possess'd of what with care you save,
The wanton boys would piss upon your grave.
    "Your sons of latitude that court your grace,   [160]
Tho' most resembling you in form and face,
Are far the worst of your pretended race.
And, but I blush your honesty to blot,
Pray God you prove 'em lawfully begot:
For in some Popish libels I have read,
The Wolf has been too busy in your bed;   1460
At least their hinder parts, the belly-piece,
The paunch, and all that Scorpio claims, are his.
Their malice too a sore suspicion brings;
For, tho' they dare not bark, they snarl at kings: [170]
Nor blame 'em for intruding in your line;
Fat bishoprics are still of right divine.
    "Think you your new French proselytes are come
To starve abroad, because they starv'd at home?
Your benefices twinkled from afar;
They found the new Messiah by the star: 1470
Those Swisses fight on any side for pay,

And 't is the living that conforms, not they.
Mark with what management their tribes divide;
Some stick to you, and some to t'other side,   [*180*]
That many Churches may for many mouths provide.
More vacant pulpits would more converts make;
All would have latitude enough to take:
The rest unbenefic'd your sects maintain;
For ordinations without cures are vain,
And chamber practice is a silent gain.   *1480*
Your sons of breadth at home are much like these;
Their soft and yielding metals run with ease:
They melt, and take the figure of the mold,
But harden and preserve it best in gold."   [*190*]
    "Your Delphic sword," the Panther then replied,
"Is double-edg'd, and cuts on either side.
Some sons of mine, who bear upon their shield
Three steeples argent in a sable field,
Have sharply tax'd your converts, who, unfed,
Have follow'd you for miracles of bread;   *1490*
Such who themselves of no religion are,
Allur'd with gain, for any will declare.
Bare lies with bold assertions they can face,
But dint of argument is out of place.   [*200*]
The grim logician puts 'em in a fright;
'T is easier far to flourish than to fight.
Thus our eighth Henry's marriage they defame;
They say the schism of beds began the game,
Divorcing from the Church to wed the dame:
Tho' largely prov'd, and by himself profess'd,   *1500*
That conscience, conscience would not let him rest;
I mean, not till possess'd of her he lov'd,
And old, uncharming Catherine was remov'd.
For sundry years before did he complain,   [*210*]
And told his ghostly confessor his pain.
With the same impudence, without a ground,
They say, that look the Reformation round,
No *Treatise of Humility* is found.
But if none were, the gospel does not want;
Our Savior preach'd it, and I hope you grant,   *1510*
The Sermon in the Mount was Protestant."

"No doubt," replied the Hind, "as sure as all
The writings of Saint Peter and Saint Paul:
On that decision let it stand or fall.   [220]
Now for my converts, who, you say, unfed,
Have follow'd me for miracles of bread;
Judge not by hearsay, but observe at least,
If since their change their loaves have been increas'd.
The Lion buys no converts; if he did,
Beasts would be sold as fast as he could bid.   1520
Tax those of int'rest who conform for gain,
Or stay the market of another reign:
Your broad-way sons would never be too nice
To close with Calvin, if he paid their price;   [230]
But rais'd three steeples high'r, would change their note,
And quit the cassock for the canting-coat.
Now, if you damn this censure as too bold,
Judge by yourselves, and think not others sold.
     "Meantime my sons accus'd, by fame's report,
Pay small attendance at the Lion's court,
Nor rise with early crowds, nor flatter late;   1531
(For silently they beg who daily wait.)
Preferment is bestow'd that comes unsought;
Attendance is a bribe, and then 't is bought.   [240]
How they should speed, their fortune is untried;
For not to ask is not to be denied.
For what they have, their God and king they bless,
And hope they should not murmur, had they less.
But, if reduc'd subsistence to implore,
In common prudence they would pass your door.   1540
Unpitied Hudibras, your champion friend,
Has shown how far your charities extend.
This lasting verse shall on his tomb be read,
He sham'd you living, and upbraids you dead.   [250]
     "With odious atheist names you load your foes;
Your lib'ral clergy why did I expose?
It never fails in charities like those.
In climes where true religion is profess'd,
That imputation were no laughing jest.
But *imprimatur,* with a chaplain's name,
Is here sufficient license to defame.   1551

What wonder is't that black detraction thrives?
The homicide of names is less than lives,
And yet the perjur'd murtherer survives."   [260]
   This said, she paus'd a little, and suppress'd
The boiling indignation of her breast;
She knew the virtue of her blade, nor would
Pollute her satire with ignoble blood:
Her panting foes she saw before her lie,
And back she drew the shining weapon dry   1560
So, when the gen'rous Lion has in sight
His equal match, he rouses for the fight;
But when his foe lies prostrate on the plain,
He sheathes his paws, uncurls his angry mane,   [270]
And, pleas'd with bloodless honors of the day,
Walks over and disdains th' inglorious prey.
So JAMES, if great with less we may compare,
Arrests his rolling thunderbolts in air;
And grants ungrateful friends a lengthen'd space,
T' implore the remnants of long-suff'ring grace.   1570
   This breathing-time the matron took; and then
Resum'd the thrid of her discourse again.
"Be vengeance wholly left to pow'rs divine,
And let Heav'n judge betwixt your sons and mine: [280]
If joys hereafter must be purchas'd here
With loss of all that mortals hold so dear,
Then welcome infamy and public shame,
And, last, a long farewell to worldly fame.
'T is with ease, but, O, how hardly tried
By haughty souls to human honor tied!
O sharp convulsive pangs of agonizing pride!   1581
Down then, thou rebel, never more to rise,
And what thou didst, and dost, so dearly prize,
That fame, that darling fame, make that thy sacrifice.   [290]
'T is nothing thou hast giv'n, then add thy tears
For a long race of unrepenting years:
'T is nothing yet, yet all thou hast to give;
Then add those *may-be* years thou hast to live:
Yet nothing still; then poor and naked come,
Thy father will receive his unthrift home,   1590
And thy blest Savior's blood discharge the mighty sum.

"Thus," she pursued, "I discipline a son,
Whose uncheck'd fury to revenge would run;
He champs the bit, impatient of his loss,   [300]
And starts aside, and flounders at the cross.
Instruct him better, gracious God, to know,
As thine is vengeance, so forgiveness too:
That, suff'ring from ill tongues, he bears no more
Than what his sovereign bears, and what his Savior bore.
    "It now remains for you to school your child,   1600
And ask why God's anointed he revil'd;
A king and princess dead! Did Shimei worse?
The curser's punishment should fright the curse:
Your son was warn'd, and wisely gave it o'er,   [310]
But he who counsel'd him has paid the score:
The heavy malice could no higher tend,
But woe to him on whom the weights descend.
So to permitted ills the *daemon* flies;
His rage is aim'd at him who rules the skies:
Constrain'd to quit his cause, no succor found,   1610
The foe discharges ev'ry tire around,
In clouds of smoke abandoning the fight;
But his own thund'ring peals proclaim his flight.
    "In Henry's change his charge as ill succeeds;   [320]
To that long story little answer needs;
Confront but Henry's words with Henry's deeds.
Were space allow'd, with ease it might be prov'd
What springs his blessed Reformation mov'd.
The dire effects appear'd in open sight,
Which from the cause he calls a distant flight,   1620
And yet no larger leap than from the sun to light.
    "Now last your sons a double paean sound,
A *Treatise of Humility* is found.
'T is bound, but better it had ne'er been sought,   [330]
Than thus in Protestant procession brought.
The fam'd original thro' Spain is known,
Rodriguez' work, my celebrated son,
Which yours by ill translating made his own;
Conceal'd its author, and usurp'd the name,
The basest and ignoblest theft of fame.   1630
My altars kindled first that living coal;

Restore, or practice better what you stole:
That virtue could this humble verse inspire,
'T is all the restitution I require."   [340]
    Glad was the Panther that the charge was clos'd,
And none of all her fav'rite sons expos'd.
For laws of arms permit each injur'd man
To make himself a saver where he can.
Perhaps the plunder'd merchant cannot tell
The names of pirates in whose hands he fell;   1640
But at the den of thieves he justly flies,
And ev'ry Algerine is lawful prize.
No private person in the foe's estate
Can plead exemption from the public fate.   [350]
Yet Christian laws allow not such redress;
Then let the greater supersede the less.
But let th' abettors of the Panther's crime
Learn to make fairer wars another time.
Some characters may sure be found to write
Among her sons; for 't is no common sight,   1650
A spotted dam, and all her offspring white.
    The salvage, tho' she saw her plea controll'd,
Yet would not wholly seem to quit her hold,
But offer'd fairly to compound the strife,   [360]
And judge conversion by the convert's life.
" 'T is true," she said, "I think it somewhat strange,
So few should follow profitable change;
For present joys are more to flesh and blood,
Than a dull prospect of a distant good.
'T was well alluded by a son of mine,   1660
(I hope to quote him is not to purloin,)
Two magnets, heav'n and earth, allure to bliss;
The larger lodestone that, the nearer this:
The weak attraction of the greater fails;   [370]
We nod a while, but neighborhood prevails;
But when the greater proves the nearer too,
I wonder more your converts come so slow.
Methinks in those who firm with me remain,
It shows a nobler principle than gain."
    "Your inf'rence would be strong," the Hind replied, 1670
"If yours were in effect the suff'ring side:
Your clergy sons their own in peace possess,

Nor are their prospects in reversion less.
My proselytes are struck with awful dread;   [380]
Your bloody comet-laws hang blazing o'er their head:
The respite they enjoy but only lent,
The best they have to hope, protracted punishment.
Be judge yourself, if int'rest may prevail,
Which motives, yours or mine, will turn the scale.
While pride and pomp allure, and plenteous ease,   1680
That is, till man's predominant passions cease,
Admire no longer at my slow encrease.
   "By education most have been misled;
So they believe, because they so were bred.   [390]
The *priest* continues what the nurse began,
And thus the child imposes on the man.
The rest I nam'd before, nor need repeat;
But int'rest is the most prevailing cheat,
The sly seducer both of age and youth:
They study that, and think they study truth.   1690
When int'rest fortifies an argument,
Weak reason serves to gain the will's assent;
For souls already warp'd receive an easy bent.
   "Add long prescription of establish'd laws,   [400]
And pique of honor to maintain a cause,
And shame of change, and fear of future ill,
And zeal, the blind conductor of the will;
And chief, among the still-mistaking crowd,
The fame of teachers obstinate and proud,
And, more than all, the private judge allow'd;   1700
Disdain of Fathers, which the daunce began,
And last, uncertain whose the narrower span,
The clown unread, and half-read gentleman."
   To this the Panther, with a scornful smile: [410]
"Yet still you travail with unwearied toil,
And range around the realm without control,
Among my sons for proselytes to prole,
And here and there you snap some silly soul.
You hinted fears of future change in state;
Pray Heav'n you did not prophesy your fate!   1710
Perhaps you think your time of triumph near,
But may mistake the season of the year;
The Swallows' fortune gives you cause to fear."

"For charity," replied the matron, "tell   [420]
What sad mischance those pretty birds befell."
    "Nay, no mischance," the salvage dame replied,
"But want of wit in their unerring guide,
And eager haste, and gaudy hopes, and giddy pride.
Yet, wishing timely warning may prevail,
Make you the moral, and I'll tell the tale.   1720
    "The Swallow, privileg'd above the rest
Of all the birds, as man's familiar guest,
Pursues the sun in summer brisk and bold,
But wisely shuns the persecuting cold: [430]
Is well to chancels and to chimneys known,
Tho' 't is not thought she feeds on smoke alone.
From hence she has been held of heav'nly line,
Endued with particles of soul divine.
This merry chorister had long possess'd
Her summer seat, and feather'd well her nest: 1730
Till frowning skies began to change their cheer,
And time turn'd up the wrong side of the year;
The shedding trees began the ground to strow
With yellow leaves, and bitter blasts to blow.   [440]
Sad auguries of winter thence she drew,
Which by instinct, or prophecy, she knew:
When prudence warn'd her to remove betimes,
And seek a better heav'n and warmer climes.
    "Her sons were summon'd on a steeple's height,
And, call'd in common council, vote a flight;
The day was nam'd, the next that should be fair;   1741
All to the gen'ral rendezvous repair;
They try their flutt'ring wings, and trust themselves in air,
But whether upward to the moon they go,   [450]
Or dream the winter out in caves below,
Or hawk at flies elsewhere, concerns not us to know.
    "Southwards, you may be sure, they bent their flight,
And harbor'd in a hollow rock at night:
Next morn they rose, and set up ev'ry sail;
The wind was fair, but blew a *mack'rel* gale:
The sickly young sat shiv'ring on the shore,
Abhorr'd salt water never seen before,   1752
And pray'd their tender mothers to delay
The passage, and expect a fairer day.   [460]

"With these the Martin readily concurr'd,
A church-begot, and church-believing bird;
Of little body, but of lofty mind,
Round-bellied, for a dignity design'd,
And much a dunce, as Martins are by kind:
Yet often quoted canon-laws, and code,
And Fathers which he never understood;   1761
But little learning needs in noble blood.
For, sooth to say, the Swallow brought him in,
Her household chaplain, and her next of kin;   [470]
In superstition silly to excess,
And casting schemes by planetary guess:
In fine, short-wing'd, unfit himself to fly,
His fear foretold foul weather in the sky.
     "Besides, a Raven from a wither'd oak,
Left of their lodging, was obscrv'd to croak.   1770
That omen lik'd him not; so his advice
Was present safety, bought at any price;
(A seeming pious care that cover'd cowardice.)
To strengthen this, he told a boding dream   [480]
Of rising waters and a troubled stream,
Sure signs of anguish, dangers, and distress;
With something more, not lawful to express,
By which he slily seem'd to intimate
Some secret revelation of their fate.
For, he concluded, once upon a time,   1780
He found a leaf inscrib'd with sacred rhyme,
Whose antique characters did well denote
The Sibyl's hand of the Cumaean grot:
The mad divineress had plainly writ,   [490]
A time should come (but many ages yet)
In which, sinister destinies ordain,
A *dame* should drown with all her feather'd train,
And seas from thence be call'd the Chelidonian main.
At this, some shook for fear; the more devout
Arose, and bless'd themselves from head to foot.   1790
     " 'T is true, some stagers of the wiser sort
Made all these idle wonderments their sport:
They said, their only danger was delay,
And he who heard what ev'ry fool could say,   [500]
Would never fix his thoughts, but trim his time away.

The passage yet was good; the wind, 't is true,
Was somewhat high, but that was nothing new,
Nor more than usual *equinoxes* blew.
The sun (already from the Scales declin'd)
Gave little hopes of better days behind,
But change from bad to worse of weather and of wind.   *1801*
Nor need they fear the dampness of the sky
Should flag their wings, and hinder them to fly,
'T was only water thrown on sails too dry.   [*510*]
But, least of all, philosophy presumes
Of truth in dreams, from melancholy fumes:
Perhaps the Martin, hous'd in holy ground,
Might think of ghosts that walk their midnight round,
Till grosser atoms, tumbling in the stream
Of fancy, madly met, and clubb'd into a dream: *1810*
As little weight his vain presages bear
Of ill effect to such alone who fear.
Most prophecies are of a piece with these;
Each Nostradamus can foretell with ease: [*520*]
Not naming persons, and confounding times,
One casual truth supports a thousand lying rhymes.
    "Th' advice was true; but fear had seiz'd the most,
And all good counsel is on cowards lost.
The question crudely put, to shun delay,
'T was carried by the *major* part to stay.   *1820*
    "His point thus gain'd, Sir Martin dated thence
His pow'r, and from a priest became a prince.
He order'd all things with a busy care,
And cells and refectories did prepare,   [*530*]
And large provisions laid of winter fare:
But now and then let fall a word or two
Of hope that Heav'n some miracle might show,
And, for their sakes, the sun should backward go;
Against the laws of nature upward climb,
And, mounted on the Ram, renew the prime: *1830*
For which two proofs in sacred story lay,
Of Ahaz' dial, and of Joshua's day.
In expectation of such times as these,
A chapel hous'd 'em, truly call'd of ease: [*540*]
For Martin much devotion did not ask;

They pray'd sometimes, and that was all their task.
   "It happen'd (as beyond the reach of wit
Blind prophecies may have a lucky hit)
That this accomplish'd, or at least in part,
Gave great repute to their new Merlin's art.   *1840*
Some* Swifts; the giants of the swallow kind,
Large-limb'd, stout-hearted, but of stupid mind,
(For Swisses, or for Gibeonites design'd,)
These lubbers, peeping thro' a broken pane,   [550]
To suck fresh air, survey'd the neighboring plain,
And saw (but scarcely could believe their eyes)
New blossoms flourish, and new flow'rs arise;
As God had been abroad, and, walking there,
Had left his footsteps, and reform'd the year;
The sunny hills from far were seen to glow   *1850*
With glittering beams, and in the meads below
The burnish'd brooks appear'd with liquid gold to flow.
At last they heard the foolish Cuckow sing,
Whose note proclaim'd the holiday of spring.   [560]
   "No longer doubting, all prepare to fly,
And repossess their patrimonial sky.
The priest before 'em did his wings display;
And that good omens might attend their way,
As luck would have it, 't was St. Martin's day.
   "Who but the Swallow now triumphs alone?   *1860*
The canopy of heaven is all her own;
Her youthful offspring to their haunts repair,
And glide along in glades, and skim in air,
And dip for insects in the purling springs,   [570]
And stoop on rivers to refresh their wings.
Their mothers think a fair provision made,
That ev'ry son can live upon his trade:
And, now the careful charge is off their hands,
Look out for husbands, and new nuptial bands:
The youthful widow longs to be supplied;   *1870*
But first the lover is by lawyers tied
To settle jointure-chimneys on the bride.
So thick they couple, in so short a space,

---

* Otherwise call'd Martlets.

That Martin's marriage-off'rings rise apace;   [580]
Their ancient houses, running to decay,
Are furbish'd up, and cemented with clay:
They teem already; store of eggs are laid,
And brooding mothers call Lucina's aid.
Fame spreads the news, and foreign fowls appear
In flocks to greet the new returning year,   1880
To bless the founder, and partake the cheer.
    "And now 't was time (so fast their numbers rise)
To plant abroad, and people colonies.
The youth drawn forth, as Martin had desir'd,   [590]
(For so their cruel destiny requir'd,)
Were sent far off on an ill-fated day;
The rest would need conduct 'em on their way,
And Martin went, because he fear'd alone to stay.
    "So long they flew with inconsiderate haste   1889
That now their afternoon began to waste;
And, what was ominous, that very morn
The sun was enter'd into Capricorn;
Which, by their bad astronomer's account,
That week the Virgin Balance should remount;   [600]
An infant moon eclips'd him in his way,
And hid the small remainders of his day.
The crowd, amaz'd, pursued no certain mark;
But birds met birds, and justled in the dark:
Few mind the public in a panic fright;   1899
And fear increas'd the horror of the night.
Night came, but unattended with repose;
Alone she came, no sleep their eyes to close:
Alone, and black she came; no friendly stars arose.
    "What should they do, beset with dangers round,   [610]
No neighb'ring dorp, no lodging to be found,
But bleaky plains, and bare unhospitable ground.
The latter brood, who just began to fly,
Sick-feather'd, and unpractic'd in the sky,
For succor to their helpless mother call;
She spread her wings; some few beneath 'em crawl;   1910
She spread 'em wider yet, but could not cover all.
T' augment their woes, the winds began to move
Debate in air, for empty fields above,

Till Boreas got the skies, and pour'd amain   [620]
His rattling hailstones mix'd with snow and rain.
    "The joyless morning late arose, and found
A dreadful desolation reign around,
Some buried in the snow, some frozen to the ground.
The rest were struggling still with death, and lay,
The Crows' and Ravens' rights, an undefended prey: 1920
Excepting Martin's race; for they and he
Had gain'd the shelter of a hollow tree:
But, soon discover'd by a sturdy clown,
He headed all the rabble of a town,   [630]
And finish'd 'em with bats, or poll'd 'em down.
Martin himself was caught alive, and tried
For treas'nous crimes, because the laws provide
No Martin there in winter shall abide.
High on an oak, which never leaf shall bear,   1929
He breath'd his last, expos'd to open air;
And there his corps, unblest, are hanging still,
To show the change of winds with his prophetic bill."
    The patience of the Hind did almost fail,
For well she mark'd the malice of the tale: [640]
Which ribald art their Church to Luther owes;
In malice it began, by malice grows:
He sow'd the serpent's teeth, an iron harvest rose.
But most in Martin's character and fate
She saw her slander'd sons, the Panther's hate,
The people's rage, the persecuting State:
Then said: "I take th' advice in friendly part;   1941
You clear your conscience, or at least your heart:
Perhaps you fail'd in your foreseeing skill,
For Swallows are unlucky birds to kill.   [650]
As for my sons, the family is blest,
Whose ev'ry child is equal to the rest;
No Church reform'd can boast a blameless line;
Such Martins build in yours, and more than mine:
Or else an old Fanatic author lies,
Who summ'd their scandals up by centuries.   1950
But thro' your parable I plainly see
The bloody laws, the crowd's barbarity;
The sunshine that offends the purblind sight—

Had some their wishes, it would soon be night.   [660]
Mistake me not: the charge concerns not you;
Your sons are malecontents, but yet are true,
As far as nonresistance makes 'em so;
But that 's a word of neutral sense, you know,
A passive term, which no relief will bring,
But trims betwixt a rebel and a king."   1960
    "Rest well assur'd," the Pardelis replied,
"My sons would all support the regal side,
Tho' Heav'n forbid the cause by battle should be tried."
    The matron answer'd with a loud Amen,   [670]
And thus pursued her argument again:
"If, as you say, and as I hope no less,
Your sons will practice what yourself profess,
What angry pow'r prevents our present peace?
The Lion, studious of our common good,
Desires (and kings' desires are ill withstood)   1970
To join our nations in a lasting love;
The bars betwixt are easy to remove,
For sanguinary laws were never made above.
If you condemn that prince of tyranny,   [680]
Whose mandate forc'd your Gallic friends to fly,
Make not a worse example of your own;
Or cease to rail at causeless rigor shown,
And let the guiltless person throw the stone.
His blunted sword your suff'ring brotherhood
Have seldom felt; he stops it short of blood: 1980
But you have ground the persecuting knife,
And set it to a razor-edge on life.
Curst be the wit which cruelty refines,
Or to his father's rod the scorpion joins;   [690]
Your finger is more gross than the great monarch's loins.
But you, perhaps, remove that bloody note,
And stick it on the first Reformers' coat.
O let their crime in long oblivion sleep:
'T was theirs indeed to make, 't is yours to keep.
Unjust, or just, is all the question now;   1990
'T is plain that, not repealing, you allow.
    "To name the Test would put you in a rage;
You charge not that on any former age,

But smile to think how innocent you stand,   [700]
Arm'd by a weapon put into your hand.
Yet still remember that you wield a sword
Forg'd by your foes against your Sovereign Lord;
Design'd to hew th' imperial cedar down,
Defraud succession, and disheir the crown.
T' abhor the makers, and their laws approve,   2000
Is to hate traitors, and the treason love.
What means it else, which now your children say,
'We made it not, nor will we take away'?
    "Suppose some great oppressor had by slight   [710]
Of law disseiz'd your brother of his right,
Your common sire surrend'ring in a fright;
Would you to that unrighteous title stand,
Left by the villain's will to heir the land?
More just was Judas, who his Savior sold;
The sacrilegious bribe he could not hold,
Nor hang in peace before he render'd back the gold.   2011
What more could you have done than now you do,
Had Oates and Bedloe, and their Plot been true?
Some specious reasons for those wrongs were found; [720]
The dire magicians threw their mists around,
And wise men walk'd as an inchanted ground.
But now, when Time has made th' imposture plain,
(Late tho' he follow'd Truth, and limping held her train,)
What new delusion charms your cheated eyes again?
The painted harlot might a while bewitch,
But why the hag uncas'd, and all obscene with itch?   2020
    "The first Reformers were a modest race;
Our peers possess'd in peace their native place;
And when rebellious arms o'erturn'd the State,   [730]
They suffer'd only in the common fate:
But now the sov'reign mounts the regal chair,
And miter'd seats are full, yet David's bench is bare.
Your answer is, they were not dispossess'd;
They need but rub their metal on the Test
To prove their ore: 't were well if gold alone   2030
Were touch'd and tried on your discerning stone;
But that unfaithful Test unfound will pass
The dross of atheists, and sectarian brass:

As if th' experiment were made to hold   [740]
For base productions, and reject the gold.
Thus men ungodded may to places rise,
And sects may be preferr'd without disguise:
No danger to the Church or State from these;
The Papist only has his writ of ease.
No gainful office gives him the pretense   2040
To grind the subject, or defraud the prince.
Wrong conscience, or no conscience, may deserve
To thrive, but ours alone is privileg'd to sterve.
    " 'Still thank yourselves,' you cry; 'your noble race [750]
We banish not, but they forsake the place:
Our doors are open.' True, but ere they come,
You toss your censing Test, and fume the room;
As if 't were Toby's rival to expel,
And fright the fiend who could not bear the smell."
    To this the Panther sharply had replied;   2050
But, having gain'd a verdict on her side,
She wisely gave the loser leave to chide;
Well satisfied to have the 'butt and peace,'
And for the plaintiff's cause she car'd the less,   [760]
Because she sued *in forma pauperis;*
Yet thought it decent something should be said;
For secret guilt by silence is betray'd:
So neither granted all, nor much denied,
But answer'd with a yawning kind of pride.
"Methinks such terms of proffer'd peace you bring,   2060
As once Æneas to th' Italian king:
By long possession all the land is mine;
You strangers come with your intruding line,
To share my scepter, which you call to join.   [770]
You plead like him an ancient pedigree,
And claim a peaceful seat by fate's decree.
In ready pomp your sacrificer stands,
T' unite the Trojan and the Latin bands,
And, that the league more firmly may be tied,
Demand the fair Lavinia for your bride.   2070
Thus plausibly you veil th' intended wrong,
But still you bring your exil'd gods along;
And will endeavor, in succeeding space,

Those household poppits on our hearths to place. [780]
Perhaps some barb'rous laws have been preferr'd;
I spake against the Test, but was not heard;
These to rescind, and peerage to restore.
My gracious sov'reign would my vote implore:
I owe him much, but owe my conscience more."
   "Conscience is then your plea," replied the dame,   2080
"Which, well inform'd, will ever be the same.
But yours is much of the *chameleon* hue,
To change the dye with ev'ry diff'rent view.
When first the Lion sat with awful sway, [790]
Your conscience taught you duty to obey:
He might have had your statutes and your Test;
No conscience but of subjects was profess'd.
He found your temper, and no farther tried,
But on that broken reed, your Church, relied.
In vain the sects assay'd their utmost art,   2090
With offer'd treasure to espouse their part;
Their treasures were a bribe too mean to move his heart.
But when by long experience you had prov'd,
How far he could forgive, how well he lov'd; [800]
A goodness that excell'd his godlike race,
And only short of Heav'n's unbounded grace;
A flood of mercy that o'erflow'd our isle,
Calm in the rise, and fruitful as the Nile;
Forgetting whence your Egypt was supplied,
You thought your sov'reign bound to send the tide;   2100
Nor upward look'd on that immortal spring,
But vainly deem'd, he durst not be a king.
Then Conscience, unrestrain'd by fear, began
To stretch her limits, and extend the span; [810]
Did his indulgence as her gift dispose,
And made a wise alliance with her foes.
Can Conscience own th' associating name,
And raise no blushes to conceal her shame?
For sure she has been thought a bashful dame.
But if the cause by battle should be tried,   2110
You grant she must espouse the regal side:
O Proteus Conscience, never to be tied!
What Phoebus from the tripod shall disclose

Which are, in last resort, your friends or foes?   [820]
Homer, who learn'd the language of the sky,
The seeming Gordian knot would soon untie;
Immortal pow'rs the term of Conscience know,
But Int'rest is her name with men below."
  "Conscience or Int'rest be 't, or both in one,"
The Panther answer'd in a surly tone,   2120
"The first commands me to maintain the crown,
The last forbids to throw my barriers down.
Our penal laws no sons of yours admit,
Our Test excludes your tribe from benefit.   [830]
These are my banks your ocean to withstand,
Which proudly rising overlooks the land;
And, once let in, with unresisted sway,
Would sweep the pastors and their flocks away.
Think not my judgment leads me to comply
With laws unjust, but hard necessity: 2130
Imperious need, which cannot be withstood,
Makes ill authentic, for a greater good.
Possess your soul with patience, and attend:
A more auspicious planet may ascend;   [840]
Good fortune may present some happier time,
With means to cancel my unwilling crime
(Unwilling, witness all ye pow'rs above);
To mend my errors, and redeem your love:
That little space you safely may allow;
Your all-dispensing pow'r protects you now."   2140
  "Hold," said the Hind, " 't is needless to explain;
You would *postpone* me to another reign;
Till when you are content to be unjust:
Your part is to possess, and mine to trust.   [850]
A fair exchange propos'd of future chance,
For present profit and inheritance.
Few words will serve to finish our dispute;
Who will not now repeal, would persecute:
To ripen green revenge your hopes attend,
Wishing that happier planet would ascend.   2150
For shame, let Conscience be your plea no more;
To will hereafter, proves she might before;
But she's a bawd to Gain, and holds the door.

"Your care about your banks infers a fear   [860]
Of threat'ning floods and inundations near;
If so, a just reprise would only be
Of what the land usurp'd upon the sea;
And all your jealousies but serve to show
Your ground is, like your neighbor nation, low.
T' intrench in what you grant unrighteous laws,   2160
Is to distrust the justice of your cause,
And argues that the true religion lies
In those weak adversaries you despise.

"Tyrannic force is that which least you fear;   [870]
The sound is frightful in a Christian's ear:
Avert it, Heav'n! nor let that plague be sent
To us from the dispeopled continent.

"But piety commands me to refrain;
Those pray'rs are needless in this monarch's reign.
Behold, how he protects your friends oppress'd,   2170
Receives the banish'd, succors the distress'd!
Behold, for you may read an honest open breast.
He stands in daylight, and disdains to hide
An act to which by honor he is tied,   [880]
A generous, laudable, and kingly pride.
Your Test he would repeal, his peers restore;
This when he says he means, he means no more."

"Well," said the Panther, "I believe him just,
And yet——"

"And yet, 't is but because you must;
You would be trusted, but you would not trust."   2180
The Hind thus briefly; and disdain'd t' inlarge
On pow'r of kings, and their superior charge,
As Heav'n's trustees before the people's choice:
Tho' sure the Panther did not much rejoice   [890]
To hear those echoes giv'n of her once loyal voice.

The matron woo'd her kindness to the last,
But could not win; her hour of grace was past.
Whom, thus persisting, when she could not bring
To leave the Wolf, and to believe her king,
She gave her up, and fairly wish'd her joy   2190
Of her late treaty with her new ally:
Which well she hop'd would more successful prove

Than was the Pigeons' and the Buzzard's love.
The Panther ask'd what concord there could be   [*900*]
Betwixt two kinds whose natures disagree.
The dame replied: " 'T is sung in ev'ry street,
The common chat of gossips when they meet;
But, since unheard by you, 't is worth your while
To take a wholesome tale, tho' told in homely style.
    "A plain good man, whose name is understood,   2200
(So few deserve the name of plain and good,)
Of three fair lineal lordships stood possess'd,
And liv'd, as reason was, upon the best.
Inur'd to hardships from his early youth,   [*910*]
Much had he done and suffer'd for his truth:
At land and sea, in many a doubtful fight,
Was never known a more advent'rous knight,
Who oft'ner drew his sword, and always for the right.
    "As fortune would, (his fortune came, tho' late,)
He took possession of his just estate;   2210
Nor rack'd his tenants with increase of rent,
Nor liv'd too sparing, nor too largely spent;
But overlook'd his hinds; their pay was just,
And ready, for he scorn'd to go on trust: [*920*]
Slow to resolve, but in performance quick;
So true, that he was awkward at a trick,
For little souls on little shifts rely,
And coward arts of mean expedients try;
The noble mind will dare do anything but lie.
False friends, (his deadliest foes,) could find no way   2220
But shows of honest bluntness, to betray:
That unsuspected plainness he believ'd;
He look'd into himself, and was deceiv'd.
Some lucky planet sure attends his birth,   [*930*]
Or Heav'n would make a miracle on earth;
For prosp'rous honesty is seldom seen
To bear so dead a weight, and yet to win.
It looks as fate with nature's law would strive,
To shew plain-dealing once an age may thrive;
And, when so tough a frame she could not bend,   2230
Exceeded her commission to befriend.
    "This grateful man, as Heav'n encreas'd his store,

Gave God again, and daily fed his poor.
His house with all convenience was purvey'd;   [940]
The rest he found, but rais'd the fabric where he pray'd;
And in that sacred place his beauteous wife
Employ'd her happiest hours of holy life.
   "Nor did their alms extend to those alone
Whom common faith more strictly made their own;
A sort of Doves were hous'd too near their hall,   2240
Who cross the proverb, and abound with gall.
Tho' some, 't is true, are passively inclin'd,
The greater part degenerate from their kind;
Voracious birds, that hotly bill and breed,   [950]
And largely drink, because on salt they feed.
Small gain from them their bounteous owner draws;
Yet, bound by promise, he supports their cause,
As corporations privileg'd by laws.
   "That house which harbor to their kind affords
Was built, long since, God knows, for better birds;   2250
But flutt'ring there, they nestle near the throne,
And lodge in habitations not their own,
By their high crops and corny gizzards known.
Like Harpies, they could scent a plenteous board,   [960]
Then to be sure they never fail'd their lord:
The rest was form, and bare attendance paid;
They drunk, and eat, and grudgingly obey'd.
The more they fed, they raven'd still for more;
They drain'd from Dan, and left Beersheba poor.   2259
All this they had by law, and none repin'd;
The pref'rence was but due to Levi's kind;
But when some lay-preferment fell by chance,
The gourmands made it their inheritance.
When once possess'd, they never quit their claim;   [970]
For then 't is sanctified to Heav'n's high name;
And, hallow'd thus, they cannot give consent
The gift should be profan'd by worldly management.
   "Their flesh was never to the table serv'd;
Tho' 't is not thence inferr'd the birds were starv'd;   2269
But that their master did not like the food,
As rank, and breeding melancholy blood.
Nor did it with his gracious nature suit,

Ev'n tho' they were not Doves, to persecute;
Yet he refus'd (nor could they take offense)   [980]
Their glutton kind should teach him abstinence.
Nor consecrated grain their wheat he thought,
Which, new from treading, in their bills they brought;
But left his hinds each in his private pow'r,
That those who like the bran might leave the flour.
He for himself, and not for others, chose,   2280
Nor would he be impos'd on, nor impose;
But in their faces his devotion paid,
And sacrifice with solemn rites was made,   [990]
And sacred incense on his altars laid.
   "Besides these jolly birds, whose crops impure
Repaid their commons with their salt manure,
Another farm he had behind his house,
Not overstock'd, but barely for his use;
Wherein his poor domestic poultry fed,
And from his pious hands receiv'd their bread.   2290
Our pamper'd Pigeons, with malignant eyes,
Beheld these inmates, and their nurseries:
Tho' hard their fare, at ev'ning and at morn,
A cruse of water and an ear of corn;   [1000]
Yet still they grudg'd that modicum, and thought
A sheaf in ev'ry single grain was brought:
Fain would they filch that little food away,
While unrestrain'd those happy gluttons prey.
And much they griev'd to see so nigh their hall
The bird that warn'd St. Peter of his fall;
That he should raise his miter'd crest on high,   2301
And clap his wings, and call his family
To sacred rites; and vex th' ethereal pow'rs
With midnight matins at uncivil hours: [1010]
Nay more, his quiet neighbors should molest,
Just in the sweetness of their morning rest.
   "Beast of a bird, supinely when he might
Lie snug and sleep, to rise before the light!
What if his dull forefathers us'd that cry,
Could he not let a bad example die?   2310
The world was fall'n into an easier way;
This age knew better than to fast and pray.

Good sense in sacred worship would appear
So to begin, as they might end the year.   [1020]
Such feats in former times had wrought the falls
Of crowing Chanticleers in cloister'd walls.
Expell'd for this, and for their lands, they fled;
And sister Partlet, with her hooded head,
Was hooted hence, because she would not pray abed.
The way to win the restiff world to God,
Was to lay by the disciplining rod,   2321
Unnatural fasts, and foreign forms of pray'r:
Religion frights us with a mien severe.
'T is prudence to reform her into ease,   [1030]
And put her in undress to make her pleas:
A lively faith will bear aloft the mind,
And leave the luggage of good works behind.
     "Such doctrines in the Pigeon-house were taught:
You need not ask how wondrously they wrought;   2329
But sure the common cry was all for these,
Whose life and precept both encourag'd ease.
Yet fearing those alluring baits might fail,
And holy deeds o'er all their arts prevail;
(For vice, tho' frontless, and of harden'd face,   [1040]
Is daunted at the sight of awful grace,)
An hideous figure of their foes they drew,
Nor lines, nor looks, nor shades, nor colors true;
And this grotesque design expos'd to public view.
One would have thought it some Egyptian piece,
With garden-gods, and barking deities,
More thick than Ptolemy has stuck the skies.   2341
All so perverse a draught, so far unlike,
It was no libel where it meant to strike:
Yet still the daubing pleas'd, and great and small,   [1050]
To view the monster, crowded Pigeon-hall.
There Chanticleer was drawn upon his knees
Adoring shrines, and stocks of sainted trees;
And by him, a misshapen, ugly race;
The curse of God was seen on ev'ry face:
No Holland emblem could that malice mend,   2350
But still the worse the look, the fitter for a fiend.
     "The master of the farm, displeas'd to find

So much of rancor in so mild a kind,
Enquir'd into the cause, and came to know   [1060]
The Passive Church had struck the foremost blow;
With groundless fears, and jealousies possess'd,
As if this troublesome intruding guest
Would drive the birds of Venus from their nest:
A deed his inborn equity abhorr'd;
But Int'rest will not trust, tho' God should plight his word.   2360
    "A law, the source of many future harms,
Had banish'd all the poultry from the farms;
With loss of life, if any should be found
To crow or peck on this forbidden ground.   [1070]
That bloody statute chiefly was design'd
For Chanticleer the white, of clergy kind;
But after-malice did not long forget
The lay that wore the robe and coronet.
For them, for their inferiors and allies,
Their foes a deadly shibboleth devise: 2370
By which unrighteously it was decreed
That none to trust, or profit, should succeed,
Who would not swallow first a poisonous wicked weed;
Or that, to which old Socrates was curst,   [1080]
Or henbane juice to swell 'em till they burst.
The patron (as in reason) thought it hard
To see this inquisition in his yard,
By which the sovereign was of subjects' use debarr'd.
    "All gentle means he tried, which might withdraw
Th' effects of so unnatural a law;   2380
But still the Dove-house obstinately stood
Deaf to their own, and to their neighbors' good;
And which was worse (if any worse could be),
Repeated of their boasted loyalty: [1090]
Now made the champions of a cruel cause,
And drunk with fumes of popular applause;
For those whom God to ruin has design'd,
He fits for fate, and first destroys their mind.
    "New doubts indeed they daily strove to raise,
Suggested dangers, interpos'd delays;   2390
And emissary Pigeons had in store,
Such as the Meccan prophet us'd of yore,

To whisper counsels in their patron's ear;
And veil'd their false advice with zealous fear.   [*1100*]
The master smil'd to see 'em work in vain
To wear him out, and make an idle reign:
He saw, but suffer'd their protractive arts,
And strove by mildness to reduce their hearts;
But they abus'd that grace to make allies,
And fondly clos'd with former enemies;
For fools are double fools, endeav'ring to be wise.   2401
    "After a grave consult what course were best,
One, more mature in folly than the rest,
Stood up, and told 'em, with his head aside,   [*1110*]
That desp'rate cures must be to desp'rate ills applied;
And therefore, since their main impending fear
Was from th' encreasing race of Chanticleer,
Some potent bird of prey they ought to find
A foe profess'd to him and all his kind:
Some haggard Hawk, who had her eyry nigh,   2410
Well pounc'd to fasten, and well wing'd to fly;
One they might trust their common wrongs to wreak:
The Musket, and the Coystrel were too weak,
Too fierce the Falcon.—'But, above the rest,   [*1120*]
The noble Buzzard ever pleas'd me best;
Of small renown, 't is true; for, not to lie,
We call him but a Hawk by courtesy.
I know he haunts the Pigeon-house and farm,
And more, in time of war, has done us harm;
But all his hate on trivial points depends:
Give up our forms, and we shall soon be friends.   2421
For Pigeons' flesh he seems not much to care;
Cramm'd Chickens are a more delicious fare.
On this high potentate, without delay,   [*1130*]
I wish you would confer the sovereign sway:
Petition him t' accept the government,
And let a splendid embassy be sent.'
    "This pithy speech prevail'd, and all agreed,
Old enmities forgot, the Buzzard should succeed.
    "Their welcome suit was granted soon as heard,   2430
His lodgings furnish'd, and a train prepar'd,
With B's upon their breast, appointed for his guard.

He came, and, crown'd with great solemnity,
'God save King Buzzard!' was the gen'ral cry.   [1140]
    "A portly prince, and goodly to the sight,
He seem'd a son of Anak for his height:
Like those whom stature did to crowns prefer;
Black-brow'd, and bluff, like Homer's Jupiter;
Broad-back'd, and brawny-built for love's delight,
A prophet form'd to make a female proselyte.   2440
A theologue more by need than genial bent;
By breeding sharp, by nature confident.
Int'rest in all his actions was discern'd;
More learn'd than honest, more a wit than learn'd;   [1150]
Or forc'd by fear, or by his profit led,
Or both conjoin'd, his native clime he fled;
But brought the virtues of his heav'n along,
A fair behavior, and a fluent tongue.
And yet with all his arts he could not thrive;
The most unlucky parasite alive.   2450
Loud praises to prepare his paths he sent,
And then himself pursued his compliment;
But, by reverse of fortune chas'd away,
His gifts no longer than their author stay: [1160]
He shakes the dust against th' ungrateful race,
And leaves the stench of ordures in the place.
Oft has he flatter'd and blasphem'd the same,
For in his rage he spares no sov'reign's name;
The hero and the tyrant change their style
By the same measure that they frown or smile.   2460
When well receiv'd by hospitable foes,
The kindness he returns, is to expose:
For courtesies, tho' undeserv'd and great,
No gratitude in felon-minds beget;   [1170]
As tribute to his wit, the churl receives the treat.
His praise of foes is venomously nice;
So touch'd, it turns a virtue to a vice:
A Greek, and bountiful, forewarns us twice.
Sev'n sacraments he wisely does disown,
Because he knows confession stands for one;   2470
Where sins to sacred silence are convey'd,
And not for fear, or love, to be betray'd:

But he, uncall'd, his patron to control,
Divulg'd the secret whispers of his soul;   [1180]
Stood forth th' accusing Sathan of his crimes,
And offer'd to the Moloch of the times.
Prompt to assail, and careless of defense,
Invulnerable in his impudence,
He dares the world; and, eager of a name,
He thrusts about, and justles into fame.
Frontless and satire-proof he scours the streets,   2481
And runs an Indian muck at all he meets.
So fond of loud report, that not to miss
Of being known (his last and utmost bliss)   [1190]
He rather would be known for what he is.
   "Such was, and is the Captain of the Test,
Tho' half his virtues are not here express'd;
The modesty of fame conceals the rest.
The spleenful Pigeons never could create
A prince more proper to revenge their hate: 2490
Indeed, more proper to revenge, than save;
A king whom in his wrath th' Almighty gave:
For all the grace the landlord had allow'd,
But made the Buzzard and the Pigeons proud;   [1200]
Gave time to fix their friends, and to seduce the crowd.
They long their fellow-subjects to inthral,
Their patron's promise into question call,
And vainly think he meant to make 'em lords of all.
   "False fears their leaders fail'd not to suggest,
As if the Doves were to be dispossess'd;
Nor sighs, nor groans, nor goggling eyes did want,   2501
For now the Pigeons too had learn'd to cant.
The house of pray'r is stock'd with large encrease;
Nor doors, nor windows can contain the press: [1210]
For birds of ev'ry feather fill th' abode;
Ev'n atheists out of envy own a God:
And, reeking from the stews, adult'rers come,
Like Goths and Vandals to demolish Rome.
That Conscience which to all their crimes was mute
Now calls aloud, and cries to persecute;
No rigor of the laws to be releas'd,   2511
And much the less, because it was their lord's request:

They thought it great their sov'reign to control,
And nam'd their pride, nobility of soul.   [*1220*]
    " 'T is true, the Pigeons, and their prince elect,
Were short of pow'r their purpose to effect;
But with their quills did all the hurt they could,
And cuff'd the tender Chickens from their food:
And much the Buzzard in their cause did stir,
Tho' naming not the patron, to infer,   *2520*
With all respect, he was a gross idolater.
    "But when th' imperial owner did espy
That thus they turn'd his grace to villainy,
Not suff'ring wrath to discompose his mind,   [*1230*]
He strove a temper for th' extremes to find,
So to be just, as he might still be kind;
Then, all maturely weigh'd, pronounc'd a doom
Of sacred strength for ev'ry age to come.
By this the Doves their wealth and state possess,
No rights infring'd, but license to oppress: *2530*
Such pow'r have they as factious lawyers long
To crowns ascrib'd, that kings can do no wrong.
But, since his own domestic birds have tried
The dire effects of their destructive pride,   [*1240*]
He deems that proof a measure to the rest,
Concluding well within his kingly breast,
His fowl of nature too unjustly were oppress'd.
He therefore makes all birds of ev'ry sect
Free of his farm, with promise to respect
Their sev'ral kinds alike, and equally protect.   *2540*
His gracious edict the same franchise yields
To all the wild encrease of woods and fields,
And who in rocks aloof, and who in steeples builds;
To Crows the like impartial grace affords,   [*1250*]
And Choughs and Daws, and such republic birds;
Secur'd with ample privilege to feed,
Each has his district, and his bounds decreed:
Combin'd in common int'rest with his own,
But not to pass the Pigeons' Rubicon.
    "Here ends the reign of this pretended Dove;   *2550*
All prophecies accomplish'd from above,
For Shiloh comes the scepter to remove.

Reduc'd from her imperial high abode,
Like Dionysius to a private rod,   [1260]
The Passive Church, that with pretended grace
Did her distinctive mark in duty place,
Now touch'd, reviles her Maker to his face.
    "What after happen'd is not hard to guess:
The small beginnings had a large encrease,
And arts and wealth succeed (the secret spoils of peace).   2560
'T is said, the Doves repented, tho' too late,
Become the smiths of their own foolish fate:
Nor did their owner hasten their ill hour;
But, sunk in credit, they decreas'd in pow'r;   [1270]
Like snows in warmth that mildly pass away,
Dissolving in the silence of decay.
    "The Buzzard, not content with equal place,
Invites the feather'd Nimrods of his race,
To hide the thinness of their flock from sight,
And all together make a seeming goodly flight: 2570
But each have sep'rate int'rests of their own;
Two *Czars* are one too many for a throne.
Nor can th' usurper long abstain from food;
Already he has tasted Pigeons' blood,   [1280]
And may be tempted to his former fare,
When this indulgent lord shall late to heav'n repair.
Bare benting times, and molting months may come,
When, lagging late, they cannot reach their home;
Or rent in schism (for so their fate decrees)
Like the tumultuous college of the bees,   2580
They fight their quarrel, by themselves oppress'd:
The tyrant smiles below, and waits the falling feast."
    Thus did the gentle Hind her fable end,
Nor would the Panther blame it, nor commend;   [1290]
But, with affected yawnings at the close,
Seem'd to require her natural repose;
For now the streaky light began to peep,
And setting stars admonish'd both to sleep.
The dame withdrew, and, wishing to her guest
The peace of heav'n, betook herself to rest.   2590
Ten thousand angels on her slumbers wait,
With glorious visions of her future state.

Occasional
Poems

Commentary on the Occasional Poems

Upon the Death of Lord Hastings. This poem is Dryden's earliest published work, an elegy on the death at nineteen of a schoolmate of his; it was published in 1649 in a memorial volume, to which other poets, including Denham, Marvell, and Waller, contributed.

then (17): than. *Archimedes* (30), *Ptolemy* (39): ancient Greek scientists. *Tycho* (43): Tycho Brahe, the Danish astronomer, discoverer of a *new star* in 1572. *astrolabe* (45): instrument for taking altitude of sun or stars. *Ganymede* (52): Trojan youth of great beauty; Zeus's cupbearer. *Pandora's box* (54): which contained all human ills. *naeves* (54): blemishes. *constellation* (56): syllabicated con-stel-la-ti-on, in older pronunciation. *Seneca . . . Caesar* (70): Roman philosophers and rulers. *metempsuchosis* (72): transmigration (of a soul). *Phoenix* (80): unique legendary bird, one of which rises from the ashes of its predecessor. *three-legg'd* (80): that is, carrying canes. *posset* (86): hot milk drink. *virgin-widow* (93): Hasting's fiancée, whose father (95) was the physician in attendance at his death. *ideas* (100): original prototypes (in Platonic philosophy).

To Dr. Charleton. This poem, published in 1663, shows Dryden's youthful interest in science: the great chemist *Boyle* (27) was at this time organizing the Royal Society, Dryden's membership in which Dr. Charleton later sponsored. Charleton himself had written a treatise (to which Dryden's poem was prefixed) in which he argued (against the opinions of the architect Inigo Jones) that Stonehenge (a prehistoric monument in southern England) was not originally a Roman temple (as Jones had thought) but more probably a Danish coronation palace.

The poem decries ancient science, symbolized by *Aristotle* (the *Stagirite, 3*), and celebrates *Bacon, Gilbert* (author of a famous treatise on the magnet), *Harvey* (discoverer of the circulation of the blood), and *Ent* (Harvey's early admirer), as well as Boyle's *brother,* the poet and politician Lord Orrery. The conclusion refers to a visit Charles II paid to Stonehenge after being defeated by the Parliamentarians at the battle of Worcester in 1651.

Annus Mirabilis. Written during the same year as the "Essay of Dramatic Poesy," this is Dryden's most elaborate nonsatiric occasional poem. It celebrates the adequacy of Charles II's new regime in confronting national crises, predicts scientific and commercial triumphs for England, and may well have been a factor in Dryden's appointment, two years later, as poet laureate. The favorable portrait of Charles, based on fact, foreshadows Dryden's treatment of the king in "Absalom and Achitophel" in the 1680s; the imaginative mingling of myth and history in a work of panegyric and celebration foreshadows Pope's somewhat similar methods in "Windsor Forest" (1713). The immediate occasion of the poem was the second Dutch war (Dryden fails to note the then unimportant fact that Holland's defeat transformed New Netherlands into New York). To an account of England's naval victory Dryden appends his description of the great fire of London, which occurred later the same year. The poem's point of view is fairly consistently royalist and heroic; but occasional images on the verge of comedy, as in stanzas 59 and 61 (where the admiral's trousers have been shot off), give suggestive glimpses of talents to be more fully deployed in "Mac Flecknoe" and other poems a decade later.

base (8): a play on words, since "Netherlands" means "low countries." *Idumaean* (11): south Palestinian. *Belgian* (16): (Belgium = Netherlands at that time). *second Punic war* (20): Twelve years earlier Cromwell had led England to victory in a trade war with Holland. Rome had ultimately destroyed Carthage in three Punic (Carthagenian) wars in the third and second centuries B.C. *babe of Spain* (32): in the infancy of Spain's king, France's Louis XIV plotted vs. the Spanish Netherlands. *he less for it* (40): he did less for England than Cromwell had done.

charge (49): expense (navies were costly). *limbecs* (51): distilling apparatus. *assert the wat'ry ball* (53): be royally active at sea. *Proteus* (59): legendary sea deity in the Odyssey. *Whether they unctuous exhalations are* (65): the nature of comets was then under study; two had appeared in 1664, and one earlier at Charles II's birth. *York* (73): Charles II's brother James. *did confess* (75): bore witness to. *wed the main* (78): as was done by doges at Venice, who threw in a ring. *gage* (79): pledge. *Lawson* (80): vice-admiral fatally wounded 29 June 1665. *off'ring for the Grecian state* (83): the first Greek off the boats at Troy (Protesilaus) was the first battle casualty.

[THE ATTEMPT AT BERGHEN] *castors* (97): beavers (they secrete a substance used in perfume-making). *tell* (135): count. *draws* (143): draws forth. *Munster's prelate* (145): when the French entered on the Dutch side, the Bishop of Munster, previously England's ally, withdrew.

[WAR DECLARED BY FRANCE] *without the lists* (154): outside the tournament grounds. *this time* (162): January 1666. *the Danes unite* (165): in February 1666. *the French* (170): (especially Huguenots).

[PRINCE RUPERT AND DUKE ALBERMARLE SENT TO SEA] *Scipio* (197): Scipio Africanus (237–183 B.C.), the Roman general. *fasces* (199): rod-and-axe bundles symbolizing authority. *camp* (201): bilingual play on words (Latin *campus* = plain). *glass* (211): probably the "optic glass" of the *camera obscura,* a lens used to throw an inverted image of distant external objects onto a paper screen in a dark room.

[DUKE OF ALBERMARLE'S BATTLE, FIRST DAY] *straight* (213): straightway. *number* (214): (85 ships to 56). *commander:* de Ruyter. *crosses* (220): red crosses of St. George, British patron saint. *join* (227): join battle. *elephant* (235): whom the lower-slung rhinoceros was thought to jab in the belly. *built* (237): build. *All bare* (243): (not only his ship's rigging but even his own breeches had been shot off). *godlike fathers* (252): chief citizens at the sack by the Gauls in 387 B.C. *Patroclus* (253): Achilles' friend, whose body was fought over in the Iliad. *pious* (255): loyal. *squander* (266): scatter. *Berkeley* (267): killed in action, June 1666. *Creusa* (268): Aeneas' wife, who failed to escape when Troy fell. *deceive* (272): frustrate.

[SECOND DAY'S BATTLE] *mold* (287): appearance. *swordfish*

(314): reputedly ferocious. *Cacus* (330): fire-breathing monster destroyed by Hercules in the *Aeneid. stoops* (342): swoops. *at check* (344): at some lesser game. *clips it:* hastens. *careful* (395): full of cares.

[THIRD DAY] *eyry* (427): nest. *callow* (428): unfledged. *kind* (433): natural. *ken* (443): look. *Joshua's* (472): when the sun stood still over Gibeon while the Israelites defeated the Amorites (Joshua 10: 12–14).

[FOURTH DAY'S BATTLE] *breath'd* (479): rested and recuperated. *offends* (485): attacks. *volume* (492): windings. *throwing* (494): dice-throwing. *flix* (526): fur. *Batavian* (533): = Dutch (Batavia, later Jakarta, was the capital of Indonesia). *confess'd* (546): borne witness to. *essay* (558): tentative trying out.

[HIS MAJESTY REPAIRS THE FLEET] *imps* (570): repairs (literally, engrafts feathers on). *Tall Norway fir,* etc. (571–72): *Fir* and *oak* are the subjects of the verb *restore; masts, leaks,* and *planks* are the objects of this verb. *oakum* (582): hemp fiber picked out of old rope. *paid o'er* (587): coated. *dauby* (589): sticky. *marling:* marline (cord). *searcloth* (590): cover with waxed cloth (a verb). *shrouds* (591): ropes supporting the mast. *-corn'd* (595): -grained.

[*Loyal London* DESCRIB'D] *London* (601): replacement for ship blown up in 1665. *Phoenix* (602): bird that rises reborn from own ashes. *to aid him bring* (616): to bring him aid.

[DIGRESSION CONCERNING SHIPPING AND NAVIGATION] *kern* (625): peasant. *Saturn* (629): was supposed by the Roman poets to have established civilization in Rome (on the banks of the Tiber) after his overthrow by Zeus. *ken* (635): view. *rolling neighbors* (655): the planets.

[APOSTROPHE TO THE ROYAL SOCIETY] *limbecs* (663): distilling apparatus. *level'd* (664): ordinary. *Achates* (689): faithful companion to Aeneas. *fruits* (692): fresh figs brought in three days from Carthage. *succeeds* (700): causes (his right hand) to replace (his shot-off left one). *gross* (728): main fleet. *blind* (731): concealed. *officious* (735): dutiful.

[SECOND BATTLE] *linstocks* (750): cannon-lighters. *expires* (is breathed forth.) *Caesar's* (762): = Charles II's. *Varro* (775): Roman general who did not despair after the defeat at Cannae. *dar'd* (780) = terrified. *hobby:* falcon. *to the blest* (801): to heaven. *fourth Harry* (802): French king, grandfather of Louis XIV, whom he now disowns as a *Burbon foe* to England. *first*

Orange: William the Silent, who *detests* the Dutch fleet's use against his benefactors, the English.

[BURNING OF THE FLEET IN THE VLIE BY SIR ROBERT HOLMES] *several* (818): particular. *turbants* (824): turbans. *Holland:* linen. *doom* (827): consign.

[TRANSIT TO THE FIRE OF LONDON] *unsincere* (833): imperfect. *post* (836): posthaste. *one* (843): water. *another* (844): fire. *usurper* (849): this would have recalled Cromwell, an unknown from the country at the time of the Civil War: cf. Gray's "Elegy," line 60. *insulting* (877): wantonly leaping. *courtesans* (881): prostitutes. *letted of* (885): hindered from. *Bridge* (889): London Bridge, where the skulls of regicides and conspirators were exhibited. *fanatic* (890): (often applied to puritan antimonarchical extremists). *sabbath* (892): witches' sabbath, scene of demonic revelry. *choir* (914): (fire buckets were kept in churches). *pipes* (915): wooden water pipes (*cut* to fill buckets). *engines:* pumps (?). *key* (921): quay. *Simoeis* (926): river attacked with flames when it tried to drown Achilles. *urn* (928): = source. *Lombard* (944): Lombard Street. *Change:* stock exchange. *Tow'r* (945): Tower of London, east of financial district. *palace* (948): Whitehall, to the west. *pious* (958): naturally paternal. *blows up all* (977): (a policy not at first followed extensively enough, but later successful). *retire* (995): remove. *lade* (1008): load. *brother* (1011): Duke of York. *gen'ral doom* (1014): doomsday. *require* (1022): search for. *vestal* (1025): (Vesta was Rome's goddess of house and hearth). *repeat* (1028): again encounter. *obnoxious* (1030): exposed.

[KING'S PRAYER] *spotted deaths* (1066): the plague of 1665, which continued into early 1666. *frequent funerals* (1069): Latinism for "numerous bodies." *magazins* (1084): ammunition storehouses. *pious* (1090): religious and charitable. *affect* (1091): seek to obtain (the way to heaven). *Ere . . . heard* (1092): before the Protestant Reformation preached faith as a way to heaven rather than good works. *Paul's* (1097): St. Paul's cathedral, later replaced by the present Christopher Wren building. *poet's song* (1099): Waller's poem about Charles I's repairs to Paul's in the 1630s. *Theban walls* (1100): raised by the music of Amphion's lyre. *profan'd by civil war* (1103): Cromwell's soldiers vandalized it and used it as a stable. *Thrones, Dominions* (1114): orders of angels. *silence damps* (1116): (the music of the spheres stops).

genius (1127): guardian spirit. *Lares* (1128): Roman household gods.

[CITY'S REQUEST TO THE KING NOT TO LEAVE THEM] *auspice* (1150): propitious influence. *Jews* (1157): who were allowed by the Persian king Cyrus to return from exile and rebuild the temple. *trines* (1165): planets in trine (120 degrees apart) are thought favorable. *high-rais'd Jove* (1166): Jupiter in ascension (also favorable). *succeed* (1168): cause to succeed. *chymic* (1169): alchemic—having the purpose of transmuting base metals into gold. *Tagus* (1193): Spanish river reputed to have had golden sands. *would . . . join* (1195): (Louis XIV had designs on the Spanish Netherlands). *vindicate* (1204): defend. *is left behind* (1210): remains to be dealt with. *dare* (1211): (to come trade with us). *vanquish* (1212): vanquish enemies. *find:* find customers.

To the Memory of Mr. Oldham. By some critics this has been thought Dryden's finest single poem. Oldham, a talented satiric poet, died in 1683 at the age of thirty, Dryden being then the well-established laureate of fifty-two and the author of the recent, very successful *Absalom and Achitophel.* Dryden's elegy was prefixed to a volume of Oldham's writings published the next year. *Nisus* and Euryalus, the latter a youth, were friends who took part in contests celebrating Anchises' funeral in Book V of *the Aeneid;* Nisus fell in a pool of blood from a sacrificed ox, enabling Euryalus—here compared to Oldham—to win the foot race, which symbolizes both literary achievement and the successful completion of a distinguished career. *Marcellus* (23) was the Emperor Augustus' nephew, whose death at twenty Virgil lamented in *Aeneid* VI; he was to have been Augustus' successor, as Oldham (Dryden implies) might have been his own. The Virgilian analogies are beautifully linked with an extended metaphor of fruition (*ripe, abundant, fruits, prime, quickness, maturing, sweets*), which leads up to the wreaths successful poets were crowned with; *fate and gloomy night* is a classical conception of death.

Epigram on Milton. *Three poets* (1): Homer, Virgil, and Milton.

To My Dear Friend Mr. Congreve. This tribute was prefixed to Congreve's second comedy, *The Double Dealer,* on its publication in 1694, at a time when Dryden had written his last play and had for several years been no longer either Poet Laureate or

Historiographer Royal, these two posts having, for political reasons, been bestowed by the Lord Chamberlain (Dorset, still friendly to Dryden [see 49]), on Thomas Shadwell, who had later been succeeded (as Historiographer) by Thomas Rymer (see 48).

Dryden correctly recognizes *Congreve's* talents as a dramatist, comparing him not only with the Restoration playwrights, *Etherege, Southerne,* and *Wycherley,* but also with the most famous Elizabethans (*the giant race before the flood* of the Civil Wars, 5), *Fletcher, Jonson,* and even *Shakespeare.*

wit (2): creative power. *Janus* (7): God supposed to have founded Rome. *second temple* (14): that is, rebuilt in Jerusalem after the Babylonian exile. *Vitruvius* (15): famous Roman architect. *Manly* (30): name of hero of Wycherley's *Plain Dealer.* *Fabius* (35) displaced in his leadership of the campaign against Hannibal by the younger Scipio. *Romano* (39): Dryden incorrectly supposed him Raphael's teacher. *Edward . . . Edward* (45–46): Edward II was assassinated in 1327; Edward III, his successor, reigned till 1377 and defeated the French in the famous battle of Crécy (1346).

Epigram on Tonson. Dryden apparently wrote this compliment under a portrait of his publisher. One story, perhaps apocryphal, says in effect that the poet, on being refused an advance of money by Tonson, sent him the epigram with a message saying that "he who wrote these lines can write more." The anecdote does not specify the result.

To My Honor'd Kinsman, John Driden. John Driden (the family name was spelled both Driden and Dryden) was the poet's cousin, being the second son of his uncle, the baronet; he owned country property inherited from his mother (43). He was a bachelor, a Whig, and an opponent of William III's aggressive military policies after the capture of *Namur* in Belgium (152) had led to the *peace* of Ryswick in 1697 (142). William's desire for a larger army than the House of Commons wanted probably accounts for Dryden's stress on the British fleet (146–150). Dryden buttresses his military and political recommendations with references to Alexander's conquests (159–163), Hannibal's war with Rome (164–166), and the traditional policies of the Roman republic (183). His reference to *Munster* (140) is to a venal continental ally of England's in the time of Charles II. *Albion* (157) is England. It is not known precisely which ancestor of John Driden's had been imprisoned for refusing to lend money to a king (188).

Dryden spices his praise of the healthfulness of country life with personal references to physicians and apothecaries: *Gibbons* (82) was his own physician, and *Garth* (107) was a poet-doctor, author of *The Dispensary* (1699), who maintained a free clinic for the poor. *Maurus* (83) is the same unfortunate Blackmore—also a physician and a poet of little merit—dealt with in the conclusion of the Preface to the *Fables*. *M-lb-rne,* or Melbourne, (87), a clergyman who had attacked Dryden's *Virgil,* also appears in both preface and poem.

travers'd (12): opposed. *Ceres* (46): goddess of grain and agriculture. *champian* (51): open country. *Pity* (75): it's a pity that . . .

Upon the Death of the
LORD HASTINGS

Must noble Hastings immaturely die,
The honor of his ancient family,
Beauty and learning thus together meet,
To bring a *winding* for a *wedding sheet?*
Must Virtue prove Death's harbinger? must she,
With him expiring, feel mortality?
Is death, sin's wages, grace's now? shall art
Make us more learned, only to depart?
If merit be disease; if virtue death;
To be good, not to be; who'd then bequeath   10
Himself to discipline? who 'd not esteem
Labor a crime? study self-murther deem?
Our noble youth now have pretense to be
Dunces securely, ign'rant healthfully.
Rare linguist, whose worth speaks itself, whose praise,
Tho' not his own, all tongues besides do raise!
Then whom great Alexander may seem less,
Who conquer'd men, but not their languages.
In his mouth nations speak; his tongue might be
Interpreter to Greece, France, Italy.   20
His native soil was the four parts o' th' earth;

All Europe was too narrow for his birth.
A young apostle; and, (with rev'rence may
I speak it,) inspir'd with gift of tongues, as they.
Nature gave him, a child, what men in vain
Oft strive, by art tho' further'd, to obtain.
His body was an orb, his sublime soul
Did move on virtue's and on learning's pole:
Whose reg'lar motions better to our view,
Then Archimedes' sphere, the heavens did shew.   30
Graces and virtues, languages and arts,
Beauty and learning, fill'd up all the parts.
Heav'n's gifts, which do, like falling stars, appear
Scatter'd in others; all, as in their sphere,
Were fix'd and conglobate in 's soul; and thence
Shone thro' his body, with sweet influence;
Letting their glories so on each limb fall,
The whole frame render'd was celestial.
Come, learned Ptolemy, and trial make,
If thou this hero's altitude canst take: 40
But that transcends thy skill; thrice happy all,
Could we but prove thus astronomical.
Liv'd Tycho now, struck with this ray, which shone
More bright i' th' morn, then others' beam at noon,
He'd take his *astrolabe,* and seek out here
What new star 't was did gild our hemisphere.
Replenish'd then with such rare gifts as these,
Where was room left for such a foul disease?
The nation's sin hath drawn that veil, which shrouds
Our dayspring in so sad benighting clouds.   50
Heaven would no longer trust its pledge; but thus
Recall'd it; rapt its Ganymede from us.
Was there no milder way but the smallpox,
The very filth'ness of Pandora's box?
So many spots, like *naeves,* our Venus soil?
One jewel set off with so many a foil!
Blisters with pride swell'd, which thro' 's flesh did sprout,
Like rose-buds, stuck i' th' lily skin about.
Each little pimple had a tear in it,
To wail the fault its rising did commit: 60
Who, rebel-like, with their own lord at strife,
Thus made an insurrection 'gainst his life.

Or were these gems sent to adorn his skin,
The cab'net of a richer soul within?
No comet need foretell his change drew on,
Whose corpse might seem a *constellation*.
O, had he died of old, how great a strife
Had been, who from his death should draw their life?
Who should, by one rich draught, become whate'er
Seneca, Cato, Numa, Caesar, were;   70
Learn'd, virtuous, pious, great; and have by this
An universal *metempsuchosis*.
Must all these ag'd sires in one funeral
Expire? all die in one so young, so small?
Who, had he liv'd his life out, his great fame
Had swoll'n 'bove any Greek or Roman name.
But hasty winter, with one blast, hath brought
The hopes of autumn, summer, spring, to naught.
Thus fades the oak i' th' sprig, i' th' blade the corn;
Thus without young, this Phoenix dies, new-born.   80
Must then old three-legg'd graybeards with their gout,
Catarrhs, rheums, achës, live three ages out?
Time's offal, only fit for th' hospital,
Or t' hang an antiquary's room withal!
Must drunkards, lechers, spent with sinning, live
With such helps as broths, possets, physic give?
None live, but such as should die? shall we meet
With none but ghostly fathers in the street?
Grief makes me rail: sorrow will force its way;
And show'rs of tears tempestuous sighs best lay.   90
The tongue may fail, but overflowing eyes
Will weep out lasting streams of elegies.
     But thou, O *virgin-widow*, left alone,
Now thy belov'd, heaven-ravish'd *spouse* is gone,
(Whose skilful sire in vain strove to apply
Med'cines, when thy balm was no remedy,)
With greater than Platonic love, O wed
His soul, tho' not his body, to thy bed:
Let that make thee a mother; bring thou forth
Th' *ideas* of his virtue, knowledge, worth;   100
Transcribe th' original in new copies; give
Hastings o' th' better part: so shall he live
In 's nobler half; and the great grandsire be

Of an heroic divine progeny;
An issue, which t' eternity shall last,
Yet but th' irradiations which he cast.
Erect no *mausoleums;* for his best
Monument is his spouse's marble breast.

To My Honor'd Friend,
DR. CHARLTON
*On his learned and useful works, and more particularly this
of Stonehenge, by him restor'd to the true founders*

The longest tyranny that ever sway'd
Was that wherein our ancestors betray'd
Their free-born reason to the Stagirite,
And made his torch their universal light.
So truth, while only one supplied the state,
Grew scarce, and dear, and yet sophisticate;
Until 't was bought, like emp'ric wares, or charms,
Hard words seal'd up with Aristotle's arms.
Columbus was the first that shook his throne,
And found a temp'rate in a torrid zone: 10
The fev'rish air fann'd by a cooling breeze,
The fruitful vales set round with shady trees;
And guiltless men, who danc'd away their time,
Fresh as their groves, and happy as their clime.
Had we still paid that homage to a name,
Which only God and nature justly claim,
The western seas had been our utmost bound,
Where poets still might dream the sun was drown'd:
And all the stars that shine in southern skies
Had been admir'd by none but salvage eyes.   20
    Among th' asserters of free reason's claim,
Th' English are not the least in worth or fame.
The world to Bacon does not only owe
Its present knowledge, but its future too.
Gilbert shall live, till loadstones cease to draw,
Or British fleets the boundless ocean awe;
And noble Boyle, not less in nature seen,
Than his great brother read in states and men.

The circling streams, once thought but pools, of blood
(Whether life's fuel, or the body's food)   30
From dark oblivion Harvey's name shall save;
While Ent keeps all the honor that he gave.
Nor are *you,* learned friend, the least renown'd;
Whose fame, not circumscrib'd with English ground,
Flies like the nimble journeys of the light;
And is, like that, unspent too in its flight.
Whatever truths have been, by art or chance,
Redeem'd from error, or from ignorance,
Thin in their authors, like rich veins of ore,
Your works unite, and still discover more.   40
Such is the healing virtue of your pen,
To perfect cures on books, as well as men.
Nor is this work the least: you well may give
To men new vigor, who makes stones to live.
Thro' you, the Danes, their short dominion lost,
A longer conquest than the Saxons boast.
Stonehenge, once thought a temple, you have found
A throne, where kings, our earthly gods, were crown'd;
Where by their wond'ring subjects they were seen,
Joy'd with their stature, and their princely mien.   50
Our sovereign here above the rest might stand,
And here be chose again to rule the land.

      These ruins shelter'd once his sacred head,
Then when from Wor'ster's fatal field he fled;
Watch'd by the genius of this royal place,
And mighty visions of the Danish race.
His refuge then was for a temple shown;
But, he restor'd, 't is now become a throne.

ANNUS MIRABILIS
The Year of Wonders, 1666

1
In thriving arts long time had Holland grown,
    Crouching at home and cruel when abroad;

Scarce leaving us the means to claim our own;
  Our king they courted, and our merchants aw'd.

2

Trade, which like blood should circularly flow,
  Stopp'd in their channels, found its freedom lost:
Thither the wealth of all the world did go,
  And seem'd but shipwrack'd on so base a coast.

3

For them alone the heav'ns had kindly heat;
  (a) In eastern quarries ripening precious dew: 10
For them the Idumæan balm did sweat,
  And in hot Ceylon spicy forests grew.

4

The sun but seem'd the lab'rer óf their year;
  (b) Each waxing moon supplied her wat'ry store,
To swell those tides, which from the line did bear
  Their brim-full vessels to the Belgian shore.

5

Thus mighty in her ships stood Carthage long,
  And swept the riches of the world from far;
Yet stoop'd to Rome, less wealthy, but more strong;
  And this may prove our second Punic war.   20

6

What peace can be, where both to one pretend?
  (But they more diligent, and we more strong)
Or if a peace, it soon must have an end;
  For they would grow too pow'rful were it long.

7

Behold two nations then, ingag'd so far,
  That each sev'n years the fit must shake each land:

  (a) *In eastern quarries,* &c. Precious stones at first are dew, condens'd and
harden'd by the warmth of the sun or subterranean fires.
  (b) *Each waxing,* &c. According to their opinion, who think that great
heap of waters under the line is depress'd into tides by the moon, towards the
poles.

Where France will side to weaken us by war,
   Who only can his vast designs withstand.

8

See how he feeds (c) th' Iberian with delays,   *30*
   To render us his timely friendship vain:
And while his secret soul on Flanders preys,
   He rocks the cradle of the babe of Spain.

9

Such deep designs of empire does he lay
   O'er them whose cause he seems to take in hand;
And, prudently, would make them lords at sea,
   To whom with ease he can give laws by land.

10

This saw our king; and long within his breast
   His pensive counsels balanc'd to and fro:
He griev'd the land he freed should be oppress'd,   *40*
   And he less for it than usurpers do.

11

His gen'rous mind the fair ideas drew
   Of fame and honor, which in dangers lay;
Where wealth, like fruit on precipices, grew,
   Not to be gather'd but by birds of prey.

12

The loss and gain each fatally were great;
   And still his subjects call'd aloud for war;
But peaceful kings, o'er martial people set,
   Each other's poise and counterbalance are.

13

He, first, survey'd the charge with careful eyes,
   Which none but mighty monarchs could maintain;   *50*
Yet judg'd, like vapors that from limbecs rise,
   It would in richer showers descend again.

(c) *Th' Iberian.* The Spaniard.

14

At length resolv'd t' assert the wat'ry ball,
  He in himself did whole armadoes bring:
Him aged seamen might their master call,
  And choose for general, were he not their king.

15

It seems as every ship their sovereign knows,
  His awful summons they so soon obey;
So hear the scaly herd when [d] Proteus blows,
  And so to pasture follow thro' the sea.   60

16

To see this fleet upon the ocean move,
  Angels drew wide the curtains of the skies;
And Heav'n, as if there wanted lights above,
  For tapers made two glaring comets rise;

17

Whether they unctuous exhalations are,
  Fir'd by the sun, or seeming so alone;
Or each some more remote and slippery star,
  Which loses footing when to mortals shown;

18

Or one, that bright companion of the sun,
  Whose glorious aspect seal'd our newborn king,   70
And now, a round of greater years begun,
  New influence from his walks of light did bring.

19

Victorious York did first, with fam'd success,
  To his known valor make the Dutch give place:
Thus Heav'n our monarch's fortune did confess,
  Beginning conquest from his royal race.

---

  [d] *When Proteus blows* or: *Cæruleus Proteus immania ponti Armenta et magnas pascit sub gurgite phocas.*—VIRGIL.
  Under the flood sea-green Proteus pastures the ocean's immense herds and the great seals—*Georgics* IV: 388, 394, 395.

20

But since it was decreed, auspicious king,
   In Britain's right that thou shouldst wed the main,
Heav'n, as a gage, would cast some precious thing,
   And therefore doom'd that Lawson should be slain.   80

21

Lawson amongst the foremost met his fate,
   Whom sea-green Sirens from the rocks lament:
Thus as an off'ring for the Grecian state,
   He first was kill'd who first to battle went.

22

(e) Their chief blown up, in air, not waves, expir'd,
   To which his pride presum'd to give the law:
The Dutch confess'd Heav'n present, and retir'd,
   And all was Britain the wide ocean saw.

23

To nearest ports their shatter'd ships repair,
   Where by our dreadful cannon they lay aw'd: 90
So reverently men quit the open air,
   When thunder speaks the angry gods abroad.

24

And now approach'd their fleet from India, fraught   The attempt
   With all the riches of the rising sun: at Berghen.
And precious sand from (f) southern climates brought,
   (The fatal regions where the war begun.)

25

Like hunted castors, conscious of their store,
   Their waylaid wealth to Norway's coasts they bring:
There first the North's cold bosom spices bore,
   And winter brooded on the eastern spring.   100

26

By the rich scent we found our perfum'd prey,
   Which, flank'd with rocks, did close in covert lie;

(e) The Admiral of Holland.
(f) Southern climates, Guinea.

And round about their murdering cannon lay,
  At once to threaten and invite the eye.

27
Fiercer than cannon, and than rocks more hard,
  The English undertake th' unequal war:
Seven ships alone, by which the port is barr'd,
  Besiege the Indies, and all Denmark dare.

28
These fight like husbands, but like lovers those:
  These fain would keep, and those more fain enjoy;   *110*
And to such height their frantic passion grows,
  That what both love, both hazard to destroy.

29
Amidst whole heaps of spices lights a ball,
  And now their odors arm'd against them fly:
Some preciously by shatter'd porc'lain fall,
  And some by aromatic splinters die.

30
And tho' by tempests of the prize bereft,
  In heaven's inclemency some ease we find:
Our foes we vanquish'd by our valor left,
  And only yielded to the seas and wind.   *120*

31
Nor wholly lost we so deserv'd a prey;
  For storms, repenting, part of it restor'd:
Which, as a tribute from the Baltic sea,
  The British ocean sent her mighty lord.

32
Go, mortals, now, and vex yourselves in vain
  For wealth, which so uncertainly must come:
When what was brought so far, and with such pain,
  Was only kept to lose it nearer home.   *128*

33

The son, who twice three months on th' ocean toss'd,
  Prepar'd to tell what he had pass'd before,
Now sees in English ships the Holland coast,
  And parents' arms in vain stretch'd from the shore.

34

This careful husband had been long away,
  Whom his chaste wife and little children mourn;
Who on their fingers learn'd to tell the day
  On which their father promis'd to return.

35

(g) Such are the proud designs of humankind,
  And so we suffer shipwreck everywhere!
Alas, what port can such a pilot find,
  Who in the night of fate must blindly steer!   *140*

36

The undistinguish'd seeds of good and ill,
  Heav'n, in his bosom, from our knowledge hides;
And draws them in contempt of human skill,
  Which oft for friends mistaken foes provides.

37

Let Munster's prelate ever be accurst,
  In whom we seek (h) the German faith in vain:
Alas, that he should teach the English first,
  That fraud and avarice in the Church could reign!

38

Happy, who never trust a stranger's will,
  Whose friendship's in his interest understood!   *150*

(g) *Such are*, &c. From Petronius: *Si bene calculum ponas, ubique fit
naufragium.* If you reckon up things accurately, there's shipwreck everywhere
—*Satyricon* 115.

(h) *The German faith.* Tacitus saith of them: *Nullos mortalium fide aut
armis ante Germanos esse.* There are no people superior to the Germans in
faithfulness or in arms—*Annals* XIII: 54.

Since money giv'n but tempts him to be ill,
    When pow'r is too remote to make him good.

39

Till now, alone the mighty nations strove;   War declar'd
    The rest, at gaze, without the lists did stand: by France.
And threat'ning France, plac'd like a painted Jove,
    Kept idle thunder in his lifted hand.

40

That eunuch guardian of rich Holland's trade,
    Who envies us what he wants pow'r t' enjoy;
Whose noiseful valor does no foe invade,
    And weak assistance will his friends destroy: 160

41

Offended that we fought without his leave,
    He takes this time his secret hate to show;
Which Charles does with a mind so calm receive,
    As one that neither seeks nor shuns his foe.

42

With France, to aid the Dutch, the Danes unite:
    France as their tyrant, Denmark as their slave.
But when with one three nations join to fight,
    They silently confess that one more brave.

43

Lewis had chas'd the English from his shore,
    But Charles the French as subjects does invite: 170
Would Heav'n for each some Solomon restore,
    Who, by their mercy, may decide their right!

44

Were subjects so but only by their choice,
    And not from birth did forc'd dominion take.
Our prince alone would have the public voice;
    And all his neighbors' realms would desarts make.

45

He without fear a dangerous war pursues,
    Which without rashness he began before:

As honor made him first the danger choose,
    So still he makes it good on virtue's score.   *180*

46

The doubled charge his subjects' love supplies,
    Who, in that bounty, to themselves are kind:
So glad Egyptians see their Nilus rise,
    And in his plenty their abundance find.

47

With equal pow'r he does two chiefs create,   Prince Rupert and
    Two such as each seem'd worthiest when alone;   Duke Albemarle
Each able to sustain a nation's fate,   sent to sea.
    Since both had found a greater in their own.

48

Both great in courage, conduct, and in fame,
    Yet neither envious of the other's praise;   *190*
Their duty, faith, and int'rest too the same,
    Like mighty partners equally they raise.

49

The prince long time had courted Fortune's love,
    But once possess'd did absolutely reign:
Thus with their *Amazons* the *heroes* strove,
    And conquer'd first those beauties they would gain.

50

The duke beheld, like Scipio, with disdain,
    That Carthage which he ruin'd rise once more;
And shook aloft the fasces of the main,
    To fright those slaves with what they felt before.   *200*

51

Together to the wat'ry camp they haste,
    Whom matrons passing to their children show:
Infants' first vows for them to heav'n are cast,
    And [i] future people bless them as they go.

---

[i] *Future people. Examina infantium futurusque populus.*—PLIN. JUN.
in *Pan. ad Traj.* Crowds of children, and future people—*Panegyricus* XXVI.

52

With them no riotous pomp, nor Asian train,
    T' infect a navy with their gaudy fears;
To make slow fights, and victories but vain;
    But war, severely, like itself, appears.

53

Diffusive of themselves, where'er they pass,
    They make that warmth in others they expect;   210
Their valor works like bodies on a glass,
    And does its image on their men project.

54

Our fleet divides, and straight the Dutch appear,   Duke of
    In number, and a fam'd commander, bold: Albemarle's
The narrow seas can scarce their navy bear,   battle, first day.
    Or crowded vessels can their soldiers hold.

55

The duke, less numerous, but in courage more,
    On wings of all the winds to combat flies:
His murdering guns a loud defiance roar,
    And bloody crosses on his flagstaffs rise.   220

56

Both furl their sails, and strip them for the fight,
    Their folded sheets dismiss the useless air:
(j) Th' Elean plains could boast no nobler sight,
    When struggling champions did their bodies bare.

57

Borne each by other in a distant line,
    The sea-built forts in dreadful order move:
So vast the noise, as if not fleets did join,
    But (k) lands unfix'd and floating nations strove.

(j) *Th' Elean,* &c. Where the Olympic games were celebrated.
    (k) *Lands unfix'd,* from Virgil: *Credas innare revulsas Cycladas,* &c. You'd think the Cyclades Islands were uprooted, etc.—*Aeneid* VIII: 691–92.

58

Now pass'd, on either side they nimbly tack;
  Both strive to intercept and guide the wind: 230
And, in its eye, more closely they come back,
  To finish all the deaths they left behind.

59

On high-rais'd decks the haughty Belgians ride,
  Beneath whose shade our humble frigates go:
Such port the elephant bears, and so defied
  By the rhinoceros her unequal foe.

60

And as the built, so different is the fight;
  Their mounting shot is on our sails design'd:
Deep in their hulls our deadly bullets light
  And thro' the yielding planks a passage find.   240

61

Our dreaded admiral from far they threat,
  Whose batter'd rigging their whole war receives:
All bare, like some old oak which tempests beat,
  He stands, and sees below his scatter'd leaves.

62

Heroes of old, when wounded, shelter sought;
  But he, who meets all danger with disdain,
Ev'n in their face his ship to anchor brought,
  And steeple-high stood propp'd upon the main.

63

At this excess of courage, all amaz'd,
  The foremost of his foes a while withdraw: 250
With such respect in enter'd Rome they gaz'd,
  Who on high chairs the godlike fathers saw.

64

And now, as where Patroclus' body lay,
  Here Trojan chiefs advanc'd, and there the Greek;

Ours o'er the duke their pious wings display,
    And theirs the noblest spoils of Britain seek.

65

Meantime his busy mariners he hastes,
    His shatter'd sails with rigging to restore;
And willing pines ascend his broken masts,
    Whose lofty heads rise higher than before.   *260*

66

Straight to the Dutch he turns his dreadful prow,
    More fierce th' important quarrel to decide:
Like swans, in long array his vessels show,
    Whose crests, advancing, do the waves divide.

67

They charge, recharge, and all along the sea
    They drive, and squander the huge Belgian fleet.
Berkeley alone, who nearest danger lay,
    Did a like fate with lost Creüsa meet.

68

The night comes on, we eager to pursue
    The combat still, and they asham'd to leave: *270*
Till the last streaks of dying day withdrew,
    And doubtful moonlight did our rage deceive.

69

In th' English fleet each ship resounds with joy,
    And loud applause of their great leader's fame:
In fiery dreams the Dutch they still destroy,
    And, slumb'ring, smile at the imagin'd flame.

70

Not so the Holland fleet, who, tir'd and done,
    Stretch'd on their decks like weary oxen lie:
Faint sweats all down their mighty members run,
    (Vast bulks, which little souls but ill supply.)   *280*

71

In dreams they fearful precipices tread;
    Or, shipwrack'd, labor to some distant shore:

Or in dark churches walk among the dead;
    They wake with horror, and dare sleep no more.

72

The morn they look on with unwilling eyes,
    Till from their maintop joyful news they hear
Of ships, which by their mold bring new supplies,   Second day's
    And in their colors Belgian lions bear.   battle.

73

Our watchful general had discern'd from far
    This mighty succor, which made glad the foe;   *290*
He sigh'd, but, like a father of the war,
    (1) His face spake hope, while deep his sorrows flow.

74

His wounded men he first sends off to shore,
    (Never, till now, unwilling to obey:)
They not their wounds, but want of strength deplore,
    And think them happy who with him can stay.

75

Then to the rest: "Rejoice," said he, "today;
    In you the fortune of Great Britain lies:
Among so brave a people, you are they
    Whom Heav'n has chose to fight for such a prize.   *300*

76

"If number English courages could quell,
    We should at first have shunn'd, not met, our foes,
Whose numerous sails the fearful only tell:
    Courage from hearts, and not from numbers, grows."

77

He said, nor needed more to say: with haste
    To their known stations cheerfully they go;
And all at once, disdaining to be last,
    Solicit every gale to meet the foe.

---

    (1) *His face*, &c. *Spem vultu simulat, premit alto corde dolorem.*—Virgil.
In his face he pretends hope; he buries grief deep in his heart—*Aeneid* I, 209.

78

Nor did th' incourag'd Belgians long delay,
    But bold in others, not themselves, they stood: *310*
So thick, our navy scarce could sheer their way,
    But seem'd to wander in a moving wood.

79

Our little fleet was now ingag'd so far,
    That, like the swordfish in the whale, they fought:
The combat only seem'd a civil war,
    Till thro' their bowels we our passage wrought.

80

Never had valor, no, not ours, before
    Done aught like this upon the land or main,
Where not to be o'ercome was to do more
    Than all the conquests former kings did gain.   *320*

81

The mighty ghosts of our great Harries rose,
    And armed Edwards look'd, with anxious eyes,
To see this fleet among unequal foes,
    By which fate promis'd them their Charles should rise.

82

Meantime the Belgians tack upon our rear,
    And raking chase-guns thro' our sterns they send:
Close by, their fire-ships, like jackals, appear,
    Who on their lions for the prey attend.

83

Silent in smoke of cannons they come on:
    (Such vapors once did fiery Cacus hide:)
In these the height of pleas'd revenge is shown,   *331*
    Who burn contented by another's side.

84

Sometimes, from fighting squadrons of each fleet,
    (Deceiv'd themselves, or to preserve some friend,)
Two grappling Ætnas on the ocean meet,
    And English fires with Belgian flames contend.

85

Now, at each tack, our little fleet grows less;
  And, like maim'd fowl, swim lagging on the main;
Their greater loss their numbers scarce confess,
  While they lose cheaper than the English gain.   *340*

86

Have you not seen, when, whistled from the fist,
  Some falcon stoops at what her eye design'd,
And, with her eagerness the quarry miss'd,
  Straight flies at check, and clips it down the wind;

87

The dastard crow, that to the wood made wing,
  And sees the groves no shelter can afford,
With her loud caws her craven kind does bring,
  Who, safe in numbers, cuff the noble bird?

88

Among the Dutch thus Albemarle did fare:
  He could not conquer, and disdain'd to fly;   *350*
Past hope of safety, 't was his latest care,
  Like falling Caesar, decently to die.

89

Yet pity did his manly spirit move,
  To see those perish who so well had fought;
And generously with his despair he strove,
  Resolv'd to live till he their safety wrought.

90

Let other Muses write his prosp'rous fate,
  Of conquer'd nations tell, and kings restor'd;
But mine shall sing of his eclips'd estate,
  Which, like the sun's, more wonders does afford.   *360*

91

He drew his mighty frigates all before,
  On which the foe his fruitless force employs:
His weak ones deep into his rear he bore,
  Remote from guns, as sick men from the noise.

92

His fiery cannon did their passage guide,
   And foll'wing smoke obscur'd them from the foe:
Thus Israel safe from the Egyptian's pride,
   By flaming pillars, and by clouds did go.

93

Elsewhere the Belgian force we did defeat,
   But here our courages did theirs subdue;   370
So Xenophon once led that fam'd retreat,
   Which first the Asian empire overthrew.

94

The foe approach'd; and one, for his bold sin,
   Was sunk; (as he that touch'd the ark was slain:)
The wild waves master'd him and suck'd him in,
   And smiling eddies dimpled on the main.

95

This seen, the rest at awful distance stood;
   As if they had been there as servants set,
To stay, or to go on, as he thought good,   379
   And not pursue, but wait on his retreat.

96

So Libyan huntsmen, on some sandy plain,
   From shady coverts rous'd, the lion chase:
The kingly beast roars out with loud disdain,
   (m) And slowly moves, unknowing to give place.

97

But if some one approach to dare his force,
   He swings his tail, and swiftly turns him round;
With one paw seizes on his trembling horse,
   And with the other tears him to the ground.

98

Amidst these toils succeeds the balmy night;   389
   Now hissing waters the quench'd guns restore;

(m) The simile is Virgil's: *Vestigia retro improperata refert,* &c. He turns his lingering footsteps backwards, etc.—*Aeneid* IX: 797–98.

And [n] weary waves, withdrawing from the fight,
   Lie lull'd and panting on the silent shore.

99

The moon shone clear on the becalmed flood,
   Where, while her beams like glittering silver play,
Upon the deck our careful general stood,
   And deeply mus'd on the [o] succeeding day.

100

"That happy sun," said he, "will rise again,
   Who twice victorious did our navy see;
And I alone must view him rise in vain,
   Without one ray of all his star for me.   400

101

"Yet like an English gen'ral will I die,
   And all the ocean make my spacious grave:
Women and cowards on the land may lie;
   The sea's a tomb that's proper for the brave."

102

Restless he pass'd the remnants of the night,
   Till the fresh air proclam'd the morning nigh;
And burning ships, the martyrs of the fight,
   With paler fires beheld the eastern sky.

103

But now, his stores of ammunition spent,   Third day.
   His naked valor is his only guard;   410
Rare thunders are from his dumb cannon sent,
   And solitary guns are scarcely heard.

104

Thus far had Fortune pow'r, here forc'd to stay,
   Nor longer durst with virtue be at strife:

   (n) *Weary waves:* from Statius, *Sylvæ: Nec trucibus fluviis idem sonus:
occidit horror Æquoris, antennis maria acclinata quiescunt.* Fierce waves don't
make the same sound: the bristling of the smooth surface dies down, and the
seas, leaning on the lands, become quiet—*Sylvae* 4–6.
   (o) The third of June, famous for two former victories.

This, as a ransom, Albemarle did pay
    For all the glories of so great a life.

105

For now brave Rupert from afar appears,
    Whose waving streamers the glad general knows:
With full-spread sails his eager navy steers,
    And every ship in swift proportion grows.

106

The anxious prince had heard the cannon long,   *421*
    And from that length of time dire *omens* drew
Of English overmatch'd, and Dutch too strong,
    Who never fought three days, but to pursue.

107

Then, as an eagle, who with pious care
    Was beating widely on the wing for prey,
To her now silent *eyry* does repair,
    And finds her callow infants forc'd away;

108

Stung with her love, she stoops upon the plain,
    The broken air loud whistling as she flies,   *430*
She stops and listens, and shoots forth again,
    And guides her pinions by her young ones' cries:

109

With such kind passion hastes the prince to fight,
    And spreads his flying canvas to the sound;
Him, whom no danger, were he there, could fright,
    Now, absent, every little noise can wound.

110

As in a drought the thirsty creatures cry,
    And gape upon the gather'd clouds for rain;
And first the martlet meets it in the sky,
    And with wet wings joys all the feather'd train.   *440*

111

With such glad hearts did our despairing men
    Salute th' appearance of the prince's fleet;

And each ambitiously would claim the ken
    That with first eyes did distant safety meet.

112
The Dutch, who came like greedy hinds before,
    To reap the harvest their ripe ears did yield;
Now look like those, when rolling thunders roar,
    And sheets of lightning blast the standing field.

113
Full in the prince's passage, hills of sand
    And dang'rous flats in secret ambush lay,
Where the false tides skim o'er the cover'd land,   *451*
    And seamen with dissembled depths betray.

114
The wily Dutch, who, like fall'n angels, fear'd
    This new *Messiah's* coming, there did wait,
And round the verge their braving vessels steer'd,
    To tempt his courage with so fair a bait.

115
But he, unmov'd, contemns their idle threat,
    Secure of fame whene'er he please to fight:
His cold experience tempers all his heat,
    And inbred worth doth boasting valor slight.   *460*

116
Heroic virtue did his actions guide,
    And he the substance, not the appearance chose;
To rescue one such friend he took more pride
    Than to destroy whole thousands of such foes.

117
But when approach'd, in strict embraces bound,
    Rupert and Albemarle together grow;
He joys to have his friend in safety found,
    Which he to none but to that friend would owe.

118
The cheerful soldiers, with new stores supplied,
    Now long to execute their spleenful will;   *470*

And in revenge for those three days they tried,
  Wish one, like Joshua's, when the sun stood still.

119

Thus reinforc'd, against the adverse fleet,   Fourth day's battle.
  Still doubling ours, brave Rupert leads the way:
With the first blushes of the morn they meet,
  And bring night back upon the new-born day.

120

His presence soon blows up the kindling fight,
  And his loud guns speak thick like angry men:
It seem'd as slaughter had been breath'd all night,
  And Death new pointed his dull dart again.   480

121

The Dutch too well his mighty conduct knew,
  And matchless courage, since the former fight:
Whose navy like a stiff-stretch'd cord did shew,
  Till he bore in and bent them into flight.

122

The wind he shares, while half their fleet offends
  His open side, and high above him shows:
Upon the rest at pleasure he descends,
  And, doubly harm'd, he double harms bestows.

123

Behind, the gen'ral mends his weary pace
  And sullenly to his revenge he sails;   490
(p) So glides some trodden serpent on the grass,
And long behind his wounded volume trails.

124

Th' increasing sound is borne to either shore,
  And for their stakes the throwing nations fear:

(p) *So glides*, &c. From Virgil: *Quum medii nexus, extremæque agmina caudæ Solvuntur; tardosque trahit sinus ultimus orbes*, &c. While his middle twinings and the driving movements of his tail's extremity relax, and his last bending drags its slow coils along, etc.—*Georgics* III: 423–24.

Their passion double with the cannons' roar,
   And with warm wishes each man combats there.

125
Plied thick and close as when the fight begun,
   Their huge unwieldly navy wastes away;
So sicken waning moons too near the sun,
   And blunt their crescents on the edge of day.   *500*

126
And now reduc'd on equal terms to fight,
   Their ships like wasted patrimonies show;
Where the thin scatt'ring trees admit the light,
   And shun each other's shadows as they grow.

127
The warlike prince had sever'd from the rest
   Two giant ships, the pride of all the main;
Which with his one so vigorously he press'd,
   And flew so home they could not rise again.

128
Already batter'd, by his lee they lay;
   In vain upon the passing winds they call:
The passing winds thro' their torn canvas play,   *511*
   And flagging sails on heartless sailors fall.

129
Their open'd sides receive a gloomy light,
   Dreadful as day let in to shades below;
Without, grim Death rides barefac'd in their sight,
   And urges ent'ring billows as they flow.

130
When one dire shot, the last they could supply,
   Close by the board the prince's mainmast bore;
All three now, helpless, by each other lie,
   And this offends not, and those fear no more.   *520*

131
So have I seen some fearful hare maintain
   A course, till tir'd before the dog she lay;

Who, stretch'd behind her, pants upon the plain,
  Past pow'r to kill, as she to get away:

132

With his loll'd tongue he faintly licks his prey;
  His warm breath blows her flix up as she lies;
She, trembling, creeps upon the ground away,
  And looks back to him with beseeching eyes.

133

The prince unjustly does his stars accuse,
  Which hinder'd him to push his fortune on;   530
For what they to his courage did refuse,
  By mortal valor never must be done.

134

This lucky hour the wise Batavian takes,
  And warns his tatter'd fleet to follow home:
Proud to have so got off with equal stakes,
  (q) Where 't was a triumph not to be o'ercome.

135

The general's force, as kept alive by fight,
  Now, not oppos'd, no longer can pursue:
Lasting till Heav'n had done his courage right;
  When he had conquer'd, he his weakness knew.   540

136

He casts a frown on the departing foe,
  And sighs to see him quit the wat'ry field:
His stern fix'd eyes no satisfaction show
  For all the glories which the fight did yield.

137

Tho', as when fiends did miracles avow,
  He stands confess'd ev'n by the boastful Dutch;
He only does his conquest disavow,
  And thinks too little what they found too much.

(q) From Horace: *Quos opimus Fallere et effugere est triumphus.* [The Romans] whom it is the greatest triumph to deceive and avoid—*Odes* IV, iv: 51–52.

138

Return'd, he with the fleet resolv'd to stay;
   No tender thoughts of home his heart divide;   *550*
Domestic joys and cares he puts away;
   For realms are households which the great must guide.

139

As those who unripe veins in mines explore,
   On the rich bed again the warm turf lay,
Till time digests the yet imperfect ore,
   And know it will be gold another day:

140

So looks our monarch on this early fight,
   Th' essay and rudiments of great success;
Which all-maturing time must bring to light,
   While he, like Heav'n, does each day's labor bless.   *560*

141

Heav'n ended not the first or second day,
   Yet each was perfect to the work design'd:
God and kings work, when they their work survey,
   And passive aptness in all subjects find.

142

In burden'd vessels first, with speedy care,
   His plenteous stores do season'd timber send:
Thither the brawny carpenters repair,   His Majesty
   And as the surgeons of maim'd ships attend.   repairs the fleet.

143

With cord and canvas from rich Hamburg sent,
   His navies' molted wings he imps once more;   *570*
Tall Norway fir, their masts in battle spent,
   And English oak, sprung leaks and planks, restore.

144

All hands employ'd, [r] the royal work grows warm:
   Like laboring bees on a long summer's day,

---

   [r] *Fervet opus:* the same similitude in Virgil. The work proceeds rapidly
—*Aeneid* I: 436.

Some sound the trumpet for the rest to swarm,
    And some on bells of tasted lilies play;

145
With gluey wax some new foundations lay
    Of virgin combs, which from the roof are hung;
Some arm'd within doors upon duty stay,
    Or tend the sick, or educate the young.   580

146
So here, some pick out bullets from the sides,
    Some drive old oakum thro' each seam and rift:
Their left hand does the calking-iron guide,
    The rattling mallet with the right they lift.

147
With boiling pitch another near at hand,
    From friendly Sweden brought, the seams instops:
Which well paid o'er, the salt sea waves withstand,
    And shakes them from the rising beak in drops.

148
Some the gall'd ropes with dauby marling bind,
    Or searcloth masts with strong tarpauling coats: 590
To try new shrouds one mounts into the wind,
    And one, below, their ease or stiffness notes.

149
Our careful monarch stands in person by,
    His new-cast cannons' firmness to explore:
The strength of big-corn'd powder loves to try,
    And ball and cartrage sorts for every bore.

150
Each day brings fresh supplies of arms and men,
    And ships which all last winter were abroad;
And such as fitted since the fight had been,
    Or new from stocks were fall'n into the road.   600

151
The goodly London in her gallant trim,   *Loyal London*
    (The Phoenix daughter of the vanish'd old,)   describ'd.

Like a rich bride does to the ocean swim,
   And on her shadow rides in floating gold.

152

Her flag aloft, spread ruffling to the wind,
   And sanguine streamers seem the flood to fire:
The weaver, charm'd with what his loom design'd,
   Goes on to sea, and knows not to retire.

153

With roomy decks, her guns of mighty strength,
   Whose low-laid mouths each mounting billow laves: 610
Deep in her draught, and warlike in her length,
   She seems a sea-wasp flying on the waves.

154

This martial present, piously design'd,
   The loyal city give their best-lov'd king:
And, with a bounty ample as the wind,
   Built, fitted, and maintain'd, to aid him bring.

155

By viewing Nature, Nature's handmaid Art   *Digression concerning*
   Makes mighty things from small beginnings grow: *shipping and*
Thus fishes first to shipping did impart   *navigation.*
   Their tail the rudder, and their head the prow.   620

156

Some log, perhaps, upon the waters swam,
   An useless drift, which, rudely cut within,
And hollow'd, first a floating trough became,
   And cross some riv'let passage did begin.

157

In shipping such as this, the Irish *kern,*
   And untaught Indian, on the stream did glide:
Ere sharp-keel'd boats to stem the flood did learn,
   Or fin-like oars did spread from either side.

158

Add but a sail, and Saturn so appear'd,
   When from lost empire he to exile went,   630

And with the golden age to Tiber steer'd,
   Where coin and first commerce he did invent.

159

Rude as their ships was navigation then;
   No useful compass or meridian known;
Coasting, they kept the land within their ken,
   And knew no North but when the Polestar shone.

160

Of all who since have us'd the open sea,
   Than the bold English none more fame have won;
[s] Beyond the year, and out of heav'n's high way,
   They make discoveries where they see no sun.   640

161

But what so long in vain, and yet unknown,
   By poor mankind's benighted wit is sought,
Shall in this age to Britain first be shown,
   And hence be to admiring nations taught.

162

The ebbs of tides and their mysterious flow,
   We, as arts' elements, shall understand,
And as by line upon the ocean go,
   Whose paths shall be familiar as the land.

163

[t] Instructed ships shall sail to quick commerce,
   By which remotest regions are allied;   650
Which makes one city of the universe;
   Where some may gain, and all may be supplied.

164

Then, we upon our globe's last verge shall go,
   And view the ocean leaning on the sky:

---

[s] *Extra anni solisque vias.*—Virg. Beyond the course of the year and of the sun—*Aeneid* VI: 796.

[t] By a more exact measure of longitude.

From thence our rolling neighbors we shall know,
 And on the lunar world securely pry.

165

This I foretell from your auspicious care,
 Who great in search of God and Nature grow;
Who best your wise Creator's praise declare,
 Since best to praise his works is best to know.

Apostrophe to
the Royal Society.

660

166

O truly Royal! who behold the law
 And rule of beings in your Maker's mind;
And thence, like limbecs, rich ideas draw,
 To fit the level'd use of humankind.

167

But first the toils of war we must endure,
 And from th' injurious Dutch redeem the seas.
War makes the valiant of his right secure,
 And gives up fraud to be chastis'd with ease.

168

Already were the Belgians on our coast,
 Whose fleet more mighty every day became
By late success, which they did falsely boast,
 And now by first appearing seem'd to claim.

670

169

Designing, subtile, diligent, and close,
 They knew to manage war with wise delay:
Yet all those arts their vanity did cross,
 And, by their pride, their prudence did betray.

170

Nor stay'd the English long; but, well supplied,
 Appear as numerous as th' insulting foe:
The combat now by courage must be tried,
 And the success the braver nation show.

171

There was the Plymouth squadron now come in,   *681*
   Which in the Straits last winter was abroad;
Which twice on Biscay's working bay had been,
   And on the midland sea the French had aw'd.

172

Old expert Allen, loyal all along,
   Fam'd for his action on the Smyrna fleet;
And Holmes, whose name shall live in epic song,
   While music numbers, or while verse has feet;

173

Holmes, the Achates of the gen'rals' fight,
   Who first bewitch'd our eyes with Guinea gold,   *690*
As once old Cato in the Romans' sight
   The tempting fruits of Afric did unfold.

174

With him went Sprag, as bountiful as brave,
   Whom his high courage to command had brought;
Harman, who did the twice-fir'd Harry save,
   And in his burning ship undaunted fought;

175

Young Hollis, on a Muse by Mars begot,
   Born, Caesar-like, to write and act great deeds:
Impatient to revenge his fatal shot,
   His right hand doubly to his left succeeds.

176

Thousands were there in darker fame that dwell,   *701*
   Whose deeds some nobler poem shall adorn;
And tho' to me unknown, they, sure, fought well,
   Whom Rupert led, and who were British born.

177

Of every size an hundred fighting sail,
   So vast the navy now at anchor rides,

That underneath it the press'd waters fail,
    And with its weight it shoulders off the tides.

178
Now, anchors weigh'd, the seamen shout so shrill,
    That heav'n, and earth, and the wide ocean rings;   *710*
A breeze from westward waits their sails to fill,
    And rests in those high beds his downy wings.

179
The wary Dutch this gathering storm foresaw,
    And durst not bide it on the English coast:
Behind their treach'rous shallows they withdraw,
    And there lay snares to catch the British host.

180
So the false spider, when her nets are spread,
    Deep ambush'd in her silent den does lie,
And feels far off the trembling of her thread,
    Whose filmy cord should bind the struggling fly;   *720*

181
Then, if at last she find him fast beset,
    She issues forth, and runs along her loom:
She joys to touch the captive in her net,
    And drags the little wretch in triumph home.

182
The Belgians hop'd that, with disorder'd haste,
    Our deep-cut keels upon the sands might run;
Or, if with caution leisurely were pass'd,
    Their numerous gross might charge us one by one.

183
But with a fore-wind pushing them above,
    And swelling tide that heav'd them from below,   *730*
O'er the blind flats our warlike squadrons move,
    And with spread sails to welcome battle go.

184

It seem'd as there the British Neptune stood,
  With all his hosts of waters at command,
Beneath them to submit th' officious flood,
  (u) And with his trident shov'd them off the sand.

185

To the pale foes they suddenly draw near,
  And summon them to unexpected fight;
They start like murderers when ghosts appear,
  And draw their curtains in the dead of night.   740

186

Now van to van the foremost squadrons meet,   Second
  The midmost battles hast'ning up behind;   battle
Who view, far off, the storm of falling sleet,
  And hear their thunder rattling in the wind.

187

At length the adverse admirals appear;
  (The two bold champions of each country's right:)
Their eyes describe the lists as they come near,
  And draw the lines of death before they fight.

188

The distance judg'd for shot of every size,
  The linstocks touch, the pond'rous ball expires: 750
The vig'rous seaman every porthole plies,
  And adds his heart to every gun he fires.

189

Fierce was the fight on the proud Belgians' side,
  For honor, which they seldom sought before;
But now they by their own vain boasts were tied,
  And forc'd at least in shew to prize it more.

(u) *Levat ipse tridenti, El vastas aperit syrtes,* &c.—VIRG. He himself raises [the ships] with his trident, and lays open vast sand-banks, etc.—*Aeneid* I: 145–46.

190

But sharp remembrance on the English part,
   And shame of being match'd by such a foe,
Rouse conscious virtue up in every heart,
   ^(v) And seeming to be stronger makes them so.

191

Nor long the Belgians could that fleet sustain,   *761*
   Which did two gen'rals' fates, and Caesar's bear:
Each several ship a victory did gain,
   As Rupert or as Albemarle were there.

192

Their batter'd admiral too soon withdrew,
   Unthank'd by ours for his unfinished fight;
But he the minds of his Dutch masters knew,
   Who call'd that providence which we call'd flight.

193

Never did men more joyfully obey,
   Or sooner understood the sign to fly: *770*
With such alacrity they bore away,
   As if to praise them all the States stood by.

194

O famous leader of the Belgian fleet,
   Thy monument inscrib'd such praise shall wear,
As Varro, timely flying, once did meet,
   Because he did not of his Rome despair.

195

Behold that navy, which a while before
   Provok'd the tardy English close to fight,
Now draw their beaten vessels close to shore,
   As larks lie dar'd to shun the hobby's flight.   *780*

196

Whoe'er would English monuments survey,
   In other records may our courage know:

---

   ^(v) *Possunt, quia posse videntur.*—Virg. They have the power, because they seem [to themselves] to have it—*Aeneid* V: 231.

But let them hide the story of this day,
    Whose fame was blemish'd by too base a foe.

197

Or if too busily they will enquire
    Into a victory which we disdain;
Then let them know, the Belgians did retire
    (w) Before the patron saint of injur'd Spain.

198

Repenting England this revengeful day
    (x) To Philip's manes did an off'ring bring: 790
England, which first, by leading them astray,
    Hatch'd up rebellion to destroy her king.

199

Our fathers bent their baneful industry
    To check a monarchy that slowly grew;
But did not France or Holland's fate foresee,
    Whose rising pow'r to swift dominion flew.

200

In fortune's empire blindly thus we go,
    And wander after pathless destiny;
Whose dark resorts since prudence cannot know,   799
    In vain it would provide for what shall be.

201

But whate'er English to the blest shall go,
    And the fourth Harry or first Orange meet;
Find him disowning of a Burbon foe,
    And him detesting a Batavian fleet.

202

Now on their coasts our conquering navy rides,
    Waylays their merchants, and their land besets;

(w) *Patron saint:* St. James, on whose day this victory was gain'd.
(x) *Philip's manes:* Philip the Second of Spain, against whom the Hollanders, rebelling, were aided by Queen Elizabeth. *manes:* departed spirit.

Each day new wealth without their care provides;
    They lie asleep with prizes in their nets.

203
So, close behind some promontory lie
    The huge leviathans t' attend their prey;   *810*
And give no chase, but swallow in the fry,
    Which thro' their gaping jaws mistake the way.

204
Nor was this all: in ports and roads remote,
    Destructive fires among whole fleets we send;   Burning of the fleet
Triumphant flames upon the water float,   in the Vlie by
    And outbound ships at home their voyage end.   Sir Robert Holmes.

205
Those various squadrons, variously design'd,
    Each vessel freighted with a several load,
Each squadron waiting for a several wind,
    All find but one, to burn them in the road.

206
Some bound for Guinea, golden sand to find,
    Bore all the gauds the simple natives wear;   *822*
Some, for the pride of Turkish courts design'd,
    For folded *turbants* finest *Holland* bear.

207
Some English wool, vex'd in a Belgian loom,
    And into cloth of spongy softness made,
Did into France or colder Denmark doom,
    To ruin with worse ware our staple trade.

208
Our greedy seamen rummage every hold,
    Smile on the booty of each wealthier chest;   *830*
And, as the priests who with their gods make bold,
    Take what they like, and sacrifice the rest.

209
But ah! how unsincere are all our joys!
   Which, sent from heav'n, like lightning make no stay:
Their palling taste the journey's length destroys,
   Or grief, sent post, o'ertakes them on the way.   Transit to the
                                                Fire of London.

210
Swell'd with our late successes on the foe,
   Which France and Holland wanted power to cross,
We urge an unseen fate to lay us low,
   And feed their envious eyes with English loss.   *840*

211
Each element his dread command obeys,
   Who makes or ruins with a smile or frown;
Who, as by one he did our nation raise,
   So now he with another pulls us down.

212
Yet London, empress of the northern clime,
   By an high fate thou greatly didst expire:
(y)Great as the world's, which at the death of time
   Must fall, and rise a nobler frame by fire.

213
As when some dire usurper Heav'n provides
   To scourge his country with a lawless sway,   *850*
His birth perhaps some petty village hides,
   And sets his cradle out of fortune's way,

214
Till fully ripe his swelling fate breaks out,
   And hurries him to mighty mischiefs on;
His prince, surpris'd at first, no ill could doubt,
   And wants the pow'r to meet it when 't is known.

(y) *Quum mare; quum tellus correptaque regia cœli Ardeat*, &c.—Ovid.
When the sea, the land, and the kindled palace of the sky shall blaze—*Meta-morphoses* I: 257–58.

215

Such was the rise of this prodigious fire,
   Which, in mean buildings first obscurely bred,
From thence did soon to open streets aspire,
   And straight to palaces and temples spread.   *860*

216

The diligence of trades and noiseful gain,
   And luxury, more late, asleep were laid:
All was the Night's, and in her silent reign
   No sound the rest of nature did invade.

217

In this deep quiet, from what source unknown,
   Those seeds of fire their fatal birth disclose;
And first, few scatt'ring sparks about were blown,
   Big with the flames that to our ruin rose.

218

Then, in some close-pent room it crept along,
   And, smould'ring as it went, in silence fed;   *870*
Till th' infant monster, with devouring strong,
   Walk'd boldly upright with exalted head.

219

Now, like some rich or mighty murderer,
   Too great for prison, which he breaks with gold;
Who fresher for new mischiefs does appear,
   And dares the world to tax him with the old;

220

So scapes th' insulting fire his narrow jail,
   And makes small outlets into open air;
There the fierce winds his tender force assail,
   And beat him downward to his first repair.   *880*

221

(z) The winds, like crafty courtesans, withheld
   His flames from burning, but to blow them more:

(z) *Like crafty,* &c. *Hæc arte tractabat cupidum virum, ut illius animum inopia accenderet.* She artfully handled the eager fellow so that deprivation might inflame his mind—Terence, *Heautontimorumenos* II, iii: 125–26.

And, every fresh attempt, he is repell'd
 With faint denials, weaker than before.

222
And now, no longer letted of his prey,
 He leaps up at it with inrag'd desire;
O'erlooks the neighbors with a wide survey,
 And nods at every house his threat'ning fire.

233
The ghosts of traitors from the Bridge descend,
 With bold fanatic specters to rejoice;   890
About the fire into a dance they bend,
 And sing their sabbath notes with feeble voice.

224
Our guardian angel saw them where he sate
 Above the palace of our slumb'ring king:
He sigh'd, abandoning his charge to fate,
 And, drooping, oft look'd back upon the wing.

225
At length the crackling noise and dreadful blaze
 Call'd up some waking lover to the sight;
And long it was ere he the rest could raise,
 Whose heavy eyelids yet were full of night. 900

226
The next to danger, hot pursued by fate,
 Half-cloth'd, half-naked, hastily retire;
And frighted mothers strike their breasts, too late,
 For helpless infants left amidst the fire.

227
Their cries soon waken all the dwellers near;
 Now murmuring noises rise in every street;
The more remote run stumbling with their fear,
 And in the dark men justle as they meet.

228
So weary bees in little cells repose;
 But if night-robbers lift the well-stor'd hive, 910

An humming thro' their waxen city grows,
　　And out upon each other's wings they drive.

229

Now streets grow throng'd and busy as by day:
　　Some run for buckets to the hallow'd choir:
Some cut the pipes, and some the engines play;
　　And some more bold mount ladders to the fire.

230

In vain; for from the East a Belgian wind
　　His hostile breath thro' the dry rafters sent;
The flames impell'd soon left their foes behind,
　　And forward with a wanton fury went.　　　　　　920

231

A key of fire ran all along the shore,
　　(a) And lighten'd all the river with a blaze;
The waken'd tides began again to roar,
　　And wond'ring fish in shining waters gaze.

232

Old father Thames rais'd up his reverend head,
　　But fear'd the fate of Simoeis would return:
Deep in his *ooze* he sought his sedgy bed,
　　And shrunk his waters back into his urn.

233

The fire, meantime, walks in a broader gross;
　　To either hand his wings he opens wide:
He wades the streets, and straight he reaches cross,　　931
　　And plays his longing flames on th' other side.

234

At first they warm, then scorch, and then they take;
　　Now with long necks from side to side they feed;
At length, grown strong, their mother-fire forsake,
　　And a new colony of flames succeed.

(a) *Sigæa igni freta lata relucent.*—VIRG. The Sigean straits shine far and wide with fire—*Aeneid* II: 312.

235

To every nobler portion of the town
   The curling billows roll their restless tide:
In parties now they straggle up and down,
   As armies, unoppos'd, for prey divide.   940

236

One mighty squadron, with a side-wind sped,
   Thro' narrow lanes his cumber'd fire does haste,
By pow'rful charms of gold and silver led,
   The Lombard bankers and the Change to waste.

237

Another backward to the Tow'r would go,
   And slowly eats his way against the wind;
But the main body of the marching foe
   Against th' imperial palace is design'd.

238

Now day appears, and with the day the king,
   Whose early care had robb'd him of his rest: 950
Far off the cracks of falling houses ring,
   And shrieks of subjects pierce his tender breast.

239

Near as he draws, thick harbingers of smoke
   With gloomy pillars cover all the place;
Whose little intervals of night are broke
   By sparks that drive against his sacred face.

240

More than his guards his sorrows made him known,
   And pious tears, which down his cheeks did show'r:
The wretched in his grief forgot their own;
   (So much the pity of a king has pow'r.)

241

He wept the flames of what he lov'd so well,   961
   And what so well had merited his love:
For never prince in grace did more excel,
   Or royal city more in duty strove.

242
Nor with an idle care did he behold:
    (Subjects may grieve, but monarchs must redress;)
He cheers the fearful, and commends the bold,
    And makes despairers hope for good success.

243
Himself directs what first is to be done,
    And orders all the succors which they bring: 970
The helpful and the good about him run,
    And form an army worthy such a king.

244
He sees the dire contagion spread so fast,
    That, where it seizes, all relief is vain;
And therefore must unwillingly lay waste
    That country which would, else, the foe maintain.

245
The powder blows up all before the fire:
    Th' amazed flames stand gather'd on a heap;
And from the precipice's brink retire,
    Afraid to venture on so large a leap.   980

246
Thus fighting fires a while themselves consume,
    But straight, like Turks, forc'd on to win or die,
They first lay tender bridges of their fume,
    And o'er the breach in unctuous vapors fly.

247
Part stays for passage, till a gust of wind
    Ships o'er their forces in a shining sheet:
Part, creeping under ground, their journey blind,
    And, climbing from below, their fellows meet.

248
Thus to some desert plain, or old wood-side,
    Dire night-hags come from far to dance their round;   990

And o'er broad rivers on their fiends they ride,
    Or sweep in clouds above the blasted ground.

249

No help avails: for, *hydra*-like, the fire
    Lifts up his hundred heads to aim his wáy,
And scarce the wealthy can one half retire,
    Before he rushes in to share the prey.

250

The rich grow suppliant, and the poor grow proud;
    Those offer mighty gain, and these ask more:
So void of pity is th' ignoble crowd,
    When others' ruin may increase their store.   *1000*

251

As those who live by shores with joy behold
    Some wealthy vessel split or stranded nigh,
And from the rocks leap down for shipwrack'd gold,
    And seek the tempests which the others fly:

252

So these but wait the owners' last despair,
    And what's permitted to the flames invade:
Ev'n from their jaws they hungry morsels tear,
    And on their backs the spoils of Vulcan lade.

253

The days were all in this lost labor spent;
    And when the weary king gave place to night,   *1010*
His beams he to his royal brother lent,
    And so shone still in his reflective light.

254

Night came, but without darkness or repose,
    A dismal picture of the gen'ral doom;
Where souls distracted, when the trumpet blows,
    And half unready with their bodies come.

255

Those who have homes, when home they do repair,
  To a last lodging call their wand'ring friends:
Their short uneasy sleeps are broke with care,
  To look how near their own destruction tends.   *1020*

256

Those who have none, sit round where once it was,
  And with full eyes each wonted room require;
Haunting the yet warm ashes of the place,
  As murder'd men walk where they did expire.

257

Some stir up coals, and watch the vestal fire,
  Others in vain from sight of ruin run;
And, while thro' burning lab'rinths they retire,
  With loathing eyes repeat what they would shun.

258

The most in fields like herded beasts lie down,
  To dews obnoxious on the grassy floor;
And while their babes in sleep their sorrows drown,   *1031*
  Sad parents watch the remnants of their store.

259

While by the motion of the flames they guess
  What streets are burning now, and what are near,
An infant, waking, to the paps would press,
  And meets, instead of milk, a falling tear.

260

No thought can ease them but their sovereign's care,
  Whose praise th' afflicted as their comfort sing:
Ev'n those whom want might drive to just despair,
  Think life a blessing under such a king.   *1040*

261

Meantime he sadly suffers in their grief,
  Out-weeps an hermit, and out-prays a saint:

All the long night he studies their relief,
  How they may be supplied, and he may want.

262

"O God," said he, "thou patron of my days,   King's prayer.
  Guide of my youth in exile and distress!
Who me unfriended brought'st by wondrous ways,
  The kingdom of my fathers to possess:

263

"Be thou my judge, with what unwearied care
  I since have labor'd for my people's good;   *1050*
To bind the bruises of a civil war,
  And stop the issues of their wasting blood.

264

"Thou, who hast taught me to forgive the ill,
  And recompense, as friends, the good misled;
If mercy be a precept of thy will,
  Return that mercy on thy servant's head.

265

"Or, if my heedless youth has stepp'd astray,
  Too soon forgetful of thy gracious hand;
On me alone thy just displeasure lay,
  But take thy judgments from this mourning land.   *1060*

266

"We all have sinn'd, and thou hast laid us low,
  As humble earth from whence at first we came:
Like flying shades before the clouds we show,
  And shrink like parchment in consuming flame.

267

"O let it be enough what thou hast done;
  When spotted deaths ran arm'd thro' every street,
With poison'd darts, which not the good could shun,
  The speedy could out-fly, or valiant meet.

268
"The living few, and frequent funerals then,
    Proclaim'd thy wrath on this forsaken place;   1070
And now those few who are return'd again,
    Thy searching judgments to their dwellings trace.

269
"O pass not, Lord, an absolute decree,
    Or bind thy sentence unconditional;
But in thy sentence our remorse foresee,
    And, in that foresight, this thy doom recall.

270
"Thy threatings, Lord, as thine thou mayst revoke;
    But, if immutable and fix'd they stand,
Continue still thyself to give the stroke,
    And let not foreign foes oppress thy land."   1080

271
Th' Eternal heard, and from the heav'nly choir
    Chose out the cherub with the flaming sword;
And bade him swiftly drive th' approaching fire
    From where our naval magazins were stor'd.

272
The blessed minister his wings display'd,
    And like a shooting star he cleft the night;
He charg'd the flames, and those that disobey'd
    He lash'd to duty with his sword of light.

273
The fugitive flames, chastis'd, went forth to prey
    On pious structures, by our fathers rear'd;   1090
By which to heav'n they did affect the way,
    Ere faith in churchmen without works was heard.

274
The wanting orphans saw with wat'ry eyes
    Their founders' charity in dust laid low;
And sent to God their ever-answer'd cries,
    (For he protects the poor, who made them so.)

275

Nor could thy fabric, Paul's, defend thee long,
  Tho' thou wert sacred to thy Maker's praise;
Tho' made immortal by a poet's song,
  And poets' songs the Theban walls could raise.   *1100*

276

The daring flames peep'd in, and saw from far
  The awful beauties of the sacred choir;
But, since it was profan'd by civil war,
  Heav'n thought it fit to have it purg'd by fire.

277

Now down the narrow streets it swiftly came,
  And, widely opening, did on both sides prey:
This benefit we sadly owe the flame,
  If only ruin must enlarge our way.

278

And now four days the sun had seen our woes;
  Four nights the moon beheld th' incessant fire: *1110*
It seem'd as if the stars more sickly rose,
  And farther from the fev'rish north retire.

279

In th' empyrean heaven, (the blest abode,)
  The Thrones and the Dominions prostrate lie,
Not daring to behold their angry God;
  And an hush'd silence damps the tuneful sky.

280

At length th' Almighty cast a pitying eye,
  And mercy softly touch'd his melting breast:
He saw the town's one half in rubbish lie,
  And eager flames drive on to storm the rest.   *1120*

281

An hollow crystal pyramid he takes,
  In firmamental waters dipp'd above;
Of it a broad extinguisher he makes
  And hoods the flames that to their quarry strove.

282

The vanquish'd fires withdraw from every place,
    Or, full with feeding, sink into a sleep:
Each household genius shews again his face,
    And from the hearths the little Lares creep.

283

Our king this more than natural change beholds;
    With sober joy his heart and eyes abound: 1130
To the All-good his lifted hands he folds,
    And thanks him low on his redeemed ground.

284

As when sharp frosts had long constrain'd the earth,
    A kindly thaw unlocks it with mild rain;
And first the tender blade peeps up to birth,
    And straight the green fields laugh with promis'd grain:

285

By such degrees the spreading gladness grew
    In every heart which fear had froze before;
The standing streets with so much joy they view,
    That with less grief the perish'd they deplore.   1140

286

The father of the people open'd wide
    His stores, and all the poor with plenty fed:
Thus God's anointed God's own place supplied,
    And fill'd the empty with his daily bread.

287

This royal bounty brought its own reward,
    And in their minds so deep did print the sense,
That if their ruins sadly they regard,
    'T is but with fear the sight might drive him thence.

288

But so may he live long, that town to sway,   1150
    Which by his auspice they will nobler make,
As he will hatch their ashes by his stay,
    And not their humble ruins now forsake

*City's request
to the king
not to leave them.*

289

They have not lost their loyalty by fire;
   Nor is their courage or their wealth so low,
That from his wars they poorly would retire,
   Or beg the pity of a vanquish'd foe.

290

Not with more constancy the Jews of old,
   By Cyrus from rewarded exile sent,
Their royal city did in dust behold,
   Or with more vigor to rebuild it went.   1160

291

The utmost malice of their stars is past,
   And two dire comets, which have scourg'd the town,
In their own plague and fire have breath'd their last,
   Or, dimly, in their sinking sockets frown.

292

Now frequent trines the happier lights among,
   And high-rais'd Jove, from his dark prison freed,
(Those weights took off that on his planet hung,)
   Will gloriously the new-laid works succeed.

293

Methinks already, from this chymic flame,
   I see a city of more precious mold,   1170
Rich as the town which gives the [b] Indies name,
   With silver pav'd, and all divine with gold.

294

Already, laboring with a mighty fate,
   She shakes the rubbish from her mounting brow,
And seems to have renew'd her charter's date,
   Which Heav'n will to the death of time allow.

295

More great than human, now, and more [c] *august,*
   New-deified she from her fires does rise:

---

[b] Mexico.
[c] *Augusta,* the old name of London.

Her widening streets on new foundations trust,
    And, opening, into larger parts she flies.   *1180*

296
Before, she like some shepherdess did show,
    Who sate to bathe her by a river's side;
Not answering to her fame, but rude and low,
    Nor taught the beauteous arts of modern pride.

297
Now, like a maiden queen, she will behold,
    From her high turrets, hourly suitors come:
The East with incense, and the West with gold,
    Will stand, like suppliants, to receive her doom.

298
The silver Thames, her own domestic flood,
    Shall bear her vessels like a sweeping train;   *1190*
And often wind, (as of his mistress proud,)
    With longing eyes to meet her face again.

299
The wealthy Tagus, and the wealthier Rhine,
    The glory of their towns no more shall boast;
And Seine, that would with Belgian rivers join,
    Shall find her luster stain'd, and traffic lost.

300
The vent'rous merchant, who design'd more far,
    And touches on our hospitable shore,
Charm'd with the splendor of this northern star,
    Shall here unlade him, and depart no more.   *1200*

301
Our pow'rful navy shall no longer meet,
    The wealth of France or Holland to invade;
The beauty of this town, without a fleet,
    From all the world shall vindicate her trade.

302
And, while this fam'd emporium we prepare,
    The British ocean shall such triumphs boast,

That those who now disdain our trade to share,
    Shall rob like pirates on our wealthy coast.

303

Already we have conquer'd half the war,
    And the less dang'rous part is left behind;   *1210*
Our trouble now is but to make them dare,
    And not so great to vanquish as to find.

304

Thus to the eastern wealth thro' storms we go,
    But now, the Cape once doubled, fear no more;
A constant trade-wind will securely blow,
    And gently lay us on the spicy shore.

To the Memory of

MR. OLDHAM

Farewell, too little, and too lately known,
Whom I began to think and call my own:
For sure our souls were near allied, and thine
Cast in the same poetic mold with mine.
One common note on either lyre did strike,
And knaves and fools we both abhorr'd alike.
To the same goal did both our studies drive;
The last set out the soonest did arrive.
Thus Nisus fell upon the slippery place,
While his young friend perform'd and won the race.   *10*
O early ripe! to thy abundant store
What could advancing age have added more?
It might (what nature never gives the young)
Have taught the numbers of thy native tongue.
But satire needs not those, and wit will shine
Thro' the harsh cadence of a rugged line:
A noble error, and but seldom made,
When poets are by too much force betray'd.
Thy generous fruits, tho' gather'd ere their prime,
Still shew'd a quickness; and maturing time   *20*

But mellows what we write to the dull sweets of rhyme.
Once more, hail and farewell; farewell, thou young,
But ah too short, Marcellus of our tongue;
Thy brows with ivy, and with laurels bound;
But fate and gloomy night encompass thee around.

EPIGRAM ON MILTON

Three poets, in three distant ages born,
Greece, Italy, and England did adorn.
The first in loftiness of thought surpass'd,
The next in majesty, in both the last:
The force of Nature could no farther go;
To make a third, she join'd the former two.

To My Dear Friend
MR. CONGREVE
On His Comedy Called The Double-Dealer

Well then, the promis'd hour is come at last;
The present age of wit obscures the past:
Strong were our sires, and as they fought they writ,
Conqu'ring with force of arms, and dint of wit;
Theirs was the giant race, before the flood;
And thus, when Charles return'd, our empire stood.
Like Janus he the stubborn soil manur'd,
With rules of husbandry the rankness cur'd;
Tam'd us to manners, when the stage was rude;
And boist'rous English wit with art indued.   10
Our age was cultivated thus at length,
But what we gain'd in skill we lost in strength.
Our builders were with want of genius curst;
The second temple was not like the first:
Till you, the best Vitruvius, come at length;
Our beauties equal, but excel our strength.
Firm Doric pillars found your solid base;

The fair Corinthian crowns the higher space:
Thus all below is strength, and all above is grace.
In easy dialogue is Fletcher's praise;   20
He mov'd the mind, but had not power to raise.
Great Jonson did by strength of judgment please;
Yet, doubling Fletcher's force, he wants his ease.
In differing talents both adorn'd their age;
One for the study, t'other for the stage:
But both to Congreve justly shall submit,
One match'd in judgment, both o'ermatch'd in wit.
In him all beauties of this age we see,
Etherege his courtship, Southerne's purity,
The satire, wit, and strength of Manly Wycherley.   30
All this in blooming youth you have achiev'd,
Nor are your foil'd contemporaries griev'd.
So much the sweetness of your manners move,
We cannot envy you, because we love.
Fabius might joy in Scipio, when he saw
A beardless consul made against the law;
And join his suffrage to the votes of Rome,
Tho' he with Hannibal was overcome.
Thus old Romano bow'd to Raphael's fame,
And scholar to the youth he taught became.   40
    O that your brows my laurel had sustain'd;
Well had I been depos'd, if you had reign'd!
The father had descended for the son;
For only you are lineal to the throne.
Thus, when the state one Edward did depose,
A greater Edward in his room arose.
But now, not I, but poetry is curst;
For Tom the Second reigns like Tom the First.
But let 'em not mistake my patron's part,
Nor call his charity their own desert.   50
Yet this I prophesy: thou shalt be seen
(Tho' with some short parenthesis between)
High on the throne of wit; and, seated there,
Not mine—that's little—but thy laurel wear.
Thy first attempt an early promise made;
That early promise this has more than paid.
So bold, yet so judiciously you dare,

That your least praise is to be regular.
Time, place, and action, may with pains be wrought;
But genius must be born, and never can be taught.   60
This is your portion; this your native store;
Heav'n, that but once was prodigal before,
To Shakespeare gave as much; she could not give him more.
   Maintain your post: that 's all the fame you need;
For 't is impossible you should proceed.
Already I am worn with cares and age,
And just abandoning th' ungrateful stage;
Unprofitably kept at Heav'n's expense,
I live a rent-charge on his providence:
But you, whom ev'ry Muse and Grace adorn,   70
Whom I foresee to better fortune born,
Be kind to my remains; and O defend,
Against your judgment, your departed friend!
Let not the insulting foe my fame pursue,
But shade those laurels which descend to you;
And take for tribute what these lines express:
You merit more; nor could my love do less.

EPIGRAM ON TONSON

With leering look, bull faced and freckled fair,
With frowsy pores poisoning the ambient air,
With two left leggs and Judas coloured hair.

To My Honor'd Kinsman,
JOHN DRIDEN
Of Chesterton, in the County of
Huntingdon, Esquire

How blest is he, who leads a country life,
Unvex'd with anxious cares, and void of strife!
Who, studying peace and shunning civil rage,
Enjoy'd his youth, and now enjoys his age:

All who deserve his love, he makes his own;
And, to be lov'd himself, needs only to be known.
   Just, good, and wise, contending neighbors come,
From your award to wait their final doom;
And, foes before, return in friendship home.
Without their cost, you terminate the cause,   10
And save th' expense of long litigious laws:
Where suits are travers'd, and so little won,
That he who conquers is but last undone.
Such are not your decrees; but so design'd,
The sanction leaves a lasting peace behind:
Like your own soul, serene; a pattern of your mind.
   Promoting concord, and composing strife,
Lord of yourself, uncumber'd with a wife;
Where, for a year, a month, perhaps a night,
Long penitence succeeds a short delight: 20
Minds are so hardly match'd, that ev'n the first,
Tho' pair'd by Heav'n, in Paradise were curst.
For man and woman, tho' in one they grow,
Yet, first or last, return again to two.
He to God's image, she to his was made;
So, farther from the fount, the stream at random stray'd.
   How could he stand, when, put to double pain,
He must a weaker than himself sustain!
Each might have stood perhaps, but each alone;
Two wrestlers help to pull each other down.   30
   Not that my verse would blemish all the fair;
But yet if *some* be bad, 't is wisdom to beware;
And better shun the bait than struggle in the snare.
Thus have you shunn'd, and shun, the married state,
Trusting as little as you can to fate.
   No porter guards the passage of your door,
T' admit the wealthy, and exclude the poor;
For God, who gave the riches, gave the heart,
To sanctify the whole, by giving part.
Heav'n, who foresaw the will, the means has wrought,   40
And to the second son a blessing brought;
The first-begotten had his father's share,
But you, like Jacob, are Rebecca's heir.
   So may your stores and fruitful fields increase;

And ever be you blest, who live to bless.
As Ceres sow'd, where'er her chariot flew;
As Heav'n in desarts rain'd the bread of dew;
So free to many, to relations most,
You feed with manna your own Israel host.
    With crowds attended of your ancient race,   *50*
You seek the champian sports or sylvan chase;
With well-breath'd beagles you surround the wood,
Ev'n then industrious of the common good;
And often have you brought the wily fox
To suffer for the firstlings of the flocks;
Chas'd ev'n amid the folds, and made to bleed,
Like felons, where they did the murd'rous deed.
This fiery game your active youth maintain'd,
Not yet by years extinguish'd, tho' restrain'd:
You season still with sports your serious hours;   *60*
For age but tastes of pleasures, youth devours.
The hare in pastures or in plains is found,
Emblem of human life, who runs the round;
And after all his wand'ring ways are done,
His circle fills and ends where he begun,
Just as the setting meets the rising sun.
    Thus princes ease their cares; but happier he
Who seeks not pleasure thro' necessity,
Than such as once on slipp'ry thrones were plac'd;
And chasing, sigh to think themselves are chas'd.   *70*
    So liv'd our sires, ere doctors learn'd to kill,
And multiplied with theirs the weekly bill.
The first physicians by debauch were made;
Excess began, and sloth sustains the trade.
Pity the gen'rous kind their cares bestow
To search forbidden truths; (a sin to know:)
To which if human science could attain,
The doom of death, pronounc'd by God, were vain.
In vain the leech would interpose delay;
Fate fastens first, and vindicates the prey.   *80*
What help from art's endeavors can we have?
Gibbons but guesses, nor is sure to save;
But Maurus sweeps whole parishes, and peoples ev'ry grave;
And no more mercy to mankind will use,

Than when he robb'd and murder'd Maro's Muse.
Wouldst thou be soon dispatch'd, and perish whole?
Trust Maurus with thy life, and M-lb-rne with thy soul.

    By chase our long-liv'd fathers earn'd their food;
Toil strung the nerves and purified the blood:
But we, their sons, a pamper'd race of men,   90
Are dwindled down to threescore years and ten.
Better to hunt in fields for health unbought
Than fee the doctor for a nauseous draught.
The wise for cure on exercise depend;
God never made his work for man to mend.

    The tree of knowledge, once in Eden plac'd,
Was easy found, but was forbid the taste:
O had our grandsire walk'd without his wife,
He first had sought the better plant of life!
Now, both are lost; yet, wand'ring in the dark,   100
Physicians, for the tree, have found the bark.
They, lab'ring for relief of humankind,
With sharpen'd sight some remedies may find;
Th' apothecary train is wholly blind.
From files a random recipe they take,
And many deaths of one prescription make.
Garth, gen'rous as his Muse, prescribes and gives;
The shopman sells, and by destruction lives:
Ungrateful tribe! who, like the viper's brood,
From med'cine issuing, suck their mother's blood!   110
Let these obey, and let the learn'd prescribe,
That men may die without a double bribe:
Let them but under their superiors kill,
When doctors first have sign'd the bloody bill;
He scapes the best, who, nature to repair,
Draws physic from the fields, in draughts of vital air.

    You hoard not health for your own private use,
But on the public spend the rich produce;
When, often urg'd, unwilling to be great,
Your country calls you from your lov'd retreat,   120
And sends to senates, charg'd with common care,
Which none more shuns, and none can better bear.
Where could they find another form'd so fit,
To poise with solid sense a sprightly wit?

Were these both wanting, (as they both abound,)
Where could so firm integrity be found?
  Well-born, and wealthy, wanting no support,
You steer betwixt the country and the court;
Nor gratify whate'er the great desire,
Nor grudging give what public needs require.   130
Part must be left, a fund when foes invade;
And part employ'd to roll the wat'ry trade:
Ev'n Canaan's happy land, when worn with toil,
Requir'd a sabbath year to mend the meager soil.
  Good senators (and such are you) so give,
That kings may be supplied, the people thrive.
And he, when want requires, is truly wise,
Who slights not foreign aids, nor overbuys,
But on our native strength, in time of need, relies.
Munster was bought, we boast not the success;   140
Who fights for gain, for greater makes his peace.
  Our foes, compell'd by need, have peace embrac'd;
The peace both parties want is like to last:
Which if secure, securely we may trade;
Or, not secure, should never have been made.
Safe in ourselves, while on ourselves we stand,
The sea is ours, and that defends the land.
Be, then, the naval stores the nation's care,
New ships to build, and batter'd to repair.
  Observe the war, in ev'ry annual course;   150
What has been done was done with British force:
Namur subdued is England's palm alone;
The rest besieg'd, but we constrain'd the town:
We saw th' event that follow'd our success;
France, tho' pretending arms, pursued the peace;
Oblig'd, by one sole treaty, to restore
What twenty years of war had won before.
Enough for Europe has our Albion fought:
Let us enjoy the peace our blood has bought.
When once the Persian king was put to flight,   160
The weary Macedons refus'd to fight,
Themselves their own mortality confess'd,
And left the son of Jove to quarrel for the rest.
  Ev'n victors are by victories undone;

Thus Hannibal, with foreign laurels won,
To Carthage was recall'd, too late to keep his own.
While sore of battle, while our wounds are green,
Why should we tempt the doubtful die again?
In wars renew'd, uncertain of success;
Sure of a share, as umpires of the peace.   *170*

   A patriot both the king and country serves;
Prerogative and privilege preserves:
Of each our laws the certain limit show;
One must not ebb, nor t'other overflow.
Betwixt the prince and parliament we stand;
The barriers of the state on either hand:
May neither overflow, for then they drown the land!
When both are full, they feed our blest abode;
Like those that water'd once the paradise of God.

   Some overpoise of sway by turns they share;   *180*
In peace the people, and the prince in war:
Consuls of mod'rate pow'r in calms were made;
When the Gauls came, one sole dictator sway'd.

   Patriots, in peace, assert the people's right;
With noble stubbornness resisting might:
No lawless mandates from the court receive,
Nor lend by force, but in a body give.
Such was your gen'rous grandsire; free to grant
In parliaments that weigh'd their prince's want:
But so tenacious of the common cause,   *190*
As not to lend the king against his laws;
And, in a loathsome dungeon doom'd to lie,
In bonds retain'd his birthright liberty,
And sham'd oppression, till it set him free.

   O true descendant of a patriot line,
Who, while thou shar'st their luster, lend'st 'em thine,
Vouchsafe this picture of thy soul to see;
'T is so far good, as it resembles thee.
The beauties to th' original I owe;
Which when I miss, my own defects I show: *200*
Nor think the kindred Muses thy disgrace;
A poet is not born in ev'ry race.
Two of a house few ages can afford;
One to perform, another to record.

Praiseworthy actions are by thee embrac'd;
And 't is my praise, to make thy praises last.
For ev'n when death dissolves our human frame,
The soul returns to heav'n, from whence it came;
Earth keeps the body, verse preserves the fame.

Verse Translations

Commentary on the Verse Translations

Dryden's verse translations of Chaucer and the Roman poets are neither "ponies" for schoolboys uncertain of their philology nor antiquarian reconstructions for the amusement of classical scholars; they are highly sophisticated new poetic constructs of Dryden's own, in no sense intended as "substitutes" for their originals. "Lay by Virgil, I beseech your Lordship, and all my better sort of judges, when you take up my version," he wrote in his dedication of the *Aeneid* to the Earl of Mulgrave; "and it will appear a passable beauty when the original Muse is absent. But, like Spenser's false Florimel made of snow, it melts and vanishes when the true one comes in sight." Dryden was, however, a highly educated poet with a firm grounding in the classics; he had a deep respect for scholarship, as well as a poet's understanding of poetry.

He inherited from his age, furthermore, a substantial tradition of verse translating; and was able to study the methods, especially in connection with famous passages of Virgil and other poets, of his several predecessors in the sixteenth and seventeenth centuries. He performed his work with great care, procuring and studying the best contemporary editions of his authors, and consulting the previous translators, whose pages he occasionally used as a mine of phrases, rimes, and even whole lines for his own versions. As a result, he succeeded in producing a body of poetry which remains unequaled, for variety and readability, by any English verse translator before or since.

LUCRETIUS. *Queen of Love* (2): the goddess Venus, mistress of Mars, the war god (see 45 ff.). *genial* (17): generative, reproductive. *salvage* (18): savage. *Memmius* (35): Lucretius' patron, to whom his poem (*De Rerum Natura:* Of the Nature of Things) is dedicated.

HORACE: *Ninth Ode.* (VI) *pointed:* appointed.

HORACE: *Twenty-ninth Ode. Tuscan* (2): of a district in Italy early conquered by Rome. *in the lion . . . high* (29): in other words, it is August. *Syrian star* (30): the Dog Star Sirius, associated with late summer heat, and epidemics. *sylvans* (37): woodsmen.

HORACE: *Second Epode. Priapus* (33): God of male fertility, protector of vineyards. *Sylvanus* (34): forest god. *Sabine matrons* (61): the Sabines were an Italian tribe early conquered by Rome. Primitive vigor is suggested here, and in the following lines. *Apulia* (62): a district in southern Italy. *heathpout* (78): grouse. *rarer bird:* pheasant.

JUVENAL. The Sixth Satire is a volcanic indictment of women; the second extract recounts the famous story of Messalina, wife of Emperor Claudius. *fruits . . . bear* (162): that is, horns, traditional symbol of the cuckold, or deceived husband. *Juno* (169): queen of the goddesses, wife of Jupiter. *ropy:* (188): sticky. *bedight:* decked out.

The third extract concludes the satire. *buskins* (829): boots worn by actors in tragedies. *Drymon's wife* (833): poisoned her sons to inherit their property. *Medea* (838): killed her two children by Jason to revenge herself on him after he abandoned her. *pious wife* (850): Alcestis, who bargained with Death to take her life in place of her husband's. *the Belides* (854): killed their husbands on their wedding night. *Clytemnestra* (855): adulterous wife of Agamemnon, whom she murdered on his return from the Trojan wars.

OVID: *Acis, Polyphemus, and Galatea.* Polyphemus was the Cyclops (a one-eyed giant, son of Neptune) who was later blinded by Ulysses (38) in a famous episode of the *Odyssey.* Galatea was a sea nymph, and Acis, her demigod lover. The episode illustrates Ovid's graceful, witty combination of the romantic and the grotesque, a combination well matched in spirit by Dryden's rendering. *simagres* (31): grimaces. *Etna* (35): volcano in Sicily. *Phaea-*

cian (115): ideal, Utopian (refers to a quasi-divine country which Ulysses visited on his way home to Ithaca). *wildings* (117): fruits of wild plants. *salvage* (135): savage. *turtles* (137): turtledoves. *Translated* (187): transplanted.

VIRGIL: *Fourth Georgic.* The comparison of the human commonwealth to that of the bees has been a favorite theme of literature and philosophy from ancient times to those of Robert Frost, and was especially popular in the Renaissance. (Some of Virgil's information about bees was fanciful rather than scientific.) The conclusion of this extract illustrates the stoic ideas of divine prescience and of a world soul (*God,* 324). *Cyclops* (245): race of one-eyed giants, supposed to have labored in smithies at the volcanic Mt. Aetna.

VIRGIL: *Aeneid.* The opening lines state the subject of the epic: how the Trojan hero Aeneas, after the fall of Troy, traveled westward and founded Rome (*the destin'd town,* 6). In this project he was opposed by Juno, the *Queen of Heav'n* (13), who wanted Carthage, not Rome, to rule the Empire of the world in the future, and who had aided Greece against Troy because *partial Paris* (39), a Trojan prince, had adjudged her less beautiful than Venus. She was angry also at the infidelities of Jupiter, her husband (40–41), who favored Aeneas.

CHAUCER. The first selection describes the temples of Venus, Mars, and Diana, built by Theseus, Duke of Athens, in celebration of a tournament between the heroes Palamon and Arcite. *Queen of Night* (465): Diana. *Sigils* (483): goodluck signs. *Narcissus* (502): fell in love with his reflection in a pool. *turtles* (519): turtledoves. *knares* (536): knots. *Clotter'd* (577): clotted. *ides* (604): fifteenth day, on which Caesar was murdered in the Capitol at Rome. *triumvirs* (606): three-man partnership in government of Rome. *geomantic* (614): used in divination. *direct . . . retrograde* (616): referring to the apparent motion of the planet (Mars) in relation to the Zodiac.

Cynthia (621): Diana. *Calisto* (623): nymph, mistress of Jupiter, transformed into the Big Dipper to prevent her son Arcas from killing her after Juno had turned her into a bear; Arcas became the Little Dipper. *Actaeon* (627): saw Diana bathing; was transformed into a stag, devoured by his own hounds.

Caledonian beast (634): a boar sent by Diana to ravage the lands of Oeneus, who had neglected her worship; the Greek heroes assembled to destroy it (633). Meleager, Oeneus' son (*Oenides',* 635) succeeded, and gave the dead boar to the huntress *Atalanta* (636); this led to a quarrel with his two uncles, whom he slew, in revenge for which his mother caused his death (638).

Volscian queen (639): Camilla, warrior queen who opposed Aeneas in Italy; Aruns killed her by trickery. She was a favorite of Diana, who avenged her death (640). *salvage* (642): savage. *buskin'd* (646): clad in boots. *alternate sway* (652): she was also queen of the underworld. *Lucina* (654): Diana as goddess of childbirth.

LUCRETIUS
The Beginning of the First Book

Delight of humankind, and gods above,
Parent of Rome, propitious Queen of Love,
Whose vital pow'r, air, earth, and sea supplies,
And breeds whate'er is born beneath the rolling skies:
For every kind, by thy prolific might,
Springs, and beholds the regions of the light.
Thee, goddess, thee the clouds and tempests fear,
And at thy pleasing presence disappear:
For thee the land in fragrant flow'rs is dress'd;
For thee the ocean smiles, and smooths her wavy breast; 10
And heav'n itself with more serene and purer light is blest.
For when the rising spring adorns the mead,
And a new scene of nature stands display'd,
When teeming buds and cheerful greens appear,
And western gales unlock the lazy year;
The joyous birds thy welcome first express,
Whose native songs thy genial fire confess;
Then salvage beasts bound o'er their slighted food,
Strook with thy darts, and tempt the raging flood.
All nature is thy gift; earth, air, and sea: 20
Of all that breathes, the various progeny,
Stung with delight, is goaded on by thee.

O'er barren mountains, o'er the flow'ry plain,
The leavy forest, and the liquid main,
Extends thy uncontroll'd and boundless reign.
Thro' all the living regions dost thou move,
And scatter'st, where thou goest, the kindly seeds of love.
   Since then the race of every living thing
Obeys thy pow'r; since nothing new can spring
Without thy warmth, without thy influence bear,   30
Or beautiful, or lovesome can appear;
Be thou my aid, my tuneful song inspire,
And kindle with thy own productive fire;
While all thy province, Nature, I survey,
And sing to Memmius an immortal lay
Of heav'n and earth, and everywhere thy wondrous pow'r
     display:
To Memmius, under thy sweet influence born,
Whom thou with all thy gifts and graces dost adorn.
The rather, then, assist my Muse and me,
Infusing verses worthy him and thee.   40
Meantime on land and sea let barb'rous discord cease,
And lull the list'ning world in universal peace.
To thee mankind their soft repose must owe,
For thou alone that blessing canst bestow;
Because the brutal business of the war
Is manag'd by thy dreadful servant's care;
Who oft retires from fighting fields, to prove
The pleasing pains of thy eternal love;
And, panting on thy breast, supinely lies,
While with thy heavenly form he feeds his famish'd eyes;   50
Sucks in with open lips thy balmy breath,
By turns restor'd to life, and plung'd in pleasing death.
There while thy curling limbs about him move,
Involv'd and fetter'd in the links of love,
When, wishing all, he nothing can deny,
Thy charms in that auspicious moment try;
With winning eloquence our peace implore,
And quiet to the weary world restore.

     .   .   .   .

HORACE
The Ninth Ode of the First Book

I

Behold yon mountain's hoary height,
   Made higher with new mounts of snow;
Again behold the winter's weight
   Oppress the lab'ring woods below;
And streams, with icy fetters bound,
Benumb'd and cramp'd to solid ground.

II

With well-heap'd logs dissolve the cold,
   And feed the genial hearth with fires;
Produce the wine, that makes us bold,
   And sprightly wit and love inspires:
For what hereafter shall betide,
God, if 't is worth his care, provide.

III

Let him alone, with what he made,
   To toss and turn the world below;
At his command the storms invade;
   The winds by his commission blow;
Till with a nod he bids 'em cease,
And then the calm returns, and all is peace.

IV

To-morrow and her works defy,
   Lay hold upon the present hour,
And snatch the pleasures passing by,
   To put them out of Fortune's pow'r:
Nor love, nor love's delights disdain;
Whate'er thou gett'st to-day is gain.

V

Secure those golden early joys
   That youth unsour'd with sorrow bears,

Ere with'ring time the taste destroys,
   With sickness and unwieldy years.
For active sports, for pleasing rest,
This is the time to be possess'd;
The best is but in season best.

VI

The pointed hour of promis'd bliss,
   The pleasing whisper in the dark,
The half-unwilling willing kiss,
   The laugh that guides thee to the mark,
When the kind nymph would coyness feign,
And hides but to be found again;
These, these are joys the gods for youth ordain.

HORACE
The Twenty-ninth Ode of the Third Book
Paraphras'd in Pindaric Verse, and Inscrib'd to
The Right Honorable Laurence, Earl of Rochester

I

   Descended of an ancient line,
     That long the Tuscan scepter sway'd,
Make haste to meet the generous wine,
     Whose piercing is for thee delay'd:
The rosy wreath is ready made;
     And artful hands prepare
The fragrant Syrian oil, that shall perfume thy hair.

II

   When the wine sparkles from afar,
     And the well-natur'd friend cries, "Come away!"
Make haste, and leave thy business and thy care;   10
     No mortal int'rest can be worth thy stay.

III

   Leave for a while thy costly country seat;
     And, to be great indeed, forget

The nauseous pleasures of the great:
 Make haste and come;
Come, and forsake thy cloying store;
 Thy turret that surveys, from high,
The smoke, and wealth, and noise of Rome;
 And all the busy pageantry
That wise men scorn, and fools adore: 20
Come, give thy soul a loose, and taste the pleasures of the poor.

IV
Sometimes 't is grateful to the rich to try
A short vicissitude, and fit of poverty:
 A savory dish, a homely treat,
 Where all is plain, where all is neat,
 Without the stately spacious room,
The Persian carpet, or the Tyrian loom,
Clear up the cloudy foreheads of the great.

V
 The sun is in the Lion mounted high;
    The Syrian star   30
    Barks from afar,
 And with his sultry breath infects the sky;
The ground below is parch'd, the heav'ns above us fry.
 The shepherd drives his fainting flock
 Beneath the covert of a rock,
 And seeks refreshing rivulets nigh:
 The *sylvans* to their shades retire,
Those very shades and streams new shades and streams require,
And want a cooling breeze of wind to fan the raging fire.

VI
 Thou, what befits the new Lord May'r,   40
 And what the city faction dare,
 And what the Gallic arms will do,
 And what the quiver-bearing foe,
 Art anxiously inquisitive to know;
But God has, wisely, hid from human sight
 The dark decrees of future fate,
 And sown their seeds in depth of night:

He laughs at all the giddy turns of state,
When mortals search too soon, and fear too late.

VII

 Enjoy the present smiling hour,   *50*
  And put it out of Fortune's pow'r;
The tide of bus'ness, like the running stream,
 Is sometimes high, and sometimes low,
A quiet ebb, or a tempestuous flow,
  And always in extreme.
 Now with a noiseless gentle course
 It keeps within the middle bed;
 Anon it lifts aloft the head,
And bears down all before it with impetuous force;
  And trunks of trees come rolling down, *60*
  Sheep and their folds together drown:
Both house and homestead into seas are borne;
And rocks are from their old foundations torn,
And woods, made thin with winds, their scatter'd honors
   mourn.

VIII

 Happy the man, and happy he alone,
  He, who can call to-day his own;
  He who, secure within, can say:
"To-morrow do thy worst, for I have liv'd to-day.
  Be fair, or foul, or rain, or shine,
The joys I have possess'd, in spite of fate, are mine. *70*
 Not Heav'n itself upon the past has pow'r;
But what has been, has been, and I have had my hour."

IX

 Fortune, that with malicious joy
  Does man her slave oppress,
 Proud of her office to destroy,
  Is seldom pleas'd to bless:
 Still various, and unconstant still,
 But with an inclination to be ill,
  Promotes, degrades, delights in strife,
  And makes a lottery of life.   *80*

I can enjoy her while she 's kind;
But when she dances in the wind,
And shakes her wings, and will not stay,
I puff the prostitute away:
The little or the much she gave is quietly resign'd;
    Content with poverty, my soul I arm;
And virtue, tho' in rags, will keep me warm.

X

            What is 't to me,
    Who never sail in her unfaithful sea,
        If storms arise, and clouds grow black;   90
        If the mast split, and threaten wreck?
    Then let the greedy merchant fear
            For his ill-gotten gain;
    And pray to gods that will not hear,
While the debating winds and billows bear
            His wealth into the main.
    For me, secure from Fortune's blows,
        (Secure of what I cannot lose,)
    In my small pinnace I can sail,
    Contemning all the blust'ring roar;   100
        And running with a merry gale,
    With friendly stars my safety seek,
    Within some little winding creek;
        And see the storm ashore.

HORACE
The Second Epode

"How happy in his low degree,
How rich in humble poverty, is he,
Who leads a quiet country life;
Discharg'd of business, void of strife,
And from the griping scrivener free!
(Thus, ere the seeds of vice were sown,
    Liv'd men in better ages born,

Who plow'd with oxen of their own
   Their small paternal field of corn.)
Nor trumpets summon him to war,   *10*
   Nor drums disturb his morning sleep,
Nor knows he merchants' gainful care,
   Nor fears the dangers of the deep.
The clamors of contentious law,
   And court and state, he wisely shuns,
Nor brib'd with hopes, nor dar'd with awe,
   To servile salutations runs;
But either to the clasping vine
   Does the supporting poplar wed,
Or with his pruning-hook disjoin   *20*
   Unbearing branches from their head,
   And grafts more happy in their stead;
Or, climbing to a hilly steep,
   He views his herds in vales afar,
Or shears his overburden'd sheep,
   Or mead for cooling drink prepares,
   Of virgin honey in the jars.
Or, in the now declining year,
   When bounteous Autumn rears his head,
He joys to pull the ripen'd pear,   *30*
   And clust'ring grapes with purple spread.
The fairest of his fruit he serves,
   Priapus, thy rewards:
Sylvanus too his part deserves,
   Whose care the fences guards.
Sometimes beneath an ancient oak
   Or on the matted grass he lies:
No god of sleep he need invoke;
   The stream, that o'er the pebbles flies,
   With gentle slumber crowns his eyes.   *40*
The wind, that whistles thro' the sprays,
   Maintains the consort of the song;
And hidden birds, with native lays,
   The golden sleep prolong.
But when the blast of winter blows,
   And hoary frost inverts the year,
Into the naked woods he goes,

And seeks the tusky boar to rear,
  With well-mouth'd hounds and pointed spear;
Or spreads his subtile nets from sight,   50
  With twinkling glasses, to betray
The larks that in the meshes light,
  Or makes the fearful hare his prey.
Amidst his harmless easy joys
  No anxious care invades his health,
Nor love his peace of mind destroys,
  Nor wicked avarice of wealth.
But if a chaste and pleasing wife,
To ease the business of his life,
Divides with him his household care,   60
Such as the Sabine matrons were,
Such as the swift Apulian's bride,
  Sunburnt and swarthy tho' she be,
Will fire for winter nights provide,
  And without noise will oversee
  His children and his family;
And order all things till he come,
Sweaty and overlabor'd, home;
If she in pens his flocks will fold,
  And then produce her dairy store,   70
With wine to drive away the cold,
  And unbought dainties of the poor;
Not oysters of the Lucrine lake
  My sober appetite would wish,
  Nor turbet, or the foreign fish
That rolling tempests overtake,
  And hither waft the costly dish.
Not heathpout, or the rarer bird
  Which Phasis or Ionia yields,
More pleasing morsels would afford   80
  Than the fat olives of my fields;
Than shards or mallows for the pot,
  That keep the loosen'd body sound,
Or than the lamb, that falls by lot
  To the just guardian of my ground.
Amidst these feasts of happy swains,

His flock returning from the plains;
   The farmer is as pleas'd as he
To view his oxen, sweating smoke,   90
Bear on their necks the loosen'd yoke:
To look upon his menial crew,
   That sit around his cheerful hearth,
And bodies spent in toil renew
   With wholesome food and country mirth."
This Morecraft said within himself,
   Resolv'd to leave the wicked town,
   And live retir'd upon his own.
He call'd his money in;
   But the prevailing love of pelf   100
   Soon split him on the former shelf,
And put it out again.

JUVENAL

From the Sixth Satire

In Saturn's reign, at Nature's early birth,
There was that thing call'd chastity on earth;
When in a narrow cave, their common shade,
The sheep, the shepherds, and their gods were laid:
When reeds, and leaves, and hides of beasts were spread
By mountain huswifes for their homely bed,
And mossy pillows rais'd, for the rude husband's head.
Unlike the niceness of our modern dames,
(Affected nymphs with new affected names,)
The Cynthias and the Lesbias of our years,   10
Who for a sparrow's death dissolve in tears;
Those first unpolish'd matrons, big and bold,
Gave suck to infants of gigantic mold;
Rough as their savage lords who rang'd the wood,
And fat with acorns belch'd their windy food.
For when the world was buxom, fresh, and young,
Her sons were undebauch'd and therefore strong;
And whether born in kindly beds of earth,

Or struggling from the teeming oaks to birth,
Or from what other atoms they begun,   *20*
No sires they had, or, if a sire, the sun.

.   .   .   .   .

  This was a private crime; but you shall hear
What fruits the sacred brows of monarchs bear:
The good old sluggard but began to snore,
When from his side up rose th' imperial whore:
She who preferr'd the pleasures of the night
To pomps, that are but impotent delight;
Strode from the palace, with an eager pace,
To cope with a more masculine embrace;
Muffled she march'd, like Juno in a cloud,
Of all her train but one poor wench allow'd;   *170*
One whom in secret service she could trust,
The rival and companion of her lust.
To the known brothel-house she takes her way;
And for a nasty room gives double pay;
That room in which the rankest harlot lay.
Prepar'd for fight, expectingly she lies,
With heaving breasts, and with desiring eyes:
Still as one drops, another takes his place,
And baffled still succeeds to like disgrace.
At length, when friendly darkness is expir'd,   *180*
And every strumpet from her cell retir'd,
She lags behind, and, ling'ring at the gate,
With a repining sigh submits to fate:
All filth without, and all a fire within,
Tir'd with the toil, unsated with the sin.
Old Caesar's bed the modest matron seeks;
The steam of lamps still hanging on her cheeks
In ropy smut: thus foul, and thus bedight,
She brings him back the product of the night.

.   .   .   .   .

  You think this feign'd; the satire in a rage
Struts in the buskins of the tragic stage,
Forgets his bus'ness is to laugh and bite;   *830*
And will of deaths and dire revenges write.
Would it were all a fable that you read;
But Drymon's wife pleads guilty to the deed.
"I," she confesses, "in the fact was caught,

Two sons dispatching at one deadly draught."
"What two! two sons, thou viper, in one day!"
"Yes, sev'n," she cries, "if sev'n were in my way."
Medea's legend is no more a lie;
Our age adds credit to antiquity.
Great ills, we grant, in former times did reign,   840
And murthers then were done: but not for gain.
Less admiration to great crimes is due,
Which they thro' wrath, or thro' revenge pursue.
For, weak of reason, impotent of will,
The sex is hurried headlong into ill;
And, like a cliff from its foundations torn
By raging earthquakes, into seas is borne.
But those are fiends, who crimes from thought begin;
And, cool in mischief, meditate the sin.
They read th' example of a pious wife,   850
Redeeming, with her own, her husband's life;
Yet, if the laws did that exchange afford,
Would save their lapdog sooner than their lord.
   Where'er you walk, the Belides you meet;
And Clytemnestras grow in every street.
But here 's the difference; Agamemnon's wife
Was a gross butcher with a bloody knife;
But murther, now, is to perfection grown,
And subtle poisons are employ'd alone;
Unless some antidote prevents their arts,   860
And lines with balsam all the noble parts:
In such a case, reserv'd for such a need,
Rather than fail, the dagger does the deed.

OVID

The Fable of Acis, Polyphemus, and Galatea
from the Thirteenth Book of The Metamorphoses
Galatea relates the story

Acis, the lovely youth, whose loss I mourn,
From Faunus and the nymph Symethis born,
Was both his parents' pleasure; but to me
Was all that love could make a lover be.

The gods our minds in mutual bands did join;
I was his only joy, as he was mine.
Now sixteen summers the sweet youth had seen,
And doubtful down began to shade his chin;
When Polyphemus first disturb'd our joy,
And lov'd me fiercely, as I lov'd the boy.   10
Ask not which passion in my soul was high'r,
My last aversion, or my first desire:
Nor this the greater was, nor that the less;
Both were alike, for both were in excess.
Thee, Venus, thee, both heav'n and earth obey;
Immense thy pow'r, and boundless is thy sway.
The Cyclops, who defied th' ethereal throne,
And thought no thunder louder than his own;
The terror of the woods, and wilder far
Than wolves in plains, or bears in forests are;   20
Th' inhuman host, who made his bloody feasts
On mangled members of his butcher'd guests,
Yet felt the force of love and fierce desire,
And burnt for me with unrelenting fire:
Forgot his caverns, and his woolly care;
Assum'd the softness of a lover's air;
And comb'd, with teeth of rakes, his rugged hair.
Now with a crooked scythe his beard he sleeks,
And mows the stubborn stubble of his cheeks;
Now in the crystal stream he looks, to try   30
His simagres, and rolls his glaring eye.
His cruelty and thirst of blood are lost,
And ships securely sail along the coast.
    The prophet Telemus (arriv'd by chance
Where Etna's summits to the sea's advance,
Who mark'd the tracts of every bird that flew,
And sure presages from their flying drew)
Foretold the Cyclops that Ulysses' hand
In his broad eye should thrust a flaming brand.
The giant, with a scornful grin, replied: 40
"Vain augur, thou hast falsely prophesied;
Already Love his flaming brand has toss'd;
Looking on two fair eyes, my sight I lost."
Thus, warn'd in vain, with stalking pace he strode,

And stamp'd the margin of the briny flood
With heavy steps; and, weary, sought again
The cool retirement of his gloomy den.
   A promontory, sharp'ning by degrees,
Ends in a wedge, and overlooks the seas;
On either side, below, the water flows: 50
This airy walk the giant lover chose.
Here on the midst he sate; his flocks, unled,
Their shepherd follow'd, and securely fed.
A pine so burly, and of length so vast,
That sailing ships requir'd it for a mast,
He wielded for a staff, his steps to guide;
But laid it by, his whistle while he tried.
A hundred reeds, of a prodigious growth,
Scarce made a pipe proportion'd to his mouth;
Which when he gave it wind, the rocks around,   60
And wat'ry plains, the dreadful hiss resound.
I heard the ruffian shepherd rudely blow,
Where, in a hollow cave, I sat below;
On Acis' bosom I my head reclin'd;
And still preserve the poem in my mind.
  "O lovely Galatea, whiter far
Than falling snows and rising lilies are;
More flow'ry than the meads, as crystal bright;
Erect as alders, and of equal height;
More wanton than a kid; more sleek thy skin   70
Than orient shells that on the shores are seen;
Than apples fairer, when the boughs they lade;
Pleasing as winter suns or summer shade;
More grateful to the sight than goodly planes;
And softer to the touch than down of swans,
Or curds new turn'd; and sweeter to the taste
Than swelling grapes that to the vintage haste;
More clear than ice, or running streams, that stray
Thro' garden plots, but ah! more swift than they.
  "Yet, Galatea, harder to be broke   80
Than bullocks, unreclaim'd to bear the yoke;
And far more stubborn than the knotted oak:
Like sliding streams, impossible to hold;
Like them fallacious; like their fountains, cold;

More warping than the willow, to decline
My warm embrace; more brittle than the vine;
Immovable, and fix'd in thy disdain;
Rough as these rocks, and of a harder grain;
More violent than is the rising flood;
And the prais'd peacock is not half so proud;   90
Fierce as the fire, and sharp as thistles are;
And more outrageous than a mother bear;
Deaf as the billows to the vows I make;
And more revengeful than a trodden snake;
In swiftness fleeter than the flying hind,
Or driven tempests, or the driving wind:
All other faults with patience I can bear;
But swiftness is the vice I only fear.

   "Yet, if you knew me well, you would not shun
My love, but to my wish'd embraces run;   100
Would languish in your turn, and court my stay
And much repent of your unwise delay.

   "My palace, in the living rock, is made
By Nature's hand; a spacious pleasing shade,
Which neither heat can pierce, nor cold invade.
My garden fill'd with fruits you may behold,
And grapes in clusters, imitating gold;
Some blushing bunches of a purple hue:
And these, and those, are all reserv'd for you.
Red strawberries, in shades, expecting stand,   110
Proud to be gather'd by so white a hand.
Autumnal cornels latter fruit provide,
And plums, to tempt you, turn their glossy side;
Not those of common kinds, but such alone
As in Phæacian orchards might have grown;
Nor chestnuts shall be wanting to your food,
Nor garden fruits, nor wildings of the wood;
The laden boughs for you alone shall bear;
And yours shall be the product of the year.

   "The flocks you see, are all my own, beside   120
The rest that woods and winding valleys hide,
And those that folded in the caves abide.
Ask not the numbers of my growing store;
Who knows how many, knows he has no more.

Nor will I praise my cattle; trust not me,
But judge yourself, and pass your own decree:
Behold their swelling dugs; the sweepy weight
Of ewes that sink beneath the milky freight;
In the warm folds their tender lambkins lie,
Apart from kids that call with human cry.   130
New milk in nut-brown bowls is duly serv'd
For daily drink; the rest for cheese reserv'd.
Nor are these household dainties all my store:
The fields and forests will afford us more;
The deer, the hare, the goat, the salvage boar,
All sorts of ven'son; and of birds the best,
A pair of turtles taken from the nest.
I walk'd the mountains, and two cubs I found,
Whose dam had left 'em on the naked ground,
So like, that no distinction could be seen;   140
So pretty, they were presents for a queen;
And so they shall: I took 'em both away;
And keep, to be companions of your play.
    "O raise, fair nymph, your beauteous face above
The waves; nor scorn my presents, and my love:
Come, Galatea, come, and view my face;
I late beheld it in the wat'ry glass,
And found it lovelier than I fear'd it was.
Survey my tow'ring stature, and my size:
Not Jove, the Jove you dream that rules the skies,   150
Bears such a bulk, or is so largely spread.
My locks, the plenteous harvest of my head,
Hang o'er my manly face; and, dangling down,
As with a shady grove my shoulders crown.
Nor think, because my limbs and body bear
A thickset underwood of bristling hair,
My shape deform'd: what fouler sight can be
Than the bald branches of a leafless tree?
Foul is the steed, without a flowing mane;
And birds, without their feathers, and their train.   160
Wool decks the sheep; and man receives a grace
From bushy limbs, and from a bearded face.
My forehead with a single eye is fill'd,
Round as a ball, and ample as a shield.

The glorious lamp of heav'n, the radiant sun,
Is Nature's eye; and she's content with one.
Add, that my father sways your seas, and I,
Like you, am of the wat'ry family.
I make you his, in making you my own;
You I adore, and kneel to you alone: *170*
Jove, with his fabled thunder, I despise,
And only fear the lightning of your eyes.
Frown not, fair nymph; yet I could bear to be
Disdain'd, if others were disdain'd with me.
But to repulse the Cyclops, and prefer
The love of Acis, heav'ns! I cannot bear.
But let the stripling please himself; nay more,
Please you, tho' that 's the thing I most abhor;
The boy shall find, if e'er we cope in fight,
These giant limbs endued with giant might.   *180*
His living bowels, from his belly torn,
And scatter'd limbs, shall on the flood be borne:
Thy flood, ungrateful nymph; and fate shall find
That way for thee and Acis to be join'd.
For O! I burn with love, and thy disdain
Augments at once my passion and my pain.
Translated Etna flames within my heart,
And thou, inhuman, wilt not ease my smart."

    Lamenting thus in vain, he rose, and strode
With furious paces to the neighb'ring wood.   *190*
Restless his feet, distracted was his walk;
Mad were his motions, and confus'd his talk:
Mad as the vanquish'd bull, when forc'd to yield
His lovely mistress, and forsake the field.

    Thus far unseen I saw: when, fatal chance
His looks directing, with a sudden glance,
Acis and I were to his sight betray'd;
Where, naught suspecting, we securely play'd.
From his wide mouth a bellowing cry he cast:
"I see, I see; but this shall be your last."   *200*
A roar so loud made Etna to rebound;
And all the Cyclops labor'd in the sound.
Affrighted with his monstrous voice, I fled,
And in the neighb'ring ocean plung'd my head.

Poor Acis turn'd his back, and: "Help," he cried,
"Help, Galatea! help, my parent gods,
And take me dying to your deep abodes!"
The Cyclops follow'd; but he sent before
A rib, which from the living rock he tore:
Tho' but an angle reach'd him of the stone,   *210*
The mighty fragment was enough alone
To crush all Acis; 't was too late to save,
But what the fates allow'd to give, I gave:
That Acis to his lineage should return;
And roll, among the river gods, his urn.
Straight issued from the stone a stream of blood,
Which lost the purple, mingling with the flood.
Then like a troubled torrent it appear'd:
The torrent, too, in little space was clear'd.
The stone was cleft, and thro' the yawning chink   *220*
New reeds arose, on the new river's brink.
The rock, from out its hollow womb, disclos'd
A sound like water in its course oppos'd:
When (wondrous to behold) full in the flood
Up starts a youth, and navel high he stood.
Horns from his temples rise; and either horn
Thick wreaths of reeds (his native growth) adorn.
Were not his stature taller than before,
His bulk augmented, and his beauty more,
His color blue, for Acis he might pass: *230*
And Acis chang'd into a stream he was.
But mine no more; he rolls along the plains
With rapid motion, and his name retains.

VIRGIL

From the Fourth Georgic

· · · ·

As when the Cyclops, at th' almighty nod,
New thunder hasten for their angry god,
Subdued in fire the stubborn metal lies;
One brawny smith the puffing bellows plies,

And draws and blows reciprocating air:
Others to quench the hissing mass prepare;   *250*
With lifted arms they order ev'ry blow,
And chime their sounding hammers in a row;
With labor'd anvils Aetna groans below:
Strongly they strike; huge flakes of flames expire;
With tongs they turn the steel, and vex it in the fire.
If little things with great we may compare,
Such are the bees, and such their busy care;
Studious of honey, each in his degree,
The youthful swain, the grave experienc'd bee:
That in the field; this, in affairs of state   *260*
Employ'd at home, abides within the gate,
To fortify the combs, to build the wall,
To prop the ruins, lest the fabric fall:
But, late at night, with weary pinions come
The lab'ring youth, and heavy laden, home.
Plains, meads, and orchards, all the day he plies;
The gleans of yellow thyme distend his thighs:
He spoils the saffron flow'rs; he sips the blues
Of vi'lets, wilding blooms, and willow dews.
Their toil is common, common is their sleep;   *270*
They shake their wings when morn begins to peep,
Rush thro' the city gates without delay,
Nor ends their work, but with declining day.
Then, having spent the last remains of light,
They give their bodies due repose at night,
When hollow murmurs of their ev'ning bells
Dismiss the sleepy swains, and toll 'em to their cells.
When once in beds their weary limbs they steep,
No buzzing sounds disturb their golden sleep.
'T is sacred silence all. Nor dare they stray,   *280*
When rain is promis'd, or a stormy day;
But near the city walls their wat'ring take,
Nor forage far, but short excursions make.
    And as, when empty barks on billows float,
With sandy ballast sailors trim the boat;
So bees bear gravel stones, whose poising weight
Steers thro' the whistling winds their steady flight.
    But, what 's more strange, their modest appetites,

Averse from Venus, fly the nuptial rites.
No lust enervates their heroic mind,   290
Nor wastes their strength on wanton womankind;
But in their mouths reside their genial pow'rs:
They gather children from the leaves and flow'rs.
Thus make they kings to fill the regal seat,
And thus their little citizens create,
And waxen cities build and palaces of state.
And oft on rocks their tender wings they tear,
And sink beneath the burthens which they bear:
Such rage of honey in their bosom beats,
And such a zeal they have for flow'ry sweets.   300
    Thus tho' the race of life they quickly run,
Which in the space of sev'n short years is done,
Th' immortal line in sure succession reigns;
The fortune of the family remains,
And grandsires' grandsons the long list contains.
    Besides, not Egypt, India, Media, more,
With servile awe their idol king adore:
While he survives, in concord and content
The commons live, by no divisions rent;
But the great monarch's death dissolves the government.   310
All goes to ruin; they themselves contrive
To rob the honey, and subvert the hive.
The king presides, his subjects' toil surveys;
The servile rout their careful Caesar praise:
Him they extol; they worship him alone;
They crowd his levees, and support his throne;
They raise him on their shoulders with a shout;
And, when their sov'reign's quarrel calls 'em out,
His foes to mortal combat they defy,
And think it honor at his feet to die.   320
    Induc'd by such examples, some have taught
That bees have portions of ethereal thought;
Endued with particles of heavenly fires:
For God the whole created mass inspires;
Thro' heav'n, and earth, and ocean's depth he throws
His influence round, and kindles as he goes.
Hence flocks, and herds, and men, and beasts, and fowls
With breath are quicken'd and attract their souls;

Hence take the forms his prescience did ordain,
And into him at length resolve again.   *330*
No room is left for death: they mount the sky,
And to their own congenial planets fly.

.   .   .   .   .

VIRGIL

From the First Book of The Aeneis

Arms, and the man I sing, who, forc'd by fate,
And haughty Juno's unrelenting hate,
Expell'd and exil'd, left the Trojan shore.
Long labors, both by sea and land, he bore,
And in the doubtful war, before we won
The Latian realm, and built the destin'd town;
His banish'd gods restor'd to rites divine,
And settled sure succession in his line,
From whence the race of Alban fathers come,
And the long glories of majestic Rome.   *10*
    O Muse! the causes and the crimes relate;
What goddess was provok'd, and whence her hate;
For what offense the Queen of Heav'n began
To persecute so brave, so just a man;
Involv'd his anxious life in endless cares,
Expos'd to wants, and hurried into wars!
Can heav'nly minds such high resentment show,
Or exercise their spite in human woe?
    Against the Tiber's mouth, but far away,
An ancient town was seated on the sea;   *20*
A Tyrian colony; the people made
Stout for the war, and studious of their trade:
Carthage the name; belov'd by Juno more
Than her own Argos, or the Samian shore.
Here stood her chariot; here, if Heav'n were kind,
The seat of awful empire she design'd.
Yet she had heard an ancient rumor fly,
(Long cited by the people of the sky,)
That times to come should see the Trojan race

Her Carthage ruin, and her tow'rs deface;   30
Nor thus confin'd, the yoke of sov'reign sway
Should on the necks of all the nations lay.
She ponder'd this, and fear'd it was in fate;
Nor could forget the war she wag'd of late
For conqu'ring Greece against the Trojan state.
Besides, long causes working in her mind,
And secret seeds of envy, lay behind:
Deep graven in her heart the doom remain'd
Of partial Paris, and her form disdain'd;
The grace bestow'd on ravish'd Ganymed,   40
Electra's glories, and her injur'd bed.
Each was a cause alone; and all combin'd
To kindle vengeance in her haughty mind.
For this, far distant from the Latian coast
She drove the remnants of the Trojan host;
And sev'n long years th' unhappy wand'ring train
Were toss'd by storms, and scatter'd thro' the main.
Such time, such toil, requir'd the Roman name,
Such length of labor for so vast a frame.

                .   .   .   .   .

From the Sixth Book of The Aeneis

                .   .   .   .   .

  "Now fix your sight, and stand intent, to see
Your Roman race, and Julian progeny.
The mighty Caesar waits his vital hour,
Impatient for the world, and grasps his promis'd pow'r.
But next behold the youth of form divine,
Caesar himself, exalted in his line;
Augustus, promis'd oft, and long foretold,
Sent to the realm that Saturn rul'd of old;   1080
Born to restore a better age of gold.
Afric and India shall his pow'r obey;
He shall extend his propagated sway
Beyond the solar year, without the starry way,
Where Atlas turns the rolling heav'ns around,
And his broad shoulders with their lights are crown'd.

At his foreseen approach, already quake
The Caspian kingdoms and Maeotian lake:
Their seers behold the tempest from afar,
And threat'ning oracles denounce the war.   1090
Nile hears him knocking at his sev'nfold gates,
And seeks his hidden spring, and fears his nephew's fates.
Nor Hercules more lands or labors knew,
Not tho' the brazen-footed hind he slew,
Freed Erymanthus from the foaming boar,
And dipp'd his arrows in Lernaean gore;
Nor Bacchus, turning from his Indian war,
By tigers drawn triumphant in his car,
From Nisus' top descending on the plains,
With curling vines around his purple reins.   1100

.   .   .

Let others better mold the running mass
Of metals, and inform the breathing brass,
And soften into flesh a marble face;   1170
Plead better at the bar; describe the skies,
And when the stars descend, and when they rise.
But, Rome, 't is thine alone, with awful sway,
To rule mankind, and make the world obey,
Disposing peace and war thy own majestic way;
To tame the proud, the fetter'd slave to free:
These are imperial arts, and worthy thee.

.   .   .   .   .

CHAUCER
From Palamon and Arcite, II

.   .   .   .

   Eastward was built a gate of marble white;
The like adorn'd the western opposite.
A nobler object than this fabric was,   450
Rome never saw; nor of so vast a space:
For, rich with spoils of many a conquer'd land,

All arts and artists Theseus could command;
Who sold for hire, or wrought for better fame;
The master painters and the carvers came.
So rose within the compass of the year
An age's work, a glorious theater.
Then o'er its eastern gate was rais'd above
A temple, sacred to the Queen of Love:
An altar stood below; on either hand   460
A priest with roses crown'd, who held a myrtle wand.
　　The dome of Mars was on the gate oppos'd,
And on the north a turret was enclos'd,
Within the wall, of alabaster white,
And crimson coral, for the Queen of Night,
Who takes in sylvan sports her chaste delight.
　　Within these oratories might you see
Rich carvings, portraitures, and imagery,
Where ev'ry figure to the life express'd
The godhead's pow'r to whom it was address'd.   470
In Venus' temple, on the sides were seen
The broken slumbers of inamor'd men,
Pray'rs that ev'n spoke, and pity seem'd to call,
And issuing sighs that smok'd along the wall;
Complaints, and hot desires, the lover's hell,
And scalding tears that wore a channel where they fell:
And all around were nuptial bonds, the ties
Of love's assurance, and a train of lies,
That, made in lust, conclude in perjuries.
Beauty, and Youth, and Wealth, and Luxury,   480
And sprightly Hope, and short-enduring Joy;
And Sorceries to raise th' infernal pow'rs,
And Sigils fram'd in planetary hours;
Expense, and Afterthought, and idle Care,
And Doubts of motley hue, and dark Despair;
Suspicions, and fantastical Surmise,
And Jealousy suffus'd, with jaundice in her eyes,
Discoloring all she view'd, in tawny dress'd,
Down-look'd, and with a cuckow on her fist.
Oppos'd to her, on t'other side, advance   490
The costly feast, the carol, and the dance,
Minstrels, and music, poetry, and play,

And balls by night, and turnaments by day.
All these were painted on the wall, and more,
With acts and monuments of times before,
And others added by prophetic doom,
And lovers yet unborn, and loves to come:
For there th' Idalian mount, and Citheron,
The court of Venus, was in colors drawn.
Before the palace gate, in careless dress,   500
And loose array, sat portress Idleness;
There, by the fount, Narcissus pin'd alone;
There Samson was, with wiser Solomon,
And all the mighty names by love undone.
Medea's charms were there, Circean feasts,
With bowls that turn'd inamor'd youth to beasts.
Here might be seen that beauty, wealth, and wit,
And prowess, to the pow'r of love submit:
The spreading snare for all mankind is laid;
And lovers all betray, and are betray'd.   510
The goddess' self some noble hand had wrought;
Smiling she seem'd, and full of pleasing thought:
From ocean as she first began to rise,
And smooth'd the ruffled seas, and clear'd the skies;
She trode the brine all bare below the breast,
And the green waves but ill conceal'd the rest.
A lute she held, and on her head was seen
A wreath of roses red and myrtles green;
Her turtles fann'd the buxom air above;
And, by his mother, stood an infant Love,   520
With wings unfledg'd; his eyes were banded o'er;
His hands a bow, his back a quiver bore,
Supplied with arrows bright and keen, a deadly store.
    But in the dome of mighty Mars the red
With diff'rent figures all the sides were spread;
This temple, less in form, with equal grace,
Was imitative of the first in Thrace:
For that cold region was the lov'd abode
And sov'reign mansion of the warrior god.
The landscape was a forest wide and bare,
Where neither beast nor humankind repair;
The fowl that scent afar the borders fly,

And shun the bitter blast, and wheel about the sky.
A cake of scurf lies baking on the ground,
And prickly stubs, instead of trees, are found;
Or woods with knots and knares deform'd and old;
Headless the most, and hideous to behold:
A rattling tempest thro' the branches went,
That stripp'd 'em bare, and one sole way they bent.
Heav'n froze above, severe; the clouds congeal,   540
And thro' the crystal vault appear'd the standing hail.
Such was the face without: a mountain stood
Threat'ning from high, and overlook'd the wood;
Beneath the low'ring brow, and on a bent,
The temple stood of Mars armipotent:
The frame of burnish'd steel, that cast a glare
From far, and seem'd to thaw the freezing air.
A strait, long entry to the temple led,
Blind with high walls, and horror over head:
Thence issued such a blast and hollow roar,   550
As threaten'd from the hinge to heave the door.
In thro' that door, a northern light there shone;
'T was all it had, for windows there were none.
The gate was adamant; eternal frame!
Which, hew'd by Mars himself, from Indian quarries came,
The labor of a god; and all along
Tough iron plates were clench'd to make it strong.
A tun about was ev'ry pillar there;
A polish'd mirror shone not half so clear.
There saw I how the secret felon wrought,   560
And treason lab'ring in the traitor's thought,
And midwife Time the ripen'd plot to murder brought.
There the red Anger dar'd the pallid Fear;
Next stood Hypocrisy, with holy leer;
Soft smiling, and demurely looking down,
But hid the dagger underneath the gown:
Th' assassinating wife, the household fiend;
And, far the blackest there, the traitor-friend.
On t'other side there stood Destruction bare;
Unpunish'd Rapine, and a waste of war;   570
Contest, with sharpen'd knives, in cloisters drawn,
And all with blood bespread the holy lawn.

Loud menaces were heard, and foul disgrace,
And bawling infamy, in language base;
Till sense was lost in sound, and silence fled the place.
The slayer of himself yet saw I there;
The gore congeal'd was clotter'd in his hair:
With eyes half clos'd and gaping mouth he lay,
And grim, as when he breath'd his sullen soul away.
In midst of all the dome Misfortune sat,   580
And gloomy Discontent, and fell Debate,
And Madness laughing in his ireful mood,
And arm'd complaint on theft, and cries of blood.
There was the murder'd corpse, in covert laid,
And violent death in thousand shapes display'd;
The city to the soldier's rage resign'd;
Successless wars, and poverty behind;
Ships burnt in fight, or forc'd on rocky shores,
And the rash hunter strangled by the boars;
The newborn babe by nurses overlaid;   590
And the cook caught within the raging fire he made.
All ills of Mars his nature, flame, and steel;
The gasping charioteer, beneath the wheel
Of his own car; the ruin'd house that falls
And intercepts her lord betwixt the walls;
The whole division that to Mars pertains,
All trades of death that deal in steel for gains,
Were there: the butcher, armorer, and smith,
Who forges sharpen'd fauchions, or the scythe.
The scarlet conquest on a tow'r was plac'd,   600
With shouts and soldiers' acclamations grac'd;
A pointed sword hung threat'ning o'er his head,
Sustain'd but by a slender twine of thread.
There saw I Mars his ides, the Capitol,
The seer in vain foretelling Caesar's fall;
The last triumvirs, and the wars they move,
And Antony, who lost the world for love.
These, and a thousand more, the fane adorn;
Their fates were painted ere the men were born,
All copied from the heav'ns, and ruling force   610
Of the red star, in his revolving course.
The form of Mars high on a chariot stood,

All sheath'd in arms, and gruffly look'd the god;
Two geomantic figures were display'd
Above his head, a warrior and a maid,
One when direct and one when retrograde.
   Tir'd with deformities of death, I haste
To the third temple of Diana chaste.
A sylvan scene with various greens was drawn,
Shades on the sides, and on the midst a lawn: 620
The silver Cynthia, with her nymphs around,
Pursued the flying deer, the woods with horns resound;
Calisto there stood manifest of shame,
And, turn'd a bear, the northern star became;
Her son was next, and by peculiar grace
In the cold circle held the second place;
The stag Actaeon in the stream had spied
The naked huntress, and, for seeing, died;
His hounds, unknowing of his change, pursue
The chase, and their mistaken master slew.   630
Peneian Daphne too was there to see,
Apollo's love before, and now his tree.
Th' adjoining fane th' assembled Greeks express'd,
And hunting of the Caledonian beast:
Oenides' valor, and his envied prize;
The fatal pow'r of Atalanta's eyes;
Diana's vengeance on the victor shown;
The murd'ress mother, and consuming son;
The Volscian queen extended on the plain;
The treason punish'd, and the traitor slain.   640
The rest were various huntings, well designed,
And salvage beasts destroy'd, of ev'ry kind.
The graceful goddess was array'd in green;
About her feet were little beagles seen,
That watch'd with upward eyes the motions of their queen.
Her legs were buskin'd, and the left before
In act to shoot a silver bow she bore,
And at her back a painted quiver wore.
She trod a wexing moon, that soon would wane,
And, drinking borrow'd light, be fill'd again;   650
With downcast eyes, as seeming to survey
The dark dominions, her alternate sway.

Before her stood a woman in her throes,
And call'd Lucina's aid her burden to disclose.
All these the painter drew with such command,
That Nature snatch'd the pencil from his hand,
Asham'd and angry that his art could feign
And mend the tortures of a mother's pain.
Theseus beheld the fanes of ev'ry god,
And thought his mighty cost was well bestow'd.   660
So princes now their poets should regard;
But few can write, and fewer can reward.

.   .   .   .   .

CHAUCER

From The Wife of Bath, *her tale*

In days of old, when Arthur fill'd the throne,
Whose acts and fame to foreign lands were blown,
The king of elfs and little fairy queen
Gambol'd on heaths, and danc'd on ev'ry green;
And where the jolly troop had led the round,
The grass unbidden rose, and mark'd the ground:
Nor darkling did they dance; the silver light
Of Phoebe serv'd to guide their steps aright,
And, with their tripping pleas'd, prolong'd the night.
Her beams they follow'd, where at full she play'd,   10
Nor longer than she shed her horns they stay'd,
From thence with airy flight to foreign lands convey'd.
Above the rest our Britain held they dear;
More solemnly they kept their sabbaths here,
And made more spacious rings, and revel'd half the year.
  I speak of ancient times, for now the swain
Returning late may pass the woods in vain,
And never hope to see the nightly train;
In vain the dairy now with mints is dress'd,
The dairymaid expects no fairy guest,   20
To skim the bowls, and after pay the feast.
She sighs, and shakes her empty shoes in vain,
No silver penny to reward her pain:

For priests with pray'rs, and other godly gear,
Have made the merry goblins disappear;
And where they play'd their merry pranks before,
Have sprinkled holy water on the floor;
And friars that thro' the wealthy regions run,
Thick as the motes that twinkle in the sun,
Resort to farmers rich, and bless their halls,   30
And exorcise the beds, and cross the walls:
This makes the fairy choirs forsake the place,
When once 't is hallow'd with the rites of grace.
But in the walks where wicked elves have been,
The learning of the parish now is seen,
The midnight parson, posting o'er the green,
With gown tuck'd up, to wakes, for Sunday next
With humming ale encouraging his text;
Nor wants the holy leer to country girl betwixt.
From fiends and imps he sets the village free,   40
There haunts not any incubus but he.
The maids and women need no danger fear
To walk by night, and sanctity so near:
For by some haycock, or some shady thorn,
He bids his beads both evensong and morn.

    .   .   .   .   .

Criticism

An Essay of Dramatic Poesy and the *Preface to the Fables* are
Dryden's two most celebrated pieces of prose criticism, the first
written near the beginning, the second at the very end, of his
career; the first representing his learned, and at the same time
practical, interest in the stage, the second his wide reading of a
variety of narrative poets in several languages. The first is cast in
the form of a conversation among Dryden (*Neander*) and three
young literary noblemen, friends of his: his brother-in-law, the poet-
dramatist Sir Robert Howard (*Crites*); Charles Sackville, later Earl
of Dorset (*Eugenius*), and the playwright Sir Charles Sedley
(*Lisideius*). This dialogue is supposed to take place on June 3,
1665 ("that memorable day" of the opening sentence), when a
naval battle between the English and Dutch was being fought in
the Channel. A new age in the English theater was opening at this
time, and the essay discusses many of the issues being raised by
educated critics and dramatists.

The *Preface to the Fables* is reminiscent and autobiographic
in form: when he wrote it Dryden was no longer a "new man"
(the etymological meaning of "Neander") but the most famous
poet, critic, and dramatist of this period, the authentic Grand Old
Man of English letters. It introduces the volume of *Fables* (narrative
poems) themselves, and discusses problems connected with their
composition. (A list of the contents of this volume is given in the
Chronological Table of Dryden's life.)

427

Of the two, the *Essay* is the more elaborate, even pretentious, piece of prose; it is based solidly on continental critical theory—notably that of Corneille—which Dryden adapts for his own purposes; the dialogue form derives from Plato and Cicero; and the discussion is larded with Latin quotations, being intended for an educated, somewhat intellectual, audience. In the present edition these quotations have been translated in the body of the text, in bracketed passages, except where Dryden has already paraphrased them himself. Notes on specific passages will be found on pages following the *Preface to the Fables.*

AN ESSAY OF DRAMATIC POESY

It was that memorable day, in the first summer of the late war, when our navy engaged the Dutch; a day wherein the two most mighty and best appointed fleets which any age had ever seen, disputed the command of the greater half of the globe, the commerce of nations, and the riches of the universe: while these vast floating bodies, on either side, moved against each other in parallel lines, and our countrymen, under the happy conduct of his royal highness, went breaking, by little and little, into the line of the enemies; the noise of the cannon from both navies reached our ears about the city, so that all men being alarmed with it, and in a dreadful suspense of the event, which they knew was then deciding, every one went following the sound as his fancy led him; and leaving the town almost empty, some took towards the park, some cross the river, others down it; all seeking the noise in the depth of silence.

Among the rest, it was the fortune of Eugenius, Crites, Lisideius, and Neander, to be in company together; three of them persons whom their wit and quality have made known to all the town; and whom I have chose to hide under these borrowed names, and they may not suffer by so ill a relation as I am going to make of their discourse.

Taking then a barge, which a servant of Lisideius had provided for them, they made haste to shoot the bridge, and left behind them that great fall of waters which hindered them from hearing what they desired: after which, having disengaged themselves from many vessels which rode at anchor in the Thames, and almost blocked up the passage towards Greenwich, they ordered the watermen to let fall their oars more gently; and then, every one favouring his own curiosity with a strict silence, it was not long ere they perceived the air to break about them like the noise of distant thunder, or of swallows in a chimney: those little undulations of sound, though almost vanishing before they reached them, yet still seeming to retain somewhat of their first horror, which they had betwixt the fleets. After they had attentively listened till such time as the sound by little and little went from them, Eugenius, lifting up his head, and taking notice of it, was the first who congratulated to the rest that happy omen of our nation's victory: adding, that we had but this to desire in confirmation of it, that we might hear no more of that noise, which was now leaving the English coast. When the rest had concurred in the same opinion, Crites, a person of a sharp judgment, and somewhat too delicate a taste in wit, which the world have mistaken in him for ill-nature, said, smiling to us, that if the concernment of this battle had not been so exceeding great, he could scarce have wished the victory at the price he knew he must pay for it, in being subject to the reading and hearing of so many ill verses as he was sure would be made on that subject. Adding, that no argument could scape some of those eternal rhymers, who watch a battle with more diligence than the ravens and birds of prey; and the worst of them surest to be first in upon the quarry: while the better able, either out of modesty writ not at all, or set that due value upon their poems, as to let them be often desired and long expected. "There are some of those impertinent people of whom you speak," answered Lisideius, "who to my knowledge are already so provided, either way, that they can produce not only a panegyric upon the victory, but, if need be, a funeral elegy on the duke; wherein, after they have crowned his valour with many laurels, they will at last deplore the odds under which he fell, concluding that his courage deserved a better destiny." All the company smiled at the conceit of Lisideius; but Crites, more eager than before, began to make particular exceptions against some writers, and said, the public magistrate ought to send betimes to forbid them; and that it concerned the peace and quiet of all honest people, that ill poets should be as well silenced as seditious preachers. "In my opinion," replied Eugenius, "you pursue your point too far; for as to my own particular, I am so great a lover of poesy, that I could wish them all rewarded who attempt but to do well; at least, I would not have them worse used than one of their brethren was by Sylla the Dictator:—*Quem in concione vidimus* (says Tully), *cum ei libellum malus poëta de populo subjecisset, quod epigramma in eum fecisset tantummodo alternis versibus longiusculis, statim ex iis rebus quas tunc vendebat jubere ei praemium tribui, sub ea conditione ne quid postea scriberet*" [We saw that in the assembly, when a poetaster from the people presented a petition to him on the grounds that he had managed to make an epigram on him in lines of the right length, he immediately ordered a reward to be given him from the goods he was then selling, on condition that the poet should never write again]. "I could wish with all my heart," replied Crites, "that many whom we know were as bountifully thanked upon the some condition,—that they would never trouble us again. For amongst others, I have a moral apprehension of two poets, whom this victory, with the help of both her wings, will never be able to escape." " 'Tis easy to guess whom you intend," said Lisideius; "and without naming them, I ask you, if one of them does not perpetually pay us with clenches upon words, and a certain clownish kind of railery? if now and then he does not offer at a catachresis or Clevelandism, wresting and torturing a word into another meaning: in fine, if he be not one of those whom the French would call *un mauvais buffon;* one who is so much a well-willer to the satire, that he intends at least to spare no man; and though he cannot strike a blow to hurt any, yet he ought to be punished for the malice of the action, as our witches are justly hanged, because they think themselves to be such; and suffer deservedly for believing they did mischief, because they meant it." "You have described him," said Crites, "so exactly, that I am afraid to come after you with my other extremity of poetry. He is one of those who, having had some advantage of education and converse, knows better than the other what a poet should be, but puts it into practice more unluckily than any man; his style and matter are every where alike: he is the most calm, peaceable writer you ever read: he never disquiets your passions with the least concernment, but still leaves you in as even a temper as he found you; he is a very leveller in poetry: he creeps along with ten little words in every line, and helps out his numbers with *For to,* and *Unto,* and all the pretty expletives he can find, till he drags them to the end of another line; while the sense is left tired half way behind it: he doubly starves all his verses, first for want of thought, and then of expression; his poetry neither has wit in it, nor seems to have it; like him in Martial:

> Pauper videri Cinna vult, et est pauper.
> [Cinna wishes to appear a poor man—
> and he actually is one.]

"He affects plainness, to cover his want of imagination: when he writes the serious way, the highest flight of his fancy is some miserable antithesis, or seeming contradiction; and in the comic he is still reaching at some thin conceit, the ghost of a jest, and that too flies before him, never to be caught; these swallows which we see before us on the Thames are the just resemblance of his wit: you may observe how near the water they stoop, how many proffers they make to dip, and yet how seldom they touch it; and when they do, it is but the surface: they skim over it but to catch a gnat, and then mount into the air and leave it."

"Well, gentlemen," said Eugenius, "you may speak your pleasure of these authors; but though I and some few more about the town may give you a peaceable hearing, yet assure yourselves, there are multitudes who would think you malicious and them injured: especially him whom you first described; he is the very Withers of the city: they have bought more editions of his works than would serve to lay under all their pies at the lord mayor's Christmas. When his famous poem first came out in the year 1660, I have seen them reading it in the midst of 'Change time; nay so vehement they were at it, that they lost their bargain by the candles' ends; but what will you say if he has been received amongst great persons? I can assure you he is, this day, the envy of one who is lord in the art of quibbling, and who does take it well that any man should intrude so far into his province." "All I would wish," replied Crites, "is, that they who love his writings, may still admire him, and his fellow poet: *Qui Bavium non odit, etc.,* is curse sufficient." "And farther," added Lisideius, "I believe there is no man who writes well, but would think he had hard measure, if their admirers should praise anything of his: *Nam quos contemnimus, eorum quoque laudes contemnimus*" [We are scornful of those who praise poets whom we scorn]. "There are so few who write well in this age," says Crites, "that methinks any praises should be welcome; they neither rise to the dignity of the last age, nor to any of the ancients: and we may cry out of the writers of this time, with more reason than Petronius of his, *Pace vestra liceat dixisse, primi omnium eloquentium perdidistis:* you have debauched the true old poetry so far, that Nature, which is the soul of it, is not in any of your writings."

"If your quarrel," said Eugenius, "to those who now write, be grounded only on your reverence to antiquity, there is no man more ready to adore those great Greeks and Romans than I am: but on the other side, I cannot think so contemptibly of the age in which I live, or so dishonourably of my own country, as not to judge we equal the ancients in most kinds of poesy, and in some surpass them; neither know I any reason why I may not be as zealous for the reputation of our age as we find the ancients themselves were in reference to those who lived before them. For you hear your Horace saying,

> Indignor quidquam reprehendi, non quia crassé
> Compositum, illepidève putetur, sed quia nuper.
> [I am displeased when anything is condemned,
>   not because it is thought clumsy or ungrace-
>   ful, but merely recent.]

And after:

> Si meliora dies, ut vina, poemata reddit,
> Scire velim, pretim chartis quotus arroget annus?
> [If time improves poems as it does wines, then
>   how long does it take a manuscript to become
>   valuable?]

"But I see I am engaging in a wide dispute, where the arguments are not like to reach close on either side; for poesy is of so large an extent, and so many both of the ancients and moderns have done well in all kinds of it, that in citing one against the other, we shall take up more time this evening than each man's occasions will allow him: therefore I would ask Crites to what part of poesy he would confine his arguments, and whether he would defend the general cause of the ancients against the moderns, or oppose any age of the moderns against this of ours?"

Crites, a little while considering upon this demand, told Eugenius, that if he pleased, he would limit their dispute to Dramatic Poesy; in which he thought it not difficult to prove, either that the ancients were superior to the moderns, or the last age to this of ours.

Eugenius was somewhat surprised, when he heard Crites make choice of that subject. "For ought I see," said he, "I have undertaken a harder province than I imagined; for though I never judged the plays of the Greek or Roman poets comparable to ours, yet, on the other side, those we now see acted come short of many which were written in the last age: but my comfort is, if we are overcome, it will be only by our own countrymen: and if we yield to them in this one part of poesy, we more surpass them in all the other: for in the epic or lyric way, it will be hard for them to show us one such amongst them, as we have many now living, or who lately were: they can produce nothing so courtly writ, or which expresses so much the conversation of a gentleman, as Sir John Suckling; nothing so even, sweet, and flowing as Mr. Waller; nothing so majestic, so correct, as Sir John Denham; nothing so elevated, so copious, and full of spirit as Mr. Cowley; as for the Italian, French, and Spanish plays, I can make it evident, that those who now write surpass them; and that the drama is wholly ours."

All of them were thus far of Eugenius his opinion, that the sweetness of English verse was never understood or practised by our fathers; even Crites himself did not much oppose it; and every one was willing to acknowledge how much our poesy is improved by the happiness of some writers yet living; who first taught us to mould our thoughts into easy and significant words,—to retrench the superfluities of expression,—and to make our rhyme so properly a part of the verse, that it should never mislead the sense, but itself be led and governed by it.

Eugenius was going to continue this discourse, when Lisideius told him that it was necessary, before they proceeded further, to take a standing measure of their controversy; for how was it possible to be decided who writ the best plays, before we know what a play should be? But, this once agreed on by both parties, each might have recourse to it, either to prove his own advantages, or to discover the failings of his adversary.

He had no sooner said this, but all desired the favour of him to give the definition of a play; and they were the more importunate, because neither Aristotle, nor Horace, nor any other, who had writ of that subject, had ever done it.

Lisideius, after some modest denials, at last confessed he had a rude notion of it; indeed, rather a description than a definition; but which served to guide him in his private thoughts, when he was to make a judgment of what others writ: that he conceived a play ought to be, *A just and lively image of human nature, representing its passions and humours, and the changes of fortune to which it is subject, for the delight and instruction of mankind.*

This definition, though Crites raised a logical objection against it—that it was only *genere et fine,* and so not altogether perfect, was yet well received by the rest; and after they had given order to the watermen to turn their barge, and row softly, that they might take the cool of the evening in their return, Crites, being desired by the company to begin, spoke on behalf of the ancients, in this manner:—

"If confidence presage a victory, Eugenius, in his own opinion, has already triumphed over the ancients: nothing seems more easy to him, than to overcome those whom it is our greatest praise to have imitated well; for we do not only build upon their foundations, but by their models. Dramatic Poesy had time enough, reckoning from Thespis (who first invented it) to Aristophanes, to be born, to grow up, and to flourish in maturity. It has been observed of arts and sciences, that in one and the same century they have arrived to great perfection; and no wonder, since every age has a kind of universal genius, which inclines those that live in it to some particular studies: the work then, being pushed on by many hands, must of necessity go forward.

"Is it not evident, in these last hundred years, when the study of philosophy has been the business of all the Virtuosi in Christendom, that almost a new nature has been revealed to us? That more errors of the school have been detected, more useful experiments in philosophy have been made, more noble secrets in optics, medicine, anatomy, astronomy, discovered, than in all those credulous and doting ages from Aristotle to us?—so true it is, that nothing spreads more fast than science, when rightly and generally cultivated.

"Add to this, the more than common emulation that was in those times of writing well; which though it be found in all ages and all persons that pretend to the same reputation, yet poesy, being then in more esteem than now it is, had greater honours decreed to the professors of it, and consequently the rivalship was more high between them; they had judges ordained to decide their merit, and prizes to reward it; and historians have been diligent to record of Eschylus, Euripides, Sophocles, Lycophron, and the rest of them, both who they were that vanquished in these wars of the theatre, and how often they were crowned: while the Asian kings and Grecian commonwealths scarce afforded them a nobler subject than the unmanly luxuries of a debauched court, or giddy intrigues of a factious city:—*Alit aemulatio ingenia* (says Paterculus), *et nunc invidia, nunc admiratio incitatio nem accendit:* Emulation is the spur of wit; and sometimes envy, sometimes admiration, quickens our endeavours.

"But now, since the rewards of honour are taken away, that virtuous emulation is turned into direct malice; yet so slothful, that it contents itself to condemn and cry down others, without attempting to do better: it is a reputation too unprofitable, to take the necessary pains for it; yet, wishing they had it, that desire is incitement enough to hinder others from it. And this, in short, Eugenius, is the reason why you have now so few good poets, and so many severe judges. Certainly, to imitate the ancients well, much labour and long study is required; which pains, I have already shown, our poets would want encouragement to take, if yet they had ability to go through the work. Those ancients have been faithful imitators and wise observers of that nature which is so torn and ill represented in our plays; they have handed down to us a perfect resemblance of her; which we, like ill copiers, neglecting to look on, have rendered monstrous, and disfigured. But, that you may know how much you are indebted to those your masters, and be ashamed to have so ill requited them, I must remember you, that all the rules by which we practise the drama at this day (either such as relate to the justness and symmetry of the plot, or the episodical ornaments, such as descriptions, narrations, and other beauties, which are not essential to the play), were delivered to us from the observations which Aristotle made, of those poets, who either lived before him, or were his contemporaries: we have added nothing of our own, except we have the confidence to say our wit is better; of which, none boast in this our age, but such as understand not theirs. Of that book which Aristotle has left us, περὶ τῆς Ποιητικῆς, Horace his Art of Poetry is an excellent comment, and, I believe, restores to us that Second Book of his concerning Comedy, which is wanting in him.

"Out of these two have been extracted the famous Rules, which the French call *Des Trois Unités,* or, The Three Unities, which ought to be observed in every regular play; namely, of Time, Place, and Action.

"The unity of time they comprehend in twenty-four hours, the compass of a natural day, or as near as it can be contrived; and the reason of it is obvious to every one,—that the time of the feigned action, or fable of the play, should be proportioned as near as can be to the duration of that time in which it is represented: since, therefore, all plays are acted on the theatre in the space of time much within the compass of twenty-four hours, that play is to be thought the nearest imitation of nature, whose plot or action is confined within that time; and, by the same rule which concludes this general proportion of time, it follows, that all the parts of it are (as near as may be) to be equally subdivided; namely, that one act take not up the supposed time of half a day, which is out of proportion to the rest; since the other four are then to be straitened within the compass of the remaining half: for it is unnatural that one act, which being spoke or written is not longer than the rest, should be supposed longer by the audience; it is therefore the poet's duty, to take care that no act should be imagined to exceed the time in which it is represented on the stage; and that the intervals and inequalities of time be supposed to fall out between the acts.

"This rule of time, how well it has been observed by the ancients, most of their plays will witness; you see them in their tragedies (wherein to follow this rule is certainly most difficult), from the very beginning of their plays, falling close into that part of the story which they intend for the action or principal object of it, leaving the former part to be delivered by narration: so that they set the audience, as it were, at the post where the race is to be concluded; and, saving them the tedious expectation of seeing the poet set out and ride the beginning of the course, they suffer you not to behold him, till he is in sight of the goal, and just upon you.

"For the second unity, which is that of Place, the ancients meant by it, that the scene ought to be continued through the play, in the same place where it was laid in the beginning: for, the stage on which it is represented being but one and the same place, it is unnatural to conceive it many,—and those far distant from one another. I will not deny but, by the variation of painted scenes, the fancy, which in these cases will contribute to its own deceit, may sometimes imagine it several places, with some appearance of probability; yet it still carries the greater likelihood of truth if those places be supposed so near each other as in the same town or city; which may all be comprehended under the larger denomination of one place; for a greater distance will bear no proportion to the shortness of time which is allotted, in the acting, to pass from one of them to another; for the observation of this, next to the ancients, the French are to be most commended. They tie themselves so strictly to the unity of place that you never see in any of their plays a scene changed in the middle of an act: if the act begins in a garden, a street, or chamber, 'tis ended in the same place; and that you may know it to be the same, the stage is so supplied with persons, that it is never empty all the time: he who enters second, has business with him who was on before; and before the second quits the stage, a third appears who has business with him. This Corneille calls *la liaison des scènes,* the continuity or joining of the scenes; and 'tis a good mark of a well-contrived play, when all the persons are known to each other, and every one of them has some affairs with all the rest.

"As for the third unity, which is that of Action, the ancients meant no other by it than what the logicians do by their *finis,* the end or scope of any action; that which is the first in intention, and last in execution: now the poet is to aim at one great and complete action, to the carrying on of which all things in his play, even the very obstacles, are to be subservient; and the reason of this is as evident as any of the former. For two actions, equally laboured and driven on by the writer, would destroy the unity of the poem; it would be no longer one play, but two: not but that there may be many actions in a play, as Ben Jonson has observed in his *Discoveries;* but they must be all subservient to the great one, which our language happily expresses in the name of *under-plots:* such as in Terence's *Eunuch* is the difference and reconcilement of Thais and Phaedria, which is not the chief business of the play, but promotes the marriage of Chaerea and Chremes's sister, principally intended by the poet. There ought to be but one action, says Corneille, that is, one complete action, which leaves the mind of the audience in a full repose; but this cannot be brought to pass but by many other imperfect actions, which conduce to it, and hold the audience in a delightful suspence of what will be.

"If by these rules (to omit many other drawn from the precepts and practice of the ancients) we should judge our modern plays, 'tis probable that few of them would endure the trial: that which should be the business of a day, takes up in some of them an age; instead of one action, they are the epitomes of a man's life;

and for one spot of ground, which the stage should represent, we are sometimes in more countries than the map can show us.

"But if we allow the Ancients to have contrived well, we must acknowledge them to have written better. Questionless we are deprived of a great stock of wit in the loss of Menander among the Greek poets, and of Caecilius, Afranius, and Varius, among the Romans; we may guess at Menander's excellency by the plays of Terence, who translated some of his; and yet wanted so much of him, that he was called by C. Caesar the half-Menander; and may judge of Varius, by the testimonies of Horace, Martial, and Velleius Paterculus. 'Tis probable that these, could they be recovered, would decide the controversy; but so long as Aristophanes and Plautus are extant, while the tragedies of Euripides, Sophocles, and Seneca, are in our hands, I can never see one of those plays which are now written but it increases my admiration of the ancients. And yet I must acknowledge further, that to admire them as we ought, we should understand them better than we do. Doubtless many things appear flat to us, the wit of which depended on some custom or story, which never came to our knowledge; or perhaps on some criticism in their language, which being so long dead, and only remaining in their books, 'tis not possible they should make us understand perfectly. To read Macrobius, explaining the propriety and elegancy of many words in Virgil, which I had before passed over without consideration as common things, is enough to assure me that I ought to think the same of Terence; and that in the purity of his style (which Tully so much valued that he ever carried his works about him) there is yet left in him great room for admiration, if I knew but where to place it. In the meantime I must desire you to take notice that the greatest man of the last age, Ben Jonson, was willing to give place to them in all things: he was not only a professed imitator of Horace, but a learned plagiary of all the others; you track him everywhere in their snow: if Horace, Lucan, Petronius Arbiter, Seneca, and Juvenal, had their own from him, there are few serious thoughts which are new in him: you will pardon me, therefore, if I presume he loved their fashion, when he wore their clothes. But since I have otherwise a great veneration for him, and you, Eugenius, prefer him above all other poets, I will use no farther argument to you than his example: I will produce before you Father Ben, dressed in all the ornaments and colours of the ancients; you will need no other guide to our party, if you follow him; and whether you consider the bad plays of our age, or regard the good plays of the last, both the best and worst of the modern poets will equally instruct you to admire the ancients."

Crites had no sooner left speaking, but Eugenius, who had waited with some impatience for it, thus began:

"I have observed in your speech, that the former part of it is convincing as to what the moderns have profited by the rules of the ancients; but in the latter you are careful to conceal how much they have excelled them; we own all the helps we have from them, and want neither veneration nor gratitude, while we acknowledge that, to overcome them, we must make use of the advantages we have received from them: but to these assistances we have joined our own industry; for, had we sat down with a dull imitation of them, we might then have lost somewhat of the old perfection, but never acquired any that was new. We draw not therefore after their lines, but those of nature; and having the life before us, besides the experience of all they knew, it is no wonder if we hit some airs and features which they have missed. I deny not what you urge of arts and sciences, that they have flourished in some ages more than others; but your instance in philosophy makes for me: for if natural causes be more known now than in the time of Aristotle, because more studied, it follows that poesy and other arts may, with the same pains, arrive still nearer to perfection; and, that granted, it will rest for you to prove that they wrought more perfect images of human life than we; which seeing in your discourse you have avoided to make good, it shall now be my task to show you some part of their defects, and some few excellencies of the moderns. And I think there is none among us can imagine I do it enviously, or with purpose to detract from them; for what interest of fame or profit can the living lose by the reputation of the dead? On the other side, it is a great truth which Velleius Paterculus affirms: *Audita visis libentius laudamus; et praesentia invidia praeterita admiratione prosequimur; et his nos obrui, illis instrui credimus:* that praise or censure is certainly the most sincere, which unbribed posterity shall give us.

"Be pleased then in the first place to take notice that the Greek poesy, which Crites has affirmed to have arrived to perfection in the reign of the old comedy, was so far from it that the distinction of it into acts was not known to them; or if it were, it is yet so darkly delivered to us that we cannot make it out.

"All we know of it is from the singing of their Chorus; and that too is so uncertain, that in some of their plays we have reason to conjecture they sung more than five times. Aristotle indeed divides the integral parts of a play into four. First, the *Protasis,* or entrance, which gives light only to the characters of the persons, and proceeds very little into any part of the action. Secondly, the *Epitasis,* or working up of the plot; where the play grows warmer, the design or action of it is drawing on, and you see something promising that it will come to pass. Thirdly, the *Catastasis,* called by the Romans, *Status,* the height and full growth of the play: we may call it properly the counter-turn, which destroys that expectation, imbroils the action in new difficulties, and leaves you far distant from that hope in which it found you; as you may have observed in a violent stream resisted by a narrow passage,—it runs round to an eddy, and carries back the waters with more swiftness than it brought them on. Lastly, the *Catastrophe,* which the Grecians called λύσις, the French *le dénouement,* and we the discovery, or unravelling of the plot: there you see all things settling again upon their first foundations; and, the obstacles which hindered the design or action of the play once removed, it ends with that resemblance of truth and nature, that the audience are satisfied with the conduct of it. Thus this great man delivered to us the image of a play; and I must confess it is so lively, that from thence much light has been derived to the forming it more perfectly into acts and scenes: but what poet first limited to five the number of the acts, I know not; only we see it so firmly established in the time of Horace, that he gives it for a rule in comedy,—*Neu brevior quinto, neu sit productior actu.* So that you see the Grecians cannot be said to have consummated this art; writing rather by entrances than by acts, and having rather a general indigested notion of a play, than knowing how and where to bestow the particular graces of it.

"But since the Spaniards at this day allow but three acts, which they call *Jornadas,* to a play, and the Italians in many of theirs follow them, when I condemn the ancients, I declare it is not altogether because they have not five acts to every play, but because they have not confined themselves to one certain number: it is building an house without a model; and when they succeeded in such undertakings, they ought to have sacrificed to Fortune, not to the Muses.

"Next, for the plot, which Aristotle called τό μύθος, and often τῶν πραγμάτων σύνθεσις, and from him the Romans *Fabula;* it has already been judiciously observed by a late writer, that in their tragedies it was only some tale derived from Thebes or Troy, or at least something that happened in those two ages; which was worn so threadbare by the pens of all the epic poets, and even by tradition itself of the talkative Greeklings (as Ben Jonson calls them), that before it came upon the stage it was already known to all the audience: and the people, so soon as ever they heard the name of Oedipus, knew as well as the poet, that he had killed his father by a mistake, and committed incest with his mother, before the play; that they were now to hear of a great plague, an oracle, and the ghost of Laius: so that they sat with a yawning kind of expectation, till he was to come with his eyes pulled out, and speak a hundred or more verses in a tragic tone, in complaint of his misfortunes. But one Oedipus, Hercules, or Medea, had been tolerable: poor people, they escaped not so good cheap; they had still the *chapon bouillé* set before them, till their appetites were cloyed with the same dish, and, the novelty being gone, the pleasure vanished; so that one main end of Dramatic Poesy in its definition, which was to cause delight, was of consequence destroyed.

"In their comedies, the Romans generally borrowed their plots from the Greek poets; and theirs was commonly a little girl stolen or wandered from her parents, brought back unknown to the city, there got with child by some lewd young fellow, who, by the help of his servant, cheats his father; and when her times comes, to cry, —*Juno Lucina, fer opem* [Help!],—one or other sees a little box or cabinet which was carried away with her, and so discovers her to her friends, if some god do not prevent it, by coming down in a machine, and taking the thanks of it to himself.

"By the plot you may guess much of the characters of the persons. An old father, who would willingly, before he dies, see his son well married; his debauched son, kind in his nature to his mistress, but miserably in want of money; a servant or slave, who has so much wit to strike in with him, and help to dupe his father; a braggadocio captain, a parasite, and a lady of pleasure.

"As for the poor honest maid, on whom the story is built, and who ought to be one of the principal actors in the play, she is commonly a mute in it: she has the breeding of the old Elizabeth way, which was for maids to be seen and not to be heard; and it is enough you know she is willing to be married, when the fifth act requires it.

"These are plots built after the Italian mode of houses,—you see through them all at once: the characters are indeed the imitation of nature, but so narrow, as if they had imitated only an eye or an hand, and did not dare to venture on the lines of a face, or the proportion of a body.

"But in how strait a compass soever they have bounded their plots and characters, we will pass it by, if they have regularly pursued them, and perfectly observed those three unities of time, place, and action; the knowledge of which you say is derived to us from them. But in the first place give me leave to tell you, that the unity of place, however it might be practised by them, was never any of their rules: we neither find it in Aristotle, Horace, or any who have written of it, till in our age the French poets first made it a precept of the stage. The unity of time, even Terence himself, who was the best and most regular of them, has neglected: his *Heautontimorumenos,* or Self-Punisher, takes up visibly two days, says Scaliger; the two first acts concluding the first day, the three last the day ensuing; and Euripides, in tying himself to one day, has committed an absurdity never to be forgiven him; for in one of his tragedies he has made Theseus go from Athens to Thebes, which was about forty English miles, under the walls of it to give battle, and appear victorious in the next act; and yet, from the time of his departure to the return of the Nuntius, who gives the relation of his victory, Aethra and the Chorus have but thirty-six verses; which is not for every mile a verse.

"The like error is as evident in Terence his *Eunuch,* when Laches, the old man, enters by mistake into the house of Thais; where, betwixt his exit and the entrance of Pythias, who comes to give ample relation of the disorders he has raised within, Parmeno, who was left upon the stage, has not above five lines to speak. *C'est bien employer un temps si court,* says the French poet, who furnished me with one of the observations: and almost all their tragedies will afford us examples of the like nature.

"It is true, they have kept the continuity, or, as you called it, *liaison des scènes,* somewhat better: two do not perpetually come in together, talk, and go out together; and other two succeed them, and do the same throughout the act, which the English call by the name of single scenes; but the reason is, because they have seldom above two or three scenes, properly so called, in every act; for it is to be accounted a new scene, not only every time the stage is empty; but every person who enters, though to others, makes it so; because he introduces a new business. Now the plots of their plays being narrow, and the persons few, one of their acts was written in a less compass than one of our well-wrought scenes; and yet they are often deficient even in this. To go no further than Terence; you find in the *Eunuch,* Antipho entering single in the midst of the third act, after Chremes and Pythias were gone off; in the same play you have likewise Dorias beginning the fourth act alone; and after she had made a relation of what was done at the Soldiers' entertainment (which by the way was very inartificial, because she was presumed to speak directly to the audience, and to acquaint them with what was necessary to be known, but yet should have been so contrived by the poet as to have been told by persons of the drama to one another, and so by them to have come to the knowledge of the people), she quits the stage, and Phaedria enters next, alone likewise: he also gives you an account of himself, and of his returning from the country, in monologue; to which unnatural way of narration Terence is subject in all his plays. In his *Adelphi,* or Brothers, Syrus and Demea enter after the scene was broken by the departure of Sostrata, Geta, and Canthara; and indeed you can scarce look unto any of his comedies, where you will not presently discover the same interruption.

"But as they have failed both in laying of their plots, and in the management, swerving from the rules of their own art by misrepresenting nature to us, in which they have ill satisfied one intention of a play, which was delight; so in the instructive part they have erred worse: instead of punishing vice and rewarding virtue, they have often shewn a prosperous wickedness, and an unhappy piety: they have set before us a bloody image of revenge in Medea, and given her dragons to convey her safe from punishment; a Priam and Astyanax murdered, and Cassandra ravished, and the lust and murder ending in the victory of him who acted them: in short, there is no indecorum in any of our modern plays, which if I would excuse, I could not shadow with some authority from the ancients.

"And one farther note of them let me leave you: tragedies and comedies were not writ then as they are now, promiscuously, by the same person; but he who found his genius bending to the one, never attempted the other way. This is so plain, that I need not instance to you, that Aristophanes, Plautus, Terence, never any of them writ a tragedy; Aeschylus, Euripides, Sophocles, and Seneca, never meddled with comedy: the sock and buskin were not worn by the same poet. Having then so much care to excel in one kind, very little is to be pardoned them, if they miscarried in it; and this would lead me to the consideration of their wit, had not Crites given me sufficient warning not to be too bold in my judgment of it; because, the languages being dead, and many of the customs and little accidents on which it depended lost to us, we are not competent judges of it. But though I grant that here and there we may miss the application of a proverb or a custom, yet a thing well said will be wit in all languages; and though it may lose something in the translation, yet to him who reads it in the original, 'tis still the same: he has an idea of its excellency, though it cannot pass from his mind into any other expression or words than those in which he finds it. When Phaedria, in the *Eunuch,* had a command from his mistress to be absent two days, and, encouraging himself to go through with it, said, *Tandem ego non illa caream, si sit opus, vel totum triduum?* [Shall I not do without her, if necessary, even for three whole days?]—Parmeno, to mock the softness of his master, lifting up his hands and eyes, cries out, as it were in admiration, *Hui! universum triduum!* [Heavens! Three *entire* days!] the elegancy of which *universum,* though it cannot be rendered in our language, yet leaves an impression on our souls: but this happens seldom in him; in Plautus oftener, who is infinitely too bold in his metaphors and coining words, out of which many times his wit is nothing; which questionless was one reason why Horace falls upon him so severely in those verses:

> Sed proavi nostri Plautinos et numeros et
> Laudavere sales, nimium patienter utrumque.
> Ne dicam stolidè.

> [But our ancestors praised the versification and
>   wit of Plautus; too indulgently in both cases,
>   not to say stupidly.]

For Horace himself was cautious to obtrude a new word on his readers, and makes custom and common use the best measure of receiving it into our writings:

> Multa renascentur quae nunc cecidere, cadentque
> Quae nunc sunt in honore vocabula, si volet usus,
> Quem penes arbitrium est, et jus, et norma loquendi.

> [Many words will be revived that are now obsolete,
>   and many will become obsolete that are now hon-

ored, if it is so willed by usage, on which depend
the judgment and the law and the rules of speech.]

"The not observing this rule is that which the world has
blamed in our satirist, Cleveland: to express a thing hard and un-
naturally, is his new way of elocution. 'Tis true, no poet but may
sometimes use a catachresis: Virgil does it—

> Mistaque ridenti colocasia fundet acantho—
>
> [(The earth) will send forth colocasiums
> mingled with smiling acanthus.]

in his eclogue of Pollio; and in his seventh Aeneid:

> mirantur et undae,
> Miratur nemus insuetum fulgentia longe
> Scuta virum fluvio pictasque innare carinas.
>
> [The waves and the unaccustomed woods are
> surprised at the shields of men flashing
> in the distance and the painted ships to
> float upon the stream.]

And Ovid once so modestly, that he asks leave to do it:

> quem, si verbo audacia detur,
> Haud metuam summi dixisse Palatia caeli.
>
> [which, if I may use a bold phrase, I would
> scarcely fear to call the *Palatia* of the
> highest heaven.]

calling the court of Jupiter by the name of Augustus his palace;
though in another place he is more bold, where he says,—*et longas
visent Capitolia pompas* [and the Capitol shall see long processions].
But to do this always, and never be able to write a line without it,
though it may be admired by some few pedants, will not pass upon
those who know that wit is best conveyed to us in the most easy
language; and is most to be admired when a great thought comes
dressed in words so commonly received, that it is understood by the
meanest apprehensions, as the best meat is the most easily digested:
but we cannot read a verse of Cleveland's without making a face at
it, as if every word were a pill to swallow: he gives us many times
a hard nut to break our teeth, without a kernel for our pains. So
that there is this difference betwixt his Satires and doctor Donne's;
that the one gives us deep thoughts in common language, though
rough cadence; the other gives us common thoughts in abstruse

words: 'tis true, in some places his wit is independent of his words, as in that of the rebel Scot:

> Had Cain been Scot, God would have chang'd his doom;
> Not forc'd him wander, but confin'd him home.

"Si sic omnia dixisset! [If only he had said everything in that manner!] This is wit in all languages: it is like Mercury, never to be lost or killed:—and so that other—

> For beauty, like white powder, makes no noise,
> And yet the silent hypocrite destroys.

You see the last line is highly metaphorical, but it is so soft and gentle, that it does not shock us as we read it.

"But, to return from whence I have digressed, to the consideration of the ancients' writing, and their wit (of which by this time you will grant us in some measure to be fit judges). Though I see many excellent thoughts in Seneca, yet he of them who had a genius most proper for the stage, was Ovid; he had a way of writing so fit to stir up a pleasing admiration and concernment, which are the objects of a tragedy, and to show the various movements of a soul combating betwixt two different passions, that, had he lived in our age, or in his own could have writ with our advantages, no man but must have yielded to him; and therefore I am confident the *Medea* is none of his: for, though I esteem it for the gravity and sententiousness of it, which he himself concludes to be suitable to a tragedy,—*Omne genus scripti gravitate tragaedia vincit* [In its dignity tragedy surpasses every kind of writing],—yet it moves not my soul enough to judge that he, who in the epic way wrote things so near the drama as the story of Myrrha, of Caunus and Biblis, and the rest, should stir up no concernment where he most endeavoured it. The masterpiece of Seneca I hold to be that scene in the *Troades,* where Ulysses is seeking for Astyanax to kill him: there you see the tenderness of a mother so represented in Andromache, that it raises compassion to a high degree in the reader, and bears the nearest resemblance of anything in the tragedies of the ancients to the excellent scenes of passion in Shakespeare, or in Fletcher: for love-scenes, you will find few among them; their tragic poets dealt not with that soft passion, but with lust, cruelty, revenge, ambition, and those bloody actions they produced; which were more capable of raising horror than compassion in an audience: leaving love untouched, whose gentleness would have tempered them; which is the most frequent of all the passions, and which, being the private concernment of every person, is soothed by viewing its own image in a public entertainment.

"Among their comedies, we find a scene or two of tenderness, and that where you would least expect it, in Plautus; but to speak generally, their lovers say little, when they see each other, but *anima mea, vita mea* [my soul, my life]; Ζωὴ καὶ ψυχῄ [life and soul], as the women in Juvenal's time used to cry out in the fury of their kindness. Any sudden gust of passion (as an ecstasy of love in an unexpected meeting) cannot better be expressed than in a word and a sigh, breaking one another. Nature is dumb on such occasions; and to make her speak would be to represent her unlike herself. But there are a thousand other concernments of lovers, as jealousies, complaints, contrivances, and the like, where not to open their minds at large to each other, were to be wanting to their own love, and to the expectation of the audience; who watch the movements of their minds, as much as the changes of their fortunes. For the imaging of the first is properly the work of a poet; the latter he borrows from the historian."

Eugenius was proceeding in that part of his discourse, when Crites interrupted him. "I see," said he, "Eugenius and I are never like to have this question decided betwixt us; for he maintains, the moderns have acquired a new perfection in writing; I can only grant they have altered the mode of it. Homer described his heroes men of great appetites, lovers of beef broiled upon the coals, and good fellows; contrary to the practice of the French Romances, whose heroes neither eat, nor drink, nor sleep, for love. Virgil makes Aeneas a bold avower of his own virtues:

> Sum pius Aeneas, fama super aethera notus;
>
> [I am the good Aeneas, renowned on high
>   by fame;]

which, in the civility of our poets is the character of a fanfaron or Hector: for with us the knight takes occasion to walk out, or sleep, to avoid the vanity of telling his own story, which the trusty 'squire is ever to perform for him. So in their love-scenes, of which Eugenius spoke last, the ancients were more hearty, were more talkative: they writ love as it was then the mode to make it; and I will grant thus much to Eugenius, that perhaps one of their poets had he lived in our age, *si foret hoc nostrum fato delapsus in aevum* (as Horace says of Lucilius), he had altered many things; not that they were not natural before, but that he might accommodate himself to the age in which he lived. Yet in the meantime, we are not to conclude anything rashly against those great men, but preserve to them the dignity of masters, and give that honour to their memories, *quos Libitina sacravit* [whom the Goddess of Death has made holy], part of which we expect may be paid to us in future times."

This moderation of Crites, as it was pleasing to all the company, so it put an end to that dispute; which Eugenius, who seemed to have the better of the argument, would urge no farther: but Lisideius, after he had acknowledged himself of Eugenius his opinion concerning the ancient, yet told him, he had forborne, till his discourse were ended, to ask him why he preferred the English plays above those of other nations? and whether we ought not to submit our stage to the exactness of our next neighbours?

"Though," said Eugenius, "I am at all times ready to defend the honour of my country against the French, and to maintain, we are as well able to vanquish them with our pens, as our ancestors have been with their swords; yet, if you please," added he, looking upon Neander, "I will commit this cause to my friend's management; his opinion of our plays is the same with mine, and besides, there is no reason, that Crites and I, who have now left the stage, should re-enter so suddenly upon it; which is against the laws of comedy."

"If the question had been stated," replied Lisideius, "who had writ best, the French or English, forty years ago, I should have been of your opinion, and adjudged the honour to our own nation; but since that time" (said he, turning towards Neander), "we have been so long together bad Englishmen that we had not leisure to be good poets. Beaumont, Fletcher, and Jonson (who were only capable of bringing us to that degree of perfection which we have), were just then leaving the world; as if in an age of so much horror, wit, and those milder studies of humanity, had no farther business among us. But the Muses, who ever follow peace, went to plant in another country: it was then that the great Cardinal Richelieu began to take them into his protection; and that, by his encouragement, Corneille, and some other Frenchmen, reformed their theatre (which before was as much below ours, as it now surpasses it and the rest of Europe). But because Crites in his discourse for the ancients has prevented me, by observing many rules of the stage which the moderns have borrowed from them, I shall only, in short, demand of you, whether you are not convinced that of all nations the French have best observed them? In the unity of time you find them so scrupulous that it yet remains a dispute among their poets, whether the artificial day of twelve hours, more or less, be not meant by Aristotle, rather than the natural one of twenty-four; and consequently, whether all plays ought not to be reduced into that compass. This I can testify, that in all their dramas writ within these last twenty years and upwards, I have not observed any that have extended the time to thirty hours: in the unity of place they are full as scrupulous; for many of their critics limit it to that very spot of ground where the play is supposed to begin; none of them exceed the compass of the same town or city. The unity of action in all plays is yet more conspicuous; for they do not burden them with under-plots, as the English do: which is the reason why many scenes of our tragi-comedians carry on a design that is nothing of kin to the main plot; and that we see two distinct webs in a play, like those in ill-wrought stuffs; and two actions, that is, two plays, carried on together, to the confounding of the audience; who, before they are warm in their concernments for one part, are diverted to another; and by that means espouse the interest of neither. From hence likewise it arises that the one half of our actors are not known to the other. They keep their distances, as if they were Montagues and Capulets, and seldom begin an acquaintance till the last scene of the fifth act, when they are all to meet upon the stage. There is no theatre in the world has anything so absurd as the English tragi-comedy; 'tis a drama of our own invention, and the fashion of it is enough to proclaim it so; here a course of mirth, there another of sadness and passion, and a third of honour and a duel: thus, in two hours and a half, we run through all the fits of Bedlam. The French affords you as much variety on the same day, but they do it not so unseasonably, or *mal à propos,* as we: our poets present you the play and the farce together; and our stages still retain somewhat of the original civility of the Red Bull:

> Atque ursum et pugiles media inter carmina poscunt.
>
> [And in the middle of the songs they call for the bear
> and the boxers.]

The end of tragedies or serious plays, says Aristotle, is to beget admiration, compassion, or concernment; but are not mirth and compassion things incompatible? and is it not evident that the poet must of necessity destroy the former by intermingling of the latter? that is, he must ruin the sole end and object of his tragedy, to introduce somewhat that is forced into it, and is not of the body of it. Would you not think that physician mad, who, having prescribed a purge, should immediately order you to take restringents?

"But to leave our plays, and return to theirs. I have noted one great advantage they have had in the plotting of their tragedies; that is, they are always grounded upon some known history: according to that of Horace, *Ex noto fictum carmen sequar* [From familiar material I shall achieve a successful poem]; and in that they have so imitated the ancients that they have surpassed them. For the ancients, as was observed before, took for the foundation of their plays some poetical fiction, such as under that consideration could move but little concernment in the audience, because they already knew the event of it. But the French goes farther:

> Atque ita mentitur, sic veris falsa remiscet
> Primo ne medium, medio ne discrepet imum.
>
> [And he constructs his fable in such a way,
>   mingling truth and falsehood, that there
> are no discrepancies between the begin-
>   ning and the middle, or between the
>   middle and the end.]

He so interweaves truth with probable fiction that he puts a pleasing fallacy upon us; mends the intrigues of fate, and dispenses with the severity of history, to reward that virtue which has been rendered to us there unfortunate. Sometimes the story has left the success so doubtful that the writer is free, by the privilege of a poet, to take that which of two or more relations will best suit with his design: as for example, in the death of Cyrus, whom Justin and some others report to have perished in the Scythian war, but Xenophon affirms to have died in his bed of extreme old age. Nay more, when the event is past dispute, even then we are willing to be deceived, and the poet, if he contrives it with appearance of truth, has all the audience of his party; at least during the time his play is acting: so naturally we are kind to virtue, when our own interest is not in question, that we take it up as the general concernment of mankind. On the other side, if you consider the historical plays of Shakespeare, they are rather so many chronicles of kings, or the business many times of thirty or forty years, cramped into a representation of two hours and a half; which is not to imitate or paint nature, but rather to draw her in miniature, to take her in little; to look upon her through the wrong end of a perspective, and receive her images not only much less, but infinitely more imperfect than the life: this, instead of making a play delightful, renders it ridiculous:—

> Quodcunque ostendis mihi sic, incredulus odi.
>
> [Whatever you show me of this sort, incredulous I hate.]

For the spirit of man cannot be satisfied but with truth, or at least verisimility; and a poem is to contain, if not τὰ ἔτυμα [the truth], yet ἐτύμοισιν ὁμοῖα [what seems to be true], as one of the Greek poets has expressed it.

"Another thing in which the French differ from us and from the Spaniards, is that they do not embarrass, or cumber themselves with too much plot; they only represent so much of a story as will constitute one whole and great action sufficient for a play; we, who undertake more, do but multiply adventures which, not being produced from one another, as effects from causes, but rarely following, constitute many actions in the drama, and consequently make it many plays.

"But by pursuing closely one argument, which is not cloyed with many turns, the French have gained more liberty for verse, in which they write; they have leisure to dwell on a subject which deserves it; and to represent the passions (which we have acknowledged to be the poet's work), without being hurried from one thing to another, as we are in the plays of Calderon, which we have seen lately upon our theatres under the name of Spanish plots. I have taken notice but of one tragedy of ours whose plot has that uniformity and unity of design in it, which I have commended in the French; and that is *Rollo,* or rather, under the name of Rollo, the Story of Bassianus and Geta in Herodian: there indeed the plot is neither large nor intricate, but just enough to fill the minds of the audience, not to cloy them. Besides, you see it founded upon the truth of history,—only the time of the action is not reduceable to the strictness of the rules; and you see in some places a little farce mingled, which is below the dignity of the other parts, and in this all our poets are extremely peccant: even Ben Jonson himself, in *Sejanus* and *Catiline,* has given us this oleo of a play, this unnatural mixture of comedy and tragedy; which to me sounds just as ridiculously as the history of David with the merry humours of Golia's. In *Sejanus* you may take notice of the scene betwixt Livia and the physician which is a pleasant satire upon the artificial helps of beauty: in *Catiline* you may see the parliament of women; the little envies of them to one another; and all that passes betwixt Curio and Fulvia: scenes admirable in their kind, but of an ill mingle with the rest.

"But I return again to the French writers, who, as I have said, do not burden themselves too much with plot, which has been reproached to them by an ingenious person of our nation as a fault; for, he says, they commonly make but one person considerable in a play; they dwell on him, and his concernments, while the rest of the persons are only subservient to set him off. If he intends this by it, —that there is one person in the play who is of greater dignity than the rest, he must tax, not only theirs, but those of the ancients, and which he would be loth to do, the best of ours; for it is impossible but that one person must be more conspicuous in it than any other, and consequently the greatest share in the action must devolve on him. We see it so in the management of all affairs; even in the most equal aristocracy, the balance cannot be so justly poised but some one will be superior to the rest, either in parts, fortune, interest, or the consideration of some glorious exploit; which will reduce the greatest part of business into his hands.

"But, if he would have us to imagine, that in exalting one character the rest of them are neglected, and that all of them have not some share or other in the action of the play, I desire him to produce any of Corneille's tragedies, wherein every person, like so many servants in a well-governed family, has not some employment, and who is not necessary to the carrying on of the plot, or at least to your understanding it.

"There are indeed some protatic persons in the ancients, whom they make use of in their plays, either to hear or give the relation: but the French avoid this with great address, making their narrations only to, or by such, who are some way interested in the main design. And now I am speaking of relations, I cannot take a fitter opportunity to add this in favour of the French, that they often use them with better judgment and more *à propos* than the English do. Not that I commend narrations in general,—but there are two sorts of them. One, of those things which are antecedent to the play, and are related to make the conduct of it more clear to us. But 'tis a fault to choose such subjects for the stage as will force us on that rock because we see they are seldom listened to by the audience and that is many times the ruin of the play; for, being once let pass without attention, the audience can never recover themselves to understand the plot: and indeed it is somewhat unreasonable that they should be put to so much trouble, as that, to comprehend what passes in their sight, they must have recourse to what was done, perhaps, ten or twenty years ago.

"But there is another sort of relations, that is, of things happening in the action of the play, and supposed to be done behind the scenes; and this is many times both convenient and beautiful; for by it the French avoid the tumult to which we are subject in England, by representing duels, battles, and the like; which renders our stage too like the theatres where they fight prizes. For what is more ridiculous than to represent an army with a drum and five men behind it; all which the hero of the other side is to drive in before him; or to see a duel fought, and one slain with two or three thrusts of the foils, which we know are so blunted that we might give a man an hour to kill another in good earnest with them.

"I have observed that in all our tragedies, the audience cannot forbear laughing when the actors are to die; it is the most comic part of the whole play. All *passions* may be lively represented on the stage, if to the well-writing of them the actor supplies a good commanded voice, and limbs that move easily, and without stiffness; but there are many *actions* which can never be imitated to a just height: dying especially is a thing which none but a Roman gladiator could naturally perform on the stage, when he did not imitate or represent, but do it; and therefore it is better to omit the representation of it.

"The words of a good writer, which describe it lively, will make a deeper impression of belief in us than all the actor can insinuate into us, when he seems to fall dead before us; as a poet in the description of a beautiful garden, or a meadow, will please our imagination more than the place itself can please our sight. When we see death represented, we are convinced it is but fiction; but when we hear it related, our eyes, the strongest witnesses, are wanting, which might have undeceived us; and we are all willing to favour the sleight, when the poet does not too grossly impose on us. They therefore who imagine these relations would make no

concernment in the audience, are deceived, by confounding them
with the other, which are of things antecedent to the play: those are
made often in cold blood, as I may say, to the audience; but these
are warmed with our concernments, which were before awakened
in the play. What the philosophers say of motion, that, when it is
once begun, it continues of itself, and will do so to eternity, without
some stop put to it, is clearly true on this occasion: the soul being
already moved with the characters and fortunes of those imaginary
persons, continues going of its own accord; and we are no more
weary to hear what becomes of them when they are not on the
stage, than we are to listen to the news of an absent mistress. But
it is objected, that if one part of the play may be related, then why
not all? I answer, some parts of the action are more fit to be repre-
sented, some to be related. Corneille says judiciously that the poet is
not obliged to expose to view all particular actions which conduce
to the principal: he ought to select such of them to be seen, which
will appear with the greatest beauty, either by the magnificence of
the show, or the vehemence of passions which they produce, or some
other charm which they have in them; and let the rest arrive to the
audience by narration. 'Tis a great mistake in us to believe the
French present no part of the action on the stage; every alteration
or crossing of a design, every new-sprung passion, and turn of it, is
a part of the action, and much the noblest, except we conceive noth-
ing to be action till the players come to blows; as if the painting
of the hero's mind were not more properly the poet's work than
the strength of his body. Nor does this anything contradict the
opinion of Horace, where he tells us,

> Segnius irritant animos demissa per aurem,
> Quam quae sunt oculis subjecta fidelibus.
> [What is heard makes a feebler impression
>   than what is seen.]

For he says immediately after,

>   Non tamen intus
> Digna geri promes in scenam; *multaque;* tolles
> Ex oculis, quae mox narret facundia praesens.
>
> [You will not act out things better kept off
>   stage; and you will keep from sight many
>   things which an actor will soon relate.]

Among which many he recounts some:

> Nec pueros coram populo Medea trucidet,
> Aut in avem Progne mutetur, Cadmus in anguem, etc.

> [Nor should Medea publicly slay her children, nor
>   Procne be turned into a bird, nor Cadmus into a
>   snake.]

That is, those actions which by reason of their cruelty will cause
aversion in us, or by reason of their impossibility, unbelief, ought
either wholly to be avoided by a poet, or only delivered by narra-
tion. To which we may have leave to add, such as, to avoid tumult
(as we before hinted), or to reduce the plot into a more reasonable
compass of time, or for defect of beauty in them, are rather to be
related than presented to the eye. Examples of all these kinds are
frequent, not only among all the ancients but in the best received
of our English poets. We find Ben Jonson using them in his *Mag-
netic Lady,* where one comes out from dinner, and relates the
quarrels and disorders of it, to save the undecent appearance of them
on the stage, and to abbreviate the story; and this in express imita-
tion of Terence, who had done the same before him in his *Eunuch,*
where Pythias makes the like relation of what had happened within
at the Soldiers' entertainment. The relations likewise of Sejanus's
death, and the prodigies before it, are remarkable; the one of which
was hid from sight, to avoid the horror and tumult of the representa-
tion; the other, to shun the introducing of things impossible to be
believed. In that excellent play, *The King and no King,* Fletcher
goes yet farther; for the whole unravelling of the plot is done by
narration in the fifth act, after the manner of the ancients; and it
moves great concernment in the audience, though it be only a rela-
tion of what was done many years before the play. I could multiply
other instances, but these are sufficient to prove that there is no
error in choosing a subject which requires this sort of narrations;
in the ill management of them, there may.

"But I find I have been too long in this discourse, since the
French have many other excellencies not common to us; as that
you never see any of their plays end with a conversion, or simple
change of will, which is the ordinary way which our poets use to
end theirs. It shows little art in the conclusion of a dramatic poem,
when they who have hindered the felicity during the four acts, de-

sist from it in the fifth, without some powerful cause to take them off their design; and though I deny not but such reasons may be found, yet it is a path that is cautiously to be trod, and the poet is to be sure he convinces the audience that the motive is strong enough. As for example, the conversion of the Usurer in *The Scornful Lady* seems to me a little forced; for, being an Usurer, which implies a lover of money to the highest degree of covetousness,—and such the poet has represented him,—the account he gives for the sudden change is, that he has been duped by the wild young fellow; which in reason might render him more wary another time, and make him punish himself with harder fare and coarser clothes, to get up again what he had lost: but that he should look on it as a judgment, and so repent, we may expect to hear in a sermon, but I should never endure it in a play.

"I pass by this; neither will I insist on the care they take that no person after his first entrance shall ever appear, but the business which brings him upon the stage shall be evident; which rule, if observed, must needs render all the events in the play more natural; for there you see the probability of every accident, in the cause that produced it; and that which appears chance in the play, will seem so reasonable to you, that you will there find it almost necessary: so that in the exit of the actor you have a clear account of his purpose and design in the next entrance (though, if the scene be well wrought, the event will commonly deceive you); for there is nothing so absurd, says Corneille, as for an actor to leave the stage only because he has no more to say.

"I should now speak of the beauty of their rhyme, and the just reason I have to prefer that way of writing in tragedies before ours in blank verse; but because it is partly received by us, and therefore not altogether peculiar to them, I will say no more of it in relation to their plays. For our own, I doubt not but it will exceedingly beautify them; and I can see but one reason why it should not generally obtain, that is, because our poets write so ill in it. This indeed may prove a more prevailing argument than all others which are used to destroy it, and therefore I am only troubled when great and judicious poets, and those who are acknowledged such, have writ or spoke against it: as for others, they are to be answered by that one sentence of an ancient author:—*Sed ut primo ad consequendos eos quos priores ducimus, accendimur, ita ubi aut praeteriri, aut aequari eos posse desperavimus, studium cum spe*

senescit: quod, scilicet, assequi non potest, sequi desinit; . . . prae-
teritoque eo in quo eminere non possumus, aliquid in quo nitamur,
conquirimus [But just as at first we try to emulate those who seem
to be leaders, so, when we give up hope of either surpassing or
equaling them, our zeal wanes with our hope; giving up what offers
no chance of eminence, we seek a new field of effort]."

Lisideius concluded in this manner; and Neander, after a little
pause, thus answered him:

"I shall grant Lisideius, without much dispute, a great part of
what he has urged against us; for I acknowledge that the French
contrive their plots more regularly, and observe the laws of comedy,
and decorum of the stage (to speak generally), with more exactness
than the English. Farther, I deny not but he has taxed us justly in
some irregularities of ours, which he has mentioned; yet, after all,
I am of opinion that neither our faults nor their virtues are consid-
erable enough to place them above us.

"For the lively imitation of nature being in the definition of a
play, those which best fulfil that law ought to be esteemed superior
to the others. 'Tis true, those beauties of the French poesy are such
as will raise perfection higher where it is, but are not sufficient to
give it where it is not: they are indeed the beauties of a statue, but
not of a man, because not animated with the soul of poesy, which
is imitation of humour and passions: and this Lisideius himself, or
any other, however biassed to their party, cannot but acknowledge,
if he will either compare the humours of our comedies, or the
characters of our serious plays, with theirs. He who will look upon
theirs which have been written till these last ten years, or there-
abouts, will find it a hard matter to pick out two or three passable
humours amongst them. Corneille himself, their archpoet, what has
he produced except *The Liar,* and you know how it was cried up in
France; but when it came upon the English stage, though well
translated, and that part of Dorant acted to so much advantage as
I am confident it never received in its own country, the most fa-
vourable to it would not put it in competition with many of
Fletcher's or Ben Jonson's. In the rest of Corneille's comedies you
have little humour; he tells you himself, his way is, first to show
two lovers in good intelligence with each other; in the working
up of the play to embroil them by some mistake, and in the latter
end to clear it, and reconcile them.

"But of late years Molière, the younger Corneille, Quinault, and some others, have been imitating afar off the quick turns and graces of the English stage. They have mixed their serious plays with mirth, like our tragi-comedies, since the death of Cardinal Richelieu; which Lisideius and many others not observing, have commended that in them for a virtue which they themselves no longer practise. Most of their new plays are, like some of ours, derived from the Spanish novels. There is scarce one of them without a veil, and a trusty Diego, who drolls much after the rate of *The Adventures*. But their humours, if I may grace them with that name, are so thin sown, that never above one of them comes up in any play. I dare take upon me to find more variety of them in some one play of Ben Jonson's than in all theirs together; as he who has seen *The Alchemist, The Silent Woman*, or *Bartholomew-Fair*, cannot but acknowledge with me.

"I grant the French have performed what was possible on the ground-work of the Spanish plays; what was pleasant before, they have made regular: but there is not above one good play to be writ on all those plots; they are too much alike to please often; which we need not the experience of our own stage to justify. As for their new way of mingling mirth with serious plot, I do not, with Lisideius, condemn the thing, though I cannot approve their manner of doing it. He tells us, we cannot so speedily recollect ourselves after a scene of great passion and concernment, as to pass to another of mirth and humour, and to enjoy it with any relish: but why should he imagine the soul of man more heavy than his senses? Does not the eye pass from an unpleasant object to a pleasant in a much shorter time than is required to this? and does not the unpleasantness of the first commend the beauty of the latter? The old rule of logic might have convinced him, that contraries, when placed near, set off each other. A continued gravity keeps the spirit too much bent; we must refresh it sometimes, as we bait in a journey that we may go on with greater ease. A scene of mirth, mixed with tragedy, has the same effect upon us which our music has betwixt the acts; which we find a relief to us from the best plots and language of the stage, if the discourses have been long. I must therefore have stronger arguments, ere I am convinced that compassion and mirth in the same subject destroy each other; and in the meantime cannot but conclude, to the honour of our nation, that we have invented, increased, and perfected a more pleasant way of writing for the stage, than was ever known to the ancients or moderns of any nation, which is tragi-comedy.

"And this leads me to wonder why Lisideius and many others should cry up the barrenness of the French plots above the variety and copiousness of the English. Their plots are single; they carry on one design, which is pushed forward by all the actors, every scene in the play contributing and moving towards it. Our plays, besides the main design, have underplots or by-concernments, of less considerable persons and intrigues, which are carried on with the motion of the main plot: as they say the orb of the fixed stars, and those of the planets, though they have motions of their own, are whirled about by the motion of the *primum mobile,* in which they are contained. That similitude expresses much of the English stage; for if contrary motions may be found in nature to agree; if a planet can go east and west at the same time;—one way by virtue of his own motion, the other by the force of the first mover;—it will not be difficult to imagine how the under-plot, which is only different, not contrary to the great design, may naturally be conducted along with it.

"Eugenius has already shown us, from the confession of the French poets, that the unity of action is sufficiently preserved, if all the imperfect actions of the play are conducing to the main design; but when those petty intrigues of a play are so ill ordered, that they have no coherence with the other, I must grant that Lisideius has reason to tax that want of due connection; for co-ordination in a play is as dangerous and unnatural as in a state. In the meantime he must acknowledge, our variety, if well ordered, will afford a greater pleasure to the audience.

"As for his other argument, that by pursuing one single theme they gain an advantage to express and work up the passions, I wish any example he could bring from them would make it good; for I confess their verses are to me the coldest I have ever read. Neither, indeed, is it possible for them, in the way they take, so to express passion, as that the effects of it should appear in the concernment of an audience, their speeches being so many declamations, which tire us with the length; so that instead of persuading us to grieve for their imaginary heroes, we are concerned for our own trouble, as we are in tedious visits of bad company; we are in pain till they are gone. When the French stage came to be reformed by Cardinal Richelieu, those long harangues were introduced to comply with the gravity of a churchman. Look upon the *Cinna* and the *Pompey;* they are not so properly to be called plays, as long discourses of reason of state; and *Polieucte* in matters of religion is as solemn as the long stops upon our organs. Since that time it is grown into a custom, and their actors speak by the hour-glass, like our parsons; nay, they account it the grace of their parts, and think themselves disparaged by the poet, if they may not twice or thrice in a play entertain the audience with a speech of an hundred lines. I deny not but this may suit well enough with the French; for as we, who are a more sullen people, come to be diverted at our plays, so they, who are of an airy and gay temper, come thither to make themselves more serious: and this I conceive to be one reason why comedies are more pleasing to us, and tragedies to them. But to speak generally: it cannot be denied that short speeches and replies are more apt to move the passions and beget concernment in us, than the other; for it is unnatural for any one in a gust of passion to speak long together, or for another in the same condition to suffer him, without interruption. Grief and passion are like floods raised in little brooks by a sudden rain; they are quickly up; and if the concernment be poured unexpectedly in upon us, it overflows us: but a long sober shower gives them leisure to run out as they came in, without troubling the ordinary current. As for comedy, repartee is one of its chiefest graces; the greatest pleasure of the audience is a chase of wit, kept up on both sides, and swiftly managed. And this our forefathers, if not we, have had in Fletcher's plays, to a much higher degree of perfection than the French poets can reasonably hope to reach.

"There is another part of Lisideius his discourse, in which he rather excused our neighbours than commended them; that is, for aiming only to make one person considerable in their plays. 'Tis very true what he has urged, that one character in all plays, even without the poet's care, will have advantage of all the others; and that the design of the whole drama will chiefly depend on it. But this hinders not that there may be more shining characters in the play: many persons of a second magnitude, nay, some so very near, so almost equal to the first, that greatness may be opposed to greatness, and all the persons be made considerable, not only by their quality, but their action. 'Tis evident that the more the persons are, the greater will be the variety of the plot. If then the parts are managed so regularly, that the beauty of the whole be kept entire, and that the variety become not a perplexed and confused mass of accidents, you will find it infinitely pleasing to be led in a labyrinth of design, where you see some of your way before you, yet discern not the end till you arrive at it. And that all this is practicable, I can produce for examples many of our English plays: as *The Maid's Tragedy, The Alchemist, The Silent Woman:* I was going to have named *The Fox,* but that the unity of design seems not exactly observed in it; for there appear two actions in the play; the first naturally ending with the fourth act; the second forced from it in the fifth; which yet is the less to be condemned in him, because the disguise of Volpone, though it suited not with his character as a crafty or covetous person, agreed well enough with that of a voluptuary; and by it the poet gained the end at which he aimed, the punishment of vice, and the reward of virtue, both which that disguise produced. So that to judge equally of it, it was an excellent fifth act, but not so naturally proceeding from the former.

"But to leave this, and pass to the latter part of Lisideius his discourse, which concerns relations: I must acknowledge with him, that the French have reason to hide that part of the action which would occasion too much tumult on the stage, and to choose rather to have it made known by narration to the audience. Farther, I think it very convenient, for the reasons he has given, that all incredible actions were removed; but whether custom has so insinuated itself into our countrymen, or nature has so formed them to fierceness, I know not; but they will scarcely suffer combats and other objects of horror to be taken from them. And indeed, the indency of tumults is all which can be objected against fighting: for why may not our imagination as well suffer itself to be deluded with the probability of it, as with any other thing in the play? For my part, I can with as great ease persuade myself that the blows are given in good earnest, as I can that they who strike them are kings or princes, or those persons which they represent. For objects of incredibility,—I would be satisfied from Lisideius, whether we have any so removed from all appearance of truth, as are those of Corneille's *Andromede;* a play which has been frequented the most of any he has writ. If the Perseus, or the son of a heathen god, the Pegasus, and the Monster, were not capable to choke a strong belief, let him blame any representation of ours hereafter. Those indeed were objects of delight; yet the reason is the same as to the probability: for he makes it not a ballet or masque, but a play, which is to resemble truth. But for death, that it ought not to be represented, I have, besides the arguments alleged by Lisideius, the authority of Ben Jonson, who has foreborne it in his tragedies; for both the death of Sejanus and Catiline are related: though in the latter I cannot but observe one irregularity of that great poet; he has removed the scene in the same act from Rome to Catiline's army, and from thence again to Rome; and besides, has allowed a very inconsiderable time, after Catiline's speech, for the striking of the battle, and the return of Petreius, who is to relate the event of it to the senate: which I should not animadvert on him, who was otherwise a painful observer of τὸ πρέπον, or the *decorum* of the stage, if he had not used extreme severity in his judgment on the incomparable Shakespeare for the same fault.—To conclude on this subject of relations; if we are to be blamed for showing too much of the action, the French are as faulty for discovering too little of it: a mean betwixt both should be observed by every judicious writer, so as the audience may neither be left unsatisfied by not seeing what is beautiful, or shocked by beholding what is either incredible or undecent.

"I hope I have already proved in this discourse, that though we are not altogether so punctual as the French in observing the laws of comedy, yet our errors are so few, and little, and those things wherein we excel them so considerable, that we ought of right to be preferred before them. But what will Lisideius say, if they themselves acknowledge they are too strictly bounded by those laws, for breaking which he has blamed the English? I will allege Corneille's words, as I find them in the end of his Discourse of the three Unities: *Il est facile aux spéculatifs d'estre sévères, etc.* ' 'Tis easy for speculative persons to judge severely; but if they would produce to public view ten or twelve pieces of this nature, they would perhaps give more latitude to the rules than I have done, when by experience they had known how much we are limited and constrained by them, and how many beauties of the stage they banished from it.' To illustrate a little what he has said: By their servile observations of the unities of time and place, and integrity of scenes, they have brought on themselves that dearth of plot, and narrowness of imagination, which may be observed in all their plays. How many beautiful accidents might naturally happen in two or three days, which cannot arrive with any probability in the compass of twenty-four hours? There is time to be allowed also for maturity of design, which, amongst great and prudent persons, such as are often represented in tragedy, cannot, with any likelihood of truth, be brought to pass at so short a warning. Farther; by tying themselves strictly to the unity of place, and unbroken scenes, they are forced many times to omit some beauties which cannot be shown where the act began; but might, if the scene were interrupted, and the stage cleared for the persons to enter in another place; and therefore the French poets are often forced upon absurdities; for if the act begins in a chamber, all the persons in the play must have some business or other to come thither, or else they are not to be shown that act; and sometimes their characters are very unfitting to appear there: as, suppose it were the king's bed-chamber; yet the meanest man in the tragedy must come and dispatch his business there, rather than in the lobby or courtyard (which is fitter for him), for fear the stage should be cleared, and the scenes broken. Many times they fall by it in a greater inconvenience; for they keep their scenes unbroken, and yet change the place; as in one of their newest plays, where the act begins in the street. There a gentleman is to meet his friend; he sees him with his man, coming out from his father's house; they talk together, and the first goes out: the second, who is a lover, has made an appointment with his mistress; she appears at the window, and then we are to imagine the scene lies under it. This gentleman is called away, and leaves his servant with his mistress; presently her father is heard from within; the young lady is afraid the serving-man should be discovered, and thrusts him into a place of safety, which is supposed to be her closet. After this, the father enters to the daughter, and now the scene is in a house; for he is seeking from one room to another for this poor Philipin, or French Diego, who is heard from within, drolling and breaking many a miserable conceit on the subject of his sad condition. In this ridiculous manner the play goes forward, the stage being never empty all the while: so that the street, the window, the houses, and the closet, are made to walk about, and the persons to stand still. Now what, I beseech you, is more easy than to write a regular French play, or more difficult than to write an irregular English one, like those of Fletcher, or of Shakespeare?

"If they content themselves, as Corneille did, with some flat design, which, like an ill riddle, is found out ere it be half proposed, such plots we can make every way regular, as easily as they; but whenever they endeavour to rise to any quick turns and counter-turns of plot, as some of them have attempted, since Corneille's plays have been less in vogue, you see they write as irregularly as we, though they cover it more speciously. Hence the reason is perspicuous why no French plays, when translated, have, or ever can succeed on the English stage. For, if you consider the plots, our own are fuller of variety; if the writing, ours are more quick and fuller of spirit; and therefore 'tis a strange mistake in those who decry the way of writing plays in verse, as if the English therein imitated the French. We have borrowed nothing from them; our plots are weaved in English looms: we endeavour therein to follow the variety and greatness of characters which are derived to us from Shakespeare and Fletcher; the copiousness and well-knitting of the intrigues we have from Jonson; and for the verse itself we have English precedents of elder date than any of Corneille's plays. Not to name our old comedies before Shakespeare, which were all writ in verse of six feet, or Alexandrines, such as the French now use,—I can show in Shakespeare many scenes of rhyme together, and the like in Ben Jonson's tragedies: in *Catiline* and *Sejanus* sometimes thirty or forty lines,—I mean besides the Chorus, or the monologues; which, by the way, showed Ben no enemy to this way of writing, especially if you read his *Sad Shepherd,* which goes sometimes on rhyme, sometimes on blank verse, like an horse who eases himself on trot and amble. You find him likewise commending Fletcher's pastoral of *The Faithful Shepherdess,* which is for the most part rhyme, though not refined to that purity to which it hath since been brought. And these examples are enough to clear us from a servile imitation of the French.

"But to return whence I have digressed: I dare boldly affirm these two things of the English drama;—First, that we have many plays of ours as regular as any of theirs, and which, besides, have more variety of plot and characters; and secondly, that in most of the irregular plays of Shakespeare or Fletcher (for Ben Jonson's are for the most part regular), there is a more masculine fancy and greater spirit in the writing than there is in any of the French. I could produce, even in Shakespeare's and Fletcher's works, some plays which are almost exactly formed; as *The Merry Wives of Windsor,* and *The Scornful Lady:* but because (generally speaking) Shakespeare, who writ first, did not perfectly observe the laws of comedy, and Fletcher, who came nearer to perfection, yet through carelessness made many faults; I will take the pattern of a perfect play from Ben Jonson, who was a careful and learned observer of the dramatic laws, and from all his comedies I shall select *The Silent Woman;* of which I will make a short examen, according to those rules which the French observe."

As Neander was beginning to examine *The Silent Woman,*

Eugenius, earnestly regarding him; "I beseech you, Neander," said he, "gratify the company, and me in particular, so far, as before you speak of the play, to give us a character of the author; and tell us frankly your opinion, whether you do not think all writers, both French and English, ought to give place to him."

"I fear," replied Neander, "that in obeying your commands I shall draw some envy on myself. Besides, in performing them, it will be first necessary to speak somewhat of Shakespeare and Fletcher, his rivals in poesy; and one of them, in my opinion, at least his equal, perhaps his superior.

"To begin, then, with Shakespeare. He was the man who of all modern, and perhaps ancient poets, had the largest and most comprehensive soul. All the images of nature were still present to him, and he drew them, not laboriously, but luckily; when he describes anything, you more than see it, you feel it too. Those who accuse him to have wanted learning, give him the greater commendation: he was naturally learned; he needed not the spectacles of books to read nature; he looked inwards, and found her there. I cannot say he is everywhere alike; were he so, I should do him injury to compare him with the greatest of mankind. He is many times flat, insipid; his comic wit degenerating into clenches, his serious swelling into bombast. But he is always great, when some great occasion is presented to him; no man can say he ever had a fit subject for his wit, and did not then raise himself as high above the rest of poets,

> Quantum lenta solent inter viburna cupressi
> [As much (taller) as cypresses usually are,
>   among pliant viburnums.]

The consideration of this made Mr. Hales of Eaton say, that there was no subject of which any poet ever writ, but he would produce it much better done in Shakespeare; and however others are now generally preferred before him, yet the age wherein he lived, which had contemporaries with him Fletcher and Jonson, never equalled them to him in their esteem; and in the last king's court, when Ben's reputation was at highest, Sir John Suckling, and with him the greater part of the courtiers, set our Shakespeare far above him.

"Beaumont and Fletcher, of whom I am next to speak, had, with the advantage of Shakespeare's wit, which was their precedent, great natural gifts, improved by study: Beaumont especially being

so accurate a judge of plays, that Ben Jonson, while he lived, sub-
mitted all his writings to his censure, and, 'tis thought, used his
judgment in correcting, if not contriving, all his plots. What value
he had for him, appears by the verses he writ to him; and therefore
I need speak no farther of it. The first play that brought Fletcher
and him in esteem was their *Philaster:* for before that, they had
written two or three very unsuccessfully, as the like is reported of
Ben Jonson, before he writ *Every Man in his Humour.* Their plots
were generally more regular than Shakespeare's, especially those
which were made before Beaumont's death; and they understood
and imitated the conversation of gentlemen much better; whose wild
debaucheries, and quickness of wit in repartees, no poet before them
could paint as they have done. Humour, which Ben Jonson derived
from particular persons, they made it not their business to describe:
they represented all the passions very lively, but above all, love.
I am apt to believe the English language in them arrived to its
highest perfection: what words have since been taken in, are rather
superfluous than ornamental. Their plays are now the most pleasant
and frequent entertainments of the stage; two of theirs being acted
through the year for one of Shakespeare's or Jonson's: the reason is,
because there is a certain gaiety in their comedies, and pathos in
their more serious plays, which suit generally with all men's hu-
mours. Shakespeare's language is likewise a little obsolete, and Ben
Jonson's wit comes short of theirs.

"As for Jonson, to whose character I am now arrived, if we
look upon him while he was himself (for his last plays were but his
dotages), I think him the most learned and judicious writer which
any theatre ever had. He was a most severe judge of himself, as
well as others. One cannot say he wanted wit, but rather that he
was frugal of it. In his works you find little to retrench or alter.
Wit, and language, and humour also in some measure, we had
before him; but something of art was wanting to the drama till he
came. He managed his strength to more advantage than any who
preceded him. You seldom find him making love in any of his
scenes, or endeavouring to move the passions; his genius was too
sullen and saturnine to do it gracefully, especially when he knew he
came after those who had performed both to such an height. Hu-
mour was his proper sphere; and in that he delighted most to
represent mechanic people. He was deeply conversant in the
ancients, both Greek and Latin, and he borrowed boldly from

them: there is scarce a poet or historian among the Roman authors of those times whom he has not translated in *Sejanus* and *Catiline*. But he has done his robberies so openly, that one may see he fears not to be taxed by any law. He invades authors like a monarch; and what would be theft in other poets is only victory in him. With the spoils of these writers he so represents old Rome to us, in its rites, ceremonies, and customs, that if one of their poets had written either of his tragedies, we had seen less of it than in him. If there was any fault in his language, 'twas that he weaved it too closely and laboriously, in his comedies especially: perhaps, too, he did a little too much Romanise our tongue, leaving the words which he translated almost as much Latin as he found them: wherein, though he learnedly followed their language, he did not enough comply with the idiom of ours. If I would compare him with Shakespeare, I must acknowledge him the more correct poet, but Shakespeare the greater wit. Shakespeare was the Homer, or father of our dramatic poets; Jonson was the Virgil, the pattern of elaborate writing; I admire him, but I love Shakespeare. To conclude of him; as he has given us the most correct plays, so in the precepts which he has laid down in his *Discoveries,* we have as many and profitable rules for perfecting the stage, as any wherewith the French can furnish us.

"Having thus spoken of the author, I proceed to the examination of his comedy, *The Silent Woman.*

EXAMEN OF THE SILENT WOMAN

"To begin first with the length of the action; it is so far from exceeding the compass of a natural day, that it takes not up an artificial one. 'Tis all included in the limits of three hours and a half, which is no more than is required for the presentment on the stage: a beauty perhaps not much observed; if it had, we should not have looked on the Spanish translation of *Five Hours* with so much wonder. The scene of it is laid in London; the latitude of place is almost as little as you can imagine; for it lies all within the compass of two houses, and after the first act, in one. The continuity of scenes is observed more than in any of our plays, except his own *Fox* and *Alchemist.* They are not broken above twice or thrice at most in the whole comedy; and in the two best of Corneille's plays, the *Cid* and *Cinna,* they are interrupted once. The action of the play is entirely one; the end or aim of which is the settling Morose's estate on Dauphine. The intrigue of it is the greatest and most noble of any pure unmixed comedy in any language; you see in it many persons of various characters and humours, and all delightful. As first, Morose, or an old man, to whom all noise but his own talking is offensive. Some who would be thought critics, say this humour of his is forced: but to remove that objection, we may consider him first to be naturally of a delicate hearing, as many are, to whom all sharp sounds are unpleasant; and secondly, we may attribute much of it to the peevishness of his age, or the wayward authority of an old man in his own house, where he may make himself obeyed; and to this the poet seems to allude in his name Morose. Besides this, I am assured from divers persons, that Ben Jonson was actually acquainted with such a man, one altogether as ridiculous as he is here represented. Others say, it is not enough to find one man of such an humour; it must be common to more, and the more common the more natural. To prove this, they instance in the best of comical characters, Falstaff. There are many men resembling him; old, fat, merry, cowardly, drunken, amorous, vain, and lying. But to convince these people, I need but tell them that humour is the ridiculous extravagance of conversation, wherein one man differs from all others. If then it be common, or communicated to many, how differs it from other men's? or what indeed causes it to be ridiculous so much as the singularity of it? As for Falstaff, he is not properly one humour, but a miscellany of humours or images, drawn from so many several men: that wherein he is singular is his wit, or those things he says *praeter expectatum,* unexpected by the audience; his quick evasions, when you imagine him surprised, which, as they are extremely diverting of themselves, so receive a great addition from his person; for the very sight of such an unwieldy old debauched fellow is a comedy alone. And here, having a place so proper for it, I cannot but enlarge somewhat upon this subject of humour into which I am fallen. The ancients had little of it in their comedies; for the τὸ γελοῖον [source of laughter] of the old comedy, of which Aristophanes was chief, was not so much to imitate a man, as to make the people laugh at some odd conceit, which had commonly somewhat of unnatural or obscene in it. Thus, when you see Socrates brought upon the stage, you are not to imagine him made ridiculous by the imitation of his actions, but rather by making him perform something very unlike himself; something so childish and absurd, as by comparing it with the gravity of the true Socrates, makes a ridiculous object for the spectators. In their new comedy which succeeded, the poets sought indeed to express the ἦθος [character], as in their tragedies the πάθος [suffering] of mankind. But this ἦθος contained only the general characters of men and manners; as old men, lovers, serving-men, courtezans, parasites, and such other persons as we see in their comedies; all which they made alike: that is, one old man or father, one lover, one courtezan, so like another, as if the first of them had begot the rest of every sort: *Ex homine hunc natum dicas* [the one is born image of the other]. The same custom they observed likewise in their tragedies. As for the French, though they have the word *humeur* among them, yet they have small use of it in their comedies or farces; they being but ill imitations of the *ridiculum,* or that which stirred up laughter in the old comedy. But among the English 'tis otherwise: where by humour is meant some extravagant habit, passion, or affection, particular (as I said before) to some one person, by the oddness of which, he is immediately distinguished from the rest of men; which being lively and naturally represented, most frequently begets that malicious pleasure in the audience which is testified by laughter; as all things which are deviations from customs are ever the aptest to produce it: though by the way this laughter is only accidental, as the person represented is fantastic or bizarre; but pleasure is essential to it, as the imitation of what is natural. The description of these humours, drawn from the knowledge and observation of particular persons, was the peculiar genius and talent of Ben Jonson; to whose play I now return.

"Besides Morose, there are at least nine or ten different characters and humours in *The Silent Woman;* all which persons have several concernments of their own, yet are all used by the poet to the conducting of the main design to perfection. I shall not waste time in commending the writing of this play; but I will give you my opinion, that there is more wit and acuteness of fancy in it than in any of Ben Jonson's. Besides that he has here described the conversation of gentlemen in the persons of True-Wit, and his friends, with more gaiety, air, and freedom, than in the rest of his comedies. For the contrivance of the plot, 'tis extreme, elabo-

rate, and yet withal easy; for the λύσις or untying of it, 'tis so
admirable, that when it is done, no one of the audience would
think the poet could have missed it; and yet it was concealed so
much before the last scene, that any other way would sooner have
entered into your thoughts. But I dare not take upon me to com-
mend the fabric of it, because it is altogether so full of art, that
I must unravel every scene in it to commend it as I ought. And
this excellent contrivance is still the more to be admired, because
'tis comedy, where the persons are only of common rank, and their
business private, not elevated by passions or high concernments,
as in serious plays. Here every one is a proper judge of all he
sees, nothing is represented but that with which he daily converses:
so that by consequence all faults lie open to discovery, and few
are pardonable. 'Tis this which Horace has judiciously observed:

> Creditur, ex medio quia res arcessit, habere
> Sudoris minimum; sed habet Comedia tanto
> Plus oneris, quanto veniae minus.
>
> [Comedy, because of its everyday materials,
>   is thought easier to write; but since
>   fewer allowances are made for it, it takes
>   more work.]

But our poet who was not ignorant of these difficulties has
made use of all advantages; as he who designs a large leap takes
his rise from the highest ground. One of these advantages is that
which Corneille has laid down as the greatest which can arrive to
any poem, and which he himself could never compass above thrice
in all his plays; viz., the making choice of some signal and long-
expected day, whereon the action of the play is to depend. This
day was that designed by Dauphine for the settling of his uncle's
estate upon him; which to compass, he contrives to marry him.
That the marriage had been plotted by him long beforehand, is
made evident by what he tells True-Wit in the second act, that
in one moment he had destroyed what he had been raising many
months.

"There is another artifice of the poet, which I cannot here
omit, because by the frequent practice of it in his comedies he
has left it to us almost as a rule; that is, when he has any char-
acter or humour wherein he would show a *coup de Maistre,* or his
highest skill, he recommends it to your observation by a pleasant

description of it before the person first appears. Thus, in *Bartholo-mew-Fair* he gives you the pictures of Numps and Cokes, and in this those of Daw, Lafoole, Morose, and the Collegiate Ladies; all which you hear described before you see them. So that before they come upon the stage, you have a longing expectation of them, which prepares you to receive them favourably; and when they are there, even from their first appearance you are so far acquainted with them, that nothing of their humour is lost to you.

"I will observe yet one thing further of this admirable plot; the business of it rises in every act. The second is greater than the first; the third than the second; and so forward to the fifth. There too you see, till the very last scene, new difficulties arising to obstruct the action of the play; and when the audience is brought into despair that the business can naturally be effected, then, and not before, the discovery is made. But that the poet might enter-tain you with more variety all this while, he reserves some new characters to show you, which he opens not till the second and third act; in the second Morose, Daw, the Barber, and Otter; in the third the Collegiate Ladies: all which he moves afterwards in by-walks, or under-plots, as diversions to the main design, lest it should grow tedious, though they are still naturally joined with it, and somewhere or other subservient to it. Thus, like a skilful chess-player, by little and little he draws out his men, and makes his pawns of use to his greater persons.

"If this comedy and some others of his were translated into French prose (which would now be no wonder to them, since Molière has lately given them plays out of verse, which have not displeased them), I believe the controversy would soon be decided betwixt the two nations, even making them the judges. But we need not call our heroes to our aid. Be it spoken to the honour of the English, our nation can never want in any age such who are able to dispute the empire of wit with any people in the universe. And though the fury of a civil war, and power for twenty years together abandoned to a barbarous race of men, enemies of all good learning, had buried the muses under the ruins of monarchy; yet, with the restoration of our happiness, we see revived poesy lifting up its head, and already shaking off the rubbish which lay so heavy on it. We have seen since his majesty's return, many dramatic poems which yield not to those of any for-eign nation, and which deserve all laurels but the English. I will set aside flattery and envy: it cannot be denied but we have had some little blemish either in the plot or writing of all those plays which have been made within these seven years; (and perhaps there is no nation in the world so quick to discern them, or so difficult to pardon them, as ours:) yet if we can persuade ourselves to use the candour of that poet, who, though the most severe of critics, has left us this caution by which to moderate our censures—

> ubi plura nitent in carmine, non ego paucis
> Offendar maculis;—
>
> [When a poem has many beauties, I shall not be
> offended at a few blemishes;—]

if, in consideration of their many and great beauties, we can wink at some slight and little imperfections, if we, I say, can be thus equal to ourselves, I ask no favour from the French. And if I do not venture upon any particular judgment of our late plays, 'tis out of the consideration which an ancient writer gives me: *vivorum, ut magna admiratio, ita censura difficilis:* betwixt the extremes of admiration and malice, 'tis hard to judge uprightly of the living. Only I think it may be permitted me to say, that as it is no lessening to us to yield to some plays, and those not many, of our own nation in the last age, so can it be no addition to pronounce of our present poets, that they have far surpassed all the ancients, and the modern writers of other countries."

This was the substance of what was then spoken on that occasion; and Lisideius, I think, was going to reply, when he was prevented thus by Crites: "I am confident," said he, "that the most material things that can be said have been already urged on either side; if they have not, I must beg of Lisideius that he will defer his answer till another time: for I confess I have a joint quarrel to you both, because you have concluded, without any reason given for it, that rhyme is proper for the stage. I will not dispute how ancient it hath been among us to write this way; perhaps our ancestors knew no better till Shakespeare's time. I will grant it was not altogether left by him, and that Fletcher and Ben Jonson used it frequently in their Pastorals, and sometimes in other plays. Farther,—I will not argue whether we received it originally from our countrymen, or from the French; for that is an inquiry of as little benefit, as theirs who, in the midst of the great plague, were not so solicitous to provide against it, as to know whether we had it from the malignity of our own air, or by transportation from Holland. I have therefore only to affirm, that it is not allowable in serious plays; for comedies, I find you already concluding with me. To prove this, I might satisfy myself to tell you, how much in vain it is for you to strive against the stream of the people's inclination; the greatest part of which are prepossessed so much with those excellent plays of Shakespeare, Fletcher, and Ben Jonson, which have been written out of rhyme, that except you could bring them such as were written better in it, and those too by persons of equal reputation with them, it will be impossible for you to gain your cause with them, who will still be judges. This it is to which, in fine, all your reasons must submit. The unanimous consent of an audience is so powerful, that even Julius Caesar (as Macrobius reports of him), when he was perpetual dictator, was not able to balance it on the other side; but when Laberius, a Roman Knight, at his request contended in the *Mime* with another poet, he was forced to cry out *Etiam favente me victus es, Laberi* [Even with me on your side you are beaten, Laberius]. But I will not on this occasion take the advantage of the greater number, but only urge such reasons against rhyme, as I find in the writings of those who have argued for the other way. First, then, I am of opinion that rhyme is unnatural in a play, because dialogue there is presented as the effect of sudden thought: for a play is the imitation of nature; and since no man, without premeditation, speaks in rhyme, neither ought he to do it on the stage. This hinders not but the fancy may be there elevated to an higher pitch of thought than it is in ordinary discourse, for there is a probability that men of excellent and quick parts may speak noble things *extempore*: but those thoughts are never fettered with the numbers or sound of verse without study, and therefore it cannot be but unnatural to present the most free way of speaking in that which is the most constrained. For this reason, says Aristotle, 'tis best to write tragedy in that kind of verse which is the least such, or which is nearest prose: and this amongst the ancients was the Iambic, and with us is blank verse, or the measure of verse kept exactly without rhyme. These numbers therefore are fittest for a play; the others for a paper of verses, or a poem; blank verse being as much below them as rhyme is improper for the drama. And if it be objected that neither are blank verses made *extempore*, yet, as nearest nature, they are still to be preferred.—

But there are two particular exceptions, which many besides myself have had to verse; by which it will appear yet more plainly how improper it is in plays. And the first of them is grounded on that very reason for which some have commended rhyme; they say, the quickness of repartees in argumentative scenes receives an ornament from verse. Now what is more unreasonable than to imagine that a man should not only light upon the wit, but the rhyme too, upon the sudden? This nicking of him who spoke before both in sound and measure, is so great an happiness, that you must at least suppose the persons of your play to be born poets: *Arcades omnes, et cantare pares, et respondere parati* [We are all dwellers in Arcadia, ready both to sing and to reply]: they must have arrived to the degree of *quicquid conabar dicere;*—to make verses almost whether they will or no. If they are anything below this, it will look rather like the design of two, than the answer of one: it will appear that your actors hold intelligence together; that they perform their tricks like fortune-tellers, by confederacy. The hand of art will be too visible in it, against that maxim of all professions—*Ars est celare artem;* that it is the greatest perfection of art to keep itself undiscovered. Nor will it serve you to object, that however you manage it, 'tis still known to be a play; and, consequently, the dialogue of two persons understood to be the labour of one poet. For a play is still an imitation of nature; we know we are to be deceived, and we desire to be so; but no man ever was deceived but with a probability of truth; for who will suffer a gross lie to be fastened on him? Thus we sufficiently understand that the scenes which represent cities and countries to us are not really such, but only painted on boards and canvas; but shall that excuse the ill painture or designment of them? Nay, rather ought they not be laboured with so much the more diligence and exactness, to help the imagination? since the mind of man does naturally tend to truth; and therefore the nearer anything comes to the imitation of it, the more it pleases.

"Thus, you see, your rhyme is incapable of expressing the greatest thoughts naturally, and the lowest it cannot with any grace: for what is more unbefitting the majesty of verse, than to call a servant, or bid a door be shut in rhyme? and yet you are often forced on this miserable necessity. But verse, you say, circumscribes a quick and luxuriant fancy, which would extend itself too far on every subject, did not the labour which is required to well-turned and polished rhyme, set bounds to it. Yet this argument, if granted, would only prove that we may write better in verse, but not more naturally. Neither is it able to evince that; for he who wants judgment to confine his fancy in blank verse, may want it as much in rhyme: and he who has it will avoid errors in both kinds. Latin verse was as great a confinement to the imagination of those poets as rhyme to ours; and yet you find Ovid saying too much on every subject. *Nescivit* (says Seneca) *quod bene cessit relinquere* [He didn't know how to let well enough alone]: of which he gives you one famous instance in his description of the deluge:

> *Omnia pontus erat, deerant quoque litora ponto.*
> Now all was sea, nor had that sea a shore.

Thus Ovid's fancy was not limited by verse, and Virgil needed not verse to have bounded his.

"In our own language we see Ben Jonson confining himself to what ought to be said, even in the liberty of blank verse; and yet Corneille, the most judicious of the French poets, is still varying the same sense an hundred ways, and dwelling eternally on the same subject, though confined by rhyme. Some other exceptions I have to verse; but since these I have named are for the most part already public, I conceive it reasonable they should first be answered."

"It concerns me less than any," said Neander (seeing he had ended), "to reply to this discourse; because when I should have proved that verse may be natural in plays, yet I should always be ready to confess, that those which I have written in this kind come short of that perfection which is required. Yet since you are pleased I should undertake this province, I will do it, though with all imaginable respect and deference, both to that person from whom you have borrowed your strongest arguments, and to whose judgment, when I have said all, I finally submit. But before I proceed to answer your objections, I must first remember you, that I exclude all comedy from my defence; and next that I deny not but blank verse may be also used; and content myself only to assert, that in serious plays where the subject and characters are great, and the plot unmixed with mirth, which might allay or divert these concernments which are produced, rhyme is there as natural and more effectual than blank verse.

"And now having laid down this as a foundation,—to begin with Crites,—I must crave leave to tell him, that some of his arguments against rhyme reach no farther than, from the faults or defects of ill rhyme, to conclude against the use of it in general. May not I conclude against blank verse by the same reason? If the words of some poets who write in it are either ill chosen, or ill placed, which makes not only rhyme, but all kind of verse in any language unnatural, shall I, for their vicious affectation, condemn those excellent lines of Fletcher, which are written in that kind? Is there anything in rhyme more constrained than this line in blank verse?—*I heaven invoke, and strong resistance make;* where you see both the clauses are placed unnaturally, that is, contrary to the common way of speaking, and that without the excuse of a rhyme to cause it: yet you would think me very ridiculous, if I should accuse the stubbornness of blank verse for this, and not rather the stiffness of the poet. Therefore, Crites, you must either prove that words, though well chosen, and duly placed, yet render not rhyme natural in itself; or that, however natural and easy the rhyme may be, yet it is not proper for a play. If you insist on the former part, I would ask you, what other conditions are required to make rhyme natural in itself, besides an election of apt words, and a right disposition of them? For the due choice of your words expresses your sense naturally, and the due placing them adapts the rhyme to it. If you object that one verse may be made for the sake of another, though both the words and rhyme be apt, I answer, it cannot possibly so fall out; for either there is a dependence of sense betwixt the first line and the second, or there is none: if there be that connection, then in the natural position of the words the latter line must of necessity flow from the former; if there be no dependence, yet still the due ordering of words makes the last line as natural in itself as the other: so that the necessity of a rhyme never forces any but bad or lazy writers to say what they would not otherwise. 'Tis true, there is both care and art required to write in verse. A good poet never establishes the first line till he has sought out such a rhyme as may fit the sense, already prepared to heighten the second: many times the close of the sense falls into the middle of the next verse, or farther off, and he may often prevail himself of the same advantages in English which Virgil had in Latin,—he may break off in the hemistich, and begin another line. Indeed, the not observing these two last things makes plays which are writ in verse so tedious: for though, most commonly, the sense is to be confined to the couplet, yet nothing that does *perpetuo tenore fluere,* run in the same channel, can please always. 'Tis like the murmuring of a stream, which not varying in the fall, causes at first attention, at last drowsiness. Variety of cadences is the best rule; the greatest help to the actors, and refreshment to the audience.

"If then verse may be made natural in itself, how becomes it unnatural in a play? You say the stage is the representation of nature, and no man in ordinary conversation speaks in rhyme. But you foresaw when you said this, that it might be answered— neither does any man speak in blank verse, or in measure without rhyme. Therefore you concluded, that which is nearest nature is still to be preferred. But you took no notice that rhyme might be made as natural as blank verse, by the well placing of the words, etc. All the difference between them, when they are both correct, is, the sound in one, which the other wants; and if so, the sweet-ness of it, and all the advantage resulting from it, which are handled in the Preface to *The Rival Ladies,* will yet stand good. As for that place of Aristotle, where he says, plays should be writ in that kind of verse which is nearest prose, it makes little for you; blank verse being properly but measured prose. Now measure alone, in any modern language, does not constitute verse; those of the ancients in Greek and Latin consisted in quantity of words, and a determinate number of feet. But when, by the inundation of the Goths and Vandals into Italy, new languages were intro-duced, and barbarously mingled with the Latin, of which the Ital-ian, Spanish, French, and ours (made out of them and the Teu-tonic) are dialects, a new way of poesy was practised; new, I say, in those countries, for in all probability it was that of the con-querors in their own nations: at least we are able to prove, that the eastern people have used it from all antiquity. This new way consisted in measure or number of feet, and rhyme; the sweetness of rhyme, and observation of accent, supplying the place of quan-tity in words, which could neither exactly be observed by those barbarians, who knew not the rules of it, neither was it suitable to their tongues, as it had been to the Greek and Latin. No man is tied in modern poesy to observe any farther rule in the feet of his verse, but that they be dissyllables; whether Spondee, Trochee, or Iambic, it matters not; only he is obliged to rhyme:

neither do the Spanish, French, Italian, or Germans, acknowledge at all, or very rarely, any such kind of poesy as blank verse amongst them. Therefore, at most 'tis but a poetic prose, a *sermo pedestris;* and as such, most fit for comedies, where I acknowledge rhyme to be improper.—Farther; as to that quotation of Aristotle, our couplet verses may be rendered as near prose as blank verse itself, by using those advantages I lately named,—as breaks in an hemistich, or running the sense into another line,—thereby making art and order appear as loose and free at nature: or not tying ourselves to couplets strictly, we may use the benefit of the Pindaric way practised in *The Siege of Rhodes;* where the numbers vary, and the rhyme is disposed carelessly, and far from often chiming. Neither is that other advantage of the ancients to be despised, of changing the kind of verse when they please, with the change of the scene, or some new entrance; for they confine not themselves always to iambics, but extend their liberty to all lyric numbers, and sometimes even to hexameter. But I need not go so far to prove that rhyme, as it succeeds to all other offices of Greek and Latin verse, so especially to this of plays, since the custom of nations at this day confirms it; the French, Italian, and Spanish tragedies are generally writ in it; and sure the universal consent of the most civilised parts of the world, ought in this, as it doth in other customs, to include the rest.

"But perhaps you may tell me, I have proposed such a way to make rhyme natural, and consequently proper to plays, as is unpracticable; and that I shall scarce find six or eight lines together in any play, where the words are so placed and chosen as is required to make it natural. I answer, no poet need constrain himself at all times to it. It is enough he makes it his general rule; for I deny not but sometimes there may be a greatness in placing the words otherwise; and sometimes they may sound better; sometimes also the variety itself is excuse enough. But if, for the most part, the words be placed as they are in the negligence of prose, it is sufficient to denominate the way practicable; for we esteem that to be such, which in the trial oftener succeeds than misses. And thus far you may find the practice made good in many plays: where you do not, remember still, that if you cannot find six natural rhymes together, it will be as hard for you to produce as many lines in blank verse, even among the greatest of our poets, against which I cannot make some reasonable exception.

"And this, Sir, calls to my remembrance the beginnings of your discourse, where you told us we should never find the audience favourable to this kind of writing, till we could produce as good plays in rhyme as Ben Jonson, Fletcher, and Shakespeare had writ out of it. But it is to raise envy to the living, to compare them with the dead. They are honoured, and almost adored by us, as they deserve; neither do I know any so presumptuous of themselves as to contend with them. Yet give me leave to say thus much, without injury to their ashes; that not only we shall never equal them, but they could never equal themselves, were they to rise and write again. We acknowledge them our fathers in wit; but they have ruined their estates themselves, before they came to their children's hands. There is scarce an humour, a character, or any kind of plot, which they have not used. All comes sullied or wasted to us: and were they to entertain this age, they could not now make so plenteous treatments out of such decayed fortunes. This therefore will be a good argument to us, either not to write at all, or to attempt some other way. There is no bays to be expected in their walks: *tentanda via est, qua me quoque possum tollere humo* [I must seek a route that will take me also off the earth].

"This way of writing in verse they have only left free to us; our age is arrived to a perfection in it, which they never knew; and which (if we may guess by what of theirs we have seen in verse, as *The Faithful Shepherdess,* and *Sad Shepherd*) 'tis probable they never could have reached. For the genius of every age is different; and though ours excel in this, I deny not but to imitate nature in that perfection which they did in prose, is a greater commendation than to write in verse exactly. As for what you have added—that the people are not generally inclined to like this way,—if it were true, it would be no wonder, that betwixt the shaking off an old habit, and the introducing of a new, there should be difficulty. Do we not see them stick to Hopkins' and Sternhold's psalms, and forsake those of David, I mean Sandys his translation of them? If by the people you understand the multitude, the οἱ πολλοί, 'tis no matter what they think; they are sometimes in the right, sometimes in the wrong: their judgment is a mere lottery. *Est ubi plebs rectè putat, est ubi peccat* [The people are sometimes right in their judgment, sometimes wrong]. Horace says it of the vulgar, judging poesy. But if you mean the mixed audience of the populace and the noblesse, I dare confidently affirm that a great part of the latter sort are already favourable to verse; and that no serious plays written since the king's return have been more kindly received by them than *The Siege of Rhodes,* the *Mustapha, The Indian Queen,* and *Indian Emperor.*

"But I come now to the inference of your first argument. You said that the dialogue of plays is presented as the effect of sudden thought, but no man speaks suddenly, or *extempore,* in rhyme; and you inferred from thence, that rhyme, which you acknowledge to be proper to epic poesy, cannot equally be proper to dramatic, unless we could suppose all men born so much more than poets, that verses should be made in them, not by them.

"It has been formerly urged by you, and confessed by me, that since no man spoke any kind of verse *extempore,* that which was nearest nature was to be preferred. I answer you, therefore, by distinguishing betwixt what is nearest to the nature of comedy, which is the imitation of common persons and ordinary speaking, and what is nearest the nature of a serious play: this last is indeed the representation of nature, but 'tis nature wrought up to a higher pitch. The plot, the characters, the wit, the passions, the descriptions, are all exalted above the level of common converse, as high as the imagination of the poet can carry them, with proportion to verisimility. Tragedy, we know, is wont to image to us the minds and fortunes of noble persons, and to portray these exactly; heroic rhyme is nearest nature, as being the noblest kind of modern verse.

> Indignatur enim privatis et prope socco
> Dignis carminibus narrari coena Thyestae
>
> [The banquet of Thyestes refuses to be related in colloquial verses, of a style suited to comedy.]

says Horace: and in another place,

> Effutire leves indigna tragoedia versus.
> [Tragedy, unfitted to babble rival verses.]

Blank verse is acknowledged to be too low for a poem, nay more, for a paper of verses; but if too low for an ordinary sonnet, how much more for tragedy, which is by Aristotle, in the dispute betwixt the epic poesy and the dramatic, for many reasons he there alleges, ranked above it?

"But setting this defence aside, your argument is almost as strong against the use of rhyme in poems as in plays; for the epic way is everywhere interlaced with dialogue, or discoursive scenes; and therefore you must either grant rhyme to be improper there, which is contrary to your assertion, or admit it into plays by the same title which you have given it to poems. For though tragedy be justly preferred above the other, yet there is a great affinity between them, as may easily be discovered in that definition of a play which Lisideius gave us. The *genus* of them is the same—a just and lively image of human nature, in its actions, passions, and traverses of fortune: so is the end—namely, for the delight and benefit of mankind. The characters and persons are still the same, viz., the greatest of both sorts; only the manner of acquainting us with those actions, passions, and fortunes, is different. Tragedy performs it *viva voce,* or by action, in dialogue; wherein it excels the epic poem, which does it chiefly by narration, and therefore is not so lively an image of human nature. However, the agreement betwixt them is such, that if rhyme be proper for one, it must be for the other. Verse, 'tis true, is not the effect of sudden thought; but this hinders not that sudden thought may be represented in verse, since those thoughts are such as must be higher than nature can raise them without premeditation, especially to a continuance of them, even out of verse; and consequently you cannot imagine them to have been sudden either in the poet or in the actors. A play, as I have said, to be like nature, is to be set above it; as statues which are placed on high are made greater than the life, that they may descend to the sight in their just proportion.

"Perhaps I have insisted too long on this objection; but the clearing of it will make my stay shorter on the rest. You tell us, Crites, that rhyme appears most unnatural in repartees, or short replies: when he who answers (it being presumed he knew not what the other would say, yet) makes up that part of the verse which was left incomplete, and supplies both the sound and measure of it. This, you say, looks rather like the confederacy of two, than the answer of one.

"This, I confess, is an objection which is in every man's mouth, who loves not rhyme: but suppose, I beseech you, the repartee were

made only in blank verse, might not part of the same argument be
turned against you? for the measure is as often supplied there as
it is in rhyme; the latter half of the hemistich as commonly made
up, or a second line subjoined as a reply to the former; which any
one leaf in Jonson's plays will sufficiently clear to you. You will
often find in the Greek tragedians, and in Seneca, that when a
scene grows up into the warmth of repartees, which is the close
fighting of it, the latter part of the trimeter is supplied by him who
answers; and yet it was never observed as a fault in them by any of
the ancient or modern critics. The case is the same in our verse,
as it was in theirs; rhyme to us being in lieu of quantity to them.
But if no latitude is to be allowed a poet, you take from him not
only his licence of *quidlibet audendi* [trying anything], but you tie
him up in a straiter compass than you would a philosopher. This
is indeed *Musas colere severiores* [to worship Muses more severe].
You would have him follow nature, but he must follow her on
foot: you have dismounted him from his Pegasus. But you tell us,
this supplying the last half of a verse, or adjoining a whole second
to the former, looks more like the design of two, than the answer
of one. Suppose we acknowledge it: how comes this confederacy to
be more displeasing to you, than in a dance which is well con-
trived? You see there the united design of many persons to make
up one figure: after they have separated themselves in many petty
divisions, they rejoin one by one into a gross: the confederacy is
plain amongst them, for chance could never produce anything so
beautiful; and yet there is nothing in it that shocks your sight. I
acknowledge the hand of art appears in repartee, as of necessity it
must in all kind of verse. But there is also the quick and poignant
brevity of it (which is an high imitation of nature in those sudden
gusts of passion) to mingle with it; and this, joined with the
cadency and sweetness of the rhyme, leaves nothing in the soul of
the hearer to desire. 'Tis an art which appears; but it appears only
like the shadowings of painture, which being to cause the rounding
of it, cannot be absent; but while that is considered, they are lost:
so while we attend to the other beauties of the matter, the care and
labour of the rhyme is carried from us, or at least drowned in its
own sweetness, as bees are sometimes buried in their honey. When
a poet has found the repartee, the last perfection he can add to it,
is to put it into verse. However good the thought may be, however
apt the words in which 'tis couched, yet he finds himself at a little

unrest, while rhyme is wanting: he cannot leave it till that comes naturally, and then is at ease, and sits down contented.

"From replies, which are the most elevated thoughts of verse, you pass to those which are most mean, and which are common with the lowest of household conversation. In these, you say, the majesty of verse suffers. You instance in the calling of a servant, or commanding a door to be shut, in rhyme. This, Crites, is a good observation of yours, but no argument: for it proves no more but that such thoughts should be waived, as often as may be, by the address of the poet. But suppose they are necessary in the places where he uses them, yet there is no need to put them into rhyme. He may place them in the beginning of a verse, and break it off, as unfit, when so debased, for any other use: or granting the worst,—that they require more room than the hemistich will allow, yet still there is a choice to be made of the best words, and least vulgar (provided they be apt), to express such thoughts. Many have blamed rhyme in general, for this fault, when the poet with a little care might have redressed it. But they do it with no more justice than if English poesy should be made ridiculous for the sake of the Water-poet's rhymes. Our language is noble, full, and significant; and I know not why he who is master of it may not clothe ordinary things in it as decently as the Latin, if he use the same diligence in his choice of words: *delectus verborum origo est eloquentiae*. It was the saying of Julius Caesar, one so curious in his, that none of them can be changed but for a worse. One would think, *unlock the door,* was a thing as vulgar as could be spoken; and yet Seneca could make it sound high and lofty in his Latin:

> *Reserate clusos regii postes laris.*
> Set wide the palace gates.

"But I turn from this conception, both because it happens not above twice or thrice in any play that those vulgar thoughts are used; and then too (were there no other apology to be made, yet), the necessity of them, which is alike in all kind of writing, may excuse them. For if they are little and mean in rhyme, they are of consequence such in blank verse. Besides that the great eagerness and precipitation with which they are spoken, makes us rather mind the substance than the dress; that for which they are spoken, rather than what is spoken. For they are always the effect of some hasty concernment, and something of consequence depends on them.

"Thus, Crites, I have endeavoured to answer your objections; it remains only that I should vindicate an argument for verse, which you have gone about to overthrow. It had formerly been said that the easiness of blank verse renders the poet too luxuriant, but that the labour of rhyme bounds and circumscribes an over-fruitful fancy; the sense there being commonly confined to the couplet, and the words so ordered that the rhyme naturally follows them, not they the rhyme. To this you answered, that it was no argument to the question in hand; for the dispute was not which way a man may write best, but which is most proper for the subject on which he writes.

"First, give me leave, Sir, to remember you that the argument against which you raised this objection was only secondary: it was built on this hypothesis,—that to write in verse was proper for serious plays. Which supposition being granted (as it was briefly made out in that discourse, by showing how verse might be made natural), it asserted, that this way of writing was an help to the poet's judgment, by putting bounds to a wild overflowing fancy. I think, therefore, it will not be hard for me to make good what it was to prove on that supposition. But you add, that were this let pass, yet he who wants judgment in the liberty of his fancy, may as well show the defect of it when he is confined to verse; for he who has judgment will avoid errors, and he who has it not, will commit them in all kinds of writing.

"This argument, as you have taken it from a most acute person, so I confess it carries much weight in it: but by using the word judgment here indefinitely, you seem to have put a fallacy upon us. I grant, he who has judgment, that is, so profound, so strong, or rather so infallible a judgment, that he needs no helps to keep it always poised and upright, will commit no faults either in rhyme or out of it. And on the other extreme, he who has a judgment so weak and crazed that no helps can correct or amend it, shall write scurvily out of rhyme, and worse in it. But the first of these judgments is nowhere to be found, and the latter is not fit to write at all. To speak therefore of judgment as it is in the best poets; they who have the greatest proportion of it, want other helps than from it, within. As for example, you would be loth to say that he who is endued with a sound judgment has no need of history, geography, or moral philosophy, to write correctly. Judgment is indeed the master-workman in a play; but he requires many subordinate hands, many tools to his assistance. And verse I affirm to be one of these; 'tis a rule and line by which he keeps his building compact and even, which otherwise lawless imagination would raise either irregularly or loosely; at least, if the poet commits errors with this help, he would make greater and more without it: 'tis, in short, a slow and painful, but the surest kind of working. Ovid, whom you accuse for luxuriancy in verse, had perhaps been farther guilty of it, had he writ in prose. And for your instance of Ben Jonson, who, you say, writ exactly without the help of rhyme; you are to remember, 'tis only an aid to a luxuriant fancy, which his was not: as he did not want imagination, so none ever said he had much to spare. Neither was verse then refined so much, to be an help to that age, as it is to ours. Thus then the second thoughts being usually the best, as receiving the maturest digestion from judgment, and the last and most mature product of those thoughts being artful and laboured verse, it may well be inferred, that verse is a great help to a luxuriant fancy; and this is what that argument which you opposed was to evince."

Neander was pursuing this discourse so eagerly that Eugenius had called to him twice or thrice, ere he took notice that the barge stood still, and that they were at the foot of Somerset-stairs, where they had appointed it to land. The company were all sorry to separate so soon, though a great part of the evening was already spent; and stood a-while looking back on the water, upon which the moonbeams played, and made it appear like floating quick silver: at last they went up through a crowd of French people, who were merrily dancing in the open air, and nothing concerned for the noise of guns which had alarmed the town that afternoon. Walking thence together to the Piazze, they parted there; Eugenius and Lisideius to some pleasant appointment they had made, and Crites and Neander to their several lodgings.

PREFACE TO THE FABLES

'Tis with a poet, as with a man who designs to build, and is very exact, as he supposes, in casting up the cost beforehand; but, generally speaking, he is mistaken in his account, and reckons short of the expense he first intended. He alters his mind as the work proceeds, and will have this or that convenience more, of which he had not thought when he began. So has it happened to me; I have built a house where I intended but a lodge; yet with better success than a certain nobleman, who, beginning with a dog-kennel, never lived to finish the palace he had contrived.

From translating the first of Homer's Iliads (which I intended as an essay to the whole work), I proceeded to the translation of the Twelfth Book of Ovid's *Metamorphoses,* because it contains, among other things, the causes, the beginning, and ending, of the Trojan war. Here I ought in reason to have stopped; but the speeches of Ajax and Ulysses lying next in my way, I could not balk 'em. When I had compassed them, I was so taken with the former part of the Fifteenth Book (which is the masterpiece of the whole *Metamorphoses*), that I enjoined myself the pleasing task of rendering it into English. And now I found, by the number of my verses, that they began to swell into a little volume, which gave me an occasion of looking backward on some beauties of my author in his former books: here occurred to me the *Hunting of the Boar, Cinyras and Myrrha,* the good-natured story of *Baucis and Philemon,* with the rest, which I hope I have translated closely enough, and given them the same turn of verse which they had in the original; and this, I may say, without vanity, is not the talent of every poet. He who has arrived the nearest to it is the ingenious and learned Sandys, the best versifier of the former age; if I may properly call it by that name, which was the former part of this concluding century. For Spenser and Fairfax both flourished in the reign of Queen Elizabeth; great masters in our language, and who saw much further into the beauties of our numbers than those who immediately followed them. Milton was the poetical son of Spenser, and Mr. Waller of Fairfax; for we have our lineal descents and clans as well as other families. Spenser more than once insinuates that the soul of Chaucer was transfused into his body; and that he was begotten by him two hundred years after his decease. Milton has acknowledged to me that Spenser was his original; and many besides myself have heard our famous Waller own that he derived the harmony of his numbers from *Godfrey of Bulloign,* which was turned into English by Mr. Fairfax.

But to return: having done with Ovid for this time, it came into my mind that our old English poet, Chaucer, in many things resembled him, and that with no disadvantage on the side of the modern author, as I shall endeavour to prove when I compare them; and as I am, and always have been, studious to promote the honour of my native country, so I soon resolved to put their merits to the trial, by turning some of the *Canterbury Tales* into our language, as it is now refined; for by this means, both the poets being set in the same light, and dressed in the same English habit, story to be compared with story, a certain judgment may be made betwixt them by the reader, without obtruding my opinion on him. Or, if I seem partial to my countryman and predecessor in the laurel, the friends of antiquity are not few; and, besides many of the learned, Ovid has almost all the beaux, and the whole fair sex, his declared patrons. Perhaps I have assumed somewhat more to myself than they allow me, because I have adventured to sum up the evidence; but the readers are the jury, and their privilege remains entire, to decide according to the merits of the cause; or, if they please, to bring it to another hearing before some other court. In the meantime, to follow the thread of my discourse (as thoughts, according to Mr. Hobbes, have always some connection), so from Chaucer I was led to think on Boccace, who was not only his contemporary, but also pursued the same studies; wrote novels in prose, and many works in verse; particularly is said to have invented the octave rhyme, or stanza of eight lines, which ever since has been maintained by the practice of all Italian writers who are, or at least assume the title of heroic poets. He and Chaucer, among other things, had this in common, that they refined their mother-tongues; but with this difference, that Dante had begun to file their language, at least in verse, before the time of Boccace, who likewise received no little help from his master Petrarch; but the reformation of their prose was wholly owing to Boccace himself, who is yet the standard of purity in the Italian tongue, though many of his phrases are become obsolete, as in process of time it must needs happen. Chaucer (as you have formerly been told by our learned Mr. Rymer) first adorned and amplified our barren tongue from the Provençal, which was then the most polished of all the modern languages; but this subject has been copiously treated by that great critic, who deserves no little commendation from us his countrymen. For these reasons of time, and resemblance of genius, in Chaucer and Boccace, I resolved to join them in my present work; to which I have added some original papers of my own, which whether they are equal or inferior to my other poems, an author is the most improper judge; and therefore I leave them wholly to the mercy of the reader. I will hope the best, that they will not be condemned; but if they should, I have the excuse of an old gentleman, who, mounting on horseback before some ladies, when I was present, got up somewhat heavily, but desired of the fair spectators that they would count fourscore and eight before they judged him. By the mercy of God, I am already come within twenty years of his number; a cripple in my limbs, but what decays are in my mind, the reader must determine. I think myself as vigorous as ever in the faculties of my soul, excepting only my memory, which is not impaired to any great degree; and if I lose not more of it, I have no great reason to complain. What judgment I had increases rather than diminishes; and thoughts, such as they are, come crowding in so fast upon me that my only difficulty is to choose or to reject, to run them into verse, or to give them the other harmony of prose: I have so long studied and practised both that they are grown into a habit, and become familiar to me. In short, though I may lawfully plead some part of the old gentleman's excuse, yet I will reserve it till I think I have greater need, and ask no grains of allowance for the faults of this my present work but those which are given of course to human frailty. I will not trouble my reader with the shortness of time in which I write it, or the several intervals of sickness. They who think too well of their own performances are apt to boast in their prefaces how little time their works have cost them, and what other business of more importance interfered; but the reader will be as apt to ask the question, why they allowed not a longer time to make their works more perfect? and why they had so despicable an opinion of their judges as to thrust their indigested stuff upon them, as if they deserved no better?

With this account of my present undertaking, I conclude the first part of this discourse: in the second part, as at a second sitting, though I alter not the draught, I must touch the same features over again, and change the dead-colouring of the whole. In general I will only say that I have written nothing which savours of immorality or profaneness; at least, I am not conscious to myself of any such intention. If there happen to be found an irreverent expression, or a thought too wanton, they are crept into my verses through my inadvertency: if the searchers find any in the cargo, let them be staved or forfeited, like counterbanded goods; at least, let their authors be answerable for them, as being but imported merchandise, and not of my own manufacture. On the other side, I have endeavoured to choose such fables, both ancient and modern, as contain in each of them some instructive moral; which I could prove by induction, but the way is tedious, and they leap foremost into sight, without the reader's trouble of looking after them. I wish I could affirm, with a safe conscience, that I had taken the same care in all my former writings; for it must be owned that, supposing verses are never so beautiful or pleasing, yet, if they contain anything which shocks religion or good manners, they are at best what Horace says of good numbers without good sense, *Versus inopes rerum, nugaeque canorae* [Verses with nothing in them, tuneful trifles]. Thus far, I hope, I am right in court, without renouncing to my other right of self-defence, where I have been wrongfully accused, and my sense wire-drawn into blasphemy or bawdry, as it has often been by a religious lawyer, in a late pleading against the stage; in which he mixes truth with falsehood, and has not forgotten the old rule of calumniating strongly, that something may remain.

I resume the third of my discourse with the first of my translations, which was the first Iliad of Homer. If it shall please God to give me longer life, and moderate health, my intentions are to translate the whole *Ilias;* provided still that I meet with those encouragements from the public which may enable me to proceed in my undertaking with some cheerfulness. And this I dare assure the world beforehand, that I have found, by trial, Homer a more pleasing task than Virgil, though I say not the translation will be less laborious; for the Grecian is more according to my genius than the Latin poet. In the works of the two authors we may read their manners, and natural inclinations, which are wholly different. Virgil was of a quiet, sedate temper; Homer was violent, impetuous, and full of fire. The chief talent of Virgil was propriety of thoughts, and ornament of words: Homer was rapid in his thoughts, and took all the liberties, both of numbers and of expressions, which his language, and the age in which he lived, allowed him. Homer's invention was more copious, Virgil's more confined; so that if Homer had not led the way, it was not in Virgil to have begun heroic poetry; for nothing can be more evident than that the Roman poem is but the second part of the *Ilias;* a continuation of the same story, and the persons already formed. The manners of Aeneas are those of Hector, superadded to those which Homer gave him. The adventures of Ulysses in the *Odysseis* are imitated in the first Six Books of Virgil's *Aeneis;* and though the accidents are not the same (which would have argued him of a servile copying, and total barrenness of invention), yet the seas were the same in which both the heroes wandered; and Dido cannot be denied to be the poetical daughter of Calypso. The six latter Books of Virgil's poem are the four-and-twenty *Iliads* contracted; a quarrel occasioned by a lady, a single combat, battles fought, and a town besieged. I say not this in derogation to Virgil, neither do I contradict anything which I have formerly said in his just praise; for his episodes are almost wholly of his own invention, and the form which he has given to the telling makes the tale his own, even though the original story had been the same. But this proves, however, that Homer taught Virgil to design; and if invention be the first virtue of an epic poet, then the Latin poem can only be allowed the second place. Mr. Hobbes, in the preface to his own bald translation of the *Ilias* (studying poetry as he did mathematics, when it was too late), Mr. Hobbes, I say, begins the praise of Homer where he should have ended it. He tells us that the first beauty of an epic poem consists in diction; that is, in the choice of words, and harmony of numbers. Now the words are the colouring of the work, which, in the order of nature, is last to be considered. The design, the disposition, the manners, and the thoughts are all before it: where any of those are wanting or imperfect, so much wants or is imperfect in the imitation of human life, which is in the very definition of a poem. Words, indeed, like glaring colours, are the first beauties that arise and strike the sight; but, if the draught be false or lame, the figures ill disposed, the manners obscure or inconsistent, or the thoughts unnatural, then the finest colours are but daubing, and the piece is a beautiful monster at the best. Neither Virgil nor Homer were deficient in any of the former beauties; but in this last, which is expression, the Roman poet is at least equal to the Grecian, as I have said elsewhere: supplying the poverty of his language by his musical ear, and by his diligence.

But to return: our two great poets being so different in their tempers, one choleric and sanguine, the other phlegmatic and melancholic; that which makes them excel in their several ways is, that each of them has followed his own natural inclination, as well in

forming the design as in the execution of it. The very heroes show
their authors: Achilles is hot, impatient, revengeful—

> Impiger, iracundus, inexorabilis, acer, etc.,

Aeneas patient, considerate, careful of his people, and merciful to
his enemies; ever submissive to the will of heaven—

> quo fata trahunt retrahuntque, sequamur.
> [Wherever fate drags us back and forth, let
> us follow.]

I could please myself with enlarging on this subject, but am
forced to defer it to a fitter time. From all I have said, I will only
draw this inference, that the action of Homer, being more full of
vigour than that of Virgil, according to the temper of the writer, is
of consequence more pleasing to the reader. One warms you by
degrees; the other sets you on fire all at once, and never intermits
his heat. 'Tis the same difference which Longinus makes betwixt
the effects of eloquence in Demosthenes and Tully; one persuades,
the other commands. You never cool while you read Homer, even
not in the Second Book (a graceful flattery to his countrymen);
but he hastens from the ships, and concludes not that book till he
has made you an amends by the violent playing of a new machine.
From thence he hurries on his action with variety of events, and
ends it in less compass than two months. This vehemence of his, I
confess, is more suitable to my temper; and, therefore, I have trans-
lated his First Book with greater pleasure than any part of Virgil;
but it was not a pleasure without pains. The continual agitations of
the spirits must needs be a weakening of any constitution, es-
pecially in age; and many pauses are required for refreshment be-
twixt the heats; the *Iliad* of itself being a third part longer than
all Virgil's works together.

This is what I thought needful in this place to say of Homer.
I proceed to Ovid and Chaucer; considering the former only in
relation to the latter. With Ovid ended the golden age of the
Roman tongue; from Chaucer the purity of the English tongue
began. The manners of the poets were not unlike. Both of them
were well-bred, well-natured, amorous, and libertine, at least in
their writings; it may be also in their lives. Their studies were the
same, philosophy and philology. Both of them were knowing in

astronomy; of which Ovid's books of the *Roman Feasts,* and Chaucer's *Treatise of the Astrolabe,* are sufficient witnesses. But Chaucer was likewise an astrologer, as were Virgil, Horace, Persius, and Manilius. Both writ with wonderful facility and clearness; neither were great inventors: for Ovid only copied the Grecian fables, and most of Chaucer's stories were taken from his Italian contemporaries, or their predecessors. Boccace his *Decameron* was first published, and from thence our Englishman has borrowed many of his *Canterbury Tales:* yet that of *Palamon and Arcite* was, written, in all probability, by some Italian wit, in a former age, as I shall prove hereafter. The tale of *Grizild* was the invention of Petrarch; by him sent to Boccace, from whom it came to Chaucer. *Troilus and Cressida* was also written by a Lombard author, but much amplified by our English translator, as well as beautified; the genius of our countrymen, in general, being rather to improve an invention than to invent themselves, as is evident not only in our poetry, but in many of our manufactures. I find I have anticipated already, and taken up from Boccace before I come to him: but there is so much less behind; and I am of the temper of most kings, who love to be in debt, are all for present money, no matter how they pay it afterwards: besides, the nature of a preface is rambling, never wholly out of the way, nor in it. This I have learned from the practice of honest Montaigne, and return at my pleasure to Ovid and Chaucer, of whom I have little more to say.

Both of them built on the inventions of other men; yet since Chaucer had something of his own, as *The Wife of Bath's Tale, The Cock and the Fox,* which I have translated, and some others, I may justly give our countryman the precedence in that part; since I can remember nothing of Ovid which was wholly his. Both of them understood the manners; under which name I comprehend the passions, and in a larger sense, the descriptions of persons, and their very habits. For an example, I see Baucis and Philemon as perfectly before me as if some ancient painter had drawn them; and all the Pilgrims in the *Canterbury Tales,* their humours, their features, and the very dress, as distinctly as if I had supped with them at the *Tabard* in Southwark. Yet even there, too, the figures of Chaucer are much more lively, and set in a better light; which though I have not time to prove, yet I appeal to the reader, and am sure he will clear me from partiality. The thoughts and words remain to be considered, in the comparison of the two poets, and

I have saved myself one-half of the labour, by owning that Ovid lived when the Roman tongue was in its meridian, Chaucer in the dawning of our language; therefore, that part of the comparison stands not on an equal foot, any more than the diction of Ennius and Ovid, or of Chaucer and our present English. The words are given up, as a post not to be defended in our poet, because he wanted the modern art of fortifying. The thoughts remain to be considered; and they are to be measured only by their propriety; that is, as they flow more or less naturally from the persons described, on such and such occasions. The vulgar judges, which are nine parts in ten of all nations, who call conceits and jingles wit, who see Ovid full of them, and Chaucer altogether without them, will think me little less than mad for preferring the Englishman to the Roman. Yet, with their leave, I must presume to say that the things they admire are only glittering trifles, and so far from being witty, that in a serious poem they are nauseous, because they are unnatural. Would any man, who is ready to die for love, describe his passion like Narcissus? Would he think of *inopem me copia fecit* [Plenty made me poor], and a dozen more of such expressions, poured on the neck of one another, and signifying all the same thing? If this were wit, was this a time to be witty, when the poor wretch was in the agony of death? This is just John Littlewit, in *Bartholomew-Fair,* who had a conceit (as he tells you) left him in his misery; a miserable conceit. On these occasions the poet should endeavour to raise pity; but, instead of this, Ovid, is tickling you to laugh. Virgil never made use of such machines when he was moving you to commiserate the death of Dido: he would not destroy what he was building. Chaucer makes Arcite violent in his love, and unjust in the pursuit of it; yet, when he came to die, he made him think more reasonably: he repents not of his love, for that had altered his character; but acknowledges the injustice of his proceedings, and resigns Emilia to Palamon. What would Ovid have done on this occasion? He would certainly have made Arcite witty on his deathbed; he had complained he was further off from possession, by being so near, and a thousand such boyisms, which Chaucer rejected as below the dignity of the subject. They who think otherwise would, by the same reason, prefer Lucan and Ovid to Homer and Virgil, and Martial to all four of them. As for the turns of words, in which Ovid particularly excels all poets, they are sometimes a fault, and sometimes a beauty, as they are used properly or improperly; but in strong passions always to be shunned, because passions are serious, and will admit no playing. The French have a high value for them; and, I confess, they are often what they call delicate, when they are introduced with judgment; but Chaucer writ with more simplicity, and followed Nature more closely than to use them. I have thus far, to the best of my knowledge, been an upright judge betwixt the parties in competition, not meddling with the design nor the disposition of it; because the design was not their own; and in the disposing of it they were equal. It remains that I say somewhat of Chaucer in particular.

In the first place, as he is the father of English poetry, so I hold him in the same degree of veneration as the Grecians held Homer, or the Romans Virgil. He is a perpetual fountain of good sense; learn'd in all sciences; and, therefore, speaks properly on all subjects. As he knew what to say, so he knows also when to leave off; a continence which is practised by few writers, and scarcely by any of the ancients, excepting Virgil and Horace. One of our late great poets is sunk in his reputation, because he could never forgive any conceit which came in his way; but swept like a drag-net, great and small. There was plenty enough, but the dishes were ill sorted; whole pyramids of sweetmeats for boys and women but little of solid meat for men. All this proceeded not from any want of knowledge, but of judgment. Neither did he want that in discerning the beauties and faults of other poets, but only indulged himself in the luxury of writing; and perhaps knew it was a fault, but hoped the reader would not find it. For this reason, though he must always be thought a great poet, he is no longer esteemed a good writer; and for ten impressions, which his works have had in so many successive years, yet at present a hundred books are scarcely purchased once a twelvemonth; for, as my last Lord Rochester said, though somewhat profanely, *Not being of God, he could not stand.*

Chaucer followed Nature everywhere, but was never so bold to go beyond her; and there is a great difference of being *poeta* and *nimis poeta* [A poet and too much of a poet], if we may believe Catullus, as much as betwixt a modest behaviour and affectation. The verse of Chaucer, I confess, is not harmonious to us; but 'tis like the eloquence of one whom Tacitus commends, it was *auribus istius temporis accommodata* [suited to the ears of that time]: they who lived with him, and some time after him, thought it musical; and it continues so, even in our judgment, if compared with the numbers of Lidgate and Gower, his contemporaries: there is the rude sweetness of a Scotch tune in it, which is natural and pleasing, though not perfect. 'Tis true, I cannot go so far as he who published the last edition of him; for he would make us believe the fault is in our ears, and that there were really ten syllables in a verse where we find but nine: but this opinion is not worth confuting; 'tis so gross and obvious an error, that common sense (which is a rule in everything but matters of Faith and Revelation) must convince the reader that equality of numbers, in every verse which we call *heroic*, was either not known, or not always practised, in Chaucer's age. It were an easy matter to produce some thousands of his verses, which are lame for want of half a foot, and sometimes a whole one, and which no pronunciation can make otherwise. We can only say, that he lived in the infancy of our poetry, and that nothing is brought to perfection at the first. We must be children before we grow men. There was an Ennius, and in process of time a Lucilius, and a Lucretius, before Virgil and Horace; even after Chaucer there was a Spenser, a Harrington, a Fairfax, before Waller and Denham were in being; and our numbers were in their nonage till these last appeared. I need say little of his parentage, life, and fortunes; they are to be found at large in all the editions of his works. He was employed abroad, and favoured, by Edward the Third, Richard the Second, and Henry the Fourth, and was poet, as I suppose, to all three of them. In Richard's time, I doubt, he was a little dipt in the rebellion of the Commons; and being brother-in-law to John of Ghant, it was no wonder if he followed the fortunes of that family; and was well with Henry the Fourth when he had deposed his predecessor. Neither is it to be admired, that Henry, who was a wise as well as a valiant prince, who claimed by succession, and was sensible that his title was not sound, but was rightfully in Mortimer, who had married the heir of York; it was not to be admired, I say, if that great politician should be pleased to have the greatest wit of those times in his interests, and to be the trumpet of his praises. Augustus had given him the example, by the advice of Maecenas, who recommended Virgil and Horace to him; whose praises helped to make him popular while he was alive, and after his death have made him precious to posterity. As for the religion of our poet, he seems to have some little bias towards the opinions of Wicliffe, after John of Ghant his patron; somewhat of which appears in the tale of *Piers Plowman:* yet I cannot blame him for inveighing so sharply against the vices of the clergy in his age: their pride, their ambition, their pomp, their avarice, their worldly interest, deserved the lashes which he gave them, both in that, and in most of his *Canterbury Tales.* Neither has his contemporary Boccace spared them: yet both those poets lived in much esteem with good and holy men in orders; for the scandal which is given by particular priests reflects not on the sacred function. Chaucer's *Monk,* his *Canon,* and his *Friar,* took not from the character of his *Good Parson.* A satirical poet is the check of the laymen on bad priests. We are only to take care that we involve not the innocent with the guilty in the same condemnation. The good cannot be too much honoured, nor the bad too coarsely used, for the corruption of the best becomes the worst. When a clergyman is whipped, his gown is first taken off, by which the dignity of his order is secured. If he be wrongfully accused, he has his action of slander; and 'tis at the poet's peril if he transgress the law. But they will tell us that all kind of satire, though never so well deserved by particular priests, yet brings the whole order into contempt. Is then the peerage of England anything dishonoured when a peer suffers for his treason? If he be libelled, or any way defamed, he has his *scandalum magnatum* to punish the offender. They who use this kind of argument seem to be conscious to themselves of somewhat which has deserved the poet's lash, and are less concerned for their public capacity than for their private; at least there is pride at the bottom of their reasoning. If the faults of men in orders are only to be judged among themselves, they are all in some sort parties; for, since they say the honour of their order is concerned in every member of it, how can we be sure that they will be impartial judges? How far I may be allowed to speak my opinion in this case, I know not; but I am sure a dispute of this nature caused mischief in abundance betwixt a King of England and an Archbishop of Canterbury; one standing up for the laws of his land, and the other for the honour (as he called it) of God's Church; which ended in the murder of the prelate, and in the whipping of his Majesty from post to pillar for his penance. The learned and ingenious Dr. Drake has saved me the labour of inquiring into the esteem and reverence which the priests have had of old; and I would rather extend than diminish any part of it: yet I must needs say that when a priest provokes me without any occasion given him, I have no reason, unless it be the charity of a Christian, to forgive him: *prior laesit* [he was the aggressor] is justification sufficient in the civil law. If I answer him in his own language, self-defence, I am sure, must be allowed me; and if I carry it further, even to a sharp recrimination, somewhat may be indulged to human frailty. Yet my resentment has not wrought so far but that I have followed Chaucer in his character of a holy man, and have enlarged on that subject with some pleasure; reserving to my-self the right, if I shall think fit hereafter, to describe another sort of priests, such as are more easily to be found than the Good Parson; such as have given the last blow to Christianity in this age, by a practice so contrary to their doctrine. But this will keep cold till another time. In the meanwhile, I take up Chaucer where I left him.

He must have been a man of a most wonderful comprehensive nature, because, as it has been truly observed of him, he has taken into the compass of his *Canterbury Tales* the various manners and humours (as we now call them) of the whole English nation in his age. Not a single character has escaped him. All his pilgrims are severally distinguished from each other, and not only in their inclinations, but in their very physiognomies and persons. Baptista Porta could not have described their natures better, than by the marks which the poet gives them. The matter and manner of their tales, and of their telling, are so suited to their different educations, humours, and callings, that each of them would be improper in any other mouth. Even the grave and serious characters are distinguished by their several sorts of gravity: their discourses are such as belong to their age, their calling, and their breeding; such as are becoming of them, and of them only. Some of his persons are vicious, and some virtuous; some are unlearn'd, or (as Chaucer calls them) lewd, and some are learn'd. Even the ribaldry of the low characters is different: the Reeve, the Miller, and the Cook, are several men, and distinguished from each other as much as the mincing Lady-Prioress and the broad-speaking, gap-toothed Wife of Bath. But enough of this; there is such a variety of game springing up before me that I am distracted in my choice, and know not which to fol-low. 'Tis sufficient to say, according to the proverb, that *here is God's plenty.* We have our forefathers and grant-granddames all be-fore us, as they were in Chaucer's days: their general characters are still remaining in mankind, and even in England, though they are called by other names than those of Monks, and Friars, and Canons, and Lady Abbesses, and Nuns; for mankind is ever the same, and nothing lost out of Nature, though everything is altered. May I have leave to do myself the justice (since my enemies will do me none, and are so far from granting me to be a good poet, that they will not allow me so much as to be a Christian, or a moral man), may I have leave, I say, to inform my reader that I have confined my choice to such tales of Chaucer as savour nothing of immodesty. If I had desired more to please than to instruct, the *Reeve,* the *Miller,* the *Shipman,* the *Merchant,* the *Sumner,* and, above all, the *Wife of Bath,* in the Prologue of her *Tale,* would have procured me as many friends and readers as there are beaux and ladies of pleasure in the town. But I will no more offend against good manners: I am sensible as I ought to be of the scandal I have given by my loose writings; and make what reparation I am able, by this public acknowledgment. If anything of this nature, or of profaneness be crept into these poems, I am so far from defending it that I disown it. *Totum hoc indictum volo* [I wish all this unsaid]. Chaucer makes another manner of apology for his broad speaking, and Boccace makes the like; but I will follow neither of them. Our countryman, in the end of his *Characters,* before the *Canterbury Tales,* thus excuses the ribaldry, which is very gross in many of his novels—

> But firste, I pray you, of your courtesy,
> That ye ne arrete it not my villany,
> Though that I plainly speak in this mattere,
> To tellen you her words, and eke her chere:
> Ne though I speak her words properly,
> For this ye knowen as well as I,
> Who shall tellen a tale after a man,
> He mote rehearse as nye as ever he can:
> Everich word of it ben in his charge,
> All speke he, never so rudely, ne large:
> Or else he mote tellen his tale untrue,
> Or feine things, or find words new:
> He may not spare, altho he were his brother,
> He mote as wel say o word as another.
> Crist spake himself ful broad in holy Writ,
> And well I wote no villany is it,
> Eke Plato saith, who so can him rede,
> The words mote been cousin to the dede.

Yet if a man should have inquired of Boccace or of Chaucer what need they had of introducing such characters, where obscene words were proper in their mouths, but very indecent to be heard; I know not what answer they could have made; for that reason, such tales shall be left untold by me. You have here a specimen of Chaucer's language, which is so obsolete, that his sense is scarce to be understood; and you have likewise more than one example of his unequal numbers, which were mentioned before. Yet many of his verses consist of ten syllables, and the words not much behind our present English: as for example, these two lines, in the description of the Carpenter's young wife—

> Wincing she was, as is a jolly colt,
> Long as a mast, and upright as a bolt.

I have almost done with Chaucer, when I have answered some objections relating to my present work. I find some people are offended that I have turned these tales into modern English; because they think them unworthy of my pains, and look on Chaucer as a dry, old-fashioned wit, not worth reviving. I have often heard the late Earl of Leicester say that Mr. Cowley himself was of that opinion; who, having read him over at my Lord's request, declared he had no taste of him. I dare not advance my opinion against the judgment of so great an author; but I think it fair, however, to leave the decision to the public. Mr. Cowley was too modest to set up for a dictator; and being shocked perhaps with his old style, never examined into the depth of his good sense. Chaucer, I confess, is a rough diamond, and must first be polished ere he shines. I deny not likewise, that, living in our early days of poetry, he writes not always of a piece; but sometimes mingles trivial things with those of greater moment. Sometimes also, through not often, he runs riot, like Ovid, and knows not when he has said enough. But there are more great wits besides Chaucer, whose fault is their excess of conceits, and those ill sorted. An author is not to write all he can, but only all he ought. Having observed this redundancy in Chaucer (as it is an easy matter for a man of ordinary parts to find a fault in one of greater), I have not tied myself to a literal translation; but have often omitted what I judged unnecessary, or not of dignity enough to appear in the company of better thoughts. I have presumed further, in some places, and added somewhat of my own where I thought my author was deficient, and had not given his thoughts their true lustre, for want of words in the beginning of our language. And to this I was the more emboldened, because (if I may be permitted to say it of myself) I found I had a soul congenial to his, and that I had been conversant in the same studies. Another poet, in another age, may take the same liberty with my writings; if at least they live long enough to deserve correction. It was also necessary sometimes to restore the sense of Chaucer, which was lost or mangled in the errors of the press. Let this example suffice at present: in the story of *Palamon and Arcite,* where the temple of Diana is described, you find these verses in all the editions of our author:—

> There saw I Danè turned unto a tree,
> I mean not the goddess Diane,
> But Venus daughter, which that hight Danè.

Which, after a little consideration, I knew was to be reformed into this sense, that *Daphne,* the daughter of Peneus, was turned into a tree. I durst not make thus bold with Ovid, lest some future Milbourne should arise and say I varied from my author because I understood him not.

But there are other judges who think I ought not to have translated Chaucer into English, out of a quite contrary notion: they suppose there is a certain veneration due to his old language, and that it is little less than profanation and sacrilege to alter it. They are farther of opinion, that somewhat of his good sense will suffer in this transfusion, and much of the beauty of his thoughts will infallibly be lost, which appear with more grace in their old habit. Of this opinion was that excellent person, whom I mentioned, the late Earl of Leicester, who valued Chaucer as much as Mr. Cowley despised him. My Lord dissuaded me from this attempt (for I was thinking of it some years before his death) and his authority prevailed so far with me, as to defer my undertaking while he lived, in deference to him: yet my reason was not convinced with what he urged against it. If the first end of a writer be to be understood, then, as his language grows obsolete, his thoughts must grow obscure—

> Multa renascentur, quae nunc cecidere; cadentque
> Quae nunc sunt in honore vocabula, si volet usus,
> Quem penes arbitrium est et jus et norma loquendi.

[Many words will be revived that are now obsolete;
many will be become obsolete that are now hon-
ored; if it is so willed by usage, on which depend
the judgment and the law and the rules of our
speech.]

When an ancient word, for its sound and significancy, deserves
to be revived, I have that reasonable veneration for antiquity to
restore it. All beyond this is superstition. Words are not like land-
marks, so sacred as never to be removed; customs are changed, and
even statutes are silently repealed, when the reason ceases for which
they were enacted. As for the other part of the argument, that his
thoughts will lose of their original beauty by the innovation of
words; in the first place, not only their beauty, but their being is
lost, where they are no longer understood, which is the present case.
I grant that something must be lost in all transfusion, that is, in
all translations; but the sense will remain, which would otherwise
be lost, or at least be maimed, when it is scarce intelligible, and
that but to a few. How few are there who can read Chaucer so as
to understand him perfectly? And if imperfectly, then with less
profit, and no pleasure. It is not for the use of some old Saxon
friends that I have taken these pains with him: let them neglect my
version, because they have no need of it. I made it for their sakes,
who understand sense and poetry as well as they, when that poetry
and sense is put into words which they understand. I will go farther,
and dare to add, that what beauties I lose in some places, I give to
others which had them not originally; but in this I may be partial
to myself; let the reader judge, and I submit to his decision. Yet I
think I have just occasion to complain of them, who because they
understand Chaucer, would deprive the greater part of their country-
men of the same advantage, and hoard him up, as misers do their
grandam gold, only to look on it themselves, and hinder others from
making use of it. In sum, I seriously protest, that no man ever had,
or can have, a greater veneration for Chaucer than myself. I have
translated some part of his works, only that I might perpetuate his
memory, or at least refresh it, amongst my countrymen. If I have
altered him anywhere for the better, I must at the same time
acknowledge that I could have done nothing without him. *Facile
est inventis addere* [It is easy to add to things that have already
been invented] is no great commendation; and I am not so vain
to think I have deserved a greater. I will conclude what I have to

say of him singly, with this one remark: A lady of my acquaintance, who keeps a kind of correspondence with some authors of the fair sex in France, has been informed by them that Mademoiselle de Scudery, who is as old as Sibyl, and inspired like her by the same God of Poetry, is at this time translating Chaucer into modern French. From which I gather that he has been formerly translated into the old Provençal; for how she should come to understand old English, I know not. But the matter of fact being true, it makes me think that there is something in it like fatality; that, after certain periods of time, the fame and memory of great Wits should be renewed, as Chaucer is both in France and England. If this be wholly chance, 'tis extraordinary; and I dare not call it more, for fear of being taxed with superstition.

Boccace comes last to be considered, who, living in the same age with Chaucer, had the same genius, and followed the same studies. Both writ novels, and each of them cultivated his mother tongue. But the greatest resemblance of our two modern authors being in their familiar style and pleasing way of relating comical adventures, I may pass it over, because I have translated nothing from Boccace of that nature. In the serious part of poetry, the advantage is wholly on Chaucer's side, for though the Englishman has borrowed many tales from the Italian, yet it appears that those of Boccace were not generally of his own making, but taken from authors of former ages, and by him only modelled; so that what there was of invention, in either of them, may be judged equal. But Chaucer has refined on Boccace, and has mended the stories, which he has borrowed, in his way of telling; though prose allows more liberty of thought, and the expression is more easy when unconfined by numbers. Our countryman carries weight, and yet wins the race at disadvantage. I desire not the reader should take my word; and, therefore, I will set two of their discourses, on the same subject, in the same light, for every man to judge betwixt them. I translated Chaucer first, and, amongst the rest, pitched on *The Wife of Bath's Tale;* not daring, as I have said, to adventure on her Prologue, because 'tis too licentious. There Chaucer introduces an old woman, of mean parentage, whom a youthful knight, of noble blood, was forced to marry, and consequently loathed her. The crone being in bed with him on the wedding-night, and finding his aversion, endeavours to win his affection by reason, and speaks a good word for herself (as who could blame her?) in hopes to mollify the sullen bridegroom. She takes her topics from the benefits of poverty, the advantages of old age and ugliness, the vanity of youth, and the silly pride of ancestry and titles, without inherent virtue, which is the true nobility. When I had closed Chaucer, I returned to Ovid, and translated some more of his fables; and, by this time, had so far forgotten *The Wife of Bath's Tale,* that, when I took up Boccace, unawares I fell on the same argument, of preferring virtue to nobility of blood and titles, in the story of *Sigismonda;* which I had certainly avoided, for the resemblance of the two discourses, if my memory had not failed me. Let the reader weigh them both; and, if he thinks me partial to Chaucer, 'tis in him to right Boccace.

I prefer, in our countryman, far above all his other stories, the noble poem of *Palamon and Arcite,* which is of the epic kind, and perhaps not much inferior to the *Ilias,* or the *Aeneis.* The story is more pleasing than either of them, the manners as perfect, the diction as poetical, the learning as deep and various, and the disposition full as artful: only it concludes a greater length of time, as taking up seven years at least; but Aristotle has left undecided the duration of the action; which yet is easily reduced into the compass of a year, by a narration of what preceded the return of Palamon to Athens. I had thought, for the honour of our nation, and more particularly for his, whose laurel, though unworthy, I have worn after him, that this story was of English growth, and Chaucer's own: but I was undeceived by Boccace; for, casually looking on the end of his seventh *Giornata,* I found Dioneo (under which name he shadows himself), and Fiametta (who represents his mistress, the natural daughter of Robert, King of Naples), of whom these words are spoken: *Dioneo e Fiametta gran pezza cantarono insieme d'Arcita, e di Palemone* [Dioneo and Fiametta would sing together much of the story of Arcite and Palamon]; by which it appears that this story was written before the time of Boccace; but the name of its author being wholly lost, Chaucer is now become an original; and I question not but the poem has received many beauties, by passing through his noble hands. Besides this tale, there is another of his own invention, after the manner of the Provençals, called *The Flower and the Leaf,* with which I was so particularly pleased, both for the invention and the moral, that I cannot hinder myself from recommending it to the reader.

As a corollary to this preface, in which I have done justice to others, I owe somewhat to myself; not that I think it worth my time to enter the lists with one M——, and one B——, but barely to take notice that such men there are, who have written scurrilously against me, without any provocation. M——, who is in orders, pretends, amongst the rest, this quarrel to me, that I have fallen foul on priesthood: if I have, I am only to ask pardon of good priests, and am afraid his part of the reparation will come to little. Let him be satisfied that he shall not be able to force himself upon me for an adversary. I contemn him too much to enter into competition with him. His own translations of Virgil have answered his criticisms on mine. If (as they say, he has declared in print) he prefers the version of Ogilby to mine, the world has made him the same compliment; for 'tis agreed, on all hands, that he writes even below Ogilby. That, you will say, is not easily to be done; but what cannot M—— bring about? I am satisfied, however, that, while he and I live together, I shall not be thought the worst poet of the age. It looks as if I had desired him underhand to write so ill against me; but upon my honest word I have not bribed him to do me this service, and am wholly guiltless of his pamphlet. 'Tis true, I should be glad if I could persuade him to continue his good offices, and write such another critique on anything of mine; for I find, by experience, he has a great stroke with the reader, when he condemns any of my poems, to make the world have a better opinion of them. He has taken some pains with my poetry; but nobody will be persuaded to take the same with his. If I had taken to the Church, as he affirms, but which was never in my thoughts I should have had more sense, if not more grace, than to have turned myself out of my benefice, by writing libels on my parishioners. But his account of my manners and my principles are of a piece with his cavils and his poetry; and so I have done with him for ever.

As for the City Bard, or Knight Physician, I hear his quarrel to me is, that I was the author of *Absalom and Achitophel,* which, he thinks, is a little hard on his fanatic patrons in London.

But I will deal the more civilly with his two poems, because nothing ill is to be spoken of the dead; and therefore peace be to the *Manes* of his *Arthurs.* I will only say, that it was not for this noble Knight that I drew the plan of an epic poem on *King Arthur,* in my preface to the translation of *Juvenal.* The Guardian Angels of kingdoms were machines too ponderous for him to manage; and therefore he rejected them, as Dares did the whirl-bats of Eryx when they were thrown before him by Entellus: yet from that preface, he plainly took his hint; for he began immediately upon the story, though he had the baseness not to acknowledge his benefactor, but instead of it, to traduce me in a libel.

I shall say the less of Mr. Collier, because in many things he has taxed me justly; and I have pleaded guilty to all thoughts and expressions of mine, which can be truly argued of obscenity, profaneness, or immorality, and retract them. If he be my enemy, let him triumph; if he be my friend, as I have given him no personal occasion to be otherwise, he will be glad of my repentance. It becomes me not to draw my pen in the defence of a bad cause, when I have so often drawn it for a good one. Yet it were not difficult to prove that in many places he has perverted my meaning by his glosses, and interpreted my words into blasphemy and bawdry, of which they were not guilty. Besides that, he is too much given to horse-play in his raillery, and comes to battle like a dictator from the plough. I will not say, *the zeal of God's house has eaten him up;* but I am sure it has devoured some part of his good manners and civility. It might also be doubted whether it were altogether zeal which prompted him to this rough manner of proceeding; perhaps it became not one of his function to rake into the rubbish of ancient and modern plays: a divine might have employed his pains to better purpose than in the nastiness of Plautus and Aristophanes, whose examples, as they excuse not me, so it might be possibly supposed that he read them not without some pleasure. They who have written commentaries on those poets, or on Horace, Juvenal, and Martial, have explained some vices, which, without their interpretation, had been unknown to modern times. Neither has he judged impartially betwixt the former age and us. There is more bawdry in one play of Fletcher's, called *The Custom of the Country,* than in all ours together. Yet this has been often acted on the stage, in my remembrance. Are the times so much more reformed now than they were five-and-twenty years ago? If they are, I congratulate the amendment of our morals. But I am not to prejudice the cause of my fellow poets, though I abandon my own defence: they have some of them answered for themselves; and neither they nor I can think Mr. Collier so formidable an enemy, that we should shun him. He has lost ground, at the latter end of the day, by pursuing his point too far, like the Prince of Condé, at the battle of Senneph: from immoral plays to no plays, *ab abusu ad usum, non valet con-*

sequentia [The fact that a thing is misused does not prove it may not be well used]. But, being a party, I am not to erect myself into a judge. As for the rest of those who have written against me, they are such scoundrels that they deserve not the least notice to be taken of them. B—— and M—— are only distinguished from the crowd by being remembered to their infamy:—

> Demetri, teque, Tigelli
> Discipulorum inter jubeo plorare cathedras.

> [You, Demetrius and you too, Tegellius, I order to weep among the benches of your pupils.]

Notes
on
The Criticism

PAGE

427 *his royal highness* (7–8): the Duke of York.

429 *conceit* (34): flight of imagination.

430 *Tully* (4): Marcus Tullius Cicero, first-century B.C. Roman orator and philosopher; cf. his *Arch*. x. 25.

430 *easy to guess* (17–18): an overstatement. Modern editors conjecture Robert Wild, author of a poem praising the Cromwellian General Monk; and (possibly) Richard Flecknoe.

430 *clenches* (19): plays, quibbles.

430 *clownish* (20): boorish.

430 *catachresis or Clevelandism* (21): farfetched metaphors such as were used by the metaphysical poet Cleveland.

430 *un mauvais buffon* (23): "an ill-natured chap."

430 *numbers* (38): verses.

431 *Martial* (3): first-century Roman writer of epigrams (cf. viii, 19).

431 *conceit* (10): imaginative expression.

431 *Withers* (21): actually, George Wither (1588–1667), a minor poet.

431 *city* (22): commercial section of London.

431 *poem* (25): the eulogy of Monk[?]

431 *'Change* (26): stock exchange.

431 *candles' ends* (27): bids were accepted until the candle burned out.

431 *Qui Bavium non odit* (33): Virgil *Ecl*. iii. 90. "Let him who doesn't detest Bavius love your poems, Maevius."

432 *Petronius* (2): *Sat*. 2.

432 *Nature* (4): reality.

432 *Horace* (14): first-century B.C. Roman poet and critic. See his *Ep*. ii, 1, 76, 34.

433 *ought* (2): anything.

433 *Suckling, Waller, Denham, Cowley* (12–15): poets of the mid-seventeenth century. Suckling was a cavalier love poet; Cowley, of the metaphysical school; and Denham and

Waller are credited by Dryden with having perfected the heroic couplet.

433   *Eugenius his* (18): Eugenius's.

433   *Aristotle* (36): major Greek philosopher (fourth-century B.C.); author of a treatise on poetics.

434   *humours* (3): idiosyncrasies.

434   *genere et fine* (6): i.e., "not specific enough": giving only the general class [*genere*]—literature—to which plays belong, and its purpose [*fine*].

434   *Thespis* (17): reputed founder of drama in the sixth century B.C.

434   *Aristophanes* (17): fifth-century Athenian comic dramatist.

434   *Virtuosi* (25): experts.

434   *the school* (27): medieval philosophy.

434   *philosophy* (28): (here) natural science.

434   *Eschylus, Euripides, Sophocles* (39): greatest Athenian writers of tragedies.

434   *Lycophron* (39): third-century B.C. Alexandrian grammarian and dramatist.

435   *Paterculus* (4): cf. his *Hist. Rom.* i. 17.

435   περὶ τῆς Πσιηιχῆς (33–34): *Concerning the Poetic Art.*

437   *Corneille* (11): he had published a discourse on the three unities in 1660.

437   *Discoveries* (25–26): fourth section from the end; ed. Hereford and Simpson.

437   *Terence* (28): Roman comic dramatist, second century B.C.

438   *Menander* (5): fourth-century B.C. Athenian writer of comedies.

438   *Caecilius, Afranius, Varius* (6): Roman dramatists of whom little is now known.

438   *Plautus* (12): Roman comic dramatist, third century B.C.

438   *Seneca* (13): Greatest Roman tragic dramatist, first century A.D.

438   *Macrobius* (22): Roman philosopher, *ca.* 400 A.D.; see his *Saturnalia.*

438   *Lucan, Juvenal* (32–33): first- and second-century Roman poets.

439   *Paterculus* (31): *Hist. Rom.* ii. 92.

440   *Neu…actu* (27–28): Horace *Ars P.* 189.

440   τῶν συνθεσις (41): "the arrangements of what happens."

PAGE

441 *late writer* (1): not certainly identified.

441 *chapon bouillé* (16): "warmed-over hash."

441 *Juno . . . opem* (25): "Juno, goddess of childbirth, accomplish this matter." Terence *And.* Act iii, Sc. 1. 15.

422 *Scaliger* (16): sixteenth-century Italian critic; cf. his *Poet.* i. 13 and vi. 3.

442 *one of his tragedies* (18–19): the *Suppliants* (598–633).

442 *C'est bien . . .* (29–30): "It's good work to make use of so short time"—Corneille, *Third Discourse.*

444 *sock, buskin* (1): symbols of comedy and tragedy, respectively.

444 *Tandem . . .* (16): Terence, *Eunu.* Act ii, Sc. 1. 18.

444 *Horace* (33): *Ars P.* 270–272.

444 *Multa . . .* (36): 70–72.

445 *Virgil* (6): *Ecl.* iv. 20.

445 *mirantur* (11): *Aen.* viii. 91–93.

445 *Ovid* (18): in *Met.* i. 175–176.

445 *et* (25): *ibid.,* 561.

446 *Si sic . . .* (5): Juvenal *Sat.* x. 123.

446 *White powder* (8): gunpowder discharged with no report [?]; arsenic [?]. Dryden believed that *Rupertismus,* from which these lines come, was by Cleveland.

446 *Omne . . .* (24): Ovid, *Tr.* ii. 381.

446 *Astyanax* (30): infant son of Hector and Andromache.

446 *Fletcher* (35): Next to Shakespeare, Fletcher was the Elizabethan dramatist Dryden's age most admired for tragedies.

447 *Juvenal's time* (9): cf. his *Sat.* vi. 195.

447 *Virgil* (28): cf. *Aen.* i. 378–379.

447 *fanfaron . . .* (33): vulgar boaster.

448 *Horace* (2): *Sat.* i. 10. 68.

448 *quos . . .* (7): cf. Horace *Epist.* ii. 1. 49.

448 *horror* (33): referring to the Civil War in the 1640's and Commonwealth government in the 50's

448 *Richelieu* (36): French statesman, d. 1642.

448 *Corneille* (38): he, Molière, and Racine were the chief French dramatists of the seventeenth century.

449 *mal à propos* (32): "inappropriately, clumsily."

449 *Red Bull* (34): popular London playhouse, later used for prize fights.

449 *atque . . .* (35): Horace *Epist.* ii. 1. 185.

PAGE

450   *Horace* (9): *Ars P.* 240.

450   *atque* ... (16): *ibid,* 151.

450   *Cyrus* (29): sixth-century B.C. Persian king.

450   *Justin* (29): Roman historian (second or third century).

450   *Xenophon* (30–31): fifth-century B.C. Greek historian.

451   *perspective* (3): telescope.

451   *Quodcunque* ... (7): Horace *Ars P.* 188.

451   *One of the Greek poets* (12): Homer (*Od.* xix. 203); Hesiod *Theog.* 27.

451   *Calderón* (27): seventeenth-century Spanish dramatist.

451   *Rollo* (31): John Fletcher's *The Bloody Brother* [1639].

451   *Herodian* (32): second-century Greek grammarian, author of work on prosody.

451   *oleo* (39): mixture, hash.

452   *Golia* (2): Goliath.

452   *an ingenious person* (11): Thomas Sprat, author of *Observations on M. de Sorbier's Voyage into England* (1665), a reply to a 1664 French attack on English plays as formless.

452   *parts* (22): talents.

452   *protatic* (32): introductory, appearing only in the beginning of a play.

452   *à propos* (38): "appropriately, neatly."

453   *sleight* (39): trick.

454   *philosophers* (5): scientists.

454   *Segnius* ... (28): *Ars P.* 180–187.

456   *The Scornful Lady* (5–6): by Beaumont and Fletcher (*ca.* 1610).

456   *ancient author* (38): Velleius Paterculus *Hist. Rom.* i. 17.

457   *humour* (29): idiosyncrasy of character.

458   *Diego* (8): comic servant.

459   *primum mobile* (10): "first mover," an outer sphere, containing those of the stars and planets—an hypothesis of astronomy down to Milton's and Dryden's time.

459   *Cinna, Pompey, Polieucte* (39, 41): by (the elder) Corneille.

461   *The Maid's Tragedy* (2–3): by Beaumont and Fletcher. The other three plays named are Jonson's.

461   *indecency* (23–24): vulgarity.

463   *one of their newest plays* (12–13): Thomas Corneille's *L'Amour à la Mode,* 1651, certain details of which Neander

PAGE

apparently confuses with a similar scene in Quinault's *L'Amant Indiscret.*

464 *examen* (38): analysis.

465 *Quantum* ... (26): Virgil *Ecl.* i. 25.

465 *Hales* (29): John Hales (d. 1656), a former fellow of Eton; *The Golden Remains of the Ever Memorable Mr. John Hales* was published in 1659.

466 *Philaster* (6): acted *ca.* 1608.

466 *mechanic people* (39): artisans, manual laborers.

467 *translation* (31): i.e., adaptation from Spanish (of a play attributed to Calderón).

470 *Horace* (14): *Epist.* II. i. 168–170.

471 *out of* (27): not in.

472 *poet* (6): Horace (*Ars P.* 351).

472 *writer* (16): Velleius Paterculus ii. 36.

473 *Macrobius* (14): *Sat.* ii. 13.

473 *Aristotle* (33): see his *Poetics,* 1449 a 23.

474 *happiness* (9): piece of luck.

474 *Arcades* ... (11): Virgil *Ecl.* vii. 4.

474 *quicquid* ... (13): cf. Ovid *Tr.* iv. 10. 25.

475 *Seneca* (8): M. Seneca, *Controv.* ix. 5.

475 *instance* (10): from Ovid *Met.* i. 292.

475 *person* (29): Aristotle.

476 *election* (21): choice.

476 *break off in the hemistich* (40): put a fragmentary line between two couplets, on the analogy of the half-lines in Virgil's *Aeneid.* Dryden's use of this device (cf. *Absalom and Achitophel,* 87) is one of the differences between his versification and Pope's.

477 *perpetuo* ... (3): Cicero, *Or.* vi. 21.

477 *Preface* (19): i.e., in his Epistle Dedicatory of *The Rival Ladies* (1664), in which Dryden had earlier defended the use of rime in plays.

478 *Siege of Rhodes* (11): an opera by Davenant (1656).

479 *bays* (18): laurel branches (used for crowning a successful poet).

479 *tentanda* ... (19–20): cf. Virgil *Georg.* iii. 8.

479 *Hopkins and Sternhold* (33–34): Elizabethan versifiers of the Psalms.

479   *Est.ubi* ... (38): cf. Horace *Epist.* ii. 1. 63.

480   *Siege of Rhodes* ... (3–4): the first play by Davenant, the second by Sir Roger Boyle, the third by Dryden and Howard, the fourth by Dryden.

480   *Horace* (31): *Ars P.* 90–91, 231.

480   *sonnet* (36): any lyric poem.

481   *genus* (11): general nature.

481   *if rhyme be proper for one* (20–21): Davenant's *Gondibert* (1651) and Cowley's *Davideis* (1656) were recent examples of rimed epics in English; *Paradise Lost* had not been published by 1665 (the date when Neander's words are supposed to be spoken); and when it was published, Milton considered it necessary to defend his choice of blank verse, which had ordinarily been used only for the stage, as Neander says.

481   *Verse* (21): note that the term "verse" throughout the essay includes the idea of rime (hence the necessity for the term *blank* verse, to make a distinction from ordinary, or rimed, verse).

482   *Quidlibet audendi* (13): Horace *Ars P.* 10.

482   *Musas* ... (15): Martial ix, 19.

482   *Pegasus* (17): winged horse, symbol of poetic inspiration.

483   *Water-poet* (20): John Taylor, an Elizabethan boatman-poet.

483   *Caesar* (24): attributed to him by Cicero (*Brut.* 72, 253).

483   *Seneca* (26): *Hippol.* 863.

484   *person* (25): Seneca, see note above, p. 483 (26).

PREFACE
TO THE FABLES

486   *a certain nobleman* (4): the Duke of Buckingham (Zimri in "Absalom and Achitophel").

486   *essay* (7): tentative beginning, "trial balloon."

486   *Sandys* (24): George Sandys' translation of the *Metamorphoses* appeared in 1626; it was enormously popular in the seventeenth century.

486   *Spenser* (26): Edmund Spenser (*ca.* 1552–1599), author of

PAGE

The Faerie Queene. Fairfax: translator of the sixteenth-century Italian epic, Tasso's *Jerusalem Delivered,* under the title of *Godfrey of Bulloign.*

486 *Waller* (30): Edmund Waller (1606–1687), one of the earliest successful practitioners of the heroic couplet.

487 *Hobbes* (18): greatest English philosopher of the mid-century; author of *Leviathan.*

487 *Boccacce* (19): Boccaccio; three of the tales from his *Decameron* were included, in Dryden's English verse paraphrase, in the *Fables.*

487 *novels* (20): i.e., short stories.

487 *Thomas Rymer* (21): an influential scholarly critic of the late seventeenth century.

489 *Horace* (11): *Ars P.* 322.

489 *religious lawyer* (16): Jeremy Collier, who had recently (1698) published his *Short View of the Immorality and Profaneness of the English Stage;* Dryden was a leading target of his attack.

489 *first Iliad* (21): i.e., first book of the *Iliad.*

490 *too late* (18): he completed his translation at eighty-six; he was no better a mathematician than poet.

491 *Impiger . . .* (3): Horace *Ars P.* 121.

491 *quo . . .* (6): *Aen.* v. 709.

491 *Longinus* (15): most famous late classical critic; see his *On the Sublime,* ch. 12.

491 *Demosthenes, Tully* (16): the former the greatest Greek orator; the latter (Cicero), the greatest Roman orator.

491 *Second Book* (18): it contains an extensive catalogue of the membership in the Greek expeditionary force.

491 *machine* (20): supernatural event. (The second book contains a significant dream of Agamemnon's.)

492 *Persius* (3–4): first-century Roman satiric poet. *Manilius:* first-century Roman didactic poet.

492 *thence* (8): Chaucer knew some of Boccaccio's works but probably not his *Decameron.*

492 *some Italian wit* (10): actually, Boccaccio.

492 *invention of Petrarch* (11): Petrarch did send Boccaccio a Latin version of this story, but he had himself translated it from Boccaccio's Italian.

PAGE

497   *Baptista Porta* (20–21): an Italian physiognomist.

498   *my enemies* (3): see the conclusion of the Preface.

498   *Reeve* . . . (8–10): referring to the more ribald parts of the *Canterbury Tales.*

498   *Characters, before* (20): i.e., the Prologue.

500   *Milbourne* (17–18): who had published an attack on Dryden's recent translation of Virgil.

500   *Multa* . . . (36): cf. Horace *Ars P.* 70–72.

502   *de Scudéry* (3–4): author of very popular French romances.

503   *its author* (33): actually, Boccaccio himself, whose *Teseide* Dryden did not know.

503   *another* (35): wrongly attributed to Chaucer.

504   *M——* (2): Milbourne (see above).

504   *B——* (2): Richard Blackmore, physician and poet, who had attacked Dryden for indecency.

504   *Ogilby* (12): whose translation of Virgil was a byword for pedestrian verse.

504   *City Bard* (31): Blackmore; "City" refers to the commercial, largely Puritan classes of London, attacked as fanatical by Dryden in several satires.

504   *two poems* (34): *Prince Arthur* (1695), and *King Arthur* (1697).

504   *whirl-bats* (40): a kind of iron-lined boxing glove which the aged fighter Entellus offers the challenger Dares in the funeral games of *Aeneid* v; but Dares finds them too heavy for him to wear.

505   *zeal* . . . (17): Psalm 69:9.

505   *Senneph* (39): fought in 1674 in Flanders.

506   *Demetri* (7): Horace *Sat.* i. 10. 90–91. Blackmore had been a schoolmaster. In Horace the pupils are female.

Rinehart Editions